To Liz & Jay

Best Wishes

From Joe & Oliver

Thomas Briody

The Road to Avondale
The memoirs of an Irish forester
(Volume 1)

Thomas (Tosty) Briody

Edited: Mícheál Briody

ISBN: 978-1-907107-25-2

A CIP catalogue for this book is available from the National Library.

This publication has received support from the Heritage Council under the 2009 Publications grant Scheme.

Front-cover photograph of Kilshelan forest and the Comeragh Mountains taken from the slopes of Slievenamon above Kilcash village as well as back-cover photograph of Thomas (Tosty) Briody (August 2009) by Tuula Sakaranaho.

The photograph of Avondale House on back cover was taken by the editor.

This book was published in cooperation with
Choice Publishing & Book Services Ltd, Drogheda, Co Louth, Ireland
Tel: 041 9841551 Email: info@choicepublishing.ie
www.choicepublishing.ie

In memory of Nora, my companion of fifty seven years

Acknowledgements

In writing his memoirs my father has received assistance and encouragement from many different people. A third or more of this first volume of his memoirs deals with Cavan, but his writings as a whole are firmly based in Cavan soil. Some ten years ago he visited his native Mullahoran on the occasion of the funeral of his eldest brother Hugh P., after a gap of many years. But for that visit he might never have begun writing his memoirs. Feeling the 'cool Cavan Breeze' again stirred something within him, and seeing the old home place and meeting all the friendly Briodys of Callanagh, made it easier for him to reminisce over the Cavan of long ago without being overcome with emotion. Since then he has visited Mullahoran once a year.

In writing his memoirs my father has benefited greatly from the research of his late niece, Patricia Gilligan, into the Briody and O'Reilly family histories, as well as her research into the 1821 census for his home area. Patricia also provided him with many photographs, some of which are reproduced in this book. We would like to thank her husband, Thomas Gilligan, for permission to publish these photographs. His brother, Paul Briody, has continued Patricia's research into family history and this has also been availed of. Paul has also provided my father down the years with newspaper cuttings and such like, and on numerous occasions has discussed local lore over the phone with him. This regular contact with his Cavan past has been of great help to my father down the years, years when he rarely saw his native place. For the past decade or so my father meets his younger brother Austin and younger sister Anna Celia, as well as Paul, once a year at a family reunion in Mullahoran. He has benefited from discussing, and indeed disputing, various memories and items of local lore with them, and also with his two first cousins, Sister Elizabeth Brady and her brother, Eddie Brady. My father looks forward to this annual gathering and to meeting all his nephews and nieces and their spouses and children, as well as neighbours and friends in Mullahoran. Three of Patricia's siblings, Annette Gannon, Josie Briody and Tony Briody, have also contributed in various substantive ways to this book.

My father's feeling of the 'cool Cavan breeze' again in August 1999 was what first inspired him to write about his childhood, but he could not have completed his memoirs without the support and encouragement of his children and in-laws, who each, in numerous ways, have contributed to his writing of this work and my editing of it. Rather than enumerate the contribution of each, I will simply list them: his daughters Joan, Anne, Máire and Geraldine; his sons Tomás, Mattie and the late Eamonn; his daughters-in-law Sheelagh and Tuula; and his sons-in-law Tom Dunne, Oliver Murphy and Paul Roach.

As editor I have also benefited from the assistance of the above, and from feeling the 'cool Cavan breeze'. I list below others who have contributed to my editing of this work. First and foremost I have to thank Paddy Sammon for proofreading the work and for much solid advice. The following offered advice and assistance of various kinds: Proinnsíos Ó Duigneáin, Michael Coady, Éamon Ó Ciosáin, Willie Nolan, Mary Maguire, Jean Costello, Seamus Helferty, Maura Cronin, Jukka Saarinen, and Pat Sullivan. I would also like to thank my wife Tuula and son Tuomas for much needed help with the maps, photographs and index. On behalf of my father and myself I would like to especially thank Amanda Ryan of the Heritage Council of Ireland for all her help, as well as the board of the Council for a grant towards the publication of this work.

A special word of thanks is also due Emma Verling, Pat O'Sullivan and Donal Magnar for last-minute help in procuring certain photographs dealing with Avondale Forestry School.

The permission of the Trustees of the National Archive of Ireland to utilise the 1901 census and the 1911 census in connection with the appendix of the book is duly acknowledged, as is that of the Ordnance Survey of Ireland to reproduce and adapt an Ordnance Survey map of part of my father's home area.

Finally, as editor, I have to thank my father for all his patience and putting up with my endless questioning, as well as a certain amount of abuse, as I went through his long text with him.

Introduction and editorial note

Born in Mullahoran, south-west Cavan, on October 28, 1913, less than a year before the outbreak of the Great War, my father's earliest memories relate to that war and to the political upheavals that followed in the wake of the 1916 Rising. He started school when Southern Ireland was still administered from Dublin Castle, and he witnessed the War of Independence and the setting up of the Irish Free State. Like many of the generation that came of age in the first decade or so of independent Ireland he was imbued with idealism. In time he was to devote his life to the re-afforestation of Ireland, and make many personal sacrifices for that ideal.

Although later in his life there were years when circumstances kept him away, and far away, from to his beloved Mullahoran and Cavan, he always carried the memories of his native place around with him in his head, and often when in a tight spot he would murmur to himself 'Mullahoran!' as a form of exhortation. It is no surprise therefore that in the first volume of his memoirs, his native parish, as well as the surrounding area, feature prominently. The Cavan of his youth made him, to a large extent, what he is, as did the years of the Economic War when times were hard not just for cash-strapped farmers but for the young in general. His experience at home in Cavan during that war helped steel him for the hard life that lay ahead.

When he finally left home in Autumn 1936 on a path that was to lead him within a year or so to Forestry, he could hardly have imagined that he would not only be blessed with long life, but that he would survive all the Avondale Forestry class of 1937-40 and one day in his nineties set pen to paper to tell his story and much of theirs as well.

My father first began writing an account of the world of his youth when he was in his late eighties in Autumn 1999. For a year or more he continued writing down his recollections of his childhood, up until his confirmation at age twelve. He may have had the intention of writing more at this juncture, but it is not entirely clear if he contemplated writing about his adult life. Much of these early writings consist of journeys down memory lane along the roads of his childhood, in the magical drumlin country of Mullahoran and Ballymachugh. Some of these early recollections about aspects of traditional life (amounting to some two hundred pages of foolscap) have been incorporated into this book, but many have not. It is hoped to publish them separately at some stage as they constitute a unit in themselves.

The bulk of my fathers memoirs proper, some thousand pages of foolscap, were written from Spring 2005 onwards, after he had reached the age of 92. In the meantime, fearing that he would never get down to writing about the rest of his long life, in July 2001, I began recording on mini-disc his recollections of Forestry and his circuitous path to Forestry, as well as memories of his youth, early manhood and the traditional way of life he was witness to. The bulk of these recordings were made between July 2001 and January 2005, and amount to more than forty hours in all. There are also some hours of video-recordings of him reminiscing on aspects of his life.

This is not all. There are in addition hundreds of pages of notes he has dictated to me over the years as well as extensive field-diary entries of mine for all his recordings. Among other things these diary entries contain much extra detail such as comments by him on his recordings, as well as additions and corrections. Subsequent to each recording session, he would diligently listen to what he had recorded. I have also kept extensive notes of numerous conversations we have had on his childhood, his career in Forestry, and other matters. My father has not just documented and recorded much of his life, he is also a very well-documented man. He once said to me that he is a guinea pig, and in a sense he is.

I believe the extensive recordings we made together over a period of almost four years helped him to focus on his life and structure it when he later came to write about it. Once he began writing his memoirs proper, he would record no more. Even though he had enjoyed immensely our recording sessions, he seemed to value the written more than the spoken word. Be that as it may, he had by this stage set himself the task of writing about his years in Forestry and nothing was going to distract him from that goal.

He began his account in Spring 1943, just prior to his

marriage, with an incident that almost ended his life, when one evening he went astray and became disorientated on the Slieve Bloom Mountains. His going astray on the Slieve Blooms is something he had refused to record for me, saying he could only do justice to it in writing. The process of describing the events of that long, terrifying night on the mountainside, would appear to have inspired him to write about what ensued when he came down off the mountain the following morning. Given up for dead by the people down below, he was to go on and marry that Summer and start a family and work the area as forester for the next three years, before being transferred to Mount Bellow, Co. Galway in 1946. There were to be two other transfers after that before he was eventually transferred to the Carrick-on-Suir area in 1960, where he was to remain until he retired in 1978. Before he could go ahead, however, and write about his subsequent career in Forestry, he had to go back, and dealt somewhat briefly with his path to Forestry via Ballyhaise Agricultural College and Albert College, Glasnevin, as well as with his training in Avondale Forestry School and his early years as a forester.

This left a gap in his writings between his Confirmation in 1925 and his going to Ballyhaise Agricultural College in 1936. He then went back diligently and filled this gap. In addition, realising that his treatment of his path to Forestry and his training as a forester had been somewhat a rushed job, he rewrote the section of his memoirs dealing with the period 1936-1943.

At this stage we had the makings of two books: one on his life up until 1943 and the other on his career as forester from 1943 to 1978. When I pointed out to him, however, that his earlier writings on his childhood would not constitute a suitable introduction for the first book, he wrote a lengthy new section on his childhood. He also rewrote and expanded a number of other sections for this first volume of his memoirs.

Thus, my father's memoirs have a somewhat convoluted history. They have also a deeper dimension because of the existence of a substantial corpus of related recordings and notes. In editing this first volume of his memoirs, it has been necessary to reorder sections of his text somewhat. This has sometimes involved the addition of a sentence or two, but any substantive changes to the text have been vetted by him. Not only has he read and commented on each section as it was edited, he has also read the final complete text twice. No mean achievement for a man of almost 96 years of age, not to mention his great achievement in writing such a lengthy document in the first place!

A few short extracts from his recordings have silently been included in this volume, but the bulk of these recordings have been left for another day. There is much on the mini-disc recordings that are not in his writings and much in his writings that are not in his recordings. They complement each other, and at times contradict each other, and this is as it should be. Memory is not a simply matter of recall. People view the past through the lense of the present and there is much in my father's writings and recordings that are influenced by more recent events, and indeed by his day-to-day life, as well as by his personality, which is very positive. This corpus of texts, notes and recordings constitute a veritable goldmine for the study of memory. Hopefully, in time to come it will be availed of by scholars, but for the present here is the first volume of his story as he tells it.

Mícheál Briody
Helsinki, 2nd September, 2009

Contents

Part I: Childhood

Earliest memories 1
Parents and relatives 4
Sponsors and neighbours 16
Farm, house and household 21
Play and pastimes 42
Religion 47
Early school years 52
Deaths in the family 57
The Troubles and aftermath 60
At School in the Irish Free State 77
Football in the Twenties 84
Confirmation and final years at school 90

Part II: Coming to manhood

Leaving school and the Wall Street Crash 105
Caffrey's College Dublin 1931–1932 113
The Economic War in Cavan 130

Part III: The path to Forestry

Ballyhaise Agricultural College 160
Albert College, Glasnevin 198

Part IV: Forestry trainee

Avondale Forestry School 211
A practical year:
Kilsheelan 249
Aughrim 255
Kinnity 266
Woodford 273
Avondale, final year 286

Part V: A qualified forester

Clonmel-Kilshelan/ forest foreman 305
Slievenamon/ forester-in-charge 314

Maps
1. Location of author's home area   329
2. Briody farm, Callanagh Middle, Mullahoran   330

Appendix: 'Like Snow off the Ditches': the decline   331
of Irish in south-west Cavan, Mícheál Briody

Photo Gallery   357

Index   364

Part I: Childhood

Earliest memories

I was born on October 28th, 1913. It is often difficult to date one's earliest memories. In my case, however, an incident occurred some year and a half before the end of the First World War that impressed itself on my memory. I was three and a half years of age at the time and it was Spring 1917.

We lived in the townland of Callanagh, in the parish of Mullahoran in south-west Cavan. We were about go set off by horse and trap for the second Mass at Our Lady of Lourdes Church, Mullahoran. My mother, whom we called Mama, was the driver. With us were my brothers Hugh P., a lad of seven, and Edward, aged five. They were both itching to get hold of the reins. Mama refused to yield. Their time would come. My father was not with us. He was an auctioneer and valuer, in addition to owning a farm, and he used be away all week during the day. He loved to walk to the first Mass with a neighbour called Tommy 'a Park (Smith) to the church two miles away. Dad would have all the news from the towns of Granard and Cavan. Tommy would have all the local news. They were great pals.

On this particular morning Tommy had come into our kitchen for a cup of tea after returning from Mass. Dad was now accompanying him to the road while we were leaving. Mama was about to salute Tommy when two aeroplanes appeared over the horizon. It was the first time I had seen an aeroplane and I was fascinated. Suddenly the planes swooped down menacingly towards us as if they were trying to identify us. We could actually see the occupants. I became frightened. Dad shouted at Mama: 'Stay at home Annie! The Germans have arrived.' I heard Mama say: 'I'm going Thomas. I have a special message for Aunt Kate. I have to go.' Mama gave a flip to the reins and off we went to Mass. When we arrived at the church, Hugh P. and Edward brought the pony and trap towards the stable. Mama took me by the hand and we ascended to the gallery of the church where we met Aunt Kate. She had a handshake for me and we took our seats. There was also a choir in the gallery. Mass was about to begin and it was a time for prayer. After Mass everybody filed out. Aunt Kate, Mama and I remained in the gallery. It was a very long chat. I was waiting to hear about the two aeroplanes but the subject never came up.

Remaining on in the gallery, where they always heard Mass, was an opportunity for both of them to solve their little problems. They had been born along the shores of Lough Sheelin and used go to Mass in Carrick, which was in the parish of Ballymachugh. Now they were married and lived in the Parish of Mullahoran. They considered that they were very fortunate in being able to go to Mass together, even to a strange chapel.

When we eventually came out, Hugh P. and Edward were waiting patiently for our arrival. Hugh P. had the reins. The road was now empty and Mama allowed him to drive us home. Mama and Kate were also great pals. Mama was the elder of the two by six years. Aunt Kate cycled growing up. Mama preferred to use the boat on her shopping trips to Finnea. As a married woman she loved driving by horse and trap, especially on her trips to Cavan Town when she would be selling a firkin of butter.

At the end of the nineteenth century and the beginning of the twentieth, bicycles were treated with great respect. Only the main roads were hard-surfaced. The rest were surfaced with gravel. In Winter the gravel roads were muddy. In Summer a passing car raised a cloud of dust which got on our clothes. Bicycles were taken apart at the advent of Winter and hung up pending their re-assembly. There were only four motorcars in our area then. There were three types of horse-drawn cars of different sizes to accommodate the different sizes of horses and ponies. Our type was the horse and trap. It was said to be called a trap because if the horse bolted and ran away, the occupants would be trapped inside the box. The trap had a door at the rear; inside was a semicircular seat. The occupants could face each other while chatting.

The next type of horse-drawn car was a back-to-back car. The driver and two others sat in front. Three could also be accommodated at the rear. These sat back-to-back with those in front – hence the name back-to-back. The third type was called a side-car. This was of older vintage than the other two. It was back-to-back but the seats were lengthwise instead of crosswise. The seats hung over the wheels of the car. The running-board on which the occupants place their feet was at the right height for them to jump on and off with ease. Between the seats were two wells: the one to the fore for luggage and the one to the rear for transporting a dog. As time went on, gradually all the iron rims of the wheels were being covered with rubber. It was no longer acceptable to make too much noise. The tip-tap of the horse's feet should be accompanied by the soft purr of the rubber covered wheels. A man who had been away in Australia for forty years was asked did he see any difference in the people at Mass. His reply was that the people in horse-drawn cars were still in horse-drawn cars but the people who went on foot were now in motorcars.

Before I proceed further with my story I should say something about the part of Ireland I was born in and grew up in. Later in life as a forester, I worked among mountains: the Wicklow Mountains, Slievenamon in Tipperary, the Comeraghs in Waterford, the Slieve Blooms bordering Laois/Offaly and the Slieve Aughty Mountains in south-east Galway. The terrain of my home area was very different. Looking north from the gate of our yard one could see Ardkill Mountain, which is really only a five-hundred-foot high hill. To the north one could see another high hill known as Bruse Hill. My home area of south-west Cavan is essentially a land of little hills very few of which are more than 500 feet high, and most of them much lower than that. The Cavan hills are interspersed with small lakes, one for every day in the year, it is said. It has some beautiful large lakes too, one of which comes into this story, namely Lough Sheelin, which is seven miles long and three miles wide. At a lower level there are many bogs. Those in our vicinity were the Clonloaghan bog, the Callanagh Upper bog and Boston (Callanagh Lower) bog. These were gradually being cut away and reclaimed. Callanagh Lower was called 'Boston' because most of the people living there had been to America and back.

On the highest part of our farm, the Sheep Field, one could see for a distance of many miles, taking in the Leitrim

Hills, the gleaming spire of the church in Granard and a fleeting glimpse of the waters of Lough Sheelin. In all we could see four counties from this hill: Westmeath, Longford, Leitrim and Cavan. On a clear day it was uplifting to climb up to the Sheep Field and view this great vista of counties. Although from our yard, which was much lower down, one had a much less spectacular view of the surrounding countryside, at night as one looked towards Drumbrucklis, north-east from our yard gate, one could see a sea of light from all the little houses.

Because of the absence of a mountain range in its path the wind blew fiercely over Mullahoran. People were beginning to plant shelter belts a distance away from their houses, in order to lift the wind. The prevailing wind was from the south-west. The north-west and the north winds were strong too. If at all possible, it was essential to build a house in the shelter of a hill. The little hills served to lift the wind. Our house was built in the shelter of a hill. This offered us protection in stormy weather. Although we were sheltered from the south-west wind, the other winds often stole a march on us. The Winters in the 1920s were excessively cold.

Parents and relatives

Mama was from a family of eleven. She was born in 1882. Her father (Edward O'Reilly) had a large farm at Carrick, on the shores of Lough Sheelin, for which he paid rent to the Deases of Turbotstown. He also had the rents of a number from townlands in Carnaross and Baskinagh, Co. Meath, which had been bequeathed to his grandmother, who was a Dease. The Deases were Catholic landowners who lived in the shadow of the Protestant Pakenhams. Edward in turn was married to Eliza O'Reilly, one of the New Inn O'Reillys. He seems to have been a well-educated man and it is said he was offered a commission in the British Army but declined the offer. Mama showed me documents, which I would love to possess now, which would seem to indicate that the family had Fenian sympathies. The Land War and the passing of various Land Acts proved a double-edged sword for my grandfather. While he achieved a lower rent

4

on his own farm and eventual ownership, the rents from Carnaross and Baskinagh were reduced as his tenants took him to court, and the family were in time to lose these properties.

The older children had enjoyed a higher standard of living. The younger children, one of whom was Mama, had to make do with less. They were helped by a relative, an officer in the American Army, who was a New Inn O'Reilly. He brought some of them to America and educated them there. Mama might have gone with some of her siblings had she not met Dad. When she was in her late teens her mother's health deteriorated. Mama, who called her own mother MaMa, stepped into the breach. She began to do the shopping and the housekeeping. Her rowing skills came in useful on her trips to Finnea. This was a large village to the west of Lough Sheelin and lay in Co. Westmeath. By boat it would only have been a distance of some three quarters of a mile, but three miles by road.

Lough Sheelin, which lies between Cavan and Westmeath, is quite a big lake, seven miles long and three miles wide. It was famous for its fishing in those years. The River Inny flows out of Lough Sheelin and goes past Finnea on its way to the River Shannon. It has been called the singing river and has been immortalised in the song 'The Rising of the Moon': 'Murmurs pass along the valley, like the banshee's lonely croon / And our pikes must be together at the rising of the moon'.

Lough Sheelin also forms the boundary between Cavan and Westmeath. At Finnea there is a bridge which joins the two counties. The Bridge of Finnea has become famous because of an encounter there in the mid-seventeenth century between Myles the Slasher O'Reilly (a soldier in Owen Rua O'Neill's army) and the English. The Scots-English force had come along the southern shore of Lough Sheelin. They were hoping to cross the River Inny at Finnea and to outflank O'Neill's army at Granard. It all seemed so easy. There was only a small force of Irish at Finnea under Myles the Slasher O'Reilly. It was a David and Golliath affair. The Irish were helped by the fact that the bridge was so narrow that only two could fight abreast. Myles the Slasher was said to have borne the brunt of the fighting. The Scotch-English failed to eject the small force lead by the Slasher and had to withdraw.

In Mama's youth a commemoration of the skirmish was held every year on the first Sunday of August. Finnea was the inspiration of how a small band of men when properly motivated could defeat a larger force. It became a sort of Mecca for physical-force nationalists of the period. It was addressed by such speakers as Bulmer Hobson and Darrel Figgis. One of Hobson's great sayings was: 'We should never despair of Ireland's freedom: Chicago was burned by the kick of a cow.'

Seán MacEoin, who was leader of the IRA in our area during the War of Independence, has said that it was while listening to speeches at Finnea that he was inspired to fight for Ireland's freedom. The holding of the commemoration on the first Sunday in August became an important date in the calendar of the period. Mama told me it was the highlight of her early years. Expatriates would take their holidays to coincide with the Finnea commemoration. For older people it was a rare opportunity to meet each other. The occasion brought life to a sleepy little village. The few pubs did a roaring trade. People came from Granard and erected stalls at convenient places. As well as speeches, there would also be athletics. Mama was one of the few girl runners in the locality in her time and won a number of trophies. Eyebrows were raised at girls running at all. Mama had to be careful. She must have realised that she was breaking new ground. At an early age she was also indoctrinated into the Fenian philosophy.

I have given Finnea more space than I should. I have done so because it comes later into my story. Adults tended only to speak about events they witnessed among themselves. We children were told relatively little of what happened in the previous generation. What I know has been mainly gleaned from talking to Mama, my godmother, Mrs Henry, a girl who worked in our kitchen, Maggie Coyle, and our farmhand, Tom McDermott. My Aunt Kate Brady also told me a lot about the events of those days.

Mama and Aunt Kate would talk of the changes that occurred in the first twenty years of their lives. Corn had sometimes to be threshed with flails. Potatoes were planted in ridges. They had to be labouriously dug out with spades. In my youth they were planted mainly in drills. On our farm we continued to plant in ridges only where the topsoil was shallow, and in reclaimed bogland where it was difficult to bring a horse and plough. A mechanical potato digger could now achieve in a day what it had taken a week to do in their youth. Similarly with the corn: a threshing machine could slip around from farm to farm and thresh the corn in no time. There were some large farms in Ballymachugh and Carrick which required extra manual labour from outside the area. This was supplied by the spalpeens who came from the west of Ireland. After they had sown their own crops they came across to help out. Similarly at harvest time, they came after they had saved their own. About ten spalpeens came to our area in the Spring and twenty at harvest time in their youth. The spalpeens were highly skilled. They also had a fund of stories and were welcomed at many a fireside. In my youth, Aunt Kate and Mama spoke nostalgically of them and wondered where the younger men had gone. I suppose many had emigrated to England, America, and Australia. Year after year, the numbers of spalpeens decreased until they no longer came. I never saw any of them. In Mama's youth the bigger farms grew more crops than later on. This necessitated more manual labour – hence the spalpeens. The advent of machinery changed all that.

Mama often spoke of the coming of the old-age pension. The Old-Age Pension Act was passed in 1908 and at first the pension was only five shillings. It was a wonderful boon for the elderly, some of whom felt themselves in the way of the family coming up. Soon they found themselves as people to be cared for. It is a yardstick of the times that 5/- per week could mean so much. People, especially women, who liked to keep young in the sight of their neighbours, now found that growing old had its benefits. The difficulty was that births and deaths had only been recorded by the State since 1864. In many places Catholic church registers did not go back that far. Now there was a gap of 35 years to be accounted for as one had to have reached the age of 70 to be eligible for the pension.

It became the custom for old people to be asked by officials could they remember the Night of the Big Wind in

7

1839, and if they could, who else alive was there in the house that night or in a neighbouring house. Their claim was then corroborated. Naturally, nobody denied anybody's claim to have been alive on that night.

You had to be assessed for the pension. Inspectors would call to check how many cattle were on the farm and who owned the farm. There were gates between farms through which cattle could be passed during the inspection. People were warned of the approach of an inspector by a particular method. An empty bottle was quarter-filled with lime or bread soda. When heated over the fire the bottom dropped out of the bottle and this could be used as a type of trumpet with which to warn of approaching inspectors. On several occasions a deliberate false alarm was given by some blackguard, which engendered great rage. My dad recalls that more old people were out and about after the passing of the Old Age Pension Act and some he thought were some distance from 70 had suddenly aged. Nevertheless, one woman was heard to remark that getting the pension was a messenger of death.

In the Twenties we used often visit 'Lake View' with Mama; her old home. Mama loved to see the old lake again. Uncle Hugh, her brother, who was still single, lived there. While there we would call in to see Aunt Maria, Mama's eldest sister, who lived nearby in Carrick. She was married to Bernard Reynolds. They had fourteen children in all, most of whom were in America. I was friendly with two of the younger girls, who were of my own age. Both went to Carrick National School, or the 'School on the Rock' as it was called. It was built into a hill. They had a gallery of photographs from America in their parlour. These had special significance for me, for my sights were already on America .

My maternal grandfather had a brother who was called Farmer O'Reillly. He had a family of one son and four daughters. At fifteen, his son, in the spirit of adventure joined the British Army, some time prior to the outbreak of the First World War. There was a large depot of soldiers in Granard. At that time joining the Army was an opportunity for a lot of young men to see the world. Very few of them associated the Army with war.

8

Six months after the Great War erupted, the young man was reported missing. We never gave up hope and he was included in the family rosary every night. After the War ended he resurfaced. He had been captured. One of his arms had been shot off just below the elbow. The Germans had made an iron hand for him and put him ploughing. He had been treated well and had a fund of stories to tell.

The trouble started when he came back to Ireland. In the space of a few short years it had become unfashionable to fight for England. As the saying went:

'The meanest, vilest wretch who walks the earth today
Is an Irish born hireling who works for English pay.'

Within a short time of his returning home he was made to feel unwelcome and even felt threatened in the locality. He had to keep out of sight until people forgot him or forgave him. His case was common enough. Because Mama was his first cousin, his presence in our house would have been noticed, but he was hidden in our barn. I think the situation eased when he married a girl who was in the Sinn Féin movement. I never heard the details of his life discussed in my home. Suffice to say that he worked a very good farm and reared a fine family.

I will now let my dad's people into the picture. Some two hundred and twenty five years ago my great-grandfather Harry Rua Briody was born in 1783. My grandfather was born in 1819 and my father in 1864. Harry Rua was born in Clonloaghan in the parish of Ballymachugh, but his father had come to the locality after being dispossessed of his farm in Co. Meath. Harry Rua, who was a very progressive farmer, in time leased a neighbouring farm for his other son, Andrew. This should not have happened. According to the custom on the Farnham Estate, a Protestant farm could only be leased by a Protestant. However, Lord Farnham's agent, Maxwell, sided with Harry Rua and Lord Farnham eventually gave his blessing. Harry Rua was also made the 'life of the townland'. This meant that while he lived, the rents of any farm in the townland could not be raised. This was a great bonus. It meant that tenants could improve their holdings. There were some landlords who saw every improvement as an opportunity to raise the rent. Wise landlords consolidated their estates by allowing tenants to improve. Harry Rua lived to be a great age, dying at the age of eighty five in 1868.

Dad was the second son in a family of five. The other siblings were Henry, Patrick, Anna and Hugh. At the time of the 1901 census only Henry, Thomas, and Anna were living at home. Patrick had become a policeman and Hugh had emigrated to Australia. In the next decade Anna married J. O'Brien of Sonnagh, Mullingar, County Westmeath. They were now without a housekeeper. Then Henry married Margaret Brady from Killinkere in east Cavan.

Dad was a very tall boy and at the age of fifteen he started collecting the Grand Jury Cess. This was a small sum to be paid by each householder and was easily collected. The area, however, was very large and Dad had to ride a pony on his rounds. The cess was to cover the administration of the Grand Jury. During the Land War of the late 1870s and early 1880s, Dad found it impossible to collect the cess any more. He was at a loose end. He became active in resisting evictions and in organising boycotts. Mama was very proud of him and always said that he did his bit. He was very popular in the surrounding counties in the years that followed. His mother was a Creevy O'Reilly. They were one of the county families (in other words, very well-to-do) in Longford and they may have helped him financially to get on his feet.

Still in his twenties, he became an agent for Hunters of Dublin, a firm that provided farmers with fertilisers, seeds and feeding-stuff for animals. Half of his customers were credit worthy. The other half were not and they sheltered under his umbrella. He also procured 'waste' from Guinness's Brewery for pig-feed. He was politically motivated. He saw that the farmers had to be given a leg up to get ahead. Later he was to join with one of the Creevy O'Reillys and found the Briody & O'Reilly firm of auctioneers, based in Granard. The experience he gained working for Hunters subsequently helped him when he went into the auctioneering business.

I really know very little about my father. He lived in a great era. The Land League, which he took an active part in, is said by historians to have been one of the most motivated rural movements in nineteenth-century Europe. He was later a member of the Ancient Order of Hibernians (AOH, Hibernians) and was a supporter of Home Rule. He spent a lot of time in Dublin over the years, both in connection with his work for Hunters and visiting my Uncle Patrick. His travels must also have taken him to Wicklow. It was only when I joined Forestry that I realised that he knew every turn of the roads at Avondale. He may have been somewhat bitter about the lukewarm support certain of the Catholic clergy gave the Land League and about the Church's role in the downfall of Parnell. However, when he came to live in Mullahoran, he worked with Fr Thomas O'Reilly to build the new church of Our Lady of Lourdes.

On the Callanagh crossroads up from our house there was a hawthorn hedge inside a ditch. There was a seat on the bank. Dad, when a he was getting on in years, would go out of an evening and after a while a curl of smoke would come across the hedge. Later a second curl of smoke would come when he would be joined by Tommy 'a Park Smith or some other neighbour.

I never heard Dad mention the commemoration at Finnea, supported by physical-force nationalists, although it came up in many a chat by the fireside. The Home Rule Movement pointed the other way. I know he was there once because it came into one of Mama's stories. Granddad, my mother's father, often attended the Finnea commemoration. It was an occasion to meet old friends. On this occasion, however, he had a cold and did not go. Dad had seen him in the distance but had never met him. He went to Finnea to ask him for Mama's hand. Instead he only met Mama. When he told her of his intention she invited him home. The boat was laden and could not take him and his friends. He said that they would cycle around by road. This gave Mama an opportunity to apprise the household of Dad's coming.

Mama loved to tell the story. She despaired of Dad and his friends arriving. She went out the road to meet them. She saw them coming along wheeling their bikes. They were trying to get sober. She may have delayed them even more. Eventually she got them to the house, fearful of what might be the consequence. Granddad and MaMa gave them a great welcome. Dad had

11

brought a bottle of whiskey and soon everyone was merry. That was the last time that Mama saw Dad under the influence. Dad did not mind anybody drinking provided they did not waste time doing so.

Mama and Dad were married in 1910. She was 28 years, he was 47. There was a gap of 18 years between them. They were married in the beautiful church near the rock of Carrick. The church had been built sixty years before. It was bequeathed to the Ballymachugh parish by the Dease family, whom Mama was related to. Mama and Dad spent the first few years of their married life in a house that had been a police barracks, Capragh House. Hugh P. and Edward were born there. They had no land there except for a flower and vegetable garden. Uncle Patrick spent his holidays with them and they spent a lot of time in Dublin near the Phoenix Park with him.

Both my parents had a regard for the Irish language, particularly Dad. He had been at an Irish class in Ballynarry in the late 1870s, but only remembered a few words. The teacher was the local Ballymachugh curate. During the years that followed he probably hit upon the dying language here and there. When I was learning Irish at school he would often ask me the Irish for such and such, and learned to count in Irish. Often at an auction when the bidding was slow Dad would liven things up with a few bits of Irish. When asked where he got his Irish he would reply that he got it from meeting the scholars.

Uncle Patrick was in the Dublin Metropolitan Police (DMP). This was an unarmed police force. When he was training in the Depot in Dublin, he happened to be on duty near the Viceregal Lodge, where a party was being held. It was quite a big party and when it was breaking up in the early hours of the morning, there was a big number of horses and carriages on the road. Suddenly, a horse bolted and everyone was attempting to get out of the way. Patrick pulled the horse down and prevented a lot of carnage. His boyhood with horses stood to him. The Viceroy, on hearing of his heroism, asked Patrick where he would like to serve. He asked to be posted to Parkgate Station, where he was put in charge of the mess. That is why Mama and Dad could visit him there. He was an expert gardener.

I recall his stories of the poor children in the 1913 lock-out and his efforts to have their prison sentences mitigated when brought before the courts accused of theft. Those children stole because they were hungry. Patrick retired from the DMP in 1920 while he had still eight years to serve. I don't know for certain, but he most likely saw the writing on the wall, and wanted to avoid been embroiled in conflict with fellow-countrymen. He was unmarried. Many also left the Royal Irish Constabulary (RIC) around this time. There were policemen in the DMP and the RIC who were married with families. Many of them had no option but to remain at a their posts.

Uncle Patrick's retirement had a big effect on our lives. He used to spend some of his time in his boyhood home at Clonloaghan. He would sleep there, and then come down to us during the day. One would imagine that his coming home would have met with IRA hostility. Not so. Down the years he had kept contact with his native place and he had recommended many a young boy wishing to be a barman in Dublin. This was remembered and he merged into the locality in a few weeks. He too was a storyteller. Uncle Henry's stories had been heard before. Patrick's were about Dublin, and that was something new. Everything has a special place, and Dublin was very much in the news.

Uncle Henry was one of the best shanachies in the district. He could also step-dance and play the violin. He had little interest in politics, yet he figures in one of my earliest memories, which involves a political procession. Arthur Griffith had won the bye-election in East Cavan for Sinn Féin, defeating the Irish Parliamentary Party candidate, who was editor of *The Anglo-Celt*. Sinn Féin in our area, which belonged to the West Cavan constituency, decided to organise a torchlight victory procession. The local men who had helped in East Cavan were to be met at Drumhawnagh Railway Station. From there the march would wind its way through AOH strongholds. The train was to arrive at the station at 9.30, where a large number of supporters were assembling. The procession would be led by a band and proceed through Killydoon, Grousehall, past Drumension hill, and on to Callanagh Lower. It would then pass through the AOH stronghold in Callanagh Middle (where we lived) and on to finish in the Sinn Féin stronghold in Boston, or to give it its official name, Lower Callanagh. It was a lovely night with a strong breeze. Dogs were barking everywhere and one sensed that a lot of people were on the move. We waited.

We had an unexpected visitor for the torchlight procession that night, namely Uncle Henry. His object in coming to us that night was to gather the makings of another story and to be able to say that he was there. Rockets were fired to signal the arrival of the train. A solitary shot fired gave us to understand that someone meant business. Then the band struck up and we knew they were on the way. We did not see them for a good while. Then the sky seemed to light up. The music was almost drowned out by the din and shouting. Mama, Dad, Maggie Coyle, Hugh P., Edward and myself were crouched down in a dyke, peering through a hedge. Not Uncle Henry. He was standing on the garden wall with a grandstand view of the oncoming procession. To our amazement he was standing to attention as if about to salute, which he did. To my child's eye what I witnessed was an amazing sight. There were about thirty men carrying pitchforks on top of which were sods of turf soaked in paraffin. They were shouting 'Up Griffith!'. Two men carried the tricolour attached to two guns. The AOH flag was green. It was a night to remember.

We all went in and had a cup of tea. Strange how nobody seemed to ask Uncle Henry about his behaviour in saluting. It became one of his greatest stories. Years later I heard him tell it. Maybe that helped me to remember it so well. Words were magic to him as he told his listeners how he had deliberately gone down that night to save the thatched farmhouse that might 'be accidentally burned on purpose'. He told us how he stood on the garden wall and calmed down the situation. For me the jury is out; I don't know. That for me will always be a memory of 1917 and of Uncle Henry. *Ar dheis Dé go raibh a anam!*

A family that played an important part in our lives were the Creevy O'Reillys, who were considered a county family. They lived at Creevy Lodge two miles from Granard in Co. Longford on the Cavan border. They had a large farm, which was

14

also a freehold, and were very well-to-do. My paternal grandmother, Rose O'Reilly of Creevy Lodge married my grandfather Hugh Briody of Clonloaghan, County Cavan. Hugh was the son of my great-grandfather Harry Rua Briody, who was born in 1783 and died in 1868.

At the turn of the twentieth century Creevy Lodge was owned by T. P. O'Reilly, a first cousin of my father's. I remember him as a highly-educated man with a great love of books and horses. He got married in his twenties, which was rare at that time. He married an O'Ferrel, also of county standing. It was a love match, which was also rare in those days. As mentioned, Dad and T.P. O'Reilly set up an auctioneering business at Granard. Dad brought to it his wealth of knowledge of the people, T.P. O'Reilly his wealth. It worked well for both of them, although Dad was many years older than his cousin. T.P. O'Reilly had three boys. Looking back it seems that there was a gap of six years between his youngest and my eldest brother. That would account for the fact that we had not as much to do with them as we had with other cousins of our own age.

The Creevy farm consisted of dry cattle, hunters, and race-horses. Our much smaller farm was a mixed one of poultry, pigs, milch cows, a few cattle, a horse, a pony, and a donkey. We had one cattle-dog. They had half a dozen different breeds of dog. We grew our own corn and hay. We cut and reared our own supply of turf. They burned coal and bought in supplies of corn and hay for the horses and cattle. They went to races and often had their own horses running. I remember one such called 'Annalee Aboo'. They went hunting too. They were a charming family and despite the difference in our positions had quite a time for us.

T.P. O'Reilly and his wife would have been the same age as Mama. The two women accommodated one another. Mrs O'Reilly was an authority on the Royal Family. Mama did not care about the Royal Family but she made herself acquainted with all their different names to be able to maintain a conversation with the other lady on the subject. Mrs O'Reilly had a lovely flower-garden, but she had not the knowledge of flowers, shrubs and weeds that Mama had. She nevertheless took time to listen and educated herself on the matter. T.P. was the real gentleman and he was a great man to help someone in need. He did not seem to have any political allegiance, but he was a sort of Irish Irelander. It was the age of pamphleteering and he was an avid reader of pamphlets. Pearse's pamphlet *The Murder Machine*, which called for a radical change in the direction of Irish education, made an impression on him. He could talk endlessly to Mama of Lady Gregory and her plays. Mama often spoke of seeing Lady Gregory's plays performed at Ballywillan near Granard.

T.P. did not seem, as far as I am aware, to have had any stories. Dad had a fund of stories, but only told them on certain occasions. Mrs O'Reilly loved to get Dad going. Needless to say he was able to pick the ones that suited her. She appreciated that he kept an eye on how things were going at Creevy. Dad disapproved of T.P.'s gambling. For a time his sleep was disturbed at night. He would wake up having dreamt of seeing T.P.'s dead father pointing in the direction of the stables. When he eventually told T.P. of this recurrent dream, it had a big effect on him. He got the message and mended his ways. It was one of the stories that Mama used to raise her eyebrows on hearing. Twenty years later I asked Dad about those dreams. He smiled and asked me not to press him on the matter.

The Creevy O'Reillys used get three of the British dailies. We would get these papers from them two days later. I recall reading *The Sketch* and *The Daily Mail* that came from them. The three O'Reilly boys loved to come across. To them our farm was a sort of menagerie which intrigued them. One day, the youngest boy asked his mother could they have a pond like ours with ducks and geese. Her answer was: 'You will be looking for the moon next.' Mrs. O'Reilly would have loved to have had a girl along with her three boys and when my sister Elizabeth was born she was forever paying attention to her.

Sponsors and neighbours

I was the first of the children to be born in the old thatched house in Callanagh. A week after my birth I was baptised at Our Lady of Lourdes Church, Mullahoran and my sponsors were Margaret Briody and Michael Galligan. My godmother, Margaret Briody, was my Uncle Henry's wife. She later wrote to me often when I was away from home. She always insisted on a reply. Oftentimes when I would be in a strange place I would buy a local paper and send it to Margaret. She used to pretend to Mama that she knew more about me than anyone else. My godparents dominated my early life to a degree which would be inconvenient today. They felt a duty towards me and said many a prayer on my behalf. My godfather, Michael Gilligan, was of the family who had originally owned our farm. He was a great favourite of everyone's. He used assist Dad at furniture auctions. He was a skilled climber and in the struggle for Independence was responsible for hoisting the tricolour flag on trees which were out of reach to most. He also succeeded in putting a tricolour on the chimney of the RIC Barracks. His climbing skills were in time to be a great asset to him. He escaped to America where he had a very successful career as a tree-doctor.

We never met again. Strange how both of our lives were connected with trees! From America he kept in touch with me and sent me many a letter and dollar bill. I always replied to his letters. To be able to write a good letter was of extreme importance for boys and girls emigrating, and was a skill emphasised at school. Emigrants from Cavan in my youth were not impoverished and illiterate like those of a hundred years before. They also had people to meet them when they landed in America. Most of them were planning to continue at night-school while they worked by day.

For the purpose of telling my story I have to tell of the lovely neighbours who lived alongside us. They were known as the 'a Parks. Their name was really Smith, but there were a lot of Smiths around so they were known as the Park Smiths or the 'a Park Smith. In the parlance of the day the old man was known as Brian 'a Park. His young wife was called Mrs 'a Park, and so on. The name ''a Park' probably derives from the Irish 'na páirce'. They had a family of four, two boys and two girls, much younger than we were. A bachelor uncle and a spinster aunt lived with them. Their farm was a much bigger farm than ours. They kept more cattle and horses than we did, but less poultry and pigs. They kept a bull, which we always had to be on the look out for. We brought their kids to school in turn and also looked after them. We were very much together.

The bachelor brother Tom (Tommy) was known as 'My Dear Man' because he always began his conversations thus. He had money but he was for ever waiting to buy a suitable farm, which never turned up. His sister Kate had turned down many a good match and mostly contented herself with the young family. She was a nice person. Some said she was a gossip, but I would say that she was very interested in news. The bachelor Tom helped out on the farm but he had a special project on hand which endeared him to all. It was a fertile farm, but there were two acres of rocky ground which lay to the north-west of the house. He built a ditch around these and then he proceeded to remove the rocks as far as possible. He even used dynamite on the larger ones. He then planted the area with trees. He was before his time. He tried to procure as many different species as possible. They were both deciduous and coniferous. He also had different shrubs on the perimeter. The work was new and we all loved to help. For me it was a case of 'coming events cast their shadow before', for in later life I became a forester. Later he introduced beehives to the area, which kept us from falling in love with the place. The plantation, planted seventy years ago, has since been cut down. The beautiful rambling thatched house with its three chimneys is also gone.

Like Dad, the Smiths belonged to the Ancient Order of Hibernians, except for Brian's young wife who held the same political views as Mama. She came from Co. Longford. Both women were great friends. There used to come back now and again a younger brother of Brian's and Tom's. He was a refined, well-spoken man. He had great time for the young family and for us. He was a single man and was in the RIC. One night in 1920, the barracks in which he was stationed was attacked by the IRA. He rushed to put on the Veery Lights, which were used to signal for help. Instead of turning them up, he turned them down and got electrocuted. His death to us was like a family bereavement. Even his Sinn Féin neighbours from Boston came along to the wake. I never saw so many people crying. We were not to be left alone in our grief. On the day of the funeral, when even the sun did not shine, a lorry of Black and Tans aggressively arrived with a firing party from the RIC. The poor family looked on dumbfounded as three volleys of shots were fired over the grave. It was a day we had all to forget.

Another sad sweet memory concerns the Dolan family. They lived in a small house in a little garden between our farm and the road. They were what was called labourers in those days. They had not even got a County Council cottage. If they had, they would have had a half acre of land to grow vegetables. It was a family of eleven. The father was a stonemason, but he was only able to obtain employment for a few days in the week. The hardships of the Twenties meant that houses were not being built to any extent. Today he would be called a craftsman. Then, he only got a half-crown for a day's work. Three of his boys were over fourteen and were already working on the neighbouring farms, where they were fed. The money they got barely kept them in clothes and boots. In the 1920s farmers had food to give. They had not money for themselves.

Some say that the Dolan family were reared on our farm. That is not true. They were a proud family and one of great principle too. Never did they get a gallon of milk but they did something for it in return. It might have been the cleaning of windows or the sweeping of the street (as the farmyard was called). They would not have it otherwise. The old man got a few drills in one of our fields where he grew potatoes, cabbage, parsnips and onions. He kept the surrounding crops free of weeds. Sometimes they might be given an extra side of bacon which we did not need. Mama was careful. She would make sure to stress that it was left over.

Another family in our vicinity were the Galligans. They had once owned our farm, but due to bad management had to sell part of it to save the rest for the family. The son, John, who got what remained, had to rent it to a neighbour while he himself went managing another farm. When he had enough capital saved, he returned and took over his own farm. It is at this point that he now joins my story. John was our 'co-man'. This meant that we each had a horse and together we did the ploughing of both farms with our team of horses. This was normal practice. A farmer who owned a horse '*co*-ed' with his neighbour. They might even do the ploughing of a third farm where there was no horse. Farmers with no horse did extra work for those who helped them out with ploughing, especially in the cutting and rearing of turf on the bogs. It made for a wonderful togetherness. Moreover, by working alongside each other people honed their different skills and working methods. The absence of electricity meant that a great deal of work had to be done manually. There were big families on most of the farms and these were stretched to the limit to get things done. Cooperation among farmers was essential. John Galligan knew every field of ours as well as his own. This was invaluable. The taste of potatoes varied from field to field. It was important to know where to plant those that would be for the table. Table-potatoes were grown in suitable soils with plenty of farmyard manure. John had a lovely sister Mary. She married the son of the man for whom John had managed the farm. The Galligans move in and out of my memories of the Twenties. They were real friends.

Another family which figured very much in our lives was the Wilson family. Although their farm lay at the back of our farm, we could not be described as near neighbours. We met them going to Mass and the Wilson children passed our house on their way to school. Mama and Mrs Wilson loved to chat. They both had an uncle a priest. Their husbands did not seem to meet. They had different political views. The Wilsons were strong Republicans. When a young child, I went to Mass with Mama, but from the age of eight I walked to Mass by myself. I was the first of the boys to go to the first Mass. I preferred to walk to Mass because there was a better opportunity to meet the men and boys who talked football. Football was very near to being a religion of its own in the Cavan of the 1920s. I rarely accepted a lift from anybody except from Mr Wilson, who had great time for me and I for him. I cannot tell at this distance in time was his name John or James, but younger people then 'Mistered' and 'Missed' the older generation. You always said 'Missus' to a married woman and 'Mister' to an adult male. I found him to be an avid reader like myself. He must have found me unusual. I had access to the British papers through the Creevy O'Reillys and to the American *Irish World* and *Irish Echo* that my aunts used send us. He in turn had a brother in Belfast, a city he seemed to know a lot about. He had a different angle on things than I had. I considered he had a very fine, balanced view of things. A son of his brother in Belfast became a priest, Fr Des Wilson, and played an active part in efforts to find peace during the recent Troubles in the North. I never exchanged newspapers with Mr Wilson, but I exchanged views. I had a feeling that there was a Fenian tradition in the family.

One of his sons, John, became an academic and later a Fianna Fáil TD. He rose to ministerial rank, and ended up as Tánaiste. Had Fianna Fáil realised the vulnerability of Brian Lenihan in time, John might have been President of Ireland. After I left Cavan, the Wilsons and Briodys were the footballers of the area. John was very friendly with my brother Austin. On his way home from school he used drop in to our house to read newspapers or borrow books. There was always a lot of books in our house. Some had come from relatives in America; others were waiting to be auctioned by Dad's firm, and had belonged to parish priests and such like. Once on a hurried visit back to Cavan, I got the idea that I should call to see Mrs Wilson. I told Mama of my intention. She took a 'Thank you card' out of the drawer, telling me that Mrs Wilson had passed on. I had left the visit too late.

Farm, house and household

After Mama and Dad had been living in Capragh House for about two years, something occurred which caused the family to move residence. Charles Galligan of Callanagh had sold half his farm to a man near Drumhawnagh some years before. This man decided to resell it. On the day of the auction it was sold for a satisfactory price. The transaction was done by Dad's firm, Briody & O'Reilly. It was customary for the buyer to put down a quarter of the purchase price as a deposit. The remainder was to be paid later. This time the buyer had not the required deposit on hand. He was waiting for the full sum to come from America. This happened with buyers now and again. Dad would pay the deposit and get it back later. This time, however, the money did not come from America. If Dad did not pay the full price for the farm, he would lose the deposit. He paid the full price of the farm intending to sell it at a later stage.

However, when Mama saw the farm she fell in love with it. On the farm was a big thatched house. Maybe it could be slated later on, to her satisfaction. She did not realise that some of her children would fall in love with that beautiful thatched house. It was a very long house extending from the road to a dairy at the upper end. At the road was a bedroom where I slept. Next was the parlour. A long, slated annex projected from this room. This was a later addition and was built to allow access to the house for a Galligan priest. As a student or as a priest he would not be supposed to enter from the kitchen, or so the folklore goes. In the parlour there were two large mirrors, one on the mantel and the other on a sideboard opposite. This gave the appearance of a very large room.

The house had three chimneys but the middle chimney, between the parlour and the kitchen, was false, being simply for decoration. There was a fireplace in every room. Unlike many thatched houses in the locality our house had no loft. The wood-panelled ceilings were high, slanting at first and level on top. The kitchen itself was the biggest room in the house. It was built in the heyday of the Galligan farm, to accommodate a number of tables of men working on the threshing and tillage. It had an open hearth where all the cooking was done. There was a hob at the back. To the right was a crane from which could be hung pots and kettles. On each side of the fire was an oven pot, which seemed to have been there permanently. When a cake was being baked a few coals of turf were taken from the fire and put under the oven pot. A cake of bread was then thrown in. Half-way through the baking a few coals were placed on the lid of the oven. When the lid was seen to rise the cake was considered to be baked. It was then taken out to cool on the window sill. In time, I learned how to make bread myself. It was slow progress at first but I got there. At an early age I became aware of the difference in the taste of bread. A slice of bread at the 'a Park Smiths was very different from that of Mrs Henry's of Clonloaghan. As I grew up and travelled further afield, I was astonished at the variety in the taste of home-made bread. Some of the women who had been to America used Bex Tartar, which bleached the flour, to make a much whiter cake.

We also ate a lot of oaten-meal bread. This dough was kneaded on a special board on the table. It was pressed down until it was just an inch thick. The oaten-cake stand was made of a few slats of strong tin with a support at the back to allow it to be stood on the hearth. There was a flat edge at the bottom to hold the cake as it lay back against the stand at an angle of 20 degrees. The cake was turned as required.

Beyond the kitchen was a large room divided by partitions into three sleeping cubicles and a passageway to allow access. Each cubicle was lit by a small window in the front of the house. The passageway was at the back. My parents and the younger children slept in this partitioned room. Hugh P. and Edward slept with me in the room beyond the parlour.

During the Twenties the Travellers were also tinsmiths. They used make oaten-cake stands, buckets, gallons and tin mugs. The latter were called porringers. They were ideal for children to eat porridge from but too hot for tea-drinking. During the First World War when tin was unavailable, tinsmiths made buckets out of sheets of galvanised iron. We used have a great welcome for the Travellers. They had always something to make or mend.

There was a big pot in the yard over a grate where the potatoes for the hens and pigs were cooked. The pot could take from ten to twelve stone. There was a seat there and a cover over it to provide shelter when it rained. We called this partially-enclosed structure the boiling-house. Many a tramp slept there. It was not an uncommon sight to see a knight of the road sweeping the yard after a good night's sleep. He would then call in to see if there was anything else that required doing. Of course, he would end up getting a breakfast.

What we called 'the street' lay on the south-west of the house and was really the farmyard; beyond which was the apple garden. There every Spring we took down about twenty rose bushes from the wall of the old house and put them up again after lime-washing. The result in June was a riot of colour against dazzling white. At the upper end of the house was the dairy, and being the dairy of a farm which at one time had consisted of some one hundred and twenty acres, it was fairly big to cater for pre-creamery days. It had a long stone bench to accommodate milk crocks. There was a very large churn at the side. This was operated by a fly-wheel, which in turn was accelerated by a spin-wheel on an axle which protruded out to the haggard, where it was connected overhead by a series of shafts and cogwheels to a draw-bar. At the end of this bar was an attachment for a donkey or pony who went around in a ring, inside a low circular hedge. The pony of my childhood needed nobody to drive him. He went rapidly around for a certain period of time depending on the size of the churning. Then, as he felt a change on the pull, he slowed down as the butter gathered. The draw-bar was painted and the circular hedge kept trimmed even long after the creamery days had come along. All that disappeared with the building of the new house.

Our surplus butter was packed into what was known as a 'firkin' (a small wooden cask). It could contain around sixty pounds. This was sold at the open market in Cavan town. Mama went shopping on the first Tuesday of every month by train to Cavan. She brought a different son with her each time. We very much appreciated the run. The selling of the firkins was different: a firkin had to be sold as soon as it became ready. Mama was very fond of driving and she loved going in the pony and trap to Cavan with her firkin. On arrival at the Market House, an official would take the firkin to the weighing scales. An inspector would be on hand to inspect the butter. He had a corkscrew-type of instrument which he would insert into the firkin and which revealed every inch of butter from top to bottom. We always got top price for our butter. We would then stable the pony in some shopkeeper's yard. After getting something to eat and doing a bit of shopping we would tackle the pony and make for home. On our way to Cavan, we kept to the main road known as the 'New Line'. On our way home we would take the old, but now less frequented road, that wound in and out among the lovely Breifne hills.

We did not start going to the creamery until about 1925, although some of our neighbours went. I do not know why exactly. It could be that initially Mama did not want to deprive Hugh P. and Edward of the pleasure of churning with the pony and donkey. She was, however, very proud of the calves she reared. The skim milk that came back from the creamery in Killydoon after the milk had been processed was not very suitable for calves. That left over from our own butter-making was much more nutritious for them. Later on a meal came on the market which put a body into the creamery skim milk. Sometime before we started going to the creamery we stopped selling butter in firkins in Cavan Town. As more and more people started going to the creamery, there developed a brisk demand locally for home-made butter. We sold it by the pound at the dairy door. Children were not taking to the white creamery butter. Parents bought our yellow butter and mixed a small portion of it with a larger portion of creamery butter and thus got their children 'over the hill'. Later when calf meal became available we started going to the creamery. Butter-making became but a memory.

Most of the farmers in our vicinity had four or five cows. The 'a Park Smiths had ten. Cows calved mostly in the springtime and they gave milk all during the Summer and Autumn. Some of them gave milk in the Winter, some did not. We were relying on a single cow who might have calved during the Summer. Generally it worked out all right, but one Winter it did not. The 'a Park Smiths supplied all their Boston neighbours. We generally supplied the Galligan family and they in turn supplied us when the need arose.

On the north-east of the house and enclosing the annex lay the flower-garden. It was fenced around by high netting wire to protect it from intruding hens. It ran the full length of the old house. On the other side of the wire fence was a track leading to the haggard. There is a surviving photograph of Mama and my younger brother Paul taken in this garden (see photo-gallery). When I first saw it some years ago, it brought back many memories. In was there that Mama taught me the names of many weeds. This lore was to come in useful in my Forestry days when it helped me to select suitable tree species for planting.

Further back and in line with the flower-garden fence ran a small stream which came from a well further up. This stream went under the public roadway and flowed into 'The Sheugh', a pond which accommodated a large number of ducks and geese. In the corner of the Sheugh Field across the road, was the Low Garden, where we grew vegetables. This was also enclosed by netting wire. Crops like potatoes, turnips, cabbage and corn were grown out on the farm, but vegetables needed in less quantity such as carrots, parsnips and onions were grown in this garden. The crops in the fields were rotated every year.

Turf which was got from a bog a mile away provided the fuel for the house. A large amount of fuel was required for the house fires and in addition for the outside boiling-house where potatoes for the pigs and hens were cooked.

Except for the purchase of flour, sugar and tea, the farm was self-sufficient in respect of food and my memories are of full and plenty. Pig-meat was used principally on the farm. We killed our own pigs. The more fleshy parts of the animal were cured as bacon. Cutlets from the more bony parts were salted and stored in crocks in the dairy. The soup there from made parsnips and onions taste delicious. We also made our own pork sausages and black puddings. Bacon and cabbage was a very common meal. We only ate beef when someone came back with a quantity of it after a fair, and at Christmas. Beef when purchased long ago had a lot of fat attached. The crisp roasted fat was very tasty. Nowadays the   butcher removes much of this fat. At Christmas time we might also have mutton. We rarely ate mutton otherwise. On a Sunday we sometimes ate some of our chickens for dinner, but we did not stoop to eating our lovely ducks, geese or turkeys. They were part of our play world. Unfortunately our turkeys were reared for the Christmas market. This was something we tried not to think about. Salted fish, mainly herring, was eaten on Fridays and fast days. It was delivered on a Thursday in a horse and spring-van by some local trader. In the late Twenties men selling a greater variety of fish used sometimes come from Poolbeg in Dublin. They would always get a cup of tea in our house.

Our breakfast before going to school consisted of an egg, home-made bread with butter or jam washed down with tea, milk or cocoa. We preferred oaten-meal bread for our school lunch. We would also bring oaten-meal cakes with us when rearing turf on the bog. You did not eat them as such. You more or less nibbled at them, as they were quite hard. Sometimes oaten-meal cakes were enriched by a handful of sugar or a handful of caraway seeds. Both types were nice but we preferred it plain. To wash the oaten-meal cakes down we brought a can of new milk to school to share amongst us.

The nicest meal of the day came in the evening when we all sat down at the end of the day to eat our fill of porridge. We called it 'stirabout'. It was eaten with buttermilk. We never had porridge in the morning. If you were still hungry, you could have porridge again later if you liked. A large family required a ton of oatmeal annually for making porridge and for baking. A handful of oatmeal was also thrown into pork soups (stews). For a week or so at Christmas we would have rice porridge, with raisins and currants mixed through it. We liked this but we nevertheless looked forward to having the oaten-meal porridge again.

Slices of bacon fried with eggs and onions was the fare on Sunday morning. The pièce de résistance of a fry was boxty. This was made from grated new potatoes mixed with flour, which held on to their unique raw taste after cooking. It was first made into a roll, wrapped in gauze and boiled. It was then sliced and fried as required. I have eaten boxty in several counties. All are very different. For me I look back nostalgically to the Mullahoran 'vintage-boxty'. Sometimes the potatoes that were left over after the dinner were mixed with flour and milk to make potato bread for the evening tea. If the men were working out in the fields at harvest time, pancakes made from flour, milk and eggs were sent out with the tea to take the edge off their appetite.

The humble potato was an important factor in our self-sufficiency. It was the first crop in rotating land. It got all the farmyard manure, enriched by loads of peat mould from the bogs. The second and third crop would be oats, barely or rye. A crop or two of hay would then be got from it before it was returned to grassland. Thus, at least four years would elapse before it was cropped again for potatoes. I never saw artificial fertiliser being used in growing potatoes in the Twenties. People were very choosy about the taste of potatoes. They would not accept the poor quality of the potatoes of today. In those days no meal was complete without a nicely flavoured potato. In Ballybaise Agriculture College, I saw twice the yield of potatoes produced than at home with the aid of artificial fertilisers, but the taste suffered greatly. Similarly, vegetables, especially turnips, that we buy today in the supermarket appear tasteless. They require so much dressing that one is sometimes at a loss to know what one is eating.

After digging we put the potatoes in pits in the field which were then covered by a pile of clay. When the fields were needed for further cropping we took the 'spuds' into the barn. Then we covered them with a layer of straw, to exclude the sunlight. A barrel was also procured and a layer of medium-sized potatoes were placed edge-to-edge at the bottom. This was covered with a layer of sand or peat about two inches thick. The next row of potatoes was placed on top of this. Then sand or peat again until the top of the barrel was reached. When June came, those potatoes came out as fresh as they went in and we looked forward to eating them. The new potatoes did not come until the first week of July. In June we often ate rice to supplement our diminishing supply of edible potatoes. This was different from the rice porridge (sweetened with currants and raisons) we ate at Christmas time, but nevertheless eaten in porridge form, not like savoury rice is prepared today.

We had an apple garden and a bed of rhubarb, from which we made pies for the Sunday evening. We had always visitors then. Our jam was made from black-and red-currants and gooseberries, which we grew, and from wild raspberries from Boston Bog. The latter could be collected there in bucketfuls. Often we would go there of a Sunday and have great fun. We might sometimes come home without any berries. The secret of jam consumption was to make different kinds and to alternate between different kinds of jam. There were also many crab-apple trees growing along the ditches of the Black Meadow. Crab-apple jelly was made from these. The Apple Garden was at the far side of the street. It also contained fruit bushes. Above the Apple Garden was the High Garden, where we had a clothes line. Pigs were also left root around there, and sometimes young calves were let in to pass the time.

Before water was supplied to rural Ireland by various schemes, wells were very important and were kept clean. No animals were allowed near them. They were regularly emptied, cleaned and limed. Every well had its regular trippers, and it was a great place to have a chat or hear news. There were different opinions about each well. Some were better for making tea with than others. Later I found this out myself in going round to the various gangs in Forestry and getting a cup of tea here and there. People knew where the good wells were. We had a well of our own in the Drilling Field. We had a second well in the Rock Field. It was close to a mearing fence, which means that it bordered a neighbour's field. He had no water, so we allowed him to make an opening on his side and avail of the water. Brian Smith had a well that was availed of by all the 'Bostonians'. It made a lovely cup of tea. Galligans had a fine well too with a nice built-in surround. The travelling people were very conscious of where the good wells were.

Going to my cousins, the Brady family, at Shanvalla in Cloncovet meant walking three miles there and three miles back. There was a well to every mile. The well near Donohoe's forge in Glen was the first one. There was a mug hanging on a bush by the well. I preferred to lean on two rocks, lower myself and suck up the precious liquid. Even when I was not thirsty, there was that strange impulse to go in to the well for a drink anyhow. You never heard of water being polluted back then. Those wells are now no longer needed by us. Maybe we should have kept a few of them open for that nostalgic cup of tea. There is an old saying: 'Never keep all your eggs in the one basket.' In time we may realise the foolishness of relying on one source of water. These wells may again be opened up. Then we might have our chat again at the well. Who knows? Instead of turning a tap, we may take our bucket and meet some interesting person at a well.

The immediate previous owner of our farm, an O'Reilly

from Drumhawnagh, did not live on the farm but worked it from a distance. We brought a bit of life to the place when we came. Ours was a farm of thirty four acres with an extra fifteen on lease. As I have mentioned above, we started '*co*-ing' with the Galligans in ploughing the two farms. The word '*co*-ing' comes from *co*operation. The Galligan family were a little older than ours and they kept a special watch over us at school and at the football matches.

Dad was a very busy man and was away most of the day. He got away early in the morning. Sometimes he used his bicycle. More times he would bring the pony and trap. He did not take any of us with him during our school years. Mama ran the farm. She had learned a lot during her rearguard action at home when fortunes changed for her father. She had not a poultry station, but she kept up to one hundred hens. She used get pedigree cockerels from a poultry station. She gradually built up a name for herself. There was a practice in our locality, which I have not seen or heard of since, of 'swapping' eggs. A boy or girl would arrive at the farm with twelve to fifteen eggs. They would always be very large eggs, possibly selected from ten dozen. Unlike their eggs, our eggs were fertilised by a cockerel. There was no money exchanged. The customer would be giving us big eggs for small eggs. Maggie Coyle, who worked in the kitchen, always came on hand with a cup of tea and a scone. I often saw half a dozen swappers come on the same day. It was all part of Mama's ingenuity.

Every farm had its half-acre of bog to supply the turf for the year. Our half-acre lay in Upper Callanagh. To get there we had first to pass through the Galligan farm. From there we would pass through the Luke and Philip Tierney farms. My brother Hugh P. married Mary Jane Tierney. In time, our half-acre no longer contained enough turf to be worth harvesting and we had to get another plot. We used the old plot to rejuvenate our potatoes and corn. We always had a few ridges of potatoes growing there. The next year we brought bog potatoes back to the farm for sowing, where they produced a bumper crop. The first year they might not be suitable for human consumption. They would be given to the pigs and poultry. The second year they would be edible. Every time a cart went to the bog, it brought back a load of peat mould to be added to the farmyard manure heap.

I cannot recall when I first realised the presence of Maggie Coyle in our kitchen. She came from a cottage adjacent to Clonoose School. She must have been around seventeen years of age when she came to us. Her kindness to me I will never forget. It was she who taught me to read. She also taught me a host of tricks in counting eggs. Later when I became an expert shopper I used help Paddy Lynch count eggs for the eggler (a man who buys and sells eggs).

The Coyle house was a pleasant house to drop into for a chat. The teachers at Clonoose school had their lunch there. Maggie's siblings were in America and she was heading there also. Her father was elderly and read quite a bit. I remember getting *Speeches from the Dock* from him. He was also a storyteller, but unlike most storytellers he would sometimes fall asleep just when you were most eager to hear what happened. His wife was very adamant that we should not wake him up. Many of his stories were thus put on ice. We often had to guess the endings for ourselves.

All Maggie needed was a slip of paper to certify that she was proficient in domestic skills, including needlework and sewing. She was already very skilled when she came to us except that she had never worked a sewing machine. She was not long in picking up that skill too. She went home every night during the summer months. She stayed with us during the wet and cold spells of Winter. In the second and third decades of the twentieth century, the Winters were exceptionally cold and the roads were often frozen over. The climate has become milder since. Maggie Coyle was like one of the family. She left for America in late 1920. She came back in the late Twenties to see one of her parents, who was dying. She left again for America where she remained.

Everyone on the farm had chores to do. We had no electricity to help us out. My chores were to help in feeding the poultry, keeping the nests clean and bringing the eggs to the shop. Even during the school term I had still to help out at home as far a possible. The eggs were brought on Wednesday evening to the shop and also on Saturday morning. Initially Maggie Coyle brought me with her and showed me how to do the shopping. We went to Paddy Lynch's shop in Grousehall. On a Saturday evening Maggie shopped for her own parents and then she went to Matt McGee's shop near Clonoose School. I sometimes went with her to McGee's shop. Mr and Mrs McGee were a childless couple. I was only a boy of three years at the time. Mrs McGee delighted in kissing me. I hated this. After a while I began to tolerate it because there was a follow-up of sweets and chocolates.

I did not like shopping at first, but later I became very proficient at it. From the age of seven I did shopping on my own. In those days every farmer was self-sufficient in food. All that was normally needed extra was tea, sugar, flour and maize meal. The sale of eggs helped buy much of these essentials. Most of the maize meal was to feed the pigs. Shopping gave me a great grasp of how to deal with money. We never got into debt.

Our farm hand, as I have said, was Tom McDermott. When I first knew him he would appear to have been in his late fifties or thereabouts. He must have been with us since we came to Callanagh in 1912. At the turn of the century he was the owner of a corn mill which had got burned down. This was situated in Glen, about half a mile up from Mullahoran church. This together with a small farm which he possessed had given him a handy living. After the fire, he slipped off to the America to get enough cash to start anew. His family remained at home. When he came back he realised that corn-milling was a dying trade and so he did not start up again. Cheap imports of maize were taking the place of native corn. Sadly all those corn-mills are now gone. Out of every six mills it would be nice to see one preserved to show future generations what Ireland was like in the early twentieth century. Water mills of one type or another must have functioned for over a thousand years. They were covered by the Brehon Laws. Some of these mills were on fast-flowing streams and could have been adapted to generate electricity for the local area. This would have helped to conserve the past with the present.

There were single and double mills depending on the amount of water available. I never went up to see what kind of mill the McDermott mill was, but it must have been a double one. The river that turned the millwheel and crossed the road at Daly's public house was fast-flowing. Maybe I should explain the difference between the single and the double mill. Well, the double mill shelled, hulled, ground and made oatmeal of the oats all at the one time. The single mill shelled and hulled the oats first, then when the millstones were lowered it ground it and made it into oatmeal.

We had our corn ground at Creighton's mill. This mill was a single one and was on the Legwee River in Loughduff. The corn had to be kiln-dried for a few hours before milling. The kiln, as far as I can recall, would have been twenty foot by twelve feet. It had a steel floor and under it was a turf fire. It was a great place for the middle-aged and elderly to gather. There were plenty of bags of unground corn to sit on. The kiln-man was a real shanachie and used regale those waiting with his stories. The men at the open fire probably gave him a hand with the bags. The miller was paid so much for every hundredweight of oatmeal made. The kiln man got a scoop or two from each customer. He also got a tip which varied from farmer to farmer. All that is no more. In fact, it would be well nigh impossible to get into Creighton's mill now. It is in ruins. The sluicegate, which intrigued us at the time, is no longer. A few lines of a riddle come to mind, which I do not recall seeing in print:

'There are   two pigs in yonder sty
One of them wet the other dry
The more they get the more they cry
Give them more and quiet the boy.'

One pig was the millwheel which the water turned, the other was the millstone on which the corn was   ground.

But to return to Tom McDermott. He had a fund of children's stories, which we loved to hear. It did not matter how many times he told a story, it seemed ever-new. He also had great stories of America. He never told any local stories. The burned-out mill was never mentioned. Everyone seemed to be avoiding speaking about it when the subject cropped up in a

33

conversation. Dad was very nice to Tom McDermott. They never spoke of politics, which was rare at the time. McDermott was very well-up about politics and spoke well. He liked to read the American papers which came in, especially *The Irish World*. He knew history inside out. In the War of Independence he kept his distance from the IRA. It was difficult to know where he stood. He was a proud man. Milling may have gone back hundreds of years in his family. He never worked with anybody else but us. Mama was very kind to him. He got eggs, milk and sometimes a chicken outside of his wages. Maggie Coyle used raise her eyebrows when he was around and her stories were always told against him. It was from her that I heard that the burning of the mill was malicious not accidental. One of her stories was of the last years of the First World War when sugar was almost unobtainable. Mama always managed to have that extra bit for Tom. He was very fond of sugar. This morning when he arrived there was none. He tasted the tea. Then he stirred the spoon to the right. He tasted it again. No luck. Then he stirred to the left. No luck!

Daly's public house in Glen was then a beautiful old-world thatched pub. Nowadays there is a nice modern pub there with a family home alongside. I never frequented the pub except when I would call with my donkey and cart to take a quarter-barrel of porter home for a threshing. The river that worked Tom McDermott's mill flows under the road here. The walls of the bridge are low. People used sit there and talk. I used sit on the left hand side when breaking my journey to Aunt Kate's. From there I could look upwards and dimly see the ruins of Tom McDermott's mill and wonder again about how it came to be burned. On the right hand side there was a shallow opening where a horse could drink. If I were barefooted and the road was hot, I could slip in and paddle in the lovely water and come out refreshed. Just beyond the bridge was an opening for a short cut to Kilcogy village. It was used by the people on foot coming from football matches. It is not used now and the opening is closed in with furze bushes.

Early on I became conscious of train noises in the distance, although I had never seen a train. I could hear the noise of shunting down at the Drumhawnagh Railway Station. Every morning, I could hear the shrill whistle of the train as it entered the station. There would be a lot of people to get on there. I observed there did not seem to be the same amount of whistling where freight trains were concerned. The extra whistling was a signal for people to keep clear, or so Maggie said. The whistling of the passenger trains seemed to have an unnerving effect on her. On hearing the full blast she would rush into the kitchen and check with the big clock there. To this day I have never found out what she was attempting to check. Was it the train or the clock?

I became interested in going on the train myself. Mama had promised to take me on a shopping trip to Cavan and I was looking forward to it. I was to see a train before that, however. On one occasion, Mama asked Edward and me to come with her to see Aunt Kate at Shanvalla. The two of us were sitting opposite each other in the front of the trap. Mama had the reins and she was seated to the rear. She had perfect control from there. The reins lay between us. When nearing Dundevan Bridge, we suddenly heard the noise of a train coming down the line. Mama halted the pony, opened the rear door of the trap and stepped from the car-step on to the road. Still holding the reins she whisked them across Edward's head. Keeping the reins taut she advanced yard by yard until she was at the pony's head. She kept a tight grip on him until the train passed. I did not know what to expect. I just gazed at the monster as it flashed by down the line. Mama stopped on Dundevan Bridge. She let us alight to allow us to look up and down the railway line. I have often travelled by train since, but to me the wonder caused by my first sight of a train that day has remained uppermost in my memory.

The bridge at Dundavan had been built in the early 1850s to allow a road pass over the new railway line. When I was older I heard many stories about the building of the bridge from two old men. I will call them Dick and Jim. One of them used sit on the wall leading up to the bridge and look up and down the road while the other would rest against the wall, lean his arms on it and look down the railway line. They used look at one another when something controversial cropped up in their conversation.

Storytelling is the art of painting pictures in the minds of your listeners. When these two men were speaking to you, they were trying to paint a picture of the past. They could go back and forth in the past without any bother. They were probably children around the time of the Famine. At any rate, they must have heard a lot of stories about it. I was unable to get any information about it from them. They were strangely silent about it. Dad was born fifteen years after the Famine. When I used ask him about it, I sensed it was time to change the subject. I wonder why. I heard a great deal from Dick and Jim about hedge schools in the area, something Dad knew little about. These two men could go back and tell stories of the hedge schools that existed prior to the State system of primary education established in the 1830s.

In 1962 the railway line was closed. Dundavan bridge should have been left. No! For some strange reason the bridge had to go too. Sixty years later people speak of bringing back the railway line to relieve the heavy traffic on the Cavan-Longford route. Is it possible that I may see Dundavan railway bridge again?

A settle bed was very much a part of the kitchens on the small farms, where space had to be utilised to the full. If you were looking at one when closed, it would appear box-like with a lid that could be pulled up to form a back to rest on. In fact, children could sit on it with their legs dangling down or they could move back and their legs would be resting on the front of the seat. You had two positions to choose from. It was mostly children who sat on it. It got them out of the way. It was a handy seat if there was an extra lot of people in. The children could also get their meals on the settle. When pulled out at night   it formed a bed. It was about six feet long. Now if one person was being accommodated, he or she could sleep lengthwise. However, the mattress inside was such that it could be stretched out on the kitchen floor and three or four kids could be accommodated in this way. It was only used as a bed in case of necessity. It could be used to put up some traveller of the roads for the night.

In the Twenties there would be a traveller along at least once a fortnight. They were a harmless lot and came from various walks of life. They all seemed to know a lot about the weather. If the weather was unsuitable for haymaking, they might have seen an orange-coloured frog along the way. If the farmer needed rain, they might have seen a convenient black frog or such like. Maybe it was their way of paying for their keep. We enjoyed having those lonely men and women. Some of them had a song. They all prayed for us. They always had a bit of news. I suppose they told us what suited us. I am not saying that they made it up. Their good news was mostly of the parish and about people who were thinking of getting married or maybe going to America or Australia. They were meeting people who had been back from both countries. They seemed to know as much about foreign parts as if they had been there. Their bad news was of places twenty miles away. This gave us a feeling of security.

We had no settle bed, but we had an armchair by the fire. We had another one in the boiling-house. If there happened to be two travellers overnighting together, they would prefer the latter. They would get a fire going and cook some potatoes. Sometimes they fed the pigs before they moved on. There are no men or women on the road now. That was another age – the age I grew up in!

Our kitchen table as well as many of the settle beds and other household furniture of the area were made by a local carpenter name Kane. At Tom McDermott's there is a sharp turn to the right. There is a farmhouse at the cross and further down was Kane's carpentry shop. The family consisted of two brothers and a sister – all in their fifties. There were no children. They were lovely people to meet and talk to. You arrived there with a note in your hand. There was a Kerry Blue dog who growled at you. This was a sign for the door to open. Mr Kane greeted you kindly, took your note, closed the door, retreated inside, and came out again with another note telling you when to return. I would love to describe that shop for you. I cannot. I never got inside. There were nights when I was returning from Aunt Kate's that he would be working late and the shop would be lit up. I would steal over to get a glance at what was inside. Just when I would be on the point of seeing something, the infernal dog would growl from the inside and I would start running uphill. There was a saw pit in the garden behind. Very few ever saw this pit, but none saw it when the brothers were working there. The Kane family have gone, but sometimes their names crop up in the folklore of the place. Kane was very honest. He gave credit, often in lieu of a cheque from America. He made coffins too for all. Some said he only charged the well-off for coffins. Maybe they had to be charged that little extra to balance the books. Was he a sort of Robin Hood? I don't know.

Apart from travelling men and women, there were other frequent visitors to our house, both neighbours and relatives. One such visitor deserves to be recalled as he later comes into my story. He was also a Briody and may have been a relation of the family. Mama always had a great welcome for him. He was nicknamed 'The Smiler'. I was never at his farmhouse. I only saw it in the distance. 'The Smiler' was in his late twenties when I first met him. He was unmarried. He was a handsome man. I once heard him tell Mama that he had forty acres from 'river to river'. The Glen River would be one boundary and the Blind Lake the other. He would appear to have lived on his own, but I cannot be certain. His father and mother could still have been alive.

In those days people dressed well on Sundays. They would wear any old clothes working on the farms or on the bogs. Children would dress neatly going to school. They would be barefooted from April to September. 'The Smiler' always dressed neatly. He would be about five foot eight inches in height. He had a long stride and he always gave you the impression that he was in a hurry. He did not have a walking stick, but carried a light stick in his hand. This was about three feet long. He gave you the impression that he was after locking a herd of cattle into a field somewhere. He had polished boots, something which was rarely seen except on a Sunday. He was a very friendly man. I understood that he sold a lot of his meadows. They would be good along the river. The small farmers in his vicinity would pay good prices for meadows to make hay. Dad did a big business auctioning meadows.

Before entering the kitchen he would leave his little cane at the door. He would be invited to sit down. No. He had not time for that. There was always a teapot beside the turf fire which a stranger could lift, get a mug for himself and as they say 'wet his lips'. In those days you were supposed to be entitled to a cup of tea if you had seen nine chimneys. The treatment for 'The Smiler' was different. He would not be expected to treat himself to a cup of tea from the pot. Instead, Maggie Coyle would boil a fresh kettle of water and brew a special cup for him. There was a great emphasis in those days on freshly boiled water when tea was being made. If a guest did not arrive on time, the kettle was emptied and refilled. I still do it.

All the time 'The Smiler' would be standing in the centre of the kitchen floor. He would be holding the back of the chair he had been invited to sit on. Now and again he would rest an elbow on the top of the chair. He would cup his face in his hand and stare into the turf fire. He would then shrug himself and stand erect as if concluding that life must go on. The cup of tea would now arrive. He would not sit to the table. He was in too great a hurry. Instead, he sat on the edge of the chair. Maggie would keep an eye on him. If he drank the tea and walked out he was really in a hurry. But if he looked towards the press, Maggie would get a bread-plate. She would cut a few slices of home-made bread, butter it with home-made butter, and finished it off with home-made jam. He would talk to Mama and often ask her opinion about something. He was actually a listener. He had a habit of interjecting some little quip of his own at some laughable part of the story. In fact, he often stole the show. Storytellers had to be on the alert when he was around. No time for tall tales. But then he was mostly in a hurry. On one occasion, our dog took his little cane away. He did not mind as he was a special dog in a special house.

My sister Elizabeth was born in 1916. She was a beautiful girl. She was a favourite of my Uncle Patrick. When I think of her I think of a Trojan task he took on some time after he came to live with us in 1920. Patrick loved to keep fit and could not find enough digging to keep going. Although invited in, he did not go into Mama's flower-garden. At first, he contented himself with growing vegetables and caring for the fruit trees. He was a very skilled gardener. He must have felt like a conqueror with nothing else to conquer. All that was to change.

He became alive. Right on our farm was something he had dreamed about. Let me explain. The field next to the haggard was known as the Black Meadow or the Well Field. In the corner of this field, diagonally across from the haggard entrance, was a gate. Inside was a spring well. The Well Field was so called because to get to this well you had to go through this field, although the well itself was actually in the Drilling Field. This well brings back many memories, as does the little rustic wooden bridge one crossed to get to it. Above the Well Field was the Rock Field. At the bottom of the latter there lay a large pond which grew from a rood of ground in Summer to an acre in Winter. The Galligans remembered when there was no pond there.

Clearly to Uncle Patrick's expert way of thinking the drainage must be at fault. I had better explain to the younger generation used to Wavin piping what was done in yesteryear. Well, you could dig a trench and leave it open. This was the easiest solution, but farm animals might fall in. You could line both sides of the trench with suitable stones and then put flagging stones across. The water flowed in the gullet underneath. A third method was the most common. Every year stones had to be picked off the grain crops. These were everywhere and found their way into what was called a French shore. If a drainage trench was six foot deep, it was filled with stones up to four feet. It was topped with heather scraws from the bogs. The remainder was topsoil to carry farm crops or grass.

Uncle Patrick's project was to convert an existing French shore into a gullet-shore. It was a challenging task. Dad offered to lend a man to help. Patrick declined. He wished to have the pleasure of completing the task on his own. The trench would be only one hundred and forty yards long. We were his audience to see him do it. There was an open drain running outside the upper ditch of the haggard. A French shore flowed into this. This is the drain that he sought to open up, thinking that it would connect directly with the pond further up. He had great success on the first day. He actually progressed twenty yards. Seven days like that and the water would be flowing. Time enough to think of what there would be to be done next. It was mid-Spring and the weather was ideal. The next day he started again. He seemed to be singing as he went along. For our part we were intrigued by the round small stones which came out. They were rounded like you would see in a river. They must have been all edges whenever they went in, many years before. Patrick himself was a great dresser, but for this job he wore an old trousers and coat. His face was black with the mud of the drain. You would hardly recognise him. What matter? This evening he would get a wash and get back into his proper clothes again.

The second day everything changed. To his surprise, he met with a rock and the shore swung to the right. What harm, it would swing back again when it had passed the rock. Day followed day. The rock persisted on the left keeping the shore to the right. It now seemed to be heading for the stream that flowed from the well, between the Well Field and the Drilling Field. Then when it was almost at the stream, the rock on the left stopped and the shore swung uphill to the left. He was now only another eighty yards from getting there. He was delighted. He had kept his cool. Elizabeth had now joined our gang. He adored her. To him she was 'Queenie'. One clap of her little hands meant more to him than all our applause. The name 'Queenie' was strange to our ears. We had never heard such a name. Mama used to look away whenever he used it. Did she know something or did she know anything? Did she, Elizabeth, remind him of someone he had known before? She was a lovely kid with her Harry Rua hair. They say that the Briodys have a sense of humour. I still remember her mischievous smile. Patrick always found something to say to her. The rest of us came second. He loved to have her watch him as he worked.

And then he struck another big rock. The shore turned to the right towards the Rock Field pond, but soon veered drunkenly to the left again. He must be admired for not using strong language that day. This time there was no doubt where it was going. It was going towards the ditch of the Limekiln Field, on the other side of which there was another stream of water. Patrick kept going. He consoled himself that he would at least succeed in draining the Limekiln Field, if not the Rock Field pond. The upper right-hand corner of the Limekiln Field was very boggy. He kept on. After a day, he found himself in the Limekiln Field and by this time a certain amount of water was flowing in the drain but not enough. It was Hugh P. who further back saw water oozing from the upper side of the French shore at a point where it was joined by another blocked shore. Patrick went back to examine it. He had not noticed the opening of this other shore on the way up. This shore appeared to connect with the pond. Clearing this would complete his work. The riddle had been solved. There was now only four feet to go and darkness was falling. Patrick decided to leave it for another day. He got up out of the trench. He was lucky and we were lucky, for as we moved away the tons of water pressing behind the bank swept the remainder of the shore away and gushed down the field with a roar. We had all to jump to safety. It was a narrow escape. The Well Field, the Rock Field, and the Limekiln Field are still clear in my memory. But most of all the beautiful red-headed girl who watched Patrick dig and shovel in that shore. She seems to be forever expectantly watching for something new to come out of that drain. So full of fun and life, with all her life ahead of her. Ah dear!

Play and pastimes

A lovely feature of my childhood was our little playground. It lay between the flower-garden and the stream which came down from a well further up. The stream had been diverted years previous leaving our playground in the hollow where once the water had flowed. It was shaded by three Lawson's cypresses. We called them 'Savins' because someone at their time of planting mistook the 'C' of Cavan on the label of the bag they came in by rail for 's'. Years later in Forestry I mystified people by still calling Lawson's Cypresses 'Savins'. It is so hard to change.

My eldest brother, Hugh P., had built a large playhouse for us. He had dug deeply into the bank. This already gave it a back wall and two side ones. He then built a front wall of different coloured stones. The roof was of timber and thatch. It even had a window. Edward was my second eldest brother and he had helped in the digging. He was big and strong. He it was who searched the different fields for the coloured stones. I was the reader of the company and I also minded my sister Elizabeth and young brother Patrick Vincent. The Gilligan, Dolan, Smith and Briody children held their little parliament there during those hot Cavan Summers. The Summers in Cavan were so different from the cold, long Winters of ice, sleet and snow.

Hugh P. was very handy and in later life put in his own central heating into the new house. He dammed up the stream which lay beyond the baby-house and erected a waterwheel. Unknown to anyone he could affix a piece of leather to the wheel which would make a clap-clop sound. At night he would slip out and get the clap-clop going. He may have been responsible for making late-night drinkers hurry homewards.

I used intrigue the company by reading comics, which used come from Creevy. We had a few seats to sit on and a few rugs to lie on. Then one of the neighbours' children would ask Hugh P. to tell a story. He had many and we always hoped it would be a new one. Both Hugh P. and Edward had great stories of Capragh and Dublin   None of the rest of the children had been to Dublin, nor lived at Capragh. Uncle Patrick on one of his visits from Dublin to Capragh had built Hugh P. a playhouse. So you see he had a model to go on. Uncle Patrick also taught the boy football and especially the skill of the crooked kick. Many an opponent in later years was mesmerised by the same. Strangely enough, although a good forward, Hugh P. played mainly in the halfback line. He had a sure pair of hands, was able to get the short kick from a team-mate, and then distribute the ball to a telling point. He was very effective and won many a game.

Those early years at Capragh were never to be outclassed by anything which happened later at Callanagh. Hugh P.'s favourite story was that of the friendly donkey. We had a donkey in Callanagh but he was dull and stupid. Maybe he was too well cared for. The donkey at Capragh belonged to a man up the road who worked him hard and then turned him out on the public road to fend for himself. It was thus he got to know Hugh P. It was not too clear from Hugh P.'s stories whether the donkey was able to open the gate or whether he would be obligingly left in. He became a constant visitor to their garden. Each day would be different from the previous day. On one occasion, Hugh P. hid him for a week in a shed. Dad had to diplomatically step in to avoid a court case. We had no stairs in our house and a lot of Hugh P.'s stories involved going up and coming down stairs. In fact, everything at Callanagh took second place to what had occurred at Capragh. He had spent a few days in Dublin. He would start one of his stories: 'I was away and I *come de back*'. But then none of us except he and Edward had been to the 'Big Smoke'. The magic of his stories lay in the imagination of his listeners. One day we too would see Dublin.

To the north of our house lay the Callanagh crossroads. It was at the merging of the Clonoose, Mullahoran and Killydream roads. The Clonoose road came from the Ballymachugh parish. The Mullahoran one led to the Drumhawnagh Railway Station. There was also a small byroad or lane leading to the farms of Cairn O'Reilly, James Smith and Con Galligan. It was a wide crossroads and in the centre was a triangle of green grass. This was an oasis for us in a warm Summer. We could lie down there and stare up at a blue sky. On the northern side of the crossroads, in front of Cairn O'Reilly's house, was a neat hedge. The hedge on the roadside had been clipped to admit of people sitting on the earthen bank.

Crossroads and roads featured greatly in the Cavan of my youth. The crossroads which impinge most on my memories were the Callanagh, Killykeen and Clonloaghan crossroads. None of these were real crossroads. Rather they were junctions where one road joined another. The real crossroads were down below where roads crossed the main Cavan-Longford road. These three crossroads were mostly used because there was a bank to sit on and a good view of the linking roads. There was no stream of traffic, unlike nowadays. There was the occasional stroller, a few bikes, a horse and cart, and maybe a pony and trap or a sidecar. Very rarely a motorcar. Sometimes an unattended horse or cow would stroll along as some of the very small farmers tended to graze their animals on the 'long acre', which was another name for the side of the road. On the right of our crossroads was the McDonald farm. Later a shop was opened there and that added to our enjoyment.

Unlike other parts of Ireland, we never danced at the crossroads, although dances had been held prior to my time. A large crowd would gather on a Saturday evening before a coming football match. A few of the senior men would deal with tactics, etc., while we youngsters would listen in with awe and reverence. We depended a lot on their coaching. The present boys in football have videos of matches to help them along. We had no such aids. We would gather again on a Sunday evening after the games to talk about a victory or a defeat. Then credit or blame was dished out. The crossroads would be quiet most evenings with the odd game of skittles now and again. Generally the work on the farm, especially the milking, stole a good part of the evening. In the Winter work was slack but evenings were shorter and nights darker and the farmhouses more inviting with their chat and music and occasionally a dance thrown in.

Skittles were not played at the Callanagh crossroads but on a level part of the road in between our house and the crossroads. Another favourite pastime in the Twenties was handball. This was also played against the gable wall of our thatched house. As our gable was at an angle to the road this allowed handballers a greater stretch of road. It was there I learned my first handballing. Later on I played against the back wall of Clonoose School when there was no teaching in session. On one occasion the parish priest got someone to dig holes in the ground behind the school to stop people playing handball there, but they were filled in. The actual handball alleys were at Killydoon and Kilcogy. Only the very skilled were allowed play there. There was another suitable gable down at the 'a Park Smiths. The wall of the old Mullahoran chapel was also suitable for playing handball, and it was there that we competed against the western part of the parish. There was no golf or little tennis then. Every stratum of society played handball. I saw Larry Kiernan, a brother of the famous Kitty Kiernan, represent a team from Granard there. That was 1924. Handball was not a physical game and it appealed to us. It also served to keep the local football team fit.

Although we did not have music and dance at our crossroads, the Cairn O'Reilly house nearby was a place for music. In a line with the well-kept thatched house was a barn. It was there that the Wolfe Tone fife and drum band did their training and rehearsals. Two of the family played the violin. On a summer evening they would play outside. I can still remember hearing that beautiful *céilidh* music floating across the crossroads to our house. It was a house of hospitality. I first visited the house with Maggie Coyle. We were children who listened and made little noise, and consequently welcome. We always got tea and cake. The trouble was that there were three of us: Hugh P., Edward and myself. Maggie would only bring two at any one time. We had to bide our time and wait our turn. We also had to behave ourselves and help Maggie with her chores. If we stepped out of line we had to accept the consequences. It was one of our first lessons in life. Later I used go there with Ellie McCann, who succeeded Maggie in the kitchen, as well as to relatives of theirs, the Kiernans of Callanagh Lower. Ellie was related to the Cairn O'Reillys.

Certain farmhouses lent themselves to *céilidh*ing, music and dancing. Generally those who frequented houses where music was played could play music or sing themselves or had an appreciation of music. One did not have to be a talker or a storyteller to frequent such a house. A favourite house for *céilidh*ing would be where the family had grown up. On no account, except where invited, would one go where there was a crowd of children. A house occupied by old people was a favourite haunt. Often there would be a card-school in such a house. Between them the players would manage to provide a supply of turf. In those days no old person would be left without company. Men and women slipped from one house to another; a night here and a night there. The secret of the *céilidh* was that visitors should not outstay their welcome. When it was getting late the woman of the house would take down the rosary beads as a signal that people should go. Although men used go *céilidh*ing more than women, in wintertime women often gathered in particular houses to make quilts and chat.

Our house was not a *céilidh* house, but it was a house

where many people would drop in. There was always a daily newspaper, an English one and sometimes an American one, lying on the kitchen table. In the morning a fellow would step in, look at the papers, and then fold them neatly back again. He would thank you and leave. The next man might spend a little more time. A reader might sometimes comment on what was in the paper or exchange a bit of news. Maybe a dozen men would drop in this way during the course of the day. I cannot recall a woman among the visitors. These visitors were all so mannerly and caused us no trouble. We provided a service for them and they in turn were company for us. In time, Hugh P. and Edward used go out visiting. I used remain in. I was regarded as a bookworm. Some people at the time would have considered my behaviour unhealthy. Later, when older, I rarely went out dancing.

I first heard a radio in Larry Kiernan's pub in Granard in 1923. I was ten years of age at the time. I was a bit disappointed at first as I thought it would be possible to send messages as well as receive them. We ourselves got a battery-operated radio a few years later. People would drop in to hear the news or to listen to football matches. Once when an old man was listening to an All-Ireland Final in our kitchen he went outside and could be seen looking up mesmerised at the roof of the house trying to discover a wire somewhere.

Religion

Religion was an essential part of our lives. The vast majority of the population of the parish were Catholics. Going to Mass was an important manifestation of our Catholic faith, but our everyday lives were infused by religious belief, and at night-time we had the family rosary before going to bed. Long before I ever went to school I was being instructed, consciously and unconsciously, in the basics of Catholic religion.

The Catholic chapel was three miles away and drew its congregation from a radius of five. In order to cut the distance to Mass, many people availed of short-cuts. There were two traditional Mass paths and there were several unofficial paths in the parish. One of these got you to the church in less than a mile from our house. The ringing of the Mass bell decided the route those on foot would take.

As a young boy I also recall going to Mass in a trap with both my parents. Then I used go with Mama after Dad started walking to the eight o'clock Mass with Tommy 'a Park Smith. Both men could cycle, but they preferred to walk to Mass, part of the way by road and part by Mass path. It was an opportunity for them, as I have said, to exchange news. They loved the walk to the chapel on a Sunday morning. In time Hugh P. and Edward were allowed take hold of the reins on the way to Mass. I never handled the reins, but I also got a new job. My chore was to get a cup of tea for Dad and Tommy on their return from Mass. Tommy would only take a cup out of his hand. His breakfast would be waiting further on. My second chore was to bring in the horse for the second Mass.

There was no farm work on a Sunday and farm-horses loved the rest. They hated having to pull a trap on a Sunday. I know, for our mare would be hiding in a far-off field. I would take a small saucepan of oats and a drumstick. I would then proceed, making as much noise as possible. She would not appear to be anywhere. Suddenly she would rear her head from out of the bushes – her love of oats having overcome her first resolve. I would only give her one mouthful of the corn. I would give her the rest when we reached the stable. I never worked with our mare on the farm. However, when I would be passing by the stable at night, she would give a little neigh on recognising my footfall. It is strange what sticks in the memory.

The Cavan-Granard-Longford road lay to the north of Mullahoran Church and was known as the New Line. Our road came from the south and joined the New Line a half a mile beyond the church. Most of the side-cars and traps came from the New Line. They went up to the old church where there were excellent stables to cater for the horses. Sunday was a special day of the week in the Twenties. It was a day of rest – a day to go to the Church or to visit your friends. It was like an oasis in a desert. The Sabbath was strictly kept. Only the barest essential domestic or farm work was permitted. The only exception to this was when a football match had to be played. Everyone appeared in his or her Sunday best. The men and boys wore blue serge suits with brown or black shoes. They all wore either a hat or a cap. None was bareheaded. The men who came back from America, Australia, Canada or Patagonia generally had some article of attire to show that they had travelled. The older women wore lovely hats and veils. The younger women were more up-to-date with their high heels and their silk stockings. Nowadays, Sunday and the rest of the week are not so different. Sunday was a special part of the Twenties.

At church we had the beautiful Latin Mass. Even the altar boys responded in Latin. I can still hear those haunting, nostalgic Latin hymns. We did not know what those beautiful words meant but they were calming and restful. A returned exile from South America once told me that his greatest consolation was that the Mass there was the same as in Mullahoran. To me the Latin Mass is part of a great past. We also had rosary and Benediction in the church of a Sunday evening, except when we would have a football match. The evening devotions on Sunday broke up the latter part of the day. It was mainly the young people who went to these devotions. It was an opportunity to meet friends. Sometimes afterwards we would have a game of handball at the old church. Every so often young people would go on to a farmhouse dance. I was too young to go. In those days the dancers danced all night and came home in the morning light.

And what of Canon Egan, who ruled the parish? When I first knew him he was Fr Egan. He was a product of Maynooth. There he had got his sympathy for the Irish language from Dr Michael O'Hickey. He did not speak the language, however, but he saw to it that all the prayers were taught in Irish in his schools. He was a great man to attend *feiseanna*, but never a football match. He was a good priest. Everyone in the flock was his special care. He made no distinction. There was a lot of middle-class nonsense in Mullahoran too, but he ignored it. He was very keen on punctuality at Mass. The curate used to say the second Mass. This would give Fr Egan the opportunity to stroll outside to see who was coming late. On one occasion he espied a group coming along who were five minutes late. One of them was unshaven.

'Why Patsy, have you not shaved?' asked the priest.

'Our Lord never shaved Father,' replied Patsy.

Canon Egan was a Republican. I can still remember him smiling to himself when the Bishop at Confirmation day during the Civil War was giving a scorching sermon on the IRA. Dad and he were on opposite sides politically, but they had great respect for one another. They became close friend in later years when the rancour of the Civil War had ebbed.

The saying of the family rosary was very important in keeping the family together. It was a very private affair. Those who were visiting us went home and our own family members came back to join the prayers. The rosary itself was always said in full but what were called 'the trimmings' could be shortened or lengthened as the occasion demanded. The trimmings consisted of a series of *Pater Nosters* (Our Fathers) and Hail Marys for different intentions. We young people heard of a neighbour who was sick or perhaps someone who was bereaved. Sometimes it was said for a person not heard from for a long time. The farm work depended on dry weather at certain periods and wet weather at other times. We often heard a prayer for rain when we young people were enjoying the hot weather. Our curiosity was aroused if we heard a prayer for a special intention. It could mean anything. It might even be asking for a change in our particular behaviour at the time.

There were great stories told about the rosary. I will just tell one that Mama told me. There were three unmarried sisters living together. They had a thriving dressmaking business. They were very nice to everyone but sometimes they fell out among themselves. They were even said to pull out one another's hair. One day a fight broke out. They were upstairs and through the open windows the neighbours could hear the choice language of the women as they pushed one another around. Who came along but Canon Egan on his rounds. He could hardly believe his ears. He knocked sharply on the door. After some delay the older sister came down and opened the door: 'Sorry for the delay, Canon dear,' she said, 'we were finishing the rosary.'

Even after I left the family circle, I still said the rosary. I regard it as a legacy of my childhood. Some people would consider it a repetitive prayer. It is far from that. It is contemplative. Every rosary is part of the life of that day. It can be a prayer for guidance or a prayer of thanks. My wife Nora and I said the rosary at night for the 57 years we were together. Sometimes we were too tired to say more than a decade, but the line was unbroken. I continue to say it every night.

There were two Protestant churches in the area, one in Drumluman and one in Ballymachugh. I think the latter was bigger. There was quite a lot of Protestants in Ballymachugh parish: in Clonloaghan, Killykeen, Ballinarry and on towards Ballymachugh village itself, and along the lakeshore of Lough Sheelin. I only knew of one Protestant family in Mullahoran, but there may have been more. Knight was their name and the children went to Kilcogy School. I think there was a Protestant school at Carrick.

Protestant farms were in general bigger, but they were hard-working people. A lot of Protestants did business with Dad and there were many Protestants at his funeral. They thought well of him. His firm sold and bought meadows to and from Protestants. Later during the Economic War when I was working for him, if a Protestant customer died I was often sent to the house to express the condolences of the firm. I was always given a good welcome when sent on such a call. This obtained for Catholics, Presbyterians, Church of Ireland and Methodists (or Dippers as they were known). Sometimes if I did not manage to get to the wake I went to the Protestant church. I used also meet Protestants at auctions.

Dad was also chairman of a limekiln in Moydristan – a joint-community affair – and a certain Mr Chambers, a Protestant, was the treasurer. There were one or two men employed at the kiln. When the books would come from Mr Chambers, I would look over them for Dad and return them to Mr Chambers. People paid for the lime the kiln produced, but when there was no longer enough being sold, the two men had to be left go and the kiln closed down. Lime was going out of fashion at the time, as it depleted the soil in the long run, although initially it boosted growth.

During the Economic War when I would visit Protestant houses on my rounds (while working for my father), I used find the girls very chatty. I sometimes thought from the way that the conversation would veer towards biblical matters that they were trying to convert me. I was always given tea and sandwiches when I visited a Protestant house on my rounds. It was a very segregated society and the occasions for meeting Protestants socially were few. The Protestant girls expressed the view that they should be at the Catholic dances. Young Catholics felt similarly. Protestants used not go to Gaelic football matches but these girls used ask me about them. A lot of Protestant farmers got land in north Co. Dublin subsequent to Independence and transferred there. Many Protestants also went to Belfast in this period.

Early school years

When I reached the age of four, I began wondering why I was not going to school. In fact, there were kids of three and a half passing the gate in the morning. I was soon to learn why. I was left-handed. The nearest school was at Clonoose with eighty pupils and two teachers; both were women. All left-handed children had to be taught to write with their right hand at home before coming to school. It was the first time I heard a discordant note in my home. I overheard Dad saying to Mama in the kitchen that he could not understand why a child should be asked to change from the left hand to the right hand. Some of his customers were left-handed and they managed without any bother. Mama said that she agreed with him but that the teachers were insisting that all children should write with the right hand. They were probably carrying out their inspector's wish.

When Maggie Coyle attempted to show me how to adapt to writing with my right hand, I objected and told her that Dad was not in favour. She was taken aback. Nothing happened for a day or two. Then Dad came home very early from town. He had apparently something very important to do at home. I noticed that everybody seemed to have disappeared except for Dad and myself. He was smiling from ear to ear. He began by telling me how well Hugh P. and Edward were getting on at school. The teacher was very kind to them. He would like to keep it that way. Maybe I could help out in the matter. He was only asking me to write with my right hand. I could still play football with my left foot and I could throw skittles with my left hand. I was only being asked to do a bit of writing with my right hand. It seemed so little to ask. He would show me. Then to my delight, Dad put his big hand over mine and helped move the pen clutched in my right hand across the page. We had a great evening together. Next day I slipped up to the loft above the barn and began experimenting. I could not believe how my efforts were rewarded. When Maggie Coyle attempted to teach me again, she got the surprise of her life. She rushed out to tell Mama of the miracle.

The following Monday I went to school. I had a new school bag. Thanks to Maggie Coyle I already knew how to read, and thanks to Dad's encouragement I was mastering how to write with my right hand. There was a boy beside me, who welcomed me. He smiled tolerantly at me in a grown-up sort of way. We were about the same age but he, because he was not 'handicapped', had already been a half year at school. His name was Philip Boylan. He was an orphan being taken care of by an aunt. He was to keep me in my place during his time in our school. His real teacher was at home.

I gradually became aware of the outside world when I went to school. The school itself was situated on the border of two parishes. It was actually in Ballymachugh. The site had been given free by a local farmer, a Mr Baxter. It was a one-roomed building and was painted and kept spick and span. A lot of my dreams lie there. Below the schoolhouse at a sharp turn in the road there was a very large tree growing on the ditch on the right-hand side. It was an ash tree. It had been there for a very long time. It has a place in the folklore of the locality. It was called 'The Cranwhinche' from the Irish *crann uinnse* ('ash tree'). During the War of Independence the road at this corner was dug up to prevent the Black and Tans from entering the area. Everyone heaved a sigh of relief when their beloved 'Crannwhinche' survived being felled. This old tree was sheltered by the terrain. Someone suggested that a new ash tree be planted nearby to take the place of the old one when it would go. This was never done. When I returned in the early Sixties the old tree was gone. Nowadays nobody talks about the 'Crannwhinche', which featured so much in the world of my youth.

The school catered for pupils within a radius of three miles, and was a mixed school of boys and girls. Some of these boys and girls left school after they were confirmed at twelve. Others remained on until they were sixteen or seventeen. I was one of the latter. When I first went there the school had two women teachers, a junior teacher of twenty five, and a senior teacher of sixty. They were both great teachers and they attracted pupils from far and near. There were approximately 80 on the roll. Later the number fell to 45 for a time. In Winter extra pupils, who were not on the roll, would attend school. These were farmhands, who had left school at twelve, and had time to kill in Winter. On wet days they would come into the classroom, but on good days they played football outside. They were always treated well by the teachers and were well behaved. The school consisted of a very large room without any partition. There was always a class sitting in the desks while another stood on the floor, around the walls. This changed every half hour or so and the children marched with military precision from one position to another. In the Fifties one of our Galligan neighbours, who was a nun in England, came home and spoke of experiments being carried out across the water with open schooling. We had a type of open school in the second decade of the last century.

It took time for me to get used to writing with my right hand. Once I got over this hurdle, I was promoted from first to third class. I now found myself being taught by the older lady, Miss O'Reilly. She seemed to take a special interest in me for some strange reason. She was unmarried. She had a tragic history. She had been engaged to an RIC man. They had a lovers' quarrel. One Winter's evening as she came from school, he met her near a place called the 'Dark Corner'. He fired a shot. She fell off her bike. Thinking that he had killed her, he shot himself.

She was a wonderful teacher of English. She lived for it.

It was pre-Treaty time and Irish was not taught at school. She did not know the language, and she had no time for it. She believed that most of her pupils were going out foreign and would not need it. The young teacher, Miss Smith, was training herself for what lay ahead. Miss O'Reilly suspected that the other might be spending her summer holidays in the Gaeltacht tinkering with what she called disparagingly the 'ould *seanteanga.*' Both stood on their dignity. When the change came and Irish became a compulsory subject, Miss O'Reilly retired and left them to it.

Walking was part of the magic of my childhood and youth. It was never a chore. It could be a walking run, an average walk or a stroll. It just suited the need or the mood of the hour. We walked to school, to church, to our friends and to the football matches. I was within three quarters of a mile of school. When I stepped on the road in the morning, I would be meeting boys and girls some of whom had already come a mile or two on their journey. They never appeared tired. They had acquired the rhythm of walking. Having five minutes to spare could mean the difference between a satisfying walk and a struggle. The boys would sometimes come along kicking a ball. The girls had the edge on us in the classroom. They were a purposeful lot with their minds set on a foreign shore. They helped us with our home work. They were great letter-writers and wrote to all their aunts and uncles abroad. They had the news.

We usually walked to school in twos. We may early on have discovered that a third person changed and maybe spoiled the conversation. It was a world of its own. We exchanged secrets with one another. Rarely did anybody betray a trust. I had three aunts and three uncles in America. One of my aunts was a nurse, the second was a teaching sister and the third was a company secretary. The latter sent us reams of type-written notes of a newsy American world. The other two wrote beautiful handwritten letters. I would love to have those letters now. They would be priceless. They told of the exiles who had made good and also of those who went under. My uncles (Eddie, James and John O'Reilly) in America worked in industry. They never wrote home. Instead, they sent *The Irish World* and *The Irish Echo*. They also sent magazines including *The Ave Maria. The Irish*

World was very revolutionary (in respect of Ireland) and caught the 'hunger' of the exiles for Ireland. We were longing to get out to a land of freedom and reward. In their turn, the exiles were gradually inventing an Ireland of their own.

In the evening we all came home together but at a more rapid pace. There were dinners waiting. There were also chores for everyone at home before getting down to our homework. Farm work was very demanding and we all had to play our part. All the farms, big and small, were self-sufficient in food. Whatever else we lacked, we had good food. The rosy cheeks of the girls required no paint or cream. We, who lived within half a mile or so of the school, would be considered very privileged. What of those who had to travel long distances in inclement weather? In very bad weather they simply did not come. They must have done their school work at home because they were just as good as we were. In fact, on showery or snowy mornings the roll call was delayed.

On the way to school we would often catch up with the Dolan, Kelly, Caffrey and Tierney children. There were three hills to school. We had nearly always five weeks of heavy frost, and we often had snow. We helped nature by throwing buckets and pails of water on to the freezing hills. This formed a continuous slide to and from school. We walked up one hill and we slid down the other on our way to school. In the evening we reversed the walking and sliding. We probably spent more time there in the evening than in the morning. The teacher had no time for latecomers.

The winters in Cavan as well as being very cold were also long. But when the Spring came, there was a sharp, rapid growth. We all loved to throw off our shoes at the advent of Summer. We continued doing so into the Autumn but were glad to put on our shoes when October came. The children of poor families held out until the beginning of November. They wore clogs in the Winter. There were several clogmakers in the area. Clogs were made chiefly out of poplar. They were very good for sliding on the icy roads in the Winter. They were shod with iron and that made an awful noise. The Summers in Cavan were very hot. The Summer of 1920 was especially hot and dry.

In trying to assist my memory of my schooldays I am reminded of the fact that when I was starting off at school I seemed to be in the company of tall boys and girls. Later I seemed to be of an equal size. Towards the end of my days at Clonoose I would appear to have been along with young children.

Reading was an important subject and we had to practise it at home. The teacher could instantly tell if you were new to your brief. When reading they would indicate by their hands whether you should go slower or faster. You had to be audible without disturbing the school. Parents would test their children's progress in school by their ability to read. We had a famous man in the area who was called 'the Smoke Doctor'. He used to travel over a wide area. He was a genius for treating chimney problems. He was also an infernal nuisance. He was a spelling wizard. On arrival at a home he would single out the children for a spelling quiz. He was an old rascal. If he liked you, he gave you an easy word. If he did not, he would give you a 'stunner'. If you got a spelling wrong, he would then ask the parent if you had gone to school yet. Thankfully, he would only drop in once every six weeks or so. I accidentally stumbled on the perfect cure for him. A spelling book arrived from an aunt in America. I selected a difficult word. The next time he called I asked him to spell it. He was dumbfounded. He departed hurriedly. Next day I learned he had subjected all the children of the neighbourhood to a lashing with the same word. He would appear to have lost all hope for the then system of education.

Mental arithmetic was an important subject in those days and we teased one another with problems. We had no calculators nor computers. Still we managed to get along. We had the feeling that we were being better educated than the generation that went before. We were in another century. We looked forward to the future and we kept the past for pride, as the saying goes.

Deaths in the family

My memories of my earliest years are naturally shadowy.

From an early age I was conscious that I was in the care of my older brothers, Hugh P. and Edward. I was also aware of the watchful eye of Maggie Coyle, the girl in the kitchen. I was also conscious of my sister Elizabeth. She was getting the admiration of everyone. This included Dad, Mama and my Uncle Patrick, who had joined the family. Nobody seemed to notice me or so I thought. Down the years I have been conscious of my brother John James, who died in infancy. He was born in 1915, the year before Elizabeth. I must have spoken of him to Elizabeth as she and I as children talked a lot about him. We wondered where he had gone. In those days death was concealed from children. We spoke of him as someone we would meet again somewhere.

Patrick Vincent came in the September of 1918. I have memories of him that conflict with the official record. It is stated in the Register of Deaths that he was thirteen months when he died. I remember him being older, perhaps around three. I remember him playing with Elizabeth and myself and that I was placed in charge of him. Although a child myself, I took my charge very seriously. We had an uncle named Hugh who had gone to Australia. We were told that Australia was down under. I remember the two of us deciding to dig a hole to get down there. We selected the Black Meadow where the soil was soft and easily dug. And so we started. We attempted to dig a hole which would be circular and a yard wide. Someone else must have given a hand, for the hole seemed deeper than the one we had left the previous day. Wiser councils must have prevailed. When we achieved a depth of four feet we found that our pit had mysteriously become filled with water. Tom Mac, who worked in our farmyard, told us that in some way we were interfering with the fairies. To get to Australia, we would first have to grow up and take the usual route by ship. Short-cuts were not tolerated. We persisted and drained half the pit with the aid of a little bucket. Next morning the pit was full again. We were told that there must be a spring at the bottom. We gave up the ghost. Later on, someone filled the pit with stones. Forces seem to have been sent to act against us. The years of childhood are so magical and interesting. Children should hate to grow up. Yet boys long to put on long trousers and be men. Obviously Patrick Vincent could only have been a witness to all this digging. Perhaps he learned to walk early and that is why my memories of him have become distorted. Or am I confusing him with my little sister Elizabeth? Be that as it may, I have very strong memories of Patrick Vincent being my playmate.

At thirteen months, according to the official record, Patrick Vincent got pneumonia. There was no cure for this illness at the time, though a mustard bath sometimes succeeded. My little brother died. On the night of his wake I stole up to where he was in his little cot and I pulled his ear. I thought that he would come away and play with me. It was my first brush with death. I started sobbing. Dad came in and took me away. Similar to John James, Elizabeth and I started speaking of Patrick Vincent as someone we would meet again. Tragically, at six years of age, Elizabeth also got pneumonia and died. The year was 1922.

When Elizabeth lay dying, I was sent across to Shanvalla to get me out of the way. Elizabeth was dead and buried by the time I returned home. I was very disturbed by her death. I owe a debt of gratitude to Aunt Kate and Charles Brady for their help during that awful period. At home work seemed to go on as usual except that there was a vacant seat. Back at school the teachers were very kind to me. The girls told me that they had all gone down to Callanagh to see my little sister being waked in her little cot. I did not want to hear any more. I was in my tenth year now and I was doing different jobs in the kitchen and outside before and after school. I noticed Mama going to a certain drawer as if she were looking for something. This would occur mostly in the evenings. One evening I went to that drawer. I found inside a lock of Elizabeth's hair. It was the *rua* colour of the family. Mama came behind me. She did not upbraid me for looking in the drawer. Instead she gave me part of the lock to keep. Then she did a strange thing. She brought me over and sat me down on the vacant chair. That was the moment that I grew up. I had to play my part in the family struggle and help Mama. I was to mind, read to, and teach the younger members of the family as they came along.

The Troubles and aftermath

The years 1915 to 1922 saw the deaths of three of my siblings. They were sad years for our family, but we were sustained by a warmth and love for one another that shone through our grief. On the political front, these same years were also troubled years for Ireland and our neighbourhood, and indeed for our family. The Irish Parliamentary Party had once dominated the political scene, but as a result of the 1916 Rising and subsequent developments, the Party was losing support. The countryside around us was gradually moving over to Sinn Féin. Dad's Hibernians (who were closely linked to the Irish Parliamentary Party) were growing thinner by the month. Mama was a Republican herself but she protected her man. I never heard them discuss politics. It was a difficult time for Dad.

One day in 1918, Hugh P., Edward and myself sensed that something unusual was astir. We were asked to help in cleaning out the barn. In the barn there was a winnowing machine for treating the corn. Ploughs, harrows and other farm equipment were kept there. In fact, it was a handy place for storing things. Generally the place was chock-a-block with stuff. Now we were asked to help in getting its contents out into the haggard. When we finished, to crown it all, Maggie Coyle arrived with the bucket to whitewash the interior of the barn, which had never been whitewashed before. Maggie was always forthcoming with information. This time she did not seem to know what was going on. Later on we found out that she actually did know. To whet our appetites for information she would appear to be writing, to our horror, the words 'Sinn Féin' with her whitewash brush on the wall. Then as if wrestling with her conscience she whitewashed over them. Further down she wrote AOH as if in a lapse. This she also covered over again to make everything right once more. She was enjoying herself.

Later on in the evening the situation reached boiling-point. Hugh P. was very fond of horses and I suppose he was looking forward to those great days in the future when he would be out ploughing. Now he was being asked to fill the manger in the stable with empty corn bags from the barn. He rebelled at the absurdity of what he was being asked to do. He was taken aside and told that a dance in the barn was in the offing. He gave us the strange news and from that onwards we were willing helpers.

At this point I am trying to remember and put it all together. It all came upon us so suddenly. It was as if some school, hall or church had been emptied of its seats. There were seats everywhere. Then a long wire was attached to a large ash tree and from there to the gable of the dairy. Another wire was stretched from the barn to the turf-house. Then it dawned on us that the dance would be in the street also. The street was bounded by a wall that separated it from the rest of the farm. A large number of lamps and lanterns arrived and were hung on these wires. They must have been on loan. Numerous young people assisted. Clearly there was a big crowd expected and a big crowd came. I cannot recall what day of the week it was, but it was a beautiful, magical June night. The whole place was lit up. The yard gate was shut and locked. People had to come through the garden gate, enter the parlour, then through the kitchen and onto the street and into the barn. It was clearly an invited party and mostly AOH members. The band was a fairly large one. We were near the homes of the McGuires and Cairn O'Reillys, all wonderful traditional Irish music families. It was easy to pick up a band there. Down the years I have been very fond of traditional Irish music. I enjoy it. When I hear it my memory slips back nostalgically to that magic night in June 1918. The band was placed on seats outside the kitchen door and the music floated around the street, into the barn and back into the farmhouse kitchen. There seemed to be dancers everywhere. In fact the music could be heard from afar and people came to see what was going on. Even these uninvited guests were dancing outside the gate. They were mostly Sinn Féiners. Then at twelve o'clock a strange thing happened: the yard gate was unlocked and the crowd came in. AOH and Sinn Féin danced together. I was too young to know if anyone from the opposing factions kissed in the moonlight, too. It was Maggie Coyle who opened the gate, I learned later. Her action made the night and it was one to remember.

Around two o'clock, the big drum of the local Wolfe

Tone fife and drum band, which was stored on the loft over our barn, was taken down, and the band played 'A Nation Once Again', and everyone stood to attention. The Hibernians present were looking for Home Rule, the Sinn Féiners for a Republic. Divided in their objectives, they were united in their desire that the solution to the Irish problem should take in the whole island. Alas, that was not to be. Home Rule for the thirty-two counties was unattainable because of the hostility of a large number of Unionists in the North. It would take another decade or more for the British to agree to a Republic for even part of the island of Ireland, as they feared it would signal the break-up of the Empire. It all seemed so simple on that June night, however. Almost ninety years later we are still wrestling with the impossible task of uniting Ireland.

To return to that night: the ladies got tea in the parlour. I remember two of them fixing me up in an armchair by the fire where I fell asleep. When I woke, everybody had gone. I can still recall that quiet morning.

The threat of conscription in early 1918 proved the nail in the coffin of the Irish Parliamentary Party. Some years earlier the dance in our barn would have been a prelude to a great election victory. Instead, Sinn Féin were victorious in the General Election later that year. Dad's dream ended there. Then came that unforgettable morning in 1920 when Tom Mac read out the King's Speech. The Six County Parliament had been voted in on the previous evening. The old farmhouse kitchen was packed with the neighbours who had come in the hear the speech. At a certain point Mama brought Dad away. Another dream had been, shattered because of the intransigence of the Ulster Unionists. It is one of my saddest memories. Dad must have realised that Home Rule would result in partition with a regional parliament in Belfast as well as Dublin. He would, however, have preferred an Ulster of nine counties to one of six within the United Kingdom. A parliament for the six north-eastern counties could only mean that it would always be dominated by the Unionists. Partition would be permanent. Donegal would become quite isolated, cut off from much of its natural hinterland. Cavan and Monaghan would have their links with Belfast severed.

I was seven years of age in 1920 at the height of the War of Independence. My area was one of those that figured prominently in the fight against the British. Seán MacEoin was the leader of the IRA in Longford/Cavan. The IRA operated in small units known as 'flying columns', which conducted hit-and-run attacks on troops and barracks. The summer of 1920 was very hot, which made the dirt roads of rural Ireland more accessible to British forces. As the IRA campaign intensified the British were more inclined to stay in towns than to venture into the countryside. Sinn Féin courts were the norm everywhere and the British ones were being ignored. The British had superior weaponry but suffered from lack of intelligence. The IRA suffered from lack of ammunition and this hampered them from the start. By 1921 a deadlock had been reached and a truce was agreed in July of that year.

Dad had no time for the local Sinn Féin and IRA. He had, however, a certain regard for Seán MacEoin, whom he knew to some extent from Granard. During the War of Independence Dad's bicycle was commandeered by the local IRA to be used by its dispatch riders. He got another bike, but that was also commandeered. He used a pony and trap instead in his work after that. Where his business was local, he walked. A very tall man, walking came easy to him. During the dark winter months of 1919–21, Mama would go to meet him if he was unduly late. She would put a coat on me and take me with her. It was only in after years I realised how dangerous it all was. The presence of a child obviously gave her a feeling of security. Dad carried a gun in those years for protection, a Webley revolver. It would appear the IRA did not know he had such a gun, but they knew he had a shotgun.

I was present the evening this gun was confiscated. On the deep inner ledge of the window in our kitchen, facing the flower-garden, there was enough space for two children to sit on. On this particular evening Edward and I were on this ledge. Hugh P. was seated underneath on a chair and he was talking up to us. Dad was seated at the table with the newspaper raised before him. Uncle Patrick was also reading at the table but with the paper spread out before him. Mama and Maggie Coyle were talking at the fire.

Suddenly the window behind me got a sharp thud. I looked out and saw a masked man with a gun pointing in. At the same time a knock came to the yard door. Two men burst in, armed and masked. Uncle Patrick got up and went towards them. One of them pointed to the shotgun which was hanging on the brace of the fireplace. Uncle Patrick took it down and handed it to them. They then enquired if there was any ammunition. After a whispered conversation with Dad, Uncle Patrick went to the parlour and returned with a box of cartridges. The IRA officer thanked him and regretted having to take the gun. All this time Dad never lowered his newspaper. He did not approve of their action, nor of them. Family tradition also records Mama going to the door to accost these men rather than Uncle Patrick, and that one of the party was a cousin of hers, but my memory is of Uncle Patrick getting up to deal with the intruders. Her cousin, the future Dr Plunkett, may indeed have been in the party, but I did not recognise him.

My most vivid memory of the War of Independence is of the burning of Granard by the Black and Tans in early November 1920 in revenge for the killing of District Inspector Kelleher of the RIC some days before in the Greville Arms Hotel. We heard the news the following morning from the postman. Fearing trouble, Dad stayed away from the town for a couple of days. On the day the town was burnt, he tackled the mare and set out for Granard. We went to school as normal, but at one o'clock when we came in from play the teachers had a whispered conversation and we were all told to get home as quickly as possible. Dad was there before us when we arrived. He usually came in about seven in the evening. He had not reached the town that morning, but had met the people streaming out. Caragh chapel was already full of Granard's poor, and efforts were being made to feed them. The Black and Tans were threatening to burn the town.

Darkness fell. It was a bitterly cold night. We had a watch on the top of the Sheep Field. From there the spire of Granard church could be seen on a clear day. There were neighbours in our kitchen and others sheltering in our barn and sheds ready to ascend the hill above our house if word came. It proved a long wait. Some may even have gone home. Sometime after midnight the watch came down. The burning of Granard had begun. Mama insisted we all be well wrapped up. Mrs Dolan remained behind to look after the young children. When we reached the Sheep Field there was a crowd there before us. The flames of Granard lit up the sky in the distance. There was a lot of talk at first and then the crowd fell silent. Suddenly a bright light appeared on a hill on the Granard side of the County Bridge. Just as suddenly the blackness of the night was stabbed by a light to our left on Galligan's Fort (a higher point on our neighbour's farm). On the other side of the fort another light appeared, shining towards Kilnaleck. Thus began the signalling and messaging for which the small hills of Cavan were so suitable. It was the first time I had seen such signalling. Maybe it was the first time I was up so late. I would love to have known exactly what messages were being conveyed. It was all so exciting for a young boy.

Next morning the news came through that seventeen houses had been burned as well as the Market House. The burning frenzy stopped as suddenly as it began. Nobody knew why. Maybe someone higher up had intervened. Where an ambush occurred, the Tans were wont to burn several farmhouses around. In places the IRA retaliated by burning a large manor or demesne house. It was tit for tat. Who would get cold feet first? Both sides were trying to be one step in front of the other. The towns were in the hands of the British military, but the countryside was in the hands of the IRA. It was a stalemate. Those big houses were in the countryside. It would have taken extra forces to protect them. Of course, it was a pity that any of them had to be burned. They were part of our history and could not be replaced.

Dad had found himself on the wrong side in 1918 when the country shifted to Sinn Féin. The situation eased for him with the coming of the Truce. He was asked to attend the Sinn Féin Arbitration Courts. The legal knowledge he had acquired as an auctioneer over the years as well as his knowledge of farm boundaries and rights of way was much sought after. More importantly, his great sense of fair play was recognised. His involvement in these courts during the Truce may have gained him a degree of acceptance among Sinn Féin and IRA supporters he had not hitherto enjoyed. As it was, Sinn Féin and the IRA were soon to split over the Anglo-Irish Treaty. During the Civil War and afterwards, Dad steered clear of both sides.

At the first opportunity, Hugh P. and myself went shopping to Granard after the coming of the Truce. We wanted to see what the ghost-town was like. We were also going for supplies. Seventeen shops and houses had been burned down. There was still much debris on the streets. The burned-out shops were covered with tarpaulins. The shopkeepers of the town had regrouped and were trying to start selling again. The town was packed with people trying to get provisions. The 'little men', as the Black and Tans were called, were going about unarmed in twos and threes. They were in very good humour. Their officers were very friendly and helpful. They got one of the 'little men' to hold our pony. A group of IRA came from a side street and marched past the British Army barracks. There was an exchange of salutes on both sides. There was a handclap from the bystanders. They were seeing something new.

The moat and the church in Granard were always a great attraction for us in our youthful days. Hugh P. and I went up there now. It was a great place to view the town and surrounding countryside. There was now something eerie about the place. The uphill road had been torn with machine-gun fire. Looking down, much of the town had become a shambles. Many chimneys had no smoke issuing from them. The place seemed strangely silent, unlike the Granard of previous years. Saddest of all was the crowd of war veterans on crutches. They were badly clothed too. Granard had been a great military town. It had given many recruits to the British Army. This was the other side of the coin. A snatch of a song of the period comes to mind: '"It's Tommy here" and "Tommy there" and "Tommy go away" / But it's "Good Evening Mr. Atkins" when the bands begin to play.'

Ex-British soldiers had very poor pensions. Some of them had even sold their pensions and were depending on charity to keep going.

The Truce of July 1921 was very welcome. The trains which had almost stopped were now running again. There was a holiday spirit in the air. One of the great puzzles at the time was the amount of young men who came out drilling on the roads. We were given to understand that there were only a few small units of IRA in our area. Now camps were organised. It was said there were hundreds training at a camp in Gowna. Other camps were similarly crowded. In fact baskets of food were being collected at all the farms to help keep them in provisions. Nobody could explain the amount of ammunition that suddenly became available. There appeared at any rate to be a good supply for the shooting ranges.

The truce held into the Autumn. First de Valera, President of the Republic declared in January 1919 in defiance of British rule, went over to London to initiate negotiations. Subsequently, a further delegation went over to finalise a peace settlement. Many people were unrealistic about the negotiations going on in London. They believed that a thirty-two-county republic was on the cards. They were forgetting that the Government of Ireland Act of 1920 had established a parliament for six of the counties of Ulster. The Irish delegates in London were put under tremendous pressure when Lloyd George, the British Prime Minister, threatened all-out war if they did not accept the peace terms which fell far below what the delegates were demanding. A Treaty was signed and brought back to Dublin. It did not establish a republic, but rather autonomy for twenty-six counties. The Irish Free State, which was to be established, would have quite wide powers, but elected representatives of the Dáil would have to swear allegiance to the British monarch. The Treaty, moreover, partitioned the country. This was not what many had fought for. It was debated fiercely in the Dáil and eventually in January 1922 confirmed by a vote of 64 for and 57 against. The Treaty was further confirmed by the electorate in an election in June 1922.

Some who voted for the Treaty in that election were people of means who favoured maintaining the *status quo*, but many more simply voted for peace. The anti-Treatyites were in a clear minority. The Civil War that followed on the heels of this election was to embitter Irish politics and society for more than a generation. It is said that the most bitter disputes are when friends fall out. Many in the IRA rejected the Treaty. They had taken an oath to the Republic, and that was sacrosanct. This was part of the problem. Civil war might have been avoided if people had been more realistic from the start.

Mama and myself were anti-Treaty; Dad, Hugh P. and Edward were pro-Treaty; Uncle Patrick was neutral. He said that it should not be looked on as final, and that there would be other agreements between Ireland and Britain. How right he was!

There were practically no hostilities in our area during the Civil War because Seán MacEoin, the local IRA leader, had thrown in his lot with Michael Collins, one of the signatories of the Treaty. Collins was engaged to Kitty Kiernan from Granard. He believed that the Treaty, imperfect as it was, could be a 'stepping stone to freedom'. During the Civil War he was Commander-in-Chief of the Free State Army. On August 22nd, 1922, he was shot dead in an ambush at Bealnablath in west Cork. He had been one of the great heroes of the fight for independence and his death was mourned even by political opponents.

On the morning after Collins was shot, Uncle Patrick was on his way down to our house from Uncle Henry's in Clonloaghan, where he usually slept, when he heard the news. Many he met along the way, and told the news to, decided to join him on his journey. They constituted a small crowd by the time they reached Callanagh. There was a mist of rain falling. Some of the crowd came into the kitchen. The rest stayed at the door. They were on different sides. Nobody seemed to be talking. Mama took down her beads and we all knelt down and said the rosary. She told me later that before the surrender of the G.P.O. in 1916, the rosary had been said. She had it from someone who was present, possibly a relative.

Although there was no fighting in our area during the Civil War, I recall an incident with Free State soldiers near our house. Dad had just gone to Granard in his pony and trap. The cows had been milked and we were sitting down to breakfast, when we heard the crash of a tree falling somewhere near the house. We went to the yard gate and we saw that the elm tree which grew at the mouth of Boston lane had fallen across the laneway, with its top branches blocking the public road. In fact, it had been felled deliberately, but instead of falling across the road as intended, had fallen across the lane. Under the tree was Dolans' well where we used quench our thirst when playing skittles. There we used rest in the shade and drink from a cup left by the well.

Soon we were playing among the branches. Before long we heard the roar of approaching lorries, the first of which stopped on the top of Dolans' Hill. We saw a man slipping along under the shelter of the ditch until he got near us. We saw that he was a Free State Army officer. He enquired of Hugh P. if we had a crosscut. Hugh P. said we had and he was told to go fetch it. When Hugh P. returned, he and Edward were put cutting the branches and I was ordered to clear them off the road. I must have looked hesitant for the officer tapped the revolver in his holster. Whereupon I proceeded to do as bid. After a time he helped me. When we had the way clear for a lorry to pass, we heard a shot, fired from the adjoining hillside. The lorries were in an exposed position. The first lorry came down and the officer clambered onto it. The rest of the lorries followed, six in all. They did not stop until they turned left at Callanagh crossroads and had reached a hill on the Granard road. There they fired back at the spot where the shot was supposed to have come from. We recognised three of the soldiers from our area. One of them was Pat Clarke, a lad of 18 who had been to Clonoose School a few years earlier. He came from Clonloaghan Upper. Some weeks later he was shot dead in Tobercurry, Co. Sligo. His death was an occasion for another military funeral in our area.

With the demise of the Irish Parliamentary Party, in the post Civil-War period Dad supported a local independent TD named O'Hanlon, owner of the *The Anglo-Celt*, who represented farming interests. My eldest brother, Hugh P., favoured Cumann na nGaedheal and later Fine Gael. Edward also went with the farmers. I remained a Republican. I don't know what Mama's politics were in the post-Civil War period. She had to steer her family through a difficult time. I once heard her remark, however, that it was better for us to have fought a civil war among ourselves than to gain independence and have to fight a civil war with the Unionists. She had a great friend in Mrs 'a Park Smith, who came from a Republican area of Co. Longford. It would have been interesting to hear the chats they had with one another. Mama was one of the great influences in my life.

After the Civil War, there was a period when people no longer talked about the Troubles. We seemed to be trying to get away from it all. The papers were full of accounts of bridges being repaired. We were in a new state, yet things moved on as they had before its inception. We had been very much in the English newspapers during the Troubles. Now we seemed to be ignored by them. They seemed to be treating us as if we did not exist. I was a boy of nine years at the time of the Treaty, longing to grow up. As a child I had witnessed very little of the Troubles really. I now wanted to learn more about those years. No one seemed to wish to answer my questions. My parents wanted to draw a line in the sand on the matter. Throughout the Twenties I remained an avid reader of both daily and weekly papers. We had a goodly number of newspapers coming into the house and I read as much of them as possible. I was thus aware of what was going on nationally.

The anti-Treatyite IRA dumped their arms in the Spring of 1923. Hostilities ceased, but the IRA did not go away. Later that year, Edward drew my attention to all the messages that were being sent at night by code from one Cavan hilltop to another. It was a system of signalling by lamps in the dark. I had seen it being used the night that Granard was burned. I was not aware that it was used other nights. Now it was being done over long periods every night. Edward told me that there had been a shift in political thinking. Things had been quiet in our area during the Civil War because of Seán MacEoin. Now there was an anti-Government swing and hence all the signalling.

Mama used to go shopping once a month to Cavan by train. This time she brought me with her. It was dark when we were returning. About a mile before we reached Drumhawnagh Railway Station, the train was held up. An IRA squad boarded the train and took the names of all those present. Most of the people were frightened. Mama did not seem to mind. She informed me that the IRA were just letting the Government know that they were still around. This was the Winter of 1923/24, almost a year after the Civil War had ended.

As time went by the Troubles receded and life took on an air of normality again. Visitors started coming home from America once more. Houses were usually whitewashed in late Spring or early Summer. If American visitors came early, houses were whitewashed early to receive them. Dad's customers and Mama's egg-swappers again got their cup of tea and a scone. The chat was mostly about football or getting a dance going for visiting Yankees. Nobody wanted to rock the boat and nobody did. 'My Dear Man' (as Tommy 'a Park Smith was known), who usually walked to Mass on a Sunday with Dad, now found time to visit us twice a week. Hugh P. had acquired a large selection of tools. He kept them in the barn. If a very wet day came, half a dozen cyclists would arrive to get some job or other done. It was a great place for local gossip.

Dad found time to be more at home. Our family had regrouped. We had lost three siblings within the space of a few years, but we had been joined by three others. Paul had come to us in July 1920, Rosetta in January 1922 and Gerald in July 1923. As Elizabeth died the same year Rosetta was born, Rosetta was a very important addition to the family, especially for Mama. Dad took a big interest in our homework. I looked after the eggs and did the shopping. Hugh P. did the ploughing and horse work. Edward assisted Tom McDermott on the farm. Tom had been in America and was a wonderful storyteller. Our neighbours the Dolan family helped out during the rush periods, as did Uncle Henry's boys, Hugh and Peter. The latter were wonderful footballers. For most of us during that period nothing else seemed to matter except football. It was the safety-valve which kept us sane during the Troubles and later.

Maggie Coyle had left us at the height of the Troubles. She had been like a second mother to us. She had taught us to read and write and to use the sewing machine. Apart from working in the kitchen, she helped out with the milking of cows, and the feeding of poultry and pigs. She was followed in the kitchen by Ellie McCann, who was equally good. Uncle Patrick continued taking care of the vegetable garden and we had the best of organic food. Although I had good and bad periods at school, I will always look back on those years of childhood with nostalgia. I seemed to have packed a lot into those first years of my life. A poet has said it somewhere: 'It never came a moment too soon or brought too long a day'. That was true of my childhood. It was a wonderful childhood, in many respects.

I knew, however, that my childhood would not last forever. It was in the year or two following the Civil War that my thoughts first turned to going to America. So many of my relatives and neighbours had gone. It was natural for me to think of following in their footsteps even though I was still so young. My godfather, Michael Galligan, was already there. I was writing him letters. I was also writing to my Aunt Lizzy and Rose (my mother's sisters) who were in America. They were anxious that I go out and finish my education there.

It was around 1924 that I first began earning, though not, as it turned out, money. I had been a shopper since I had been seven years of age. I had developed a great rapport with my shopkeeper, Paddy Lynch. It was a district where a lot of poultry was kept. An eggler called every week at the shop with a lorry to collect the eggs. I did my shopping early on a Saturday morning. Paddy asked me to help him count the eggs. The eggs had to be divided into two categories, big and small. I can still recall how we counted the eggs all those years ago. We had a tray that would hold ten dozen of the bigger eggs and twelve dozen of the smaller ones. It would have been too time-consuming to have counted the entire supply of eggs one by one. We only checked the trays now and again. Our system was almost perfect.

Paddy had become wealthy. He was able to afford to give credit to a lot of small farmers who might not have been able to get the same elsewhere. Although good-natured, his nickname was 'Tight', because of his difficulty in parting with money. This was true in my case at any rate. He loaded me with Woodbines, instead of giving me money for my help in the shop. These were the cheap cigarettes of the period. I should have become a heavy smoker, were I not saved by my friends. They were all badly in need of a smoke. It was common for young boys to smoke at the time. My circle of friends grew. Ellie McCann warned me that a number of mothers were talking about me. She advised me to get Paddy to give me a present of shoes or clothes instead. I felt that I could never talk to Paddy in that way. I let things drift.

Mama had trained me to address Paddy and his wife as Mr and Mrs Lynch, respectively. This I was careful to do. However, I became aware that Mrs Lynch appeared to be ignoring me. I told this to Mama. She advised me to treat her very warily. They were a childless couple. Paddy, she suggested, might be treating me as the son he might have had, and Mrs Lynch may have become jealous of me. One day I arrived at the shop. Paddy had gone to Cavan. There was only one shopper in front of me. When she had left, Mrs Lynch looked out the window. It was a difficult situation. I managed to say: 'Mrs Lynch, you are very busy, do you mind if I help you? I have weighed with Mr Lynch on many an occasion.' She seemed to be at a loss as to what to say. Then she said: 'Go ahead,' and left for the kitchen. She returned with a cup of tea and a plate of biscuits. She became a great friend of mine in the years that followed.

My friendship with Mrs Lynch was to extricate me from a difficult situation the following year. A clause in the Anglo-Irish Treaty had proposed the setting up of a Boundary Commission to make adjustments to the border between Northern Ireland and the Free State. In the battle for votes for the Treaty, each side had interpreted this clause in the way which suited them best. In accordance with the terms of the Treaty, a Boundary Commission was set up in 1925. This caught many people's attention and raised expectations. The chairman was a Mr Justice Feetham from South Africa. The Free State was represented by Eoin MacNeill. It was initially looked on as a fairly independent commission. As it progressed, however, it became apparent that it would only consider minor adjustments to the border, and might indeed favour the Unionists. The pro-Treatyites had hoped that nationalist strongholds such as Derry City, south Armagh and other areas would be transferred to the South. Now this seemed unlikely to happen. It was a tricky problem. The Protestants who occupied the fertile valley of the

River Foyle in Donegal and the Protestant farmers of Monaghan who adjoined Northern Ireland also hoped for their areas to be included with Northern Ireland just as the Nationalists of Derry, Tyrone and Armagh hoped to be joined to the Free State. When word was leaked that the recommendations of the Commission might favour the Unionists, the Commission was disbanded under pressure from the Free State. Many Nationalists came to believe that the Boundary Clause in the Treaty had been intentionally misleading. Some had even hoped that what would be left of Northern Ireland after the Commission had done its work would prove unviable and that unification would be achieved in this way. How unrealistic they were!

I never heard Dad or Mama discuss the Boundary Commission. Dad had become preoccupied with farmers' politics. Mama kept her thoughts to herself. She appeared to be very cautious as to what she said to us about politics. The papers were full of the collapse of the Boundary Commission. I was already in the donkey and cart on this particular morning and about to set out for Paddy Lynch's when Ellie McCann called me. Mama wanted to speak to me. She had been talking to Dad. They had decided that I should say nothing at the shop about the Boundary Commission. As a reader of newspapers, I would be considered to be able to talk on the subject. The trouble was that what I might say could be interpreted as the view of the household. I was asked to say nothing. It was a small favour to ask and I was glad to comply. Anyway I would only be talking to Paddy Lynch or his wife.

To explain what subsequently happened I had better describe the layout of Lynch's shop and kitchen. Both shop and kitchen occupied the same long room, but were divided by a makeshift low wall. To the left of the entrance were piled bags of maize. These were each four feet in length and were placed across the floor to a distance of ten feet. On top of these were placed other bags until the pile rose to five feet or so. These bags were replaced according as they were sold. It was all very handy and served a purpose. You could slip into the kitchen through an opening left at the end of the pile and you found yourself quite isolated from the shop. There were about ten chairs placed around a nice fire. It was a great place for talk and the exchange of news. After a customer was served in the shop, Mrs Lynch would enter the kitchen area and say 'Next please!' At the time, who could imagine that the system could be improved. Nowadays such as set-up would be laughed at.

When I entered the shop there were three customers there. Mrs Lynch signalled to me to go inside to the kitchen. I thought there would only be one or two there. However, every chair was occupied except one. I sat down on this and listened. They were discussing the Boundary Commission. Nothing could save me except a call from Mrs Lynch. I cautiously looked around. The men occupying the seats were all farmers who had voted for the Treaty. They all appeared to be vexed and disappointed. I listened while I tried to watch the antics of a small fly endeavouring to climb up the back window of the kitchen. I turned around only to find the steely stare of the man opposite upon me. I turned to the next man. He too was staring at me. I turned to where a third man was sitting. He in turn was staring at me and then he spoke:

'You're having fun, young fellow-me-lad.'

'I don't know what you are talking about,' I ventured.

'We're discussing the Boundary Commission. We would expect that a boy like you who reads the papers should have something to say,' he said.

'The Treaty was signed in 1922', I said, 'We'll find it difficult to change it now.'

They all arose from their seats and I expected a bit of a hiding. Then came the merciful words from Mrs Lynch, 'Next please!', and I fled into the shop.

Mrs Lynch must have heard more than I imagined. Before she served me she went back into the kitchen. She must have said something which calmed the situation. I half-expected that someone would follow me on the way home, but no one did. I was determined to say nothing about the incident. A direct question from Mama gave me no choice: 'Was there a discussion about the Boundary Clause in the kitchen?', she asked. I had to tell the story as it evolved. To my surprise, she smiled and remarked: 'Mrs Lynch is worth her weight in gold.'

National politics left a particular imprint on our area in 1925, which is worth recording, as it concerned something which is still a subject for much discussion, namely the state of Cavan's roads. Because Cavan was a county of small farms it had a large amount of roads and by-roads. These were farmed out to contractors who supplied gravel for the potholes. I spent many an hour watching the men in the gravel pit near my home smashing stones with a small hammer. It was actually a very skilled operation. The men sat by the gravel heaps on small bags stuffed with hay. They tossed a stone into the air with the left hand. The right hand with its hammer smashed the stone in its flight. And all the time they might have been talking to the next man. They could express their indignation by giving the stone an extra hard belt. I tried to imitate those men with my own hammer and stone. I failed dismally. Later a stone crusher came to the quarry and the dozen men were reduced to two.

A bye-election occurred in West Cavan around this time and because of the strong support for the Farmers' Party in the constituency, it was essential for the Government to win over the independent vote if it was to hold the constituency. It was thought one way of doing this was to improve the poor condition of private roads leading to farms and bogs. In our area as elsewhere in west Cavan a large number of farmhouses are a considerable distance from the public roads. These farmhouses are accessed by either avenues or lanes. Avenues would be fairly wide and might be flanked by a row of trees on either side. Lanes, bounded by ditches and hedges, on the other hand, would be so narrow as to admit of a cart only. Lanes were in particular need of attention.

A few engineers descended on our locality and soon a scheme was set in motion. A squad of men was recruited. In addition to this, the farmers who owned the lanes also decided to give a hand. Lanes were widened and given a better surface. Clay scraped from the base of the ditches, as they were narrowed, was spread on the surface of the laneways and mixed with surplus small stones which over generations had been cleared from fields and piled up along headlands and elsewhere. This mixture of clay and stones was then rolled to give a much better surface than the previous one. It was a great community effort, and certainly an improvement. When cars became the norm, these lanes could easily accommodate them.

The engineers next turned their attention to the bog roads. As bogs were cut away, the areas in which turf was being cut gradually receded. If an area was wet and low-lying, scraws cut from the high bog were used to make a temporary road. I myself brought donkey-and-cart loads along such roads. They were good in dry weather but very difficult in rainy conditions. The engineers instructed people to dig down to the original subsoil and harvest by slane all the remaining turf. This was easy enough in a cut-away area because the subsoil was not far away. Where the underlying subsoil dipped, a considerable amount of turf had to be harvested. In this way many bog roads in our area were also greatly improved.

The Government won the bye-election. To what extent all this road improvement helped them to win is difficult to say. Many public roads in Cavan have been built over an underbelly of turf, however, and these continue to pose ever-recurring problems. It is impossible to keep an even surface on such roads.

The year 1926 was an exciting year politically, and saw a development which for the first time since the Civil War offered the prospect of political change. Elements within anti-Treatyite Sinn Féin founded a new political party called Fianna Fáil. Its leader was Éamon de Valera, President of the pre-Treaty self-declared Irish Republic, who had been in the political wilderness since his defeat in the Civil War. The founding of this new party caused great excitement. At first Fianna Fáil would not take the oath of allegiance to the British monarch and were consequently prevented from entering the Dáil. However, de Valera in time developed a new attitude to the oath of allegiance: namely that it was an 'empty formula'. He entered the Dáil in the Summer of 1927. There were to be exciting times ahead. De Valera and his party come into my story later on.

At school in the Irish Free State

We all thought that Miss Smith would get the

principalship of the school when Miss O'Reilly retired. Instead a 'Patrick O'Shea from Dingle Bay' arrived and took over. This was around the year 1923. O'Shea was all for Irish and Maths. He was a native speaker of Irish from west Kerry. In his estimation what we spoke was not English; he used say that he would have to teach us English before he could teach us Irish. He had *searús* on our knowledge of the counties of Great Britain and the states and cites of the USA. He thought that we should take more interest in our own country. He held us spell-bound as he expounded on Irish history. He used sit on the table and dangle his legs. At a vital point he would get off the table and stare out the window, and then he would speak to us in a whisper. The Irish armies were only beaten by the narrowest of margins, and sometimes they had won but they did not know it. His greatest performance was of the retreat of O'Sullivan Beare from Bantry to Leitrim. Later on I was to realise that he had drawn on his imagination a good deal and that much of what he told us was what he would like to have happened.

He was liked for the most part. He rarely used the rod but he often had half a dozen of us standing on the table and the chief offender on the wide open hearth with his head stuck up the chimney, thus restricting his view. He did not seem to notice that Miss Smith existed, which suited her fine. I think she thought that he was not the full shilling. The attendance fell to 45 in his time. He then became quiet and nice and we were treated like royalty. He used rebuke us: 'What could you think of a crowd of children who have never seen the sea?' Some of the girls said that he was probably fed too much fish when he was young.

He went off somewhere, as he said himself, 'on promotion'. A Master O'Connell came after Master O'Shea. O'Connell taught me in fourth and fifth standard. He did not stay all that long either. The reason for such a turnover of male teachers was that ours was a school serving two parishes and as a result was without an official teacher's residence. It was a school for single teachers. When teachers improved their positions or got married, they moved on. The other teachers used the bicycle. Master O'Connell had a motorbike and had his digs in town. He was dealing with country children who had to be kept in order.

He was a strict disciplinarian in sharp contrast to the teachers who had gone before.

Miss Smith was on hand to open the school and get things going. O'Connell would arrive sharp on time for roll call. We could hear his noisy motorbike long before we saw him. It had an upsetting effect on the younger classes he had nothing to do with. They were in living terror of him. The older pupils had to bear the brunt of his treatment. When he came in, on no account were you to look in his direction. He had gimlet eyes seeking out his first prey. Our eyes had to be concentrated on our books. We had to forget the floor, ceiling or windows. If he wanted our individual attention, he sharply called out our name. We had to respond quickly. No dilly-dallying or time-wasting. Our duty was to obey.

He had not got the love for English of Miss O'Reilly nor the love for Irish of Mr O'Shea. He was a mathematician who espoused new methods in mathematics. Not for him the endless long division and multiplication. He would draw a long straight line on the blackboard on which he placed the figures of his problem as he went along. We were trained to use factors from 1 to 19 and to divide simultaneously with the top and bottom of the structure. The answer emerged in half the time compared to the more conventional way. Then we were shown how to prove that two was equal to one. His sanity at this stage was strongly doubted by our parents. Their fears passed when he explained the fallacy. He gave us the eleventh commandment: 'Thou shall not divide by nought!' Luckily he took his leave and we breathed again.

Master Greaney came after Master O'Connell. He was also from Kerry, and had good Irish. He believed in hitting the blackboard with the cane instead of hitting us. He used put the fear of God in us with a yell. Strangest of all, Miss Smith began smiling again. For the first half of the month, he used have us singing songs and reciting poetry. He was truly great. Then for the last part of the month a great change used come over him and we all wondered what trouble was on his mind: it was said he drank all his pay in the first half and had to live on the wind for the second half.

The highlights of our schooldays were the inspectors. One was a lady who examined the girls and tested their sewing, knitting, and darning capabilities. She was with us prior to the Treaty and she examined well into the Twenties. She spoke with a high-class English accent. In later years my wife, Nora, was to tell me that the same lady used visit her school in Portlaw, Co. Waterford. So she must have travelled the entire country. The other inspector was a man with an Oxford accent. He too preceded the Free State and remained on into the Twenties and examined us on every subject except Irish. He could walk in unannounced and examine the roll-books. There was a strict eye kept on the roll call, especially if averages were falling. For a general examination of all subjects, he gave six weeks' notice. On receipt of this knowledge, the teachers told us that our holidays were over. It was a period of intense cramming and we were loaded with homework. The exam morning came and we were asked to put our best foot forward. The teacher's life seemed to be in our hands. We did our best to help the teacher. He had already picked the helpers. I will only deal with one such helper.

The inspector took the fifth class aside and gave each of them a different composition. No chance of copying. Prearranged with the teacher, and unnoticed by the inspector, a young girl slipped in and changed the essays, giving each pupil the composition that best suited them. As pupils read out their essays the inspector was astonished at the array of talent. However, something happened that changed the situation. He remembered giving a particular title to one of the pupils and asked the boy in question to read out his essay. He introduced the boy's essay: 'And now we are going to hear a lovely letter by a boy to his aunt in New York.' You could hear a pin drop when the boy began: 'I am very fond of my donkey at home but I am in great trouble because my father is going to sell him because he is stealing the oats out of the barn.' The young girl had given the boy an essay on a donkey to suit his abilities. There was a rush by the teacher who took the inspector aside and told him that the boy was not the full shilling. The inspector seemed to understand and he took the boy by the hand and explained his great appreciation for the boy's love of a dumb animal. He asked the teacher to do something about the matter. This the teacher undertook to do and the crisis passed.

The accent of both the inspectors was so unfamiliar to our ears that we all tried to imitate them. This would be in the playground, of course. Some of the boys were very good at mimicking. This was to play an unexpected part in the afternoon of the inspector's visit. He had been testing the class on their reading ability. Until then he had been listening in a dissatisfied manner. He suddenly took over. He selected a short poem. Then we heard him say in his grandest accent:

'Oh! what do they say in Fairyland?
Oh what funny things
You might as well
Try to tell
What a birdie sings.'

He now asked Brian Smith to repeat this. He had asked the perfect mimic. Brian began to speak exactly as the inspector had said it. Our teacher grew pale and seemed unable to cope with the situation. The inspector's mouth opened and then he looked out the window as if to reassure himself that he was still in Ireland. Brian rambled on and then stopped at the end of the piece. The inspector was quiet for a moment, and then something happened which we had never experienced before. The inspector started laughing, the teacher laughed, and we all laughed. We had crossed a second bridge that day.

The examination should have gone on for another hour and a half, but the atmosphere was so friendly that the inspector took his leave. We were lucky, for the next subject would have been geography and we might have been asked about the counties of England. It was usual for the teacher to bring a large gallon of sweets on the following day. This time he brought two. Master Greaney said: '...go raibh sé tuillte againn' ('that we had deserved it'). Of course, this could only happen in the Master Greaney era.

Another aspect of my schooldays was the scrapping and sparring that schoolboys engaged in. We enjoyed it. There were strict codes. Kicking with the feet was not allowed. That would be considered brawling or mobbing. Scrapping had to be one-to-one. You fought your own age group. It warmed up many a cold day. I would consider myself average. I was always learning from seeing others scrap. Although we did not scrap in the school yard, later I was to realise that it was an important part of my education. In later life it gave you confidence. If you were ever attacked unawares, you had to know how to extricate yourself.

We also played football in the schoolyard. At first I was only a spectator. Then I started playing. Our family were very good footballers. Dad was from Ballymachugh and we had first, second, and third cousins in the parish. We could have opted to play with Ballymachugh because of our roots, but we always played with Mullahoran, and were very much appreciated in the latter parish. Some years Mullahoran were the stronger team; other years Ballymachugh were on top. We had to learn to take defeat as well as victory. The half-hour school break was too short for a game of football. When we had our lunch eaten we had only twenty minutes left. To get over this obstacle, the total aggregate score on Friday was accepted. As I grew older I found myself teaching the incoming kids the skills of football.

Often after school I used play football with Brian Smith. On our homeward walks from school, I would bring Brian in for a few apples. He invited me to his house. I got a great welcome there. His brother and sister were quite grown up by this stage. I suppose they were glad that he had somebody his own age to play with. I spent many a lovely evening there. Nobody seemed to think that I was away from home. I felt completely safe. He lived at the end of a lane which began at the Callanagh crossroads. To get there I had to pass the Cairn O'Reilly entrance and the Conny Galligan farm.

The pitch we played football on was only fifty yards long. For goalposts we put down a cap and a coat at each end. The goalmouth would be the official yardage in width. We tossed for who would start the game. If Brian was to start, he would bring the ball back to the goalmouth he was defending. It was all ground-play. Brian would tap the ball out in front of him as I was going forward. I had always to keep between him and my goalmouth. He was a real sharpshooter. All he needed was to be a yard or so out from his own goalmouth in order to score. I, on the other hand, would need to get within twenty yards of his goalmouth to shoot. I was the fastest runner of the two. Very rarely when he brought the ball from his goalmouth did he fail to shoot. I would then have the option of bringing the ball forward. I had to adopt different tactics. I would bring the ball along the side. Sometimes he would refuse to be coaxed and would remain in goalmouth to withstand my shot. It was great fun. To retain possession was essential. If we met at midfield, the boy who could hold onto the ball was generally the winner.

He was the more skilled of the two of us. I have the feeling that he let me win now and again. His aunt would sometimes come out and sit in a chair to watch us. She seemed to be backing the visitor. I very much appreciated this. We were both boys of ten or eleven. At the end of the games, I would be brought in for a nice tea, which I very much enjoyed. It is said that hunger is a good sauce. When Brian came to our house he was always given a substantial meal. Our play on these occasions though consisted of handball and skittles rather than football. He became very good at these games too. Around the age of twelve he went away to Belfast or somewhere. Twelve years later when I came back home for the Economic War, I came across him again. He had come back to the farm, married and was rearing a family. After leaving Mullahoran, I was never to come back to stay, only to visit.

On one occasion while playing football at school, I was thrown on the wall of the yard and left unconscious. Dad arrived and brought me in a horse and trap to the doctor five miles away. I must have considered myself a very troublesome boy, for I was delighted when I heard Dad say to the doctor: 'This is a very quiet boy.' I was in great pain, having narrowly escaped a broken skull. I had to remain in a darkened room for ten days and it was a further five weeks before I returned to school. The boy who caused my injury was in a terrible state and could not do enough for me when I finally returned. It was the end of the Mullahoran/Ballymachugh clash for supremacy, for me at any rate. I did not play again for a long time. In time, while convalescing, I got accustomed to the dim light and was doing some studying. I was hoping to be on an equal keel with my fellow-students when I joined school again. I would have needed some time longer but I was told that the inspector was to pay a visit to the school and I was asked to come back prematurely.

I sat beside many different boys while at school. In particular, I have many pleasant memories of Harry Briody whom I sat beside in fifth class. Harry Briody was a great friend of mine. He was more like a brother than a second cousin to me. He was sometimes known as Harry Cruise Briody as he lived with a wealthy relative named Tom Cruise, who took him to all the All-Ireland Finals of the period. Harry had a keen intellect and took in everything he saw. He enlarged our view of the world by telling us about all he saw on his trips with his uncle. Nowadays children broaden their horizons through television. It is a wonderful medium.

Some time after I arrived in Carrick-on-Suir in 1960, I heard that Harry was ill. I put everything aside and went back to Cavan. He was now living with his brother Matt. When I called I was taken upstairs. He seemed to be his old self. I had not seen him for twenty years.

'Who have I?' he asked.

'Well, I am a cousin of yours,' I replied.

'I thought I knew all my cousins,'

'I'm your second cousin.'

'You don't fit in there anywhere,' he replied.

'You are two days older than I am,' I gently said.

'Could you be Tosty?' he asked.

'Yes,' I said and we both grasped hands.

We broke down. We had met again. He died a few days later. He was unmarried. What a lovely fellow to write a book about. I have great memories to recall, but there are also those where a cloud obscures the sun. This is one.

Football in the Twenties

Football featured greatly not only in my childhood but also in my adolescence. It was a very important part of our lives in Cavan in the Twenties and Thirties. The sound of a ball in an adjacent field would be a call to arms. It interrupted many a chat and interfered quite a lot with our school homework. The chores on the farm also often got a hurried finish. Somehow or other one had to get to the playing-pitch. In fact the sound of football being played in the distance was very unwelcome for the busy farmers in the harvest evenings. In those days it was only the darkness of night which halted the ongoing farm-work. What sticks in the mind most are those particular times when you could not leave a chore and had to listen to the sound of a ball being kicked around. There could be so many different sounds. These when punctuated by a shout or a cheer would cause the imagination to run riot.

Football and handball were not given much space in the national newspapers of the period. In contrast, *The Anglo-Celt*, the weekly Cavan paper, gave football a lot of coverage. It praised us, coaxed us and criticised us in turn. It was a tonic. Looking back, I would say that the success of Cavan football in the Twenties, Thirties, Forties and Fifties was due in no small measure to *The Anglo-Celt*. We had a special interest in all the local footballers. We had a few who played for the county team and they were little gods. One of the county players was named Jack Smallhorns. He drove a CIE lorry. I often met him at Paddy Lynch's. He was a wonderful player. He was the Cavan sharpshooter. He had broken the heart of many an opposing team. We were good friends.

We were to meet in later life. Forty years later I was having a read of the Sunday papers in my car while my children were out swimming in the sea near Dungarvan. A stranger came across and asked me for the sports page of the paper. I gave it to him and then I asked if he could tell if the tide was going out or coming in.

'It's at the butty now,' he replied.

'You are a Cavan man?' I queried?

'Yes, do you not remember Smallhorns?'

We had met again. We had a lot to say to one another. His wife was dead. His only son had a thriving business and was the pride of his life. It was such a lovely Summer's evening and there were so many different tales for each of us to tell. We could have talked on into the night but my daughter had to catch a train at Dungarvan and we broke up. That was a Sunday evening. On Monday morning I heard on the radio that his son had been killed on his way to Dublin, just around the time I had been talking to his dad. My brother Hugh P. told me that everybody rallied around the old county player who had given so much pleasure to us all. His strength of character saw him through and he devoted his latter life to imparting the skills of football to the younger generation.

It is difficult to describe for a younger generation what it was like to be part of a surging crowd going to a football match in the Twenties. I was a walker up to fourteen years of age. Cycling was for the under-thirties. The older men still walked, rode on horseback or travelled by trap or side-car. At first there would appear to be only a few on the roads going to a match. That changed when the crowds came in from different areas. We made use of every available near-cut across the fields. As we neared the football pitch we could hear the local fife and drum band playing some martial music. Our day was made when we heard the thud of a ball being kicked around. The younger spectators were admitted free and this gave us scope for the purchase of sweets and biscuits at the matches

There used be a travelling boy who sang 'Patsy Fagan'. He was part of the scene. He followed the Mullahoran team and he had a few local songs to suit every occasion. He had a lovely voice. Nowadays, he would be an asset to any band. We did not know his name but we all knew him as Patsy Fagan. He travelled to all the games around. Sometimes when I hear one of the old 'Come all yes', I see him in my mind's eye going around the crowds, singing his head off and collecting with his old worn cap.

The football pitches in those days were really farmers' fields which were hired for the occasion. There was no such thing as side lines. The crowds were kept off the pitch by a band of stewards, sometimes assisted by ropes. The stewards had a difficult job, especially in a closely played match. It all seemed very normal then. There were no dressing rooms. Undressing was done in a nearby farm barn or maybe in a neighbouring field. The modern dressing rooms and well-regulated pitches are a tribute to all the hard work done by successive generations. It is a far cry from eighty years ago.

In the mid-Twenties we used play football against the Kilcogy boys in a field belonging to Pat George (further up Pat Daniel's boreen in Glen). These matches were unofficial. He was a married man with no children. He had plenty of bog-meadows, which were lovely to play on. These meadows had been reclaimed from bogland and were very springy. Better still, he bought footballs for us. Of course, we often helped him rear his turf supply. He was our referee and took no nonsense. I was told that on one occasion he even gave a boy a clip on the ear. I have never heard of any of our modern referees adopting such a practice. There could be upwards of forty boys frequenting the venue. He knew every boy's capability. If only ten boys turned up, George would select two teams of five each. Today, politicians accuse each other of changing the goalposts; we did just that in the bog meadows in the Twenties. On one occasion we played twenty-one aside, which was popular in pre-G.A.A. days. Dad told me that he had played such football in his youth.

There were some lovely footballers who never got on the official teams. They might have been 'only sons' who had to devote themselves to arduous farmwork. They might have got married young and were unable to continue practising football. Players did not have the intensive training of nowadays. Playing handball, however, kept us nimble of foot and hand. Perhaps on account of all the strenuous physical work, footballers seemed to have a shorter active span than today. I myself finished at twenty five years.

The official Mullahoran teams were accommodated at Kilcogy and Carricknabrick. They had not a playing pitch either but rented a field from a farmer. There is a lovely park now at Lisnatinny. A feature of the Twenties was the large number of clerical students, coming back at holiday time. Some would be so good that they would be a welcome asset to any team. Others, less skilled, could be kept in reserve. They would be slipped in here and there when someone got injured so as not to displace the good players of the existing teams. There was great sympathy for these clerical students who were later to work on difficult missionary work. Some of these when out foreign were to remember the magic power of football played with Mullahoran.

Sunday was a day to look forward to, but it was extra-special when there was a football match in the offing. We, the young people under fifteen, travelled by foot to every match within a radius of five miles. However, there was one venue younger children were prohibited from travelling to and that was Bruskey in Ballintemple parish. The route was mostly across country with a river to cross that was dangerous in flood. The roads beyond the river were of little use to the walker and we had to make use of Mass paths and short-cuts across fields to reach our objective. My first visit to Bruskey was on a lovely August Sunday.

Our usual walking crowd was swollen by the fact that a lot of cyclists who could make the venue by a circuitous route had joined us for the sheer fun of the trip. I will describe my first journey there, for its memories have lived with me down the years. We were travelling towards the Cavan heartland and needed upwards of two hours' walking time to reach our destination. About fifty yards from my home, we left the main road and proceeded down a lane to reach 'Boston' (Callanagh Lower) a half-mile away. Here there was a cluster of small farms on the edge of a bog. The majority of the young people were away in foreign lands. The people remaining at home made do with the minimum of farm work. Living beside a good turf bog, they specialised in cutting turf beyond their own requirements. They only sold this turf when a wet Summer created a scarcity. Their whitewashed houses and their well-trimmed hedges spoke of contentment and ease. It was in sharp contrast to living on larger farms where the work was ongoing from dawn until darkness.

We realised that we were a little late, for the place was filled with parked bicycles deserted by their riders for the trip across country. Our first task was to cross 'Boston' Bog. Half of this bog was cutaway bog. The turf had been taken out and the area was ready to be reclaimed for farming. The high bog remained and it was quite swampy in places. Sometimes we walked three abreast. Often we fell back to two and for a difficult stretch we walked in single file. We were now at a lower level. Looking back towards 'Boston', we could see the oncoming surging column of boys and girls. Some carried a flag. An odd cheer disturbed the wildlife of the area. Our behaviour was to change when we crossed the river.

At last, we reached the Drumbrucklis River, which is a tributary of the River Erne. Sometimes it was merely a lazy-flowing stream. Today it was swollen with the Lammas Floods, which occur in Cavan during the months of August. The tops of the crossing stones were barely visible. It was very intimidating, especially to non-swimmers.

About twenty girls were waiting at the riverside to be carried by the boys across to the other side. Some of them I recognised as shoppers at Paddy Lynch's. Part of the fun was seeing the girls being carried across, but I was glad that nobody fell in. A cold shiver came over me when one of Lynch's shoppers approached me and asked to be carried across. I knew who she was and that she was going out to her aunt in America that Autumn, to be educated there.

I could hardly refuse. We walked to the river's edge. I bent down and she slipped over my shoulders. She was a year or so younger but I soon realised I could not carry her on dry land not to speak of attempting to cross a river with her which I had never crossed myself. By this time we had quite an audience. We were holding up the traffic. She relieved the situation by whispering that we could cross together. She went in front. I followed with my right hand on her shoulder. She skilfully shifted her feet from one stone to another. It was then I realised that it was she who was ferrying me across. It was a journey to remember.

When we reached the other side, she turned and helped me up the bank. I found myself thanking her. Her eyes acknowledged my thanks. She looked like she was about to kiss me but then she looked away and the moment passed. There was a handclap from both banks and I knew that it was not for me. I found myself dashing ahead and taking refuge further up in the surging column. It would be nice to meet her later in Boston or New York. There might be a stream there to carry her across. I was told later that she had an uncle living on the other side of the river. She had probably crossed the river a hundred times or more. We learn slowly.

Our throng was now being joined by another one from the south. Later on we were to join another coming from the north. I cannot describe the élan of those boys and girls in their Sunday best. It was a memory to treasure. We were on our best behaviour. We were proud of Mullahoran. We were not cheering now. We were showing how civilized we were. We knew that some of the tales they told around the winter fires were about the wild men from among the Mullahoran hills. People came to the road to see us pass. Their field gates were flung open. Their dogs were held locked up. There was no bull or wicked animal to be seen. Every effort was made to be friendly and nice to the visitors. I would say that they were a little bit afraid of us. Instead of seeing a mob invading their sanctuary, to their surprise they saw something else. We were conscious of being on a stage.

To be fair to the people of Ballintemple, we really did not understand them. They were more of a stay-at-home farming class. We were a people who were thinking of foreign lands. Some of us had been across and back. We knew that we were part of their folklore. Maybe we liked it that way. If we hadn't behaved ourselves, we would have given them something to talk about. I am, a traveller myself, looking back. How nice it would be if one could span the years and cross Drumbrucklis River again.

Confirmation and final years at school

I was confirmed in 1925. Although I was from the parish of Mullahoran, my school was in the parish of Ballymachugh, although only just. It was known as the 'school in no-man's-land'. The children in Clonoose School who were from Mullahoran went to their own parish church to be confirmed. Those who were from Ballymachugh were confirmed in that parish. By this time it was the custom for children of the parish of Mullahoran who were to be confirmed to stay behind after the eleven o'clock Mass on Sunday for a Christian Doctrine class. We thought that it did not concern us as we went to school in another parish. Canon Egan had other ideas. He spoke to our parents on the matter. Our parents told us to comply, which we did unwillingly.

There were five schools in Mullahoran parish and there was intense rivalry among them as to who should get the 'red rosette' when the Bishop came around. Miss Smith was the teacher at Clonoose who prepared us for Confirmation. She had a reputation to maintain. She paid special attention to that part of her class who had to face the cold breeze of competition in Mullahoran parish. How important were such matters then! We were very good, but there are always a few weak pupils in every class and ours was no exception. The teacher at Mullahoran church got to know which of us knew our Christian Doctrine and who did not. She would first ask one of our weak pupils a question. He or she would not know it. She would then ask one of the bright pupils of the parish. Of course, they sang out the answer. She was playing a game at our expense. We spared Miss Smith by not telling her what was happening.

We tried to coach these pupils but the going was tough. Someone hit on a plan. We changed places with them to confuse the teacher. That was a day to remember. The teacher asked someone she thought was weak at Christian Doctrine a fairly hard question. She had asked our best man. It was a question on Hell. He gave the usual 'Penny Catechism' answer and then he qualified it by saying that nobody knew where it was and nobody had come back from it. She passed on to the next weak pupil with another difficult question; and then to another. All our substitute weak pupils chirped the right answers. The priest came in. He had been listening to the replies in the porch. He complemented the teacher on her pupils, paying special tribute to the boy who had spoken on Hell.

The teacher smiled and Canon Egan went off maybe to enjoy the joke to himself. I don't know. We were treated with great respect after that. The teacher was pleasant to us and we were nice to her. It is difficult to know exactly why she behaved so. She was a nice person, but she may have felt she was being imposed upon by having to take us every Sunday, when we could have been shared around among the other teachers. Like the other teachers who stayed on after second Mass she got nothing extra for this work. Moreover, the Clonoose children were regarded as 'little outlaws' by the other schools. She may have had little tolerance for us to begin with.

Time passed and in the Confirmation of 1925, Mattie Reilly and myself tied for first place. We each got a red rosette and got two lovely missals. We were from Clonoose School. We had beaten the schools of the parish. It was a situation which nobody could explain. Worse still, the class for Confirmation at Clonoose had been taught by Miss Smith, who was only 'second in command'. The Bishop thanked all the teachers in a general way but he had special praise for Miss Smith. He also noted that one of the boys had blessed himself with his left hand, but said it was perfectly all right. That boy was me!

It was a very unusual day and the children paid the penalty. During the Troubles, things had become strained between Canon Egan and the Bishop. The Bishop would appear to have thought that the Canon had leaned too much towards the Republicans. It was even said they were not on speaking terms. It was now 1925 and it was time to put the past behind them. The ceremony which would normally only have lasted an hour and a half took two hours and a half. The Canon's homily was unduly long and only the 'right things' were said. The Bishop had a fund of anecdotes which kept the congregation on their toes. When we thought the ceremony was over, we found that the Bishop was out in the front of the church mixing with the people. We had to wait to kiss his ring. And all this time we had been fasting from midnight. As they say in Cavan: 'We could have eaten the quarter sessions.'

Mama had brought a packed lunch for us but in the event it would have called for the miracle of the loaves and fishes as it had also to be shared around among other hungry children. I was lucky that I ended up with half a cut of bread. Mattie Reilly's mother also brought a packed lunch and I remember getting a piece of bread from her also. It was nice to get home for a proper meal. It was a day when the Republicans and the Free Staters talked together.

An incident that occurred some time after my confirmation has stuck in my mind. I was sent down to Drumhawnagh Railway Station. We were expecting a wagonload of slag, to be used as a fertiliser, for distribution to the people who were selling meadows. A couple of bags here and there made the difference when they were being sold for hay.

I was just coming away when two boys stopped me. They were a few years older.

'Have you your missal with you?' one queried.

'No,' I replied.

'You'll need to say a few prayers. We are going to give you a good dressing.'

'I only fight one-to-one,' I replied.

'We will hammer you in turn.'

One fellow sat down. The other lunged at me. His very weight would have carried me to the ground. I stepped aside. I must have got him somewhere on the neck. He stumbled. The other fellow got up and the two attacked me at once. I was getting the worst of it. When I avoided one, I ran into the other. I was getting a severe dressing.

One of them said: 'Maybe, you would like to kneel down and ask for mercy?' I was about to answer 'No!' when I realised something strange was happening. Two schoolgirls had joined the fray. Their swinging schoolbags were now catching the heads of my opponents. We were now joined by the station master and the two boys skedaddled. They were two young girls, who stopped at Paddy Lynch's shop. They had helped a fellow-customer. I got hell from Paddy himself when he heard of it. He made out the girls were interested in me.

I was twelve years of age in 1925, the year I was confirmed. In different circumstances I might have gone to secondary school after Confirmation, but there was no such school nearby. The three nearest secondary schools were all equidistant from me. Longford was 22 miles away. Mullingar and Cavan were also 22 miles away. The boys who were going for the Church in Mullahoran went to Longford to St Mel's

College. The thought of going to America had already occurred to me. Two of my aunts had gone to night-school there and graduated. I would do likewise. I made myself acquainted with the geography of the USA. I also studied its history and writers. I had a special interest in American history because one of my granduncles had been an officer in the American Civil War. He had fought on the Union side.

There was no alternative but to stay on in national school and study for going to America. In addition to attending school, I also availed of correspondence courses under the guidance of my teacher. I studied arduously. Sometimes I studied in the parlour but for complete peace I used climb up to the loft barn. I had completely given up football. I could be missing for hours on end. I thought that Mama would be in favour of my plans to further my education in America. I was to find out later that she was bitterly opposed to any us going there. She preferred that we all stayed at home and made a country of it.

There was an upsurge of hayshed building from the mid-Twenties onwards. Before long we had one erected. The wet summers had taught everybody the need for haysheds. The supply of hay for livestock for the Winter had previously been stored in huge ricks. The size of a rick varied with the number of stock to be fed. Bringing the hay into the haggard was a tricky operation. Generally the neighbours helped out. They went to each other in turn. Every townland had its skilled rick-maker. On the day a rick was being made, five or six farmers joined forces and together they brought the hay into the haggard. All took a hand in forking the hay but the rick specialist went up and made the rick. It is a pity that haysheds put an end to his art. Henceforth, community effort was no longer needed. Each farmer could bring in hay to his shed if he got a few hours of sunshine. It was the end of an era. It also shortened the threshing day as the straw could be piled into the shed instead of being ricked. Yes, haysheds made for more individual farming. I did not realise this at the time. I was later to see the change which they brought about. Nevertheless, I immediately appreciated that our hayshed offered me even more solitude than the barn loft. Oftentimes I would steal up into the hay to study one of my schoolbooks or with a newly-acquired book for a secret read.

Our family got two more additions in the mid-Twenties. Henry Austin was born in early 1925 and Anna Celia late in 1926. Our family now consisted of six boys and two girls. Hugh P., Edward and myself were the older members and behaved like uncles to the others. The years that ensued between 1925 and 1930 were eventful for the country and for us. Ellie McCann left us for America sometime around 1926. She was not replaced in the kitchen. I don't know for certain what was the reason for this. Hugh P. and Edward were no longer at school and had more time to help Tom Mac with the farm work. Mama was a very systematic worker, and now that there was more of us to help her, she probably found more time to devote to the kitchen and house. Dad was now in his mid-sixties and Mama never asked him for any help on the farm. We, the older children, all had our separate chores to do. As the younger children got older, they also were given duties. Everyone chipped in and helped those who found themselves behind in their work. I was still at school and I helped my younger brothers and sisters with their homework. Later, after leaving school, I was to help them more.

During the last five years of the twenties, I saw a lot of my cousins, the Brady family, at Shanvalla. There was an extra bicycle available at home and I had to get my turn on it. Hitherto I had walked across farms to reach my destination. Now ironically when I was older and better at climbing over ditches and crossing rough terrain, I had a bicycle to ride. The older people were aghast at what they considered children cycling. To add strength to their stand on the matter, a young girl aged twelve fell off her bike and got killed. This happened near Granard. So we all had to be extra heedful of our elders' advice. A common feature of cycling where young boys were concerned was the lighting of a cigarette after alighting from their bikes. It was all so grown-up. I made sure not to smoke any cigarette when in Shanvalla.

There were nine children in the Brady family, eight girls and a boy, Chassy (Charles). Chassy was the youngest, and died while still a young boy in 1933. That same year another son, Eddie, was born. When Chassy died, I was sent across to

Shanvalla to help the family in their grieving. Aunt Kate and Charles had sheltered me when my sister Elizabeth was dying more than ten years before, now I was doing something in return. I was close to all the family. The oldest of the family was Mary Francis.

From the age of seven onwards I was the bearer of messages between Mama and Aunt Kate. Then I had to cross country by foot. I had to know where a bull or stallion might be. I had also to get friendly with all the barking dogs. I was welcomed by all, especially those who lived alone. Any newspaper no matter how old was welcome. We used get quite an amount of newspapers but they all disappeared in this way. When I started cycling, I missed the chats with the old people along the route over the fields. Sometimes a bike would not be available and I would have to walk. I used get an extra welcome and maybe a cup of tea. There were only half a dozen radios on the route. This was a blessing in disguise. The people who had no radio dropped in to hear the news where there was one. Keeping a community alive can be very simple or very difficult. Or is alone ever alone?

My chief attraction in Shanvalla was the Irish language. The eldest girl, Mary Francis, had gone to the Gaeltacht and had come back with a rich Connemara *blas*. We listened and did our best to imitate her. The teacher, Master Fitzmaurice, in the local national school at Cloncovet was a keen *Gaeilgeoir* and brought his pupils to the various *feiseanna*. The Brady girls ranked among the best pupils at Irish. Our teachers taught us Irish at Clonoose but they did not bring us to the *feiseanna*. I considered myself lucky to be drinking at such an 'Irish well'.

The Brady girls were a unique bunch. They were all mad to work on the farm. Working with horses came easily to them. In the early years there used be two to three men working on the farm. In later times there were none, as extra help was not needed. All the girls went to boarding-schools. Two of them became nuns. One was a Reverend Mother in Chicago. The other, Elizabeth (Bal), taught for a time in Iceland, an unusual destination for an Irish nun. Two were to become teachers. The rest married farmers.

As I have said above, if we were short of milk in Winter, the Galligans supplied us, and we in turn supplied them when in need. On one occasion neither of us had any milk to give. Galligans had to get their supply from the Tierney family. We were left without any. I was a boy of twelve and I volunteered to go across to the Brady family for a supply. It was a distance of two miles across country or four miles by road. After coming home from school, I had a quick dinner and set off for Shanvalla. I carried two cans, which would hold a half-gallon each. I jogged down the hills and walked uphill. I had a quick cup of tea at Shanvalla and was back home as darkness was falling. This sufficed for two days and I was quite pleased with myself. I did this for weeks on end. The nights were getting darker and we were approaching the shortest days in the year. No matter, the days would be getting longer after Christmas.

Then the test came. I was on my way home from school. I was at my ease talking to another boy when I heard the sound of a stone hitting the galvanised-iron roof of Caffrey's shed. This was a considerable distance from the road and could only be reached by a catapult sling. Some boy from behind us had done the trick. Then there followed another bang and another. The Caffrey brothers, who had been in a field further down, were already on the road rushing up to meet us. We had no alternative but to jump into the adjoining field and get home by a circuitous route. I was late getting home as a result. I ate a hasty dinner and set out for Shanvalla. I knew that I could never make it before dark and was contemplating having to walk the four miles home by road. To make matters worse, I had to pass by a graveyard. I pressed on. Then I saw two girls coming towards me. Their beautiful hair gave them away. They were two of the Brady girls. They had two full gallons of milk to exchange for my empty ones. It remains one of my beautiful memories of over eighty years ago. I was home before darkness fell.

The Brady farm itself consisted of sixty acres with additional cutaway bog, which offered excellent grazing. The dwelling house was two-storey and slated. The out-offices were also all slated. They had no galvanised hayshed but they had an old slated barn that could hold all the hay they needed. My best memory of Shanvalla is of the high walls of the outbuildings. I spent many a happy hour there playing handball against those walls. The Brady girls were highly skilled at the game.

Charles Brady was a lovely man. He seemed to have read widely. He had certain ideas as to how the country should go. His views were sometimes dramatically opposite to mine, and my father's. For instance, Dad took great pride in fixing up returned emigrants with farms. In fact during the two periods I helped my father with his work in the late 1920s and early 1930s all farms had been bought with American money. The small farms could never have been kept going without help from abroad. Charles had different ideas. He seemed to think that some farmers' sons were too lazy to work in Ireland. Instead, they emigrated to America. There they worked at the most menial jobs and amassed money. Then they came home. Their money inflated the price of farms. Honest hardworking farmers who had stayed at home were not able to compete with them. Worse still, they forgot what they had been working at in America. They put on 'the brass' (airs and graces) and looked down their noses at the natives. I asked him for his remedy. He merely said: 'If a boy or girl goes to America, they should stay there.' I did not argue with him. I knew that he liked me very much. Maybe he was indirectly saying that I should not go to America. I was beginning to have some misgivings about going there. My chirpy bunch of younger brothers and sisters were a treasure which I would miss. There are certain things for which there is no compensation. The Brady girls were another consideration. They were such a vibrant cheerful bunch. They were outdoor girls. They did not need powder and paint. Their rosy cheeks got the added tan of the sun.

When cycling to Aunt Kate's in Shanvalla I used pass Donohoe's forge in Glen. I was only there on a few occasions on business along with my brother Hugh P., getting a horse shod, but on my frequent visits to Shanvalla it was handy to drop in and rest for a while at the forge. It was a great place for exchanging news. At an earlier period newspapers used be read aloud in this and other forges.

There were four forges in the parish. I knew this one and

Tommy Lynch's one at Grousehall beside Paddy Lynch's shop. Donohoe's forge was the one I liked best. It was a stone-wall building with a galvanised roof. The door was in the front, the back of the building was facing north-west. It was sheltered. Men and horses liked this. Inside there was a raised stone hearth about six feet from the end of the building. There was a large bellows at the back of this to blow the fire of coal. The fire was about two and a half feet from the ground. In front was a stone trough filled with water. The blacksmith stood to the left of the fire. He could contract and expand the bellows with his left hand. In his right was a poker three feet long with which he could poke the fire as the air came through from the bellows. An intense fire could thus be achieved in a matter of minutes. A forge fire and its scatter of sparks is something that fondles the memory. Beside the blacksmith was the anvil. It had a flat end on which the molten iron was beaten, and a rounded end to shape the object. There was an array of tongs and other implements on the bench behind. There were several vices and a cutter for heavy iron. In the forge, there was space to accommodate two horses. The floor underneath was cobbled.

There was an old retainer there who was called to deal with the troublesome horses. To me he seemed to be only talking to the animal. He was strangely effective. In addition to shoeing horses, ploughs were repaired, cartwheels shod, slanes for turf cutting made and spades and other farm implements repaired. The forge had a long history and made pikes in 1798 for rebels who fought at the battle of Ballinamuck.

On the other side of the road was Farrelly's sand pit. Mullahoran had plenty of sand deposits of high quality; the building sites of the surrounding towns were supplied from the parish. A gate beside the forge led into a field and to part of a Mass path. A throng of people used this Mass path in the 1920s. Today, nobody goes that way. This path went down to a stream where the cartwheels were shod and then up the hill to Donohoe's farmhouse. There was a special shoeing circle for the purpose at the stream. There were always cattle in the field beside the forge and the rule was that you shut the gate no matter who was coming after or coming against you. Funny how that gate sticks in my memory after all those years. I hope that the shoeing circle has been left untouched. We spent many an hour watching the wheels being shod there.

Mama was vehemently opposed to my going to America. I recall very vividly how I learned this. I was in the kitchen with Mama at the time. Then I saw her put on her coat. That was a signal that she was going for a walk uphill on the farm. She and Dad had a walk there every Sunday. They always went alone. Maggie Coyle used bring us as children almost every second day there. It would be hard for me to bring you on that walk now. The farm of thirteen small fields has been converted into four or five big fields. So I will try to bring you along the route I knew in my youth. Mama beckoned me to accompany her. This was something new. When we left the farmyard we entered the Limekiln Field. It was a hundred years since lime had been burned there but it still retained its name. We were gradually going uphill. When we reached the Rock Field, we paused and looked around. Once there had been a rock there and a pond covering about a rood. Neither were there now. Uncle Patrick when he retired from the police, looked around for something to do. He blew up the rock and drained the pond. Mama and I were now looking at a fertile piece of ground with milch cows chewing their cud. Mama looked at me and then she said something that I did not understand: 'Would it not be nice to see the old rock and pond again?' I said nothing as I could not see her line of reasoning. Now I can, after going back to places I have not seen for fifty years. Now I know that she was associating that rock and pond as areas that were there before the Troubles.

We continued uphill until we reached the Sheep Field, from the top of which I had seen Granard burning that night in late 1920. Granard was a special town to us. It was there we said goodbye to our turkeys and *banbh*s (bonham pigs) that we would never see again. This evening the sun caused the steeple on the Granard church to be lit up. It was a wonderful spectacle. I looked at Mama. She was looking towards Lough Sheelin, along whose shore she had spent her girlhood. I pointed towards Granard. She looked away. Then she took my hand, just as she had taken it during the War of Independence when we set out to meet a husband and father that might not return.

We crossed over to the other side of the hill. There we looked towards Kilnaleck and south-east Cavan. Not far away lay my old school house at Clonoose. It had been newly painted and looked as if it would remain there forever. It is now a derelict building but still holds onto its roof. Moreover, the five schools of Mullahoran parish have since been accommodated in a large school near Mullahoran church. Then we came around to Dan's Field. We were now looking towards the Drumbrucklis River and the parish of Ballintemple. Mama looked at me and laughed. I hoped that she was laughing at some incident from her own life. She left me in no doubt when she said: 'I believe there is a footbridge planned to cross the Drumbrucklis River. I understand that there were some near-drownings there.' I refused to be drawn. Eventually, we reached the field called The Orchard, though there were no apple trees in it in my time. It was in the shelter of the hill. There had been two houses there seventy years before. I was expecting some extra titbit about the area. I was disappointed when she said:
'Tosty, Dad and I have been talking about you. We don't want to interfere with your plans for going to America, but we would prefer if you stayed here. Things are looking up and the country needs everyone to make it a better place.'

I was not totally unprepared for this. I had got hints now and again. I had always heard that Mama was on the point of going to America when she had met Dad. I had also heard that she had coaxed Dad to go too, for she was fearful of coming times. He had put her off by saying that he would go after Ireland achieved Home Rule. It was the old story over again. Men and women did not mind emigrating. Many intended to come back. However, they did not want their children to emigrate. Years later I was to experience similar feelings.

I could not refuse Mama outright. I just told her that I had put in extra hours studying and that I was in touch with Aunt Lizzy and my godfather, Michael Galligan, in America. I said that if I got a job here I would stay. Otherwise I would have to go. Mama thanked me. She told me that herself and Dad would do their best to try to fit me in somewhere. It all seemed so possible.

I also remember that walk with Mama for another reason. I still remember the cup of tea that Ellie McCann poured out for us on our return. She was a very considerate girl (a girl beyond her years in many respects) and we missed her very much when she left us. When my friendship grew with my near neighbour Pat 'a Park Smith, I would take him on that route through our farm very often. Sometimes we walked there in the moonlight and enjoyed looking at the lit-up houses that dotted the Cavan hills. Later when we grew older I used walk across the Drilling Field and onto the road that led to Mullahoran Church. There I would meet Pat with his motorbike, which were very scarce then. The Drilling Field had originally consisted of nine acres, but had been divided in two by a ditch before my time. Tradition had it that a branch of the O'Reilly (Ó Raghallaigh) clan who fought alongside Owen Rua O'Neill in the 1641 Rebellion used drill their soldiers there. Another of our fields was also divided in two. There was a drain, but no ditch, running across the top of the Rock Field.

Mention of the Limekiln Field brings back a memory from late October 1927. We had a lot of pigs that year and they were out in this field before feeding-time. Some were grazing, others were lying down and enjoying the lovely balmy evening. The air seemed to stand still. Suddenly there was a rush of pigs towards the farm gate. When the gate was opened they hid in the furthest recesses of their houses. Tom McDermott and a son of Uncle Henry's, Hugh, were working there that evening. Dad was away. Mama had heard somewhere that a fierce wind was brewing. Lucky we had plenty of ropes and heavy stones. Every building was reinforced and tied down. We were beginning to think that it was all a joke. Tom, however, although it was feeding-time noted that not a single pig had come out.

The storm came. I found myself thrown into a hedge and there I remained. Everything held except the turf-shed. When the roof shook the door fell in. My brother Hugh P. and cousin Hugh of Clonloaghan attempted to hold the rising roof down. The boys were now many feet up in the air. McDermott shouted, 'Let go!'

They did. The roof kept rising. It ended up a half-mile away, but was useless for re-roofing. The storm passed and the pigs came out as hungry as ever. We felt sorry about the missing roof. Next morning the news came through. Tens of fishermen had lost their lives on the west coast of Ireland. We were warned but the poor fishermen were not. They had very small boats in those days. The tragedy deeply affected everybody at the time. Thankfully, the Irish fishermen of today have bigger and safer boats.

Mention of the plight of fishermen and the ferocity of the sea in storm, brings to mind a strange episode from my school days. Sometime before leaving school I took part in an essay competition. This was an annual competition sponsored by the Royal Lifeboat Service and many schools in our area participated in it. I was chosen as the representative of our school for this particular year. The representatives of the other schools were considered very competent. The title of the essay came in a sealed envelope. There was no limit to the time that could be spent in writing the essay. The title was 'What kind of woman should a lifeboatman's wife be.'

Along with the rest of the competitors in our area I had never seen the sea. I had never seen a lifeboat. A lifeboatman's wife was a further mystery still. I was being asked to give an opinion on a type of person I knew nothing about. I looked around. Pens were still being held aloft by everybody. It was clear that inspiration would not come. I suddenly thought of a way out of the problem. My mind went back to the troubled days of 1920 when the moon often seemed to be hiding behind dark clouds. Dad would be late coming home. Mama would be forever glancing at the clock. Then she would slip my little overcoat over me and together we would go out into the night to meet Dad. Now and again she would stop as if she was trying to hear his footsteps. Then she would trudge on again. There was always a hug when Mama and Dad met.

I began to write about Mama. She had all the qualities of a lifeboatman's wife waiting for him to come home from sea. I wrote on. I was conscious that all the desks were empty around me. In fact, some of those present gave up after half an hour. I sensed that the teachers were waiting for me to finish. Then I realised that they were behind me glancing over my shoulder. Most of the students had achieved from a half to three-quarters of a page. I was on my fourth page and still writing.

At last I finished. One of the teachers read my essay out aloud while the rest looked at one another. I heard no more for about two months. Then one day our school got a certificate of merit, which was duly framed and put in a place of honour. I had come first in Ireland and moreover very high in Britain and Ireland. More gratifying still my essay was described as having unusual merit. Those were heady days for me and my school. Then an ugly rumour spread. I could not possibly have written such a brilliant piece of writing. It was the teacher who wrote it. I had memorised it and got it onto paper. My friends stood up for me. Gradually the entire episode was forgotten. I was given the framed certificate to bring home. It was hung in an honoured place to be admired. Years later when I went home I found that it was missing.

Part II: Coming to manhood

Leaving School and the Wall Street Crash

Pat Smith was two years older than myself. His bachelor uncle had bought him a motorbike to convey him to and from Cavan Technical School. The neighbours considered that Pat was a wild young fellow and were waiting to hear of him in some accident or other. I was about thirteen and I was studying hard for my going to America. I was still at the national school but was availing of correspondence courses under the guidance of my teacher. I spent a lot of my free time studying, and no longer played any football.

Sunday evening was an exception. I would walk across the farm to where it met the road leading to the church. There I would wait until Pat Smith came along with his motorbike. We travelled the most of the roads of Cavan, Longford and Westmeath. Pat had a lot of relatives on his mother's side in Co. Longford and he always knew where to get the welcome meal. He was a great mechanic and always kept his machine in order. In fact, I became quite skilled myself and what he taught me came in very useful in my later life. One evening, as darkness was falling, we stopped at a roadside show outside Edgeworthstown. We entered. It was the end of a week-long competition for a grandfather clock. Each competitor paid for and got ten shots with a pellet gun. To win the prize, one had to get ten bull's-eyes. By our arrival nobody had yet achieved this. Pat took up the gun and shot ten bull's-eyes. For good measure he shot another ten with the same result. There was an awkward silence? A stranger had stolen the show. Then Pat tossed a coin in the air between those who had got nine and gave the clock to the winner. All the time, I did not realise what greatness I was rubbing against. Pat later joined the British Air Force (RAF). He was one of the heroes of the retreat at Dunkirk and the Battle of Britain. I thought that nobody knew that I used be travelling the countryside with Pat. His mother knew and was glad of my moderating influence. As teenagers we underestimated our parents, and so it has been down the years. We learn slowly.

It was at this stage that I became very close to Dad. It all happened over a period. I remained on at school as long as possible. One day, at the age of fifteen or so, my teacher told me that he could not teach me anything more. On finally leaving school Dad asked me to help him out surveying the conacre plots which he annually auctioned out. The strong branch of the Hibernians of which he had been chairman was now only a memory. He busied himself with farmers' affairs. He liked to ponder on things. He started talking about the events that were happening in Great Britain and Europe. For him another World War seemed inevitable. Then he started talking about the home front. His talk was not of politics, but of what was happening in rural Ireland among the common people. He brought me back to my days in Clonoose school. Many of the mothers of children there had been to America and back. They had gone to America, done a domestic stint there and come back. They had tried to save every penny possible. They had brought back dowries of from three to four hundred pounds and married farmers. All the farms that we sold were bought with American money.

After leaving national school, I still kept studying and continued doing correspondence courses. For a time I did a business course with a correspondence school in England. Then I switched over to a correspondence course with Caffrey's College in Dublin. I did everything I was asked to do on the farm or in my father's business. This gave me contact with the local paper, *The Anglo-Celt*, in connection with advertisements of sale of farms. I was very much engaged in the carriage of sales. This was a term used to cover the sale of a farm and its ultimate transfer to a new property holder.

Briody & O'Reilly was an auctioneering firm which bought and sold farms. They also handled furniture auction sales. These were few and far between and were mostly those of priests and solicitors. The firm also provided farmers with loans via the banks for the restocking of farms, supplying seeds, buying meadows, conacre and turf letting. If a farmer, either big or small, defaulted on a loan to the bank, we paid up. We kept him on our books against the time when he would be in a position to pay. Farming had its difficulties, even in the best of times, due to the vagaries of weather and the rise and fall in the price of agricultural produce. This was accentuated during the Economic War when there were sometimes fairs and markets without buyers. The very large farmers who had to obtain loans for the restocking of cattle conducted their own private dealings with the banks. We dealt with the middle and small farmer. They were creditworthy too, but the banks preferred to deal with them through us because of our local knowledge. Two-thirds of these were steady, hard-working farmers who took the rough with the smooth. The other third was on the poverty line and could not obtain credit from the banks. They were honest people with large families on poor agricultural holdings. They were really the salt of the earth. To the banks they were 'undesirables'. They sheltered under our umbrella. The people who sold meadows did not require credit. If there was a funeral or other emergency, they would look for a small loan to tide them over until the sale of the meadows. They did not go to the bank. I never saw mention of this in any of the accounts. I suspect Dad gave them this money out of his own pocket.

There was always a good demand for such meadows to make hay. Some farmers would graze their entire farms, leaving it to chance to buy some meadows in the Autumn. Others might graze most of their land but have some tillage. Tom McDermott, who worked with us, had no stock on his farm. He let his farm in meadows, which were exceptionally good as they lay along the river. They were kept manured and 'sold' by auction to other farmers in the vicinity. He came off better than if he farmed this small farm in the normal way.

Conacre meant that someone would let a field to grow crops like potatoes or vegetables or corn. If a whole field was let there was no difficulty. We knew its area from the map. If only part of a field was let, it had to be measured. Meadows, on the other hand, had to be watched for fear of trespassing, lest the grass be trampled on. Conacre was sold in the Spring. Meadows were sold in the Autumn. We sold both through the banks on credit, to be paid for eleven months hence, when farmers got paid for their stock. Even well-off farmers availed of the service.

I was gradually becoming accomplished in the skills of

auctioneering. I was lucky to have a father whose word was always taken. If a farm was not looking its best, I was detailed to see that the gates were painted, for example. What was very important on a farm was the availability of water. Piped water had not yet come on the scene. It was essential that all wells were cleaned and limed. The possibility of collection of rainwater from sheds had to be looked into and barrels provided if necessary. Every farm had a half-acre of bog to provide fuel for fires. In some cases this had been cut away and it was necessary to look around where another half-acre could be purchased. Whenever it came available, we would buy plots of turbary, amounting to ten acres or so. This could be held in hand. Half-acres could then be doled out as the occasion warranted. I learned as I went along. It was at this stage that I first came into contact with the 'dandelion boys'. At first I thought these boys were a menace. Then I realised that they were actually improving the quality of the meadows. These boys came from the cottages. They descended on the meadows when the growth was a foot high. They had a special tool which picked up the dandelion plants and a good deal of the root. It was amazing how quickly a bag got filled. Back home, they each had a pig or two. In no time they had pigs for the market. Those boys also kept goats. These were tied in pairs to prevent them trespassing. The goats kept the roadside hedges nice and neat. This enabled us to see over the hedges. It was a far cry from the present tractor-driven hedge-cutter.

On New Year's Day 1929, I was at Mass in Mullahoran. It was the first Mass and was generally got through in time to make way for the second Mass. The curate was reading the Mass. We were all expecting a few sharp reminders about making New Year resolutions. Instead, we were treated to a long, upbeat sermon. Rather than admonish us for our failings, he praised us as a generation that he was privileged to serve. We deserved the best. He told us that this year was the centenary of Catholic Emancipation. We should be proud of what had been achieved in the past hundred years in the national and religious fields. For the first time I heard Daniel O'Connell raised to the position of hero. Our teachers had barely mentioned him. This was probably

108

because he was not an advocate of physical force.

This sermon was a prelude to a year of large- and small-scale celebrations, on a national and local level. We in Mullahoran marked the centenary on April 1st. This involved a special Mass and a procession headed by the local Wolfe Tone fife and drum band. The day's activities were very much enjoyed by my younger brothers and sisters. We were made to feel invincible. We had achieved Catholic Emancipation, put the Famine behind us, fought and won the Land War and gained national Independence. We were in control of our destiny. It was up to each of us to forge ahead in the march of a nation. I was glad to have been in Ireland to celebrate Catholic Emancipation. If things had gone differently, I might already have been in New York, or be preparing to go. Soon, however, any chance that remained of my going to America was to be banished for good.

I was sixteen when the Wall Street Crash came in October 1929. A year or so earlier, towards the end of 1928, I got a note from my godfather, Michael Galligan. The economy had slowed down in America. He suggested that I defer my coming out until the Thirties. I was therefore not completely unprepared when the Wall Street crash came. It was a time when I had to count my blessings. Some of my pals who used shop at Paddy Lynch's were not so lucky. They had made definite preparations for going to America and now could not go. My godfather became unemployed because of the Wall Street Crash and again advised me to stay at home for a few years until things picked up.

The period from 1929 to 1931 is a difficult one to examine and record. What was true of our area of south-west Cavan was possibly true of Ireland as a whole. Many young people's plans for emigrating were suddenly cut short. The Wall Street Crash took most people in Cavan completely by surprise. The ordinary boy or girl who was thinking of emigrating was totally unprepared. It was as if an earthquake had occurred, leaving a wide chasm which was impossible to cross. A feature of those years were the numbers of people who crowded onto the crossroads. If I was cycling to Shanvalla, I would pass three crossroads. In the early part of the Twenties, there would probably be twenty people standing there of a Sunday evening. They would step aside to let you cycle through. Now there would be fifty to sixty there. You had to get down off your bike and walk through the crowd. The same was true if I went towards Clonloaghan. There were now restrictions on immigration into America. This accounted for the extra numbers at the crossroads. Northern Ireland, and particularly Belfast which had taken an amount of boys from our area for the pub trade, was now experiencing a recession. This was a new phenomenon there.

In spite of the slump, for a time we were still getting a lot of American money to keep the sale of farms going, as some emigrants still had savings. The trouble for us was the Irish banks. A lot of Irish emigrant men and women were still suspicious of putting their money in American banks. They sent their money back to Ireland to the local banks. A lot of their money would appear to have been invested in British dividends. As these dividends would have to be sold in England, a certain amount of time elapsed before we could get hold of this money. When a farm was sold, it was customary for a buyer to pay one quarter of the purchase money. This was not always available and we often had to do the necessary. That is, we often had to put down the money ourselves. We never got caught, but there were a few close shaves.

It was the October of 1930, I think, and I was returning home after a busy day measuring conacre plots. As I was nearing the farm yard gate I saw a man standing there. He was holding a, horse with a cart crate. I got the impression that he was waiting for Dad. Instead he hailed me. He asked if I had ever seen him before.

'No,' I said, 'I have not.'

'That's better,' he said. 'Open the gate for me.'

I did so and he brought his horse and vehicle into our yard. He took out the tailboard of the cart crate, heeled up the cart and twelve young pigs fell into the yard. I could not understand what was happening. He turned to me and I heard him say:

'There was no one to buy my pigs at the fair. I have no food for them at home. I am now giving them to your father.'

Mama came on the scene and she told me to hold the horse while she brought the demented man in for a cup of tea. Later I was to learn that she had given him my dinner while I had to do with a cup of tea. Mama always did the right thing! The stranger and Mama emerged. I heard her ask him if he had a family. He said that he had. Then I saw Mama give him three pounds. He did not want to take it at first. However, you would know by him that he was glad to get it. In those days workers were paid from twenty to twenty five shillings per week on the farms. Three pound could buy quite a lot of groceries.

He never came back. We tried to sell the pigs at the next fair but failed. We managed to get rid of them at the following fair. I later came across him accidentally and I found out who he was. Dad sent the money to him.

Historians say that the 1930 slump was the worst for sixty years. Belfast with the shipyards and the linen mills experienced it very badly. Southern Ireland with its few industries was not affected in the same way. Nevertheless, the staunching of emigration and the return of emigrants from America and Britain had a huge effect on the South. To a certain extent this slump prepared us for the hardships of the Economic War.

The Cumann na nGaedheal party, headed by William T. Cosgrave, was in power until February 1932. They were a law-and-order party. They were strapped for cash. Much money had to be spent repairing damaged buildings and infrastructure in the wake of the Civil War. The ceasing of the flow of emigrants to America greatly increased their problems. Nevertheless, Cumann na nGaedheal achieved considerable success internationally. The Irish delegation played a prominent role at the Westminster Conference in 1926, which declared the Dominions to be of equal status to Britain within the Commonwealth. Cosgrave did not seem to have the same success on the home front. In 1931, in order to balance the budget, the pay of Gardaí and teachers was reduced. It might have benefited Cumann na nGaedheal to have courted Labour and sought to alleviate social inequalities. However, it relied greatly on the middle-class vote and unlike their opponents, Fianna Fáil and Labour, did not stress social issues. When the tide began to turn against them, they resorted to a lot of scaremongering about the dangers of Communism and fell back on the old law-and-order line. Everything that was decent was within Cumann na nGaedheal; everything outside the party was suspect.

Fianna Fáil was a relatively small party at first. It became highly organised on the local level. Scattered throughout the country were small clubs called '*cumanns*'. These were not of the same size. One might cover only a townland, while another could cover a parish. They were held in houses where there might be only a couple and no children. It was often combined with a card-playing centre. These were centres for debates and were places where you could criticize your own party if you so wished. When Fianna Fáil came to power in 1932, several deputations came from these clubs to try to influence policy.

This was a time of my life when I should have been quite content. I was looking forward to getting onto the local football team. I had given up smoking and was a teetotaller. I was conscious that people were sizing me up as to what I was capable of doing. In other words I was being sounded. I felt very capable in the work I was doing. I realised that if I made it a career I would require a large sum of capital which I had not got. Hugh P. when, he eventually succeeded Dad would require all that was available to keep him going. I was being asked questions by customers who were wondering was I going to stay. I used have to ponder deeply before replying. Eventually I consulted Mama on what it was all about. She told me that if times improved, I might join up with one of T.P. O'Reilly's boys and form a new Briody & O'Reilly firm. In such an event, the new alliance would need a new name. Anyway, all that was in the future.

Towards the end of 1931, I was told by Dad and his partner, T. P. O'Reilly, that they had decided to send me to Dublin, to acquire new business methods, accountancy and shorthand skills. If things went well we could take it from there. This did not fit in with my plans exactly. I was enjoying helping the younger members of the family with their homework. I was playing a bit of football with the local lads. I was going to the odd dance or two. I loved discussing books with Mama and looked forward to being with her for some time to come. I consoled myself that I would only be going away for a year or so. Nevertheless, I was also glad of the opportunity to see Dublin. I wrote to Caffrey's College, Dublin, with whom I had earlier been doing a correspondence course, about attending their college. They told me that they could suit all my requirements.

On the Sunday before I went to Dublin, I went up to Clonloaghan to say good bye to Mrs Henry, my godmother. It was a distance of two miles. I cycled and had to pass two crossroads to get to my destination. Ten years before that I would probably have encountered a score of boys playing skittles at both Kilcogy and Clonloaghan crossroads. Now there was not far off a hundred boys and young men between both crossroads. I had to get off my bike and edge my way through the milling crowd. The young people could no longer get away to England and America, as both countries were in recession.

Caffrey's College Dublin 1931–1932

It was September 1931 when I went to Dublin. I was glad that Dad accompanied me. We went by rail via Mullingar. The railway company had availed of the worst land possible to build their railroads. After we left Mullingar we came into the Bog of Allen. I had never seen so much bog before. It stretched for miles until it reached the horizon. Dad told me that when he first saw it, it was much larger, and stretched on both sides of the railway. It was getting less conspicuous every time he travelled through it. He seemed to know people here and there who got on and off the train. When I saw it again fifty years later the Bog of Allen had receded into the distance and was now being conserved by the environmentalists. Dad was able to give me a lot of details about the towns and railway stations we passed through. Then he broke the news to me that he considered that we would be having a change of government. He asked me to be very careful. He was sure the Cosgrave party would call in the military before relinquishing office. It would be a test of their law-and-order stance.

When we alighted at the Broadstone Rail Terminus, Dad

appeared to be in familiar territory. The years seemed to have slipped away from him and he was a young man again. He took great delight in showing me around a Dublin which was much smaller then. For a country boy like myself Dublin was a place of wonder with its neon lights and its clanging trams. I may have been homesick leaving Cavan, but now I revelled in being in Dublin.

Towards evening, Dad and I arrived at a house in Dorset Street where I was to stay during the remainder of my time in Dublin. He chose it because he knew the owners, Mr. and Mrs O'Reilly. Mr O'Reilly had formerly been a Dublin Metropolitan Policeman and had known my Uncle Patrick. It was home from home. One of the lodgers was a McGerty boy from east Cavan. His first name was Eugene but his people called him Owney. He was a student at Skerry's College. I was going to Caffrey's College, which was close by. There was only one snag. Both of these colleges were on the south side of the city. The 'digs' were on the north side. This did not worry Dad. He told me that it would help me to get to know the city. I sensed, for him my getting to know Dublin was going to be part of my education. I was sorry to say goodbye to him.

I slept soundly that night. The hooting of the Guinness' boats on the River Liffey woke me up. The place was strangely silent. There seemed to be nobody around but myself. I went downstairs to the breakfast room where a girl was setting the tables for breakfast. I asked her where the rest of the ten lodgers were. She informed me that they had all gone to morning Mass. This astonished me. We only went to Mass on a Sunday in Mullahoran. We thought of ourselves as religious in Cavan, but going to Mass every day was considered somewhat extreme. A man in Mullahoran, known as Paddy Johnny, was in the habit of going to daily Mass. An old woman was heard to remark: 'Won't Paddy have a great sell, if there's no Hell!' After a while the lodgers came trooping in. They were from all walks of life, from retired people, commercial travellers, mechanics, shop assistants to students like McGerty and myself. They all seemed to be in a hurry as they ate their meal. McGerty went down to the kitchen and got two packed lunches. He told our landlady to expect us

114

when she saw us. McGerty was of immense help on that first morning.

We went by tram to St Stephen's Green. Skerry's College was on the south side of the Green. Caffrey's College was on the west side near the entrance to Harcourt Street. On arrival at Caffrey's I introduced myself to the principal, Mr Caffrey. He was, most helpful. I picked out shorthand, bookkeeping, accountancy and business methods. The trouble was that there were gaps between the classes. Luckily, all my classes were over before three o'clock in the afternoon. I seemed to be an unusual student. The others were all preparing for entrance to the University or to the Civil Service. Grinds were the main activity of the college. Some people were there for a month, others for three months, others still for a longer period. Mr Caffrey was a wonderful man for general knowledge and would ask students to throw questions at him to best him. On answering a question correctly, he used say: 'Ask me another'.

Without realising it I was being indoctrinated into a new society. For the first time I was meeting with young urban boys and girls. Everybody appeared friendly. I appreciated this. Half the students were girls. Later I realised that their friendliness was partly prompted by a curiosity because I was different and from the country. In those days Dublin people looked down on country people. Unlike them I was not going for the University or Civil Service. I found on going to Caffrey's that I knew more than many there who had done the Leaving Cert. There were other differences between us also. It was only fifteen years since the 1916 Rising, an event which was of great interest to me. Nobody I spoke to at Caffrey's knew anything about it. I tried out some salutations in Irish on a few. Most of them could read the language after a fashion but nobody attempted speaking it. It was all so different from the enthusiasm for Irish that I had encountered in Mullahoran in the 1920s. Adults approved of their children learning Irish at school and would often ask them what the Irish for such and such was.

There was no canteen in the college. It was beautiful late Autumn weather and I enjoyed having my lunch in St Stephen's Green. I made the acquaintance of some ducks there and gladly parted with a quarter of my lunch. It was an opportunity to have a quick glance at the daily newspaper. They were exciting times with a General Election less than a year off. On one occasion I was reading *The Irish Press*. I always read the Irish-language section to keep my Irish alive. There was a man beside me also enjoying his lunch. He tapped me on the shoulder and spoke to me in Irish. He told me that he was one of Caffrey's Irish teachers and recognised me from the college. He wondered why he had not seen me in any of the Irish classes. I replied that I was doing a secretarial course to fit me out for work in auctioneering. He seemed mystified.

Next day, Mr Caffrey himself invited me to join the Irish classes. No payment was asked for: it was on the house. The arrangement suited me down to the ground as it helped to fill the gaps between my other subjects. There were two distinct Irish classes: one for Matriculation and one for the Civil Service. I chose the Matriculation class. It was there I got the 'bug' for the first time. I became unsettled. Maybe I could go to the university if I got a job to support my studies. I turned my eye towards the Irish Civil Service.

In the meantime, things were turning out well for me in the 'digs'. I got on well with all the lodgers. We all turned out for Mass at seven o'clock in the morning. After breakfast Eugene McGerty and I boarded a tram to get us to Stephen's Green and from there we went our separate ways. To keep fit I decided to walk across the city in the evening. I had a map. I walked down Grafton St., College Green, Westmoreland St. and across O'Connell Bridge. I then went right down the quays and past where Busáras now stands, and home through Gardiner Street to Dorset St. I enjoyed the walk and the different aspects of the city, except for the tenements in Gardiner St. The little boys and girls swinging on the lampposts tugged at my heart. At first I always walked fast in going through the street. I was afraid of the unknown. In time I chanced talking to those children.

The drinking water in Dublin was very flat and insipid. I had been blessed with lovely drinking water from a well in our own Black Meadow. There were three equally good wells on my cross-country trip to Aunt Kate in Shanvalla. I was really spoiled. I timidly broached the matter with my landlady. She was very motherly. She invited me downstairs to the kitchen to get a cup of tea whenever I felt thirsty. Drinking it as tea made the water more palatable. It was at this stage that I made a discovery which was to serve me on many an occasion later. I chanced to bring a bottle of cold tea along with my lunch to College. I found that it was amazingly satisfying. I became a cold tea addict and in later life I may have preferred the cold to the hot cup. In Dublin I also had to get used to eating porridge for breakfast with new milk. At home we always ate porridge with buttermilk.

In addition to the hot cup and cold cup of tea, I longed for a glass of buttermilk. The digs I was in was once a Georgian house. Someone in the past had erected a small lean-to building at the front, which served as a shop. My landlady used this as an, outlet for selling milk. She only serviced this for one hour in the morning and one hour in the evening. She had a lot of customers from the tenements in Gardiner Street. I discovered that she was selling buttermilk. I offered to buy a glass. She would hear none of that. Any time I felt like having a glass, I could have it. She was so kind about the matter that I felt I had to do something in return and I found myself doing odds and ends in her little dairy.

My landlady was an admirer of Cosgrave and hated de Valera. I had to be careful not to reveal my Republican sympathies. It was evident that she loved preaching a gospel as did many another woman of that era. This held for both sides of the divide. The women from the tenements who listened to her just nodded their heads and winked at one another. On one occasion, however, when she was in full flight running down de Valera an old woman interjected: 'But Mrs O'Reilly, you forget that Dev is the greatest mathematician in the world.' 'What has that to do with it?' snapped Mrs O'Reilly. The old lady replied: 'He has solved every problem and he will solve ours.' She departed leaving Mrs O'Reilly to ponder on what she had said. It was the first time that a customer had taken her up on something. It was a sign of coming events. Subsequently my landlady was to remain silent in her dairy except to remark on the vagaries of the weather. There were times when Mrs O'Reilly would go shopping in the evenings or at weekends and I was left in charge.

I loved talking to those women and they loved talking to me. Or did they recognise the student who spoke to their children? I don't know.

I was free on a Saturday and Sunday. Eugene McGerty and I had one thing in common. We both should have been in America instead of Dublin. He was the youngest of a large family all of whom were in America, except for a brother and sister who had remained on the farm. We were of the same age and had come from the same county. I was from west Cavan and he was from east Cavan. No wonder we became bosom pals. We were intrigued to find that each of us had a different accent. He had been in Dublin for a couple of years and knew the city like the palm of his hand. In fact, he was very fond of Dublin. He was forever finding out more about its history and especially its buildings. He spoke lovingly of the great days when Dublin was the second city of the United Kingdom. My knowledge of Dublin was due to Eugene McGerty. Later in life I could speak of Dublin as if I had been there for years. They were beautiful memories except for those slum tenements and the soul-destroying appearance of the Dublin dockland. I like to think that a lot has changed.

On our first Saturday, we went to Dalymount Park to a football match or so I thought. It was only when I saw the players heading the ball that I realised that I was not at a G.A.A. match. I was actually looking at soccer being played. It was 1931 and the ban on foreign games was very strictly enforced. I was a Gaelic footballer and now found myself looking at something which should have been taboo. What astonished me was the heading of the ball. I had never seen this attempted in Gaelic football. It was one of the skills of the latter game to catch the ball from on high, especially with only one hand. In after years, when I made a close study of soccer, I noticed that heading the ball had become less frequent.

Watching soccer being played reminded me of something I had experienced while playing Gaelic football in my home parish. I had been playing on the forward line and had been whistled by the referee for holding the ball. My coach gave me a strict order not to hold onto the ball. This was resolved by my changing my style of play. Instead of waiting for the time when I would be in possession of the ball, I had to plan in advance whom I would pass the ball to. Instead of toeing up a ball, I kicked it to a comrade or goal-wards. This resulted in a saving of time. It also avoided physical contact. It was a bonus for a medium-sized man. My staying in the game depended on my ability to maintain my degree of speed. My visits to Dalymount became more pleasant as time went by. I deluded myself that it was to improve my own game. Or was this simply an excuse for looking at a foreign game? For me the jury is out. I used also enjoyed listening to the Dublin accent and especially to the Dublin wit at these soccer matches.

We often went to the Phoenix Park. In the Fifteen Acres there were pitches where soccer and Gaelic were played side by side. Despite his interest in soccer, Eugene usually brought me to the Gaelic pitches where I enjoyed a 'kick-around'. But we sometimes kicked around with those playing soccer, too. I began to appreciate Eugene. He was a rather stylish football player and had actually a few medals to his credit. I had none.

The lodgers were all very interesting in their different ways. One was a Mr Hogan. He was in the civil service. He was doing a correspondence course trying to better himself in order to go higher in the service. I used study in the dining room. I found myself helping him on a few occasions. I had already got the bug in Caffrey's College, but helping Mr Hogan made me even more eager to go to the University. I would first have to support my studies by getting a job, perhaps in the civil service. However, when I went home for Christmas I refrained from mentioning such plans. The atmosphere there was so happy and secure that I shrank from disturbing the equilibrium.

Early 1932 saw stirring times in Dublin. The existing Government had a comfortable majority and did not need to go to the country for another six months or so. Because the economic situation was getting worse they decided to go to the country sooner than later. The Eucharistic Congress to be held the following June probably also affected their decision. The election was held in February. Late January saw the campaign in full swing. Perhaps I had better make a comparison between electioneering in 2007 and 1932.

Today, the candidates are helped by radio, television and newspaper coverage. True, the politicians rush around and shake hands with as many people as possible. But there are no public speeches by the candidates. At the end, the leaders meet face to face in a television debate chaired by a neutral person. Each candidate is, moreover, allowed to send a letter outlining his proposals to each voter free of charge. A group of canvassers call to each house and drop in a card calling on people to come out to vote. It is all so civilised but nevertheless exciting.

It was so very different in 1932. Eugene McGerty and I canvassed for Fianna Fáil in that election, to the extent that our studies allowed. In this way we came face to face with many of the big names in the party, including Éamon de Valera, Seán Lemass, Seán McEntee, and Harry Colley. We also attended most of the Fianna Fáil election meetings in Dublin. These meetings were held chiefly in the evenings or at night. It was a great advantage to a candidate if he could deliver a good speech. The meetings were mostly outdoor. The back of a lorry could be used as a platform. Sometimes a platform would be improvised from half a dozen barrels and a few timber planks. It had to be a place where there was public lighting. In those early years, the constituencies were very large and had an odd number of elected representatives. Constituencies were mostly five-, seven- and nine-seaters. This resulted in a bigger number of candidates speaking at the meetings than would be the case nowadays. Dublin City was divided into two large constituencies: a nine-seat northside constituency and a seven-seat southside one. McGerty and myself canvassed in Dublin North.

De Valera was always very well dressed in the canvassing rooms (halls or private homes) where we would meet. He kept aloof from us canvassers. His colleagues were much more approachable. Candidates could make very different speeches: saying one thing at one street corner and something quite different at another. There wasn't so much media surveillance then as now to take them to task. Every meeting attracted both government and opposition supporters. Every speech was heckled. A speaker had to anticipate what might be thrown at him. A ready wit was half the battle. To give an example, a speaker talking about agriculture was asked: 'How many toes has a pig?' To which the speaker replied: 'Take off your shoe and count them.' From a modern perspective, perhaps the strangest thing of all was the absence of motorcars at these meetings. People arrived by foot or bicycle or where possible by tram. However, all meetings were held away from tramlines. On one occasion I remember Seán Lemass arriving on a bicycle. He laid his mode of conveyance against a wall, took off his bicycle clips and vaulted on to the platform. He got a great ovation. Sometimes there was a band playing music at Fianna Fáil meetings. At other times there might be a sole accordion player. The music never obtruded much. It was just there to start the proceedings. Oftentimes on reaching a meeting, we would find the young people waltzing around. The Republicans smelled victory in the air. The Government party did not seem to know what was happening.

Sinn Féin and the IRA supported Fianna Fáil in this election. I was present at a Sinn Féin meeting in Foster Place after the election when Madame Despard and Madame Gonne held forth. I was also present that night at Arbour Hill Prison when the Republican prisoners were released from captivity. Partly because of IRA involvement there was trouble at some Cumann na nGaedheal meetings. The Guards had to appear in force to control the crowds at such meetings.

The Cosgrave party had a major meeting towards the end of the campaign in College Green, when many of its leading figures were present on the one platform. Eugene and myself decided to go along. College Green was a place where countless meetings were held. We were lucky that we went early because it was an overflow meetings which gradually spread into the ends of the adjoining streets. We were used to having a band strike up at Fianna Fáil meetings. Here it was strictly business. I never saw more Guards in the one place. They seemed to be scattered at strategic points in the crowd and there was a ring of Guards around the platform itself in case it would be rushed.

Eugene and I edged our way along the railings of Trinity College until we had a good view of the platform. We were conscious that we were being scrutinised by the Guards. Suddenly a stranger came over and said:

'You are very welcome, Thomas.'

This took me completely by surprise. He shook my hand. He then extended the same treatment to Eugene. He introduced himself as Michael. He showed us a Fianna Fáil sticker at the back of the lapel of his coat. He whispered to me that they were anticipating trouble. He told me that we could heckle if we liked. Bad language was not permissible. Violence was out, especially the throwing of bottles. We were shocked.

He then asked us to move away from the railings of Trinity College. If bottles were thrown, they would not be thrown at the platform. Instead they would be thrown to smash on the railings and cause panic. I then realised how we had come so easily along the railings. I innocently asked him if there was an IRA presence. His reply astonished me: 'Yes,' he said 'they are here to control the crowd.'

We moved as far as we could away from the railings and turned our attention towards the platform. It was easy to recognise those seated there from the pictures in the national newspapers. Some of them were smoking cigarettes. One had a pipe going. There were only two women in the bunch. One of them I recognised as Mrs Collins-O'Driscoll (she was a sister of Michael Collins). One man's face will forever remain in my memory. It was that of Cosgrave. He looked terrified. Now and again he turned his face from the crowd and looked down at his feet. He looked like a man who wished for a hole to emerge to swallow him up. He must have realised that the game was up and that he would have to hand over power to the 'anti-law-and-order faction'. Within his party were those who favoured a military coup. He had brought Ireland back from anarchy to a situation where law and order prevailed. He could have pleaded that Irish society was not ready for change. Instead, he handed over power to de Valera. Historians claim that was 'his finest hour'.

I was very anxious to see Hogan, the Minister for Agriculture. He was not there. I had become conscious of him some years earlier when I was bringing the eggs to Paddy Lynch's shop. We were not allowed to wash eggs anymore.

Instead we had to concentrate on the cleanliness of the poultry runs. The bloom had to be kept on our eggs to compete with those from Denmark. Hogan's Department had advocated this.

The speeches which until then were mostly upbeat and optimistic suddenly changed in tone. A new speaker had come onto the platform. He was a real 'law-and-order' man. His opening sentence spoke volumes: 'Spare the rod and spoil the child!' On no account was the country settled yet. The present government by whatever means were to be kept there to finish the job. He was received with stunned silence at first, then the heckling came fast and furious. The man called 'Michael' tapped me on the shoulder and advised us to get away. He said that he was expecting a police baton-charge. By this stage the crowd had become thinner and it was easy to get away. We had reached the edge of the crowd when we heard the sound of bottles crashing on the Trinity railings. Then we heard the shrill noise of police whistles. The crowd ran and we ran as fast as we could go. It was a night to remember. Eugene and I were wont to go for a walk between 8 and 10 p.m. After the College Green incident we kept indoors at night until the election was over. Thankfully, everything quietened down after the election.

Perhaps I had better explain the antics of Michael. It was part of the art of politics to get to know people. We never stooped to asking somebody to introduce us to somebody else. I became very skilled at it myself. When canvassing, if I saw a stranger out in front whom I did not know, I asked somebody who he was. I then walked up to him and called him by his first name. I then gave him by first name. If he was curious as to what was my surname he had to ask somebody else. This only happened when we were canvassing. In private life I behaved differently.

The yelling of the 'paperboys' was a feature of Dublin in those days. It was a time when the latest twist in the election campaign was an opportunity for the press to bring out a 'Stop Press'. These generally consisted of a small sheet of paper. Some days there might be only four hours between news-sheets. The 'paperboys' would give the impression that the end of the world had arrived. When you bought a news-sheet three or four people attached themselves onto you.

Fianna Fáil got 44% of the vote but they still needed seven Labour deputies to form a government. There were a few days of tension. Every day there was a 'Stop Press' about something or other. Some people felt that the Irish Army might intervene and take over. Others feared that the British Army might return if things got out of control. Things normalised some weeks after the installation of the new Government thanks to the handling of the situation by Cosgrave and the shrewdness of de Valera, who was quick to stress that there would be no victimisation.

The Eucharistic Congress to be held in June turned all our attention to something new and caught Dublin on the wrong foot. The Cosgrave Government had deliberately held the General Election early in order to be able to cope with such a major event. They were now out of office and the incoming Government were new to office. Dublin as a mainly Catholic city had hungered for such an event as the Congress. The fact that Dublin had only a few large hotels seemed to have been left out of the reckoning. We were totally unprepared to cope with the influx of the million people that were expected. Panic gripped the city early in May. The accommodation problem was partly solved by ordinary people agreeing to take in visitors. A super effort of volunteer groups helped clean up the city. The people followed suit and decorated their own homes too. During the Congress, people who had hardly ever gone beyond the Phoenix Park found themselves bringing their foreign visitors out on joyrides to see the beauties of Wicklow. A great time was had by all. The Eucharistic Congress is one of my fondest memories. I often look back and laugh at some of the incidents that occurred during that time. It was a mad time.

On the Friday of the Congress a cousin of mine, Hugh Briody, called. It was the only day on which he could attend. It was Ladies' Day in the Park and we were the only non-clerical men there. Our mysterious appearance was a cause of grave concern to some of the women present. We survived. The area of the Fifteen Acres in the Phoenix Park where the final Mass was to be held had been carefully plotted. A map detailing the section which each diocese and parish should occupy was drawn up. I was a steward helping to marshal and accommodate the million who flocked to the Park on the final Sunday. Along with others I had familiarised myself with all the detail. We were placed at strategic points to meet the oncoming throngs. For me it was a great thrill to meet some of my old parishioners from Mullahoran and to guide them to their respective berths. I was glad that I could only spend a little time with each of them. They were inclined to hang onto me for fear of being lost in the vast crowd. I had to point out to them that my time was not my own and that I could only give a little of it to them. That lovely day, with its throngs of people, often came back to me later when working alone doing a selection of species on the Slieve Blooms and miles away from any fellow human being. But then alone is never alone: I had myself to talk to.

Coincidently my future wife, Nora O'Hickey, was a boarder at Sion Hill, Blackrock, Co. Dublin in Spring/Summer 1932. She and her fellow-pupils had done a great deal of volunteer work in the preparations for the Congress. We did not know of one another's existence then. In later life, after we had met, our experiences of what happened were very different. We could have been speaking of two different events, a thousand miles apart. I had to be very careful. Nora was very jealous of my being able to tell of the Congress itself. After all their good volunteer work, she and her fellow pupils had been sent home to allow the convent to house the visitors.

During the final hours of the Congress in the Phoenix Park when one million people knelt to pray, the sky was lit up by lightning flashes and thunder rolled. No rain fell and the huge throng were allowed to march down to benediction on O'Connell Bridge. The elderly marched down the shortest route. The middle-aged came down a less easy route, and so on. The group I was in had a circuitous march of seven miles. When we reached our sixth mile-point, we were handed cups of tea. I will always remember that cup of tea: it saved my life. At that point, Nora and a friend were out walking in the woods at Portlaw, Co. Waterford, her hometown. They were a mile from shelter when the thunderstorm broke and they were drenched to the skin. This was the cloudburst which should have fallen over Dublin but had decided instead to fall on the small town of Portlaw. Ah dear! Yes I have great memories of the Congress.

Dublin after the Congress was for a time like a deserted ship. On the political front, it was soon back to business. The Fianna Fáil party were certainly relieved that there had been no bloodshed on their assuming power. But the expectations of the grass roots were high and there was much to be done on the economic and social front. Dev had caught the imagination of the Irish people. I helped to elect his party in 1932 but I must admit that he made some serious mistakes. The first was to ban the importing of maize meal in order to help the barley-growing farmers in Leinster. Although his intention was to encourage tillage, it had an adverse effect on small farmers in counties such as Cavan. It took more barley to feed the same number of pigs than maize and there was a consequent reduction in profit. The pig industry in Cavan slumped before long to a new low. The position was partly saved with large quantities of maize being smuggled in from the Six Counties at extra cost.

In June 1932 de Valera also decided to withhold the payment of the Land Annuities to the British Government. The British gloves came off. They retaliated by imposing a 20% tariff on Irish livestock. Thus began the Economic War, which became a tit-for-tat affair, with the Irish Government imposing tariffs on British goods. Perhaps I had better explain what the Land Annuities were. The Land War of 1879-1881 led to the passage of a number of Land Acts and ultimately to the transfer of the land from landlord to tenant ownership. However, landlords had to be bought out. Tenants acquired ownership of their land by means of government loans. The debts incurred by farmers had to be paid back over a number of decades. This meant that the farmers (tenants) in time would own their own lands. These Land Acts also allowed for the resale of farms. The new owner simply shouldered the debt of the seller and that was that.

The reason de Valera gave for the retention of the Land Annuities was the belief, held by many Nationalists, that Ireland compared to the rest of the United Kingdom had been overtaxed

126

in the nineteenth century. In addition to refusing to forward this money to Britain, de Valera halved the Land Annuities for Irish farmers. Repayment time was also doubled. While halving the Land Annuities benefited large farmers as well as small, Britain's placing of a tariff on Irish livestock hit large farmers particularly. Our government sought to offset the British tariff on cattle by paying bounties of about the same value as the tariff. The bounties and subsidies were paid for by the Irish taxpayer through higher taxes and higher consumer prices. The British tariff on Irish cattle and the subsequent imposition of a quota for Irish cattle being imported to Britain greatly reduced the numbers of animals being exported. Large numbers of surplus fat cattle were killed and the meat distributed to the poorer sections of the community. It became known as the 'Free Beef Scheme'.

The poverty I witnessed in Dublin caused me much personal anguish. On my way home from College, I found myself dropping in to Gardiner Street church to pray for a few minutes. It gave me great peace of mind. It was a time when I was trying to find answers to many questions concerning social justice. I had been reared to full and plenty. In my home area there were also poor but nothing to compare with the Dublin slums. It was sometime after the 1932 General Election that I first met the Jesuit Fr Finlay. I had heard him speak on a few occasions in Gardiner Street church and I liked his approach to employment and kindred subjects. He was critical of capitalism as it then obtained. I had also sometimes seen him out walking. On this occasion I was passing him by when I suddenly turned and introduced myself.

I took him by surprise, but I in turn was taken by surprise when he started chatting with me. He must have had Cavan connections. He knew the Mullahoran area very well. In fact he chided me on being such a mild representative of such a fierce fighting people. It was an honour to have met Fr Finlay. He was a great preacher and had been all over the English-speaking world. He was, however, in love with Dublin and its old brick walls and 'the faith of the people behind those walls'. I have to thank Fr Finlay for all his help.

As well as opening my eyes, the city also broadened my

horizons. I had been sent to Dublin by my father and his business partner to learn accountancy and business skills. As I have said, I began thinking about going to university and to this end it was essential that I get a job first. A first cousin of my mother's, Harry Plunkett, was working in Guinness's Brewery and I investigated the possibility of getting work there, but to no avail. A first cousin of my own, Harry Briody, worked as a grocer's assistant in Dublin. He nominated me to fill a vacancy that occurred for a trade unionist in his union, but I failed to secure the required votes. This was a position I would like to have got. I often look back on what might have been. It was a very lean period and there were few jobs on offer. Suffice it to say that I sat for every job that came along, including civil service jobs. My efforts were unrewarded. I was prepared to work in any job for the time being. It was tough going for a boy of my age. Looking back on my efforts to remain in Dublin, I seem to only half-remember the many jobs I sought to obtain. I felt that I was honing my skills with each attempt and that I would land a job somehow and at some time.

I was in weekly communication with Mama but I said nothing about my efforts to get a job or of my thoughts of going to university. A letter I got from her one morning told of the effect the stiff tariff de Valera had put on maize earlier that year was having on the pig industry at home. Cavan was next to Cork in pig production. We were often referred to as the 'Cavan pig-feeders'. Beside Lough Sheelin, in the parish of Ballymachugh, there were big pig-farms employing a considerable number of people. Mama told me there was only one sow in our yard where there had been three. That meant that in six months' time our pig population would be only one third of the original. In fact she was considering increasing her poultry and having no pigs. Maybe the birds would take better than the pigs to the barley. A postscript to the letter told me the sad story: two hundred young men from the greater area had emigrated to seek work on pig-farms in England. It is only when something impinges on yourself that you feel the pain. A Cavan farm without pigs would be something new.

Mama's letter prepared me somewhat for a letter I got

from Dad some time after I resumed my studies in Caffrey's in September 1932. He told me that the business was very sluggish. There was difficulty with the cash-flow. He asked me to come home and give a hand until conditions improved. He required someone to go around to deal with the situation on the ground. He would explain how to do that same when we met. This was like a bolt from the blue. The prospect of the well-oiled business machine of Briody & O'Reilly running into trouble never occurred to me.

Before leaving Dublin I sat the exam for the Hibernian Bank. Caffrey's College did courses for the bank. Banking was considered to be a swanky middle-class occupation and was much sought after. Accordingly, I applied. The terms of employment were astonishing. The first year's salary was £52 per annum, the next was £65 and the third was £78. The snag was that the digs per week must amount to at least twenty five shillings. The sum of money earned over three years would just equal the amount paid in digs, namely £195. It was clearly a non-starter. If I got it I could still not take it. Still, it would be another examination to sit and hone my skills with. Jobs were very scarce. Everybody seemed to be doing it. Even those who were planning to go to university felt there was no harm in having an alternative. An unusual feature of the exam was that you could substitute Irish for an advanced maths paper. Although I was very strong in Irish, I felt that the Bank authorities were looking after their own interests and would favour maths. So I decided to take the maths paper. The examination was held in Dawson St. in Dublin. It had once been a Freemasons' hall and the large room was packed to capacity. I cannot say now how many posts were on offer. I would say that it was a small number.

I felt very satisfied with the examination paper. Comparing my answers with those of the other students, I considered that I had done exceptionally well. It took the pain out of having to leave Dublin. I began to entertain fresh hopes. Maybe if I got the examination, I could work in the Granard Hibernian Bank and commute from home. A few years hence, the recession might be over and I could move back to Dublin again. Everything was still to be fought for.

The Economic War in Cavan

On getting Dad's letter I put my affairs in order as quickly as I could and hurried home. When I got there I realised that life had moved on. Dad, although still an energetic man, was approaching seventy and Mama was almost fifty. I was prepared to do anything to help out. In time Dublin would become but a memory. I had determined to keep my bank dream to myself. In a weak moment, however, I told it to Mama, who in turn told it to Dad. They must have had some qualms of conscience about asking me to come home, for they did not react negatively to the news. In fact, they thought the whole matter was a dead cert. Maybe I did so too. I was about a month home and I was doing some business for Dad in the bank in Granard when the bank manager approached me. He welcomed me back. I knew by him that he was intensely curious about my homecoming. To fit him into the picture I told him that I had done the examination for the bank and that I was hoping that before long I might be working with him.

I seemed to have shocked him. He was silent. He invited me into the office and there over a cup of coffee he told me that I could not work locally for the bank. I was flabbergasted. The thought of having to work away from home on a pittance was unthinkable. Instead I would stay here and help Dad. I told the sad story to Mama. She in turn told it to Dad. He was not very optimistic, but said he would try to do something. He and his partner had nurtured the Hibernian Bank in Granard when it was only a struggling branch. Now was the time for payback. The unexpected happened. I got a letter in the post informing me that I had failed. My parents were bitterly disappointed. The whole affair was actually a relief to me when it petered out. It took its place as one of the might-have-beens of my life. I have no regrets. However, I love to talk to the young men and women in my bank branch at Carrick-on-Suir, but am relieved to be on the outside of the counter.

The position awaiting me at home is best explained by a few simple facts. Although the collapse of the Wall Street stock market in 1929 was not immediately felt in Dad's business, in time the subsequent staunching of Irish emigration to America meant that less money was coming back to help the small farmers balance their accounts. More importantly, less savings were accumulating in the Irish banks to buy future farms. Moreover, the decline of the local pig industry and the heavy tariffs on irish cattle going to Britain since Fianna Fáil came to power, had compounded the plight of farmers.

Farmers paid rents to the Land Commission and rates to the County Council, e.g., for the upkeep of the roads. On most farms money became available only in the Autumn when crops were harvested and livestock sold. We were the umbrella under which credit was provided. It was availed of by everybody and suited rich and poor. The years 1933, 1934 and 1935 were ones in which this system almost broke down, then rallied and survived. I will attempt to explain this miracle.

Dad, when he had been a seed-merchant for Hunters during the late nineteenth century, had discovered a useful way of helping farmers who were finding it difficult meeting payments. He issued small notebooks to each. Every month they paid what they could afford. When the time came for the final payment, the remainder was very small. If the crisis got worse, he would try that again. The trouble was that it meant extra manpower to supervise the system. The small farmers who had time on their hands cut more than their annual share of turf. Every fortnight they sold a crate of turf in one of the big towns. This helped them to meet their payments. This sense of initiative was what we were trying to tap. For someone approaching seventy Dad was a wonderful man to be thinking in this way. But that was Dad. He was a great community man.

The basis for Dad's business was very complex and something which I had only half-understood previously. Over the next few years I was to become intimately acquainted with it. Once home I tried to fit into the scheme of things. I did everything I was asked to do, which often meant cycling for most of the day, collecting money on my rounds. I also balanced the books. I did the shopping for Mama when possible and assisted her in the poultry runs. If required I sometimes helped out with other farm work. It would be hard to describe what my exact role was. I only knew that I was wanted at home. Even though it was hard for me to leave Dublin behind, it is such a priceless thing to be wanted.

I again came into contact with my old shopkeeper Paddy Lynch to whom I had sold eggs in the Twenties. I had been his egg-counter. I remember he used to give me oodles of cigarettes for my trouble. He had now a nephew helping him in the shop. He asked me to look into his accounts. I now had spare time to do so. It was 'money from Heaven'. He had kept his sums fairly tidy and that made my work quite easy. It was the enormity of the sums involved that took my breath away. Paddy also got me more work to do at Ballinagh and other places. It was nice at last to be earning my own money instead of getting an allowance from Dad. Smiths of Cavan Town, a firm of solicitors who dealt with legal matters for Briody & O'Reilly, also gave me bookkeeping work. Dad got this work for me. Paddy Lynch had six or seven dozen customers. He did not mind if a customer owed him a lot of money provided he stayed with him. People called him 'tight'. He should have been called a saint instead. It was men like Paddy who helped people come through the Economic War.

I came back around the first days of December 1932. We were so busy that Christmas came on me unawares. I was glad of the festive season. The clouds of depression momentarily lifted. I found time to go down to the Killydoon Hall and dance with the local girls. They had been at my school, and my shopping pals in Paddy Lynch's. In fact some of them may have helped me count eggs in days gone by. Of course, two-thirds of them were missing. They had either emigrated or gone to Dublin. There were those who had come back for Christmas, too. I was often to remember that dance in the black period that lay ahead. I only made brief visits to Clonloaghan and Shanvalla. People seemed to be waiting for some explanation from me for coming home.

January 1933 brought a big surprise. Fianna Fáil had won the General Election of 1932. Now, de Valera went again to the country to obtain a fresh mandate. January is one of those months when the farming community takes a well-earned rest before the heavy labouring work of Spring begins. People felt that this was somewhat of an imposition as they would have preferred a summer election, as it was easier to get out to vote in Summer. Moreover, while a winter election did not pose much of a problem in cities and towns where there was electric street lighting, in the countryside electioneering was especially difficult for canvassers. I did not do any canvassing on this occasion. In time, we got used to the idea of the election. The weather was not too bad and there were a few moonlit nights for the canvassers. Nevertheless, many hoped that Dev would not inflict the ordeal of a winter election on them again.

It was my first time voting. I did not support any party openly but they all knew at home where my sympathies lay. It was an astonishing turnout. Quite a large number of voters came back to vote from England. I did not go to vote until the evening. I noticed that throughout the day a number of people called to the house to say hello to Mama and Dad. They were the men who worked in England and whose families and little farms were looked after by us. They were killing two birds with one stone. They had come home to see their families and to vote for the man they called the Chief.

Some had a little present for Mama. Of course, they all got their tea and scone. I did not linger with them. I preferred to let them talk to my parents. Edward signalled to me and we went off to vote in Clonoose School where I had got my education. Apparently the polling booth catered for a big area because there were two tables there with two girls at each table. Seated at a separate chair was my old teacher Miss Smith. Apparently, she was in charge of the school. She saluted me in Irish. She mildly enquired how my left hand was getting on with my right. My classmates knew that I could still write with my left hand, and used sometimes do so for bravado. Miss Smith got a chair for me to sit down and chat with her, and as a result I nearly forgot to vote. Edward had slipped away long ago. Miss Smith had been going to the Gaeltacht for several years before Independence. We all thought that she would succeed Miss O'Reilly as Principal. A man was appointed instead. Every Friday evening when there was no fear of an inspectorial visit she would have her little Irish class. She had the ground prepared when the native Government came. People like her played their part in the early days of the State in the revival of Irish.

She pointed towards the rostrum. She informed me that all my old composition books were there. She told me that the children still availed of them when writing their little compositions. She asked me if I did any writing. In my youthful enthusiasm, I told her that if I wrote I would like to write in Irish. She suggested that I keep my Irish alive by writing an odd piece for *Scéala Éireann*. The *Irish Press/Scéala Éireann* had a half page devoted to the Irish language. Oftentimes I would stumble across something which I considered especially newsworthy. With the aid of Dineen's dictionary, I would hammer out the news item. If I was pressed for time, I would finish it in English. I had the satisfaction of often seeing the corrected pieces in print. It kept my Irish alive. Helping my younger siblings also honed it. I made the acquaintance of a Mr. Daly who was the Irish Editor of the *Irish Press*. This Mr Daly, better known as Cearbhall Ó Dálaigh, was later to became President of Ireland. Ó Dálaigh was very kind to me and I must thank him very sincerely. Before I left home again in 1936 he asked me to write about my experiences of the Economic War in Irish. I did so. It amounted to six pages. His Irish was very rich and he corrected my text and returned it to me. He told me to keep it until it was safe to publish it. Perhaps Ó Dálaigh may have felt that my writing about the hardships of the Economic War could be taken as criticism of government policy. *The Irish Press* was the official organ of Fianna Fáil.

Around this time, I also began to read regularly in Irish. There were a lot of classics translated into Irish. As I had read the original books in English, this was an advantage. After a time, I stopped reading these translations, preferring to read newer works in Irish. Yes, it was a time when many envisaged that the Irish of Connemara, Kerry and Donegal would recover and push outwards. This did not happen. Instead, we should have taken the revival of the spoken language onto the streets of the cities and towns.

My account of the Economic War got lost among others of my treasures during the dismantling of our old thatched house.

It would be of great help to me in trying to recall happenings of seventy five years ago. It would allow me to measure my then thoughts against my present ones. Much research has gone into the study of this period. It would be very innocent of me to say that I am not influenced by what others have written. I would like to read again what I wrote about the events as I lived through them. During a busy life packed with changes, I tended to forget the Thirties. I was so taken up by what happened to me and my family. I snatched happiness where I could find it.

What amazes me now is that the Twenties, Thirties and Forties are so real. Photographs of long ago are a great help. Looking at a boy of five and now seeing him as a grown man gets the memory going. When you attempt to adequately deal with one event, another comes in to crowd the other out. Instead of searching for material you have to chose from a selection.

The Callanagh of the Thirties bore no relation to the Callanagh of the Twenties. There was no longer a girl in the kitchen. Mama did the household chores with the help, as time went by, of Paul and Rosetta, who were the two next-eldest after me. We still had a large poultry farm and I helped out there too. Paul, Gerald and Austin did everything they were asked to do on the farm. Because we were relying on smuggled maize, we had only a small number of pigs. Just enough to begin with if conditions improved. In the Twenties we kept quite a number of pigs and had two men employed. We now endeavoured to carry on without any hired help. The eldest of my siblings, Hugh P., helped Dad with the auctioneering, while the second eldest, Edward, ran the farm without any hired help.

In looking back we are apt to remember the sunny days and so it seems with regard to those fighting days of 1933, '34 and '35. I was third-eldest in a family of eleven. The fourth, fifth and sixth of the family had died. I was now twenty one years of age. The seventh, Paul, was thirteen, and Anna Celia, the youngest, was six. Three other children lay in-between, Rosetta, Austin and Gerald. To the younger children I must have appeared more like an uncle than a brother. They only saw me in the evenings or on Sunday. I was on hand to help them with their homework. They were a lovely, sometimes cheeky, bunch and lapped up all I could teach them. I was glad now that I had come back. Teaching them gave me a greater knowledge of the little I knew, and I had better concede that at times I could have been their pupil and they my teachers. I cannot claim all the credit for their education. They, of course, had the interaction with school and they all helped one another.

This period at home may have been my most adverse, but Callanagh was a place to tarry in. Yes, there was still that beautiful thatched house with a slated annex and a lovely garden of flowers and herbs. The thick mud walls of the house afforded space for presses, each three feet in depth. They held numerous books and great memories. Sadly that house is no more. In its stead is a two-storey modern farmhouse

On my return home our storyteller, McDermott, was gone. It had been the latter's job to go round and see to the meadows, making sure that fences were in repair. Now and again, the travelling people with there horses were a problem. McDermott kept an eye out. Generally speaking, the Travellers because they were selling tin ware had to keep moving on to a fresh market. Nowadays, they have cars and vans. Their horses are gone. I was again given the task of inspecting meadows and I endeavoured to familiarise myself with the ins and outs of the problems involved. It put me in contact with a lot of people, especially the less well-off, as it was generally small farmers who sold meadows. My job was to ensure that no trespass occurred and that the meadows were at their best. I found a great honesty among the small farmers. Otherwise I would have had an impossible task.

I should say something more about my two older brothers with whom I had a lot to do during the Economic War. Hugh P., the eldest, was only three years older than me. In the ways of the world he could have been nine or ten years older. At the age of fourteen he started *céilidh*ing at Uncle Henry's in Clonloaghan. Eventually he moved on to the crossroads and thence into football circles. As a boy he had been trained by Uncle Patrick to play football. He was said to have a 'crooked foot'. His feet seemed normal to me. I suppose this meant his ability to score goals. Most of his kicks seemed to hit the ground before avoiding the goalkeeper. Strangely enough, his best days in football were on the back line. There he used his knowledge of forward play to help the defence.

He it was who looked after me when I was thrown in at the deep end. He spent a couple of weeks cycling around with me and introducing me to all our customers. He told them that all they said to me was strictly private and would be held in confidence. In other words, he was telling me to keep a closed mouth. Any news which I had heard and passed on should be positive. I should always try to have the good word. Always, if possible, to give a gossiper the pleasure of telling news you already knew.

Hugh P. was a very good-looking boy. He had a very friendly manner which put everybody at ease. He had everything except time. Our football coach, 'Hughie the County', was very particular about training and insisted on a full attendance. Hugh P. could never oblige. Nevertheless, he was always brought onto the team. He appeared to have been the one who trained instead of those who actually did train. He told me to solve problems as best I could. Any that I could not solve were to be passed on to him. On no account were Mama and Dad to be bothered with trivial things.

Before going to Dublin I had no experience of farm work. On my return, Edward was now my tutor. He was exact. I was very thankful to him in later life. Edward was a great man in assisting people. He sometimes helped out in the auctioneering. He was skilled at valuing cattle. Before a fair, farmers would ask him to come along to value the animals. He was also very good at valuing furniture. He earned money this way and often gave me a 'hand out'. Very early on he had injured his big toe. This precluded him from playing football. He made up for this: he could talk forever about football.

Edward was a very interesting man. He was just a year and a half older than I was. He seemed to have a hankering after the Hibernians and what they represented. He still kept the old green Hibernian flag in the loft against the time when it would be again unfurled. That flag seemed to mean more to him than the tricolour. The Hibernians were really a thing of the past in our area. Dad himself had moved on, as I have said, occupying himself with farming matters. A distant cousin of Mama's, a Major Dease, had died leading his troops on the Somme. His photograph hung in the parlour. He had been awarded the Victoria Cross. Edward kept that picture carefully cleaned. The flowers he brought to place before it were the wild flowers from the fields and bog. The nearest he could get to the poppies of Flanders were the wild foxgloves. He acted more like a father to me. I must have appeared strange to him at the time.

   With Edward you never knew what the morrow would bring. When farm operations were nearing an end he became unsettled. When you were asked by him to get up an hour earlier than usual, you could be prepared for anything. There had always been a great spirit among farmers to help one another to save and to harvest crops. During the Economic War, this communal cooperation was intensified to help those in particular need. There was a patriotic wind blowing. Edward was one of those who organised this communal help in our area. He had always a lot of projects on hand. There was always someone to be helped out. I also played my part.

   On one occasion it was a widow farmer with four young children. We moved off early in the morning in our pony and spring-van. We were carrying two packed lunches and an old tea-kettle to make tea in. We also had a sack of seed potatoes. When we arrived at the farm of the widow we were met by nine other farmers who each had a sack of seed potatoes. I was astonished how prearranged it all was. Half of the carts went to the farmyard manure heap and brought out dung for the ridges. Potatoes could be either planted in drills or in ridges. This time they were planted in ridges. My chore on that day was laying the seed potatoes. I was helped by another boy. The seed potato splits were placed twelve inches apart on the yard-wide ridge with fifteen inches between the rows. The split had to be placed with the flat side down and eyes on top. In our own field it did not matter what side I put face down. It would grow anyway. It was different where the gimlet eye of the neighbour was present. If such an event occurred, the shoveller had to lay down his implement and re-affix the 'erring split'. I had been told to keep my end up.

We were on a very small farm. The farmer was dead and his widow was carrying on as best she could. We were two hours there before I saw smoke rising from the chimney of the house. The widow came out and I saw her talking to Edward. I was called to bring in the tea-kettles. I found a nicely-kept kitchen with a family of two boys and two girls. Their ages ranged from three to ten. We were invited to have our meal there but Edward would have none of it, saying that the men liked having their tea in the open. The widow came out with us. She thanked each man in turn. We all felt it was a pleasure to do a favour for that lady and her family. It was a day of sport and good-humoured banter. The hours passed like minutes. Yet the work rarely stopped. There was an urgency to finish before dark. We got through with an hour to spare. The lady of the house came out with tea and lovely pancakes. It was a day to remember.

Another day we helped a man who was crippled with rheumatism. His wife had died, leaving him with a very young family. What struck me most was that we had a different set of helpers from the previous time. This time, the farmer insisted on our having dinner. It was like that. No two days were the same. Another day still we planted a garden for an old workman who had been with us in the early Twenties and was now invalided. Yes, they were great days. We survived the Economic War by holding one another up. On another day we crossed with the local football team to another parish to help an old goalkeeper now crippled with pain. He had been our adversary of yesteryear and had denied us many a goal. We were now his welcome friends in his 'potato patch'. That was Cavan in the Economic War.

When autumn came we found ourselves rescuing late-comers in the corn field. This was very necessary where corn had fallen with heavy rain and the scythe had to replace the reaping machine. It was then I was taught the art of scything. I was to find a place for this skill in the years which followed. It had a magic all its own.

The potato digging in the autumn had its hazzards too. The mechanised digger had only just made its appearance and was frowned on by reason of the quantity of potatoes that were cut and bruised using this method. The spade was an older and safer method. Potatoes had to be dug out and pitted before the 8th of November. There was an urgency to beat this deadline and everybody helped out.

It was a great period of community effort and it would be nice to recall that it went smoothly without any friction. On one occasion, however, we landed ourselves in trouble. It was the turf-cutting season (June/July) and Edward informed me that he and his friends had decided to cut a supply of turf for the widow for whom we had sown the potatoes in the Spring. I was not asked to participate in the operation because I was otherwise employed. I am sorry now because it would have been a lively gathering to talk about. I heard that there was great fun and laughter and that a good day's work was achieved. Every farm had a half-acre of turbary. This was essential for the annual supply of turf to the household. When this half-acre was exhausted it served for renewing potatoes and corn. Seed sown in this peat land gave bumper crops when transferred back to the farm. There were three large bogs in the area, Callanagh Upper, Boston (Callanagh Lower) and Clonloaghan. The Callanagh Upper bog had been cut away and was now serving as a seed-renewing area. Both Boston and Clonloaghan were big bogs and there were hundreds of half-acre plots there.

I was merely asked to find out where Mrs X's plot lay. I enquired where the widow's plot was. I was shown a certain plot. I made the mistake of forgetting that there could be more widows than Mrs X. The turf lay where it fell and gradually the summer sun reduced the moisture content. It was the school holidays and the delighted widow and her four children set out to win and clamp the turf. They were to discover that they had no turf to clamp. The turf had been cut on another widow's plot.

Dad came to my rescue. He advised me to talk to the two widows and to no one else. Accordingly, I spoke first to the lady I knew. She was very grateful for my offering to intervene but very firm that she and her children could not trespass on another woman's property. She was not in a position to buy the turf and had decided to leave the crop to the other lady. Dad told me to be very careful with the latter. There was a possibility she could throw me out and bring the matter to court. Instead of visiting Widow Y, I wrote her a letter explaining in detail how we had helped Widow X sow her potato crop and that we decided to cut her turf for her too. I took sole responsibility for the mistake and would call on her on such a date to thrash the matter out.

When I knocked on her door, I was fearful of what might be the outcome. When she opened the door, she looked at me as if she expected to see someone else. She barely acknowledged my salutation and asked me to come into the parlour. I sat down. She left me abruptly and went towards the kitchen. She returned with a tray on which were two cups of tea and a plate of biscuits. She asked me why I had left Dublin. I replied that I had come home to help my dad in the Economic War. She looked surprised as if she could not comprehend what she was hearing. Then she started talking. She had spent part of her youth working in the big shops in Dublin. There she had met her husband. He had been left a farm in the country by a relative and they had come here. She had no children and was thinking of selling out and going back to Dublin again. I realised that she had got someone to talk to. I found it hard to broach the object of my visit. I was taken aback when she took my hand and there was more than tears in her eyes when she said: 'Tell your friend that she has my permission to take all the turf home. It would be nice if I could swap with her and her lovely children.' I found it hard to tear myself away. In fact, I often later dropped in to say hello. She never left for Dublin but remained on to enjoy the 'Cavan breeze'.

The year 1933 seemed to pass like a flash we were so much on the go between the auctioneering business and farming. A proper yardstick of how busy we were was the family rosary. Before I went to Dublin, it had reached the late hour of 9 p.m. Now it was gradually moving later to accommodate Hugh P., Edward and me coming home late. It often reached eleven o'clock. Looking back now I realise how important we all felt was that twenty minutes when we all knelt down together to pray. The chief benefactors were our younger brothers and sisters. They could stay up later. In fact, because of the hard times, they were older than their years. They were all still at school. They still played their skittles and football. By doing their different chores, they were helping to keep the farm and farmyard ticking over.

The General Election of January 1933 gave de Valera an overall majority. The Election was also a mandate to continue what he set out to do in 1932. In March 1933 he dismissed Eoin O'Duffy, Head Commissioner of the Gardaí, who had not been cooperating with his government. Later that Summer, O'Duffy assumed the leadership of the National Guard. The National Guard, originally known as the Army Comrades Association, had been set up in February 1932. It soon adapted the blue shirt and beret as a uniform and began to take the straight-arm salute, in imitation of continental Fascist organisations. The National Guard became popularly known as the Blueshirts. They attracted to their ranks many who were opposed to Fianna Fáil. In September 1933, the National Guard joined with Cumann na nGaedheal and the Centre Party to form a new party known as Fine Gael, with O'Duffy as its leader.

The Winter of 1933, and especially the early months of 1934, were exciting months in Ireland. The Blueshirts were increasing their efforts to destabilise the government. A Blueshirt news-sheet was trust through the letterbox in the door of our annex. We learned that every household of any consequence had got one too. We did not know who delivered the paper. Its distribution was certainly well organised.

The paper was mostly about Italy and the success of the Fascist movement there, and extolled the virtues of the corporate state and sought to highlight the defects of democracy. The big farmers, although they had benefited by the halving of the Land Annuities, were suffering from the tariffs on the export of cattle to Britain. They were easy prey for the Blueshirt movement who urged non-payment of rates. The rate collectors were caught in the crossfire. These were usually people of some means who could afford to bear the burden of someone being late with their payment or defaulting.

We had not any Blueshirt parades in our area, but the

movement had its supporters. There was a rash of people wearing berets or 'berries' as they were called. Among them were ones knitted from wool. They looked so very comfortable when you met these people cycling in the biting wind, that I was half inclined to wear one myself while cycling. The fear of it being hailed as a conversion on my part kept me from doing so. Now and again we allowed ourselves to laugh. A girl who was working in Dublin came home on a week's holiday. In those days women wore a head-dress in Church. This girl came wearing a beret. It was really part of a school uniform. She had dyed it brown. She had a face that suited the beret and she stole the show. It was one of those few times when we all laughed in church.

The Blueshirt weekly news-sheet kept us abreast of all that was happening countrywide. There were Blueshirt dances and even Blueshirt weddings. In fact, it appeared that the Blueshirts were here to stay. A Blueshirt column from above Finnea in Co. Westmeath decided to march down to Kilcogy in Mullahoran parish on what they chose to term an educational tour. They numbered about sixty. When they reached Finnea Bridge, which was the entry into Co. Cavan, they observed what they described as a 'yelling mob' on the other side. Wiser council seems to have prevailed and the Blueshirt column retreated. That would appear to be the only 'incident' in our area and I would not have known about it but for the Blueshirt weekly.

Most Blueshirts did not really believe in Fascism. The movement drew a lot of its support from strong farmers who merely wanted to retain the old traditional trading ties with Britain and an end to tariffs on both sides. O'Duffy tried to destabilise the Fianna Fáil government by non-constitutional tactics but de Valera faced down the Blueshirt threat. By the Summer of 1934 the Blueshirts were on the wane. Later that year, O'Duffy resigned as head of Fine Gael. The Blueshirt movement quietly faded away.

In the year 1934, a new departure caught my attention. Seán T. O'Kelly, Minister for Local Government, was rushing through a big housing programme in Dublin to provide the tenement dwellers with new houses. A small grant was also made available to convert thatched houses in rural Ireland into slated ones. In the relative absence of thatched houses today, I will give a few details about them. Thatch on a house had to be given a fresh coat every eight years or so. The existing thatch roof remained as it was and fresh oaten straw was stitched into it. The older a house grew the higher the amount of thatch carried by the roof. The mud-walled thatched house was warm in the Winter and cool in the Summer. The thatch of the roof extended about two feet beyond the wall of the house. There were no pipes or shoots to carry the rainwater off. When a shower fell, the rain travelled down the thatch and fell in a thousand droplets at the end of the numerous straws.

When thatched houses were well kept, they looked beautiful. The brown of the thatch contrasted with the white-washed walls. A green hedge nearby and a long rick of turf completed the picture. In contrast, if thatching could only be achieved every twelve years, the result was quite different. If the thatch was slack (thin) near the wall and if the rain was getting onto the lime wash, a shocking picture emerged. We all hated the existence of these houses. Thankfully they were few and far between. Those were the first recipients of the grant and it gave us a lift to see that they were being attended to. The grant was small. It merely covered the cost of the slates and timber. It had been forgotten that the walls had to be raised two feet if a second storey were to be added. This was achieved by voluntary labour by the 'handy men' of the area.

I did not think that all this had got anything to do with me. Hugh P. thought otherwise. On my rounds he told me to look out for houses where there were just a few helping with re-roofing. He told me to go where there was a big squad and to ask some of them to help out smaller squads. Meeting the different squads at the different houses was an education in itself. It helped me in the art of motivating men later on in Forestry.

The fact that I was wearing a collar and tie and that my boots were polished may in some way have connected me in people's eyes with the grant itself. It was my first brush with roofing, about which I knew nothing. I learned as I went along. The fact that I was seeing so many different roofing squads gave me ample opportunities to observe different working techniques. Sometimes I might be asked how such a squad was doing such a thing. I told the story as I saw it. It made me more observant. I was particularly interested in the timber that roofed the old thatched houses. I had been told that it was oak which had been dug up in the bogs. It was not so. Every house was different. Some had bog oak alright, but the majority were roofed with a variety of timber such as ash, birch and native felled oak. Sometimes roofing timbers consisted of sawn planks. The majority were of various dimensions and picked from whatever timber was available and were mostly unsawn. Some of these houses would date back to the eighteenth century when out of necessity people had to make do with whatever timber was to hand on the farm. There were about a dozen houses that had been roofed with selected bog-oak beams. These beams shone like black ebony. Hugh P. urged people to hold on to this timber. Few heeded him. In discarding this timber they did not realise how valuable bog oak would one day be.

Changing from thatch to slates often caused the owner of the house to whitewash the rest of his outbuildings, in order to make the farmyard look better. A disturbing thing occurred here and there. Beautiful thatched houses were slated. I did not go near any of these. I was fearful lest my lovely thatched home would be slated. Sadly that happened five years later. Part of me went with that house.

The Economic War hit Cavan hard. One thing that helped sustain people was football. Cavan had conquered Ulster on many an occasion but an All-Ireland title had eluded them. We had held Kerry to a point at Tralee on one occasion and we had been twice foiled by Kildare in Croke Park. Our local newspaper, the *Anglo-Celt*, spurred us on. The journalist who handled the football columns in that paper had a magic pen. Even our defeats were described as if they were narrow victories. The goals and points we got were described in detail. Those of our opponents were disposed of in a few lines and were described as a result of 'up-and-down play'. We felt like a deprived lot.

We held our heads high. Cavan was improving by the season. The present team should take some beating. The trouble lay in the fact that Kerry had a super team. They had two All-Ireland medals under their belt. They were asked to go America to give a display of their skills. They had come back with a bag of trophies. They must have felt as proud ambassadors for Ireland. Better still, they gratified the Kerry exiles who cheered them on. They were now coming to Breffney Park in Cavan Town to play the Cavan team. For once *The Anglo-Celt* was cautious in the extreme. The journalist even mentioned the other semi-finalist, Galway, as a team to be feared. Of course, he was waiting and hoping that we would give Kerry a close game. He could then work his magic pen.

I went to the Semi-Final with my friend Pat 'a Park Smith. He had left his motorcycle behind and had taken his ordinary bike. It was not a day to be conspicuous. Even though in our early twenties, we had to keep our Sunday motorcycle-trips as secret as possible. We were late in arriving. It was an overflow crowd and we had to be content with a position behind one of the goalmouths. We were also standing. We were on an embankment and that helped. Otherwise it would have been especially hard to view the match. The best view is always from the side of the pitch, but we were glad to have got in at all. We soon realised that those in our vicinity were Kerry supporters. There were three Kerry boys beside us. We were anxious to identify the Kerry players and they were curious about ours. They were well dressed. One was a clerical student of about twenty years of age. The others were slightly older. It was the first time we had heard the Kerry accent and turn of phrase and it must have been the first time they had heard ours. In fact they laughed when we asked for clarification on things they said. We had similarly to laugh when they asked us to repeat what we had said. They clapped our Cavan scores and we had perforce to clap theirs. It was the first time we had clapped the opposition. Of course, our new friends were expecting only one ending to the match: one more victory on the road to another All Ireland. On the other hand, we as yet had not contemplated a Cavan victory. The most we hoped for was a good running fight by our players.

The result when it came was catastrophic. It has been recorded in song:

'Six minutes before the whistle blew
And Cavan were in arrears
Some thought that Kerry's last attack
Would settle their affairs
But for once in Gaelic history
Those visions proved untrue
When Cavan launched their last attack
For Kerry's Waterloo.'

We were too shocked to cheer. Our Kerry friends, who were young men, broke down and cried. Pat came to the rescue. He consoled them by saying that it was the first time that we had beaten Kerry and we had still to fight Galway in the All Ireland. They had won many a title, but it would be only our first if successful. It was a match to remember. It ended for us with a handshake all round. We congratulated these young men on Kerry's great record. They congratulated us on the fact that we were approaching our first All Ireland. I am glad to record this. Cavan went on beat Galway and win its first All Ireland football title. It was the first time we had got hold of the Sam Maguire Cup.

Football is a great safety valve in any county, but winning the All Ireland Football Final in 1933 was a tremendous boost to the Cavan area. We were congratulated by our Longford, Westmeath, Monaghan and Leitrim neighbours. All wished to share in our good fortune. It was very important in the Economic War. We were against the odds. Winning the All Ireland showed that the unattainable could be attained. In that period of the year which covers November, December and January, farm work winds down and it is a time for other things until the normal pace of work resumes in the Spring. It is said that it is in this period that revolution breeds. Only the arrival of work in the planting of crops eases the situation. Football rather than revolution dominated many a conversation around the fireside in the Winter of 1933-34.

We were in the All Ireland Semi-Final of 1934. We were narrowly beaten by Galway. Meanwhile Mullahoran were trying to win their first County championship. They had joined up with Ballymachugh. For the first time all the boys who played against one another at Clonoose School were together in the same senior team. I had been very good as a minor. I was consequently anxious to play on the Mullahoran/Ballymachugh team. Mullahoran was the actual name of the team. My brother Hugh P. and two first cousins, Peter Briody of Clonloaghan and his brother Hugh, and my second cousin Sammy Briody, also of Clonloaghan, were playing there. After I came back from Dublin, I played one game. To be exact, I only played for the first half. The excessive cycling, which I was not used to, had developed different leg muscles. I had always been very speedy. Now I found that I had lost pace. I decided to bow out until my muscles normalised after I got more used to cycling. I did not leave the game altogether. I studied players of opposing teams and gave what I had discovered to the coach. This came in handy to me when I was later captain of the football team in Avondale.

Nothing brings one back to earth like reality itself. My education as I worked for and among the people was eye-opening. People during the Economic War were in no position to buy many consumer goods. New clothes were a luxury that many people could not afford. Those working on the land wore any kind of clothes they could lay hands on. When Sunday came, they had nice clothes to go to Mass in. These clothes had to be strictly kept for the Sabbath. No one knew when the Economic War would end or if it would ever end at all. Britain had the knack of winning the last round. Overnight we were all realising the difference between political freedom and economic freedom.

As things turned out, the notebooks which were to help farmers pay what was due us had to be used to a lesser extent than anticipated. They were designed to help the less-well-off farmers. Well-off farmers who had never been financially embarrassed before now posed a problem for us. The banks had been more lenient towards them in the past than they were to the men who sheltered under our umbrella. This leniency had gone. We were really sorry for these strong farmers. They were all hard-working people and the conflict which now engulfed them was not of their making. We were conscious that the Economic

War was in danger of breeding a discontented rural middle class, particularly as the social policy of Fianna Fáil was seen to favour the less-well-off. Consequently, we trod carefully when dealing with these people. Were it not for the fact that there was little money available, more big farms could have changed hands in this period.

All cattle passing through Irish ports had to pay a stiff tariff. The only way of avoiding these tariffs was to smuggle the cattle into Northern Ireland. Nowadays we think of smuggling as something illegal but during the Economic War it was considered by many an economic necessity. In the newspapers there were accounts of cattle being captured by excise men as they crossed the border. There were also accounts of fairs in the North of Ireland being flooded with Southern cattle. In our area, because of Lough Sheelin, the route to the border would have to come through Finnea or Mountnugent. That meant that we saw very little actual passage of cattle. I myself witnessed directly very little smuggling. There may have been more smuggling activity going on around me than I was aware of. As I was not expected to stay in the area things may have been kept from me. I would be moving on and did not need to know. Our clients' farms were restocked by us when necessary from whatever cattle were available and some of the cattle on route to the border may have been bought for this purpose.

Much of what I know about smuggling during the Economic War I learned by way of hearsay or later. I was told that there was a 'haven' near the border (the location I can no longer recall) and that cattle were only smuggled from there in very small lots. There was another 'haven' on the other side to receive them. They often did not reach the fairs in Northern Ireland. They were bought at the 'haven' across the border. There was a great demand by the farmers in Northern Ireland for the southern cattle. All those cattle had to be fed and finished before marketing. Some of the cattle that had come long distances must have been in a very poor state. Nationalists and Unionists cooperated in smuggling, it would appear. Of course, both benefited by these transactions.

Hundreds of people who never saw the border played an

149

important part in the smuggling operations of the Economic War. Smuggling really began in the 'deep south' where cattle prices were very depressed. The nearer one got to the border the higher the prices. The movement of cattle was disguised as movements from fair to fair. As far as I know, the cattle were walked. Some of them could have been transported by lorry or rail. I don't know. The railways converged on the ports of the country. They would not have facilitated the movement of cattle from south to north.

I was to learn later that some cattle dealers who had lost their livlihood because of the changed conditions had taken to smuggling. Many did not leave their own area. Instead they sold to the next dealer who brought them to the next 'haven' and maybe sold again. The nearer you got to the border the higher rose the price.

The smuggling of cattle may have been haphazard at first but it became a cleverly marshalled operation after a period of time. The only people who could be called smugglers as such were the dealers/drovers who crossed the border. They were assisted by the fact that at that time cattle were 'untagged'. My information about the smuggling trade comes from three men I met during my Forestry days. One was from Co. Offaly, another from Co. Galway and another still from Co. Waterford. They walked their cattle. The Offaly and Galway men went as far south as possible in search of cattle. They both bought their cattle from other dealers who had come from the deep south. They invested in cattle from a year old to a finished beast. On the way up they passed through fairs where they bought and sold. Farmers were on the look out for them and bought a lot of the young cattle to replenish their stock. An essential rule of good farming practice is to keep a farm stocked up to a certain level but never overstocked. Lack of movement of cattle tended to leave farms overstocked.

Everyone had a friendly look out for the men who were walking the cattle: the farmer trying to get rid of his heavy cattle; the farmer trying to restock his herd; and the butcher who could help out if cattle were unable to travel and had to be slaughtered. The 'smugglers' I knew were honest men; their word was their bond. They were wealthy enough to to give credit where required. The Economic War was a real war with everybody playing a part.

I only came across one incident of smuggling and that remains one of my great memories. I had been on one of my usual rounds. I was after having a cup of tea in a farmhouse near home. I was standing outside the house. Coming down towards me was a long line of cattle. They seemed to be very tired. As the saying goes: 'They were lifting their legs and letting them fall.' A man came from the back with a map in his hand. He came up to me and asked me if I knew who owned the pond inside the ditch. I replied that I did. It belonged to the farm I had just visited. He told me that he wanted to water the cattle and asked would I help him. Accordingly, I went back and asked permission from the man of the house, which was readily given. The farmer came out and he opened the field gate. There were thirty cattle in the bunch and only ten were allowed in to drink at a time. I lingered on out of interest. What I noticed was that the cattle on the road all looked towards the water. When the ten had satisfied themselves, they went up the field and laid down. The next ten did the same and soon all the thirsty, tired cattle were stretched out enjoying the rest. The farmer asked the drovers in for a cup of tea. No. They could not leave the cattle. They had lunches with them and they would be obliged if he brought them out a cup of tea. And so we got talking. They had to come off their usual route because the animals were heavy and slow-moving. The other route was much faster but their animals could not stick it. They were within four miles from their next 'haven'. They would leave the cattle there for a week before pushing on. They had been walking the cattle from six o'clock in the morning. It was now four in the evening.

Suddenly I saw one of the animals getting up. There was a rush by the smugglers to get them onto the road again. One of them explained to me that the herd was quite capable of eating all the grass in the little field in a half hour. The cattle seemed different now. They had an eagerness to push on. The smugglers told me that this always happened with the approach of darkness. From past experience the cattle knew that they are nearing food

151

and water. As I wended my way home, I felt sad about our treatment of the poor dumb animals. How have we the right to assume that they are for 'man's use and benefit'?

Towards the end of 1935 the cash flow improved and took care of itself. This was partly due to money being sent home from England by young men and women working mainly in munitions factories. At the end of that year, I finished with the collecting. I had more time to help Mama with the poultry and help out otherwise on the farm. I also had more time to spend with my younger brothers and sisters. I continued to look after the advertisements in the local papers. During the Economic War we even tried to advertise sales of farms in the American newspaper *The Irish Echo*, but nothing came of it. The Great Depression had dried up money there. I used often go to Smiths Solicitors in Cavan Town in respect of carriage of sales. In this way I got to grips with the legal end of the selling of farms.

Everything was undecided. I was no longer needed at home and had to consider my future. In the Spring of 1936, I applied for the job of clerical worker in Cavan County Council and got it. The snag was that it was twenty miles from home. For a few weeks I cycled to and from work. Then I took lodgings with a Mrs Cassidy in Cavan Town. She put me in touch with certain traders in the town. I got a lot of handy jobs doing their books for them and I was careful to keep my mouth shut about what I saw and heard. My salary with the Council was not good and were it not for these extra jobs, I could not have managed. In the national school Master O'Shea had called me 'Tomás an tSíoda', which meant Silken Thomas. I was the best dressed kid in school. With my extra money I now bought new clothes and looked back indulgently at the first bleak years of the Economic war. The work suited me and did not suit. I felt imprisoned sitting behind a desk. I always managed to have my work done and my overcoat on when the door was closing. I made friends with the Secretary of the Cavan Department of Agriculture. He was responsible for my dreaming of a possible route to the university via Ballyhaise Agricultural College and Albert College, Glasnevin. I had a leaning towards Horticulture. Mama had taught me how to identify the weeds of the different seasons.

It is so nice to dream. In due course I sat an exam and secured a Cavan County Council scholarship to Ballyhaise.

Although the cash flow at home had eased and was taking care of itself, it would not be entirely true to say that times had improved. The truth was that we were getting used to hard times and were 'cutting our cloth according to our measure.' It was a time when I did not know whether I was coming or going. The golden years of youth were slipping away. I came home every weekend. It was nice to see everybody. Dad seemed more relaxed. Men of his generation had to forget the past and make most of the present. I was glad that I had come back from Dublin to help. Glad too that my coming back had given me an opportunity to help my younger brothers and sisters with their schoolwork. They were all doing well.

This was one of those weekends on which I was coming home. I was cycling and was within three hundred yards of the old thatched home when I noticed Mama walking towards me. This was unusual. Could there be something wrong? As it happened there wasn't; she was just coming out to meet me. I was somewhat late. Then the thought struck me that I had better confide in her about my future plans. To say that she was delighted would put it mildly. I must have been a puzzle to her since I came back from Dublin. At times, she had thought that I might have a late vocation for the Church. My plan to get to university via Ballyhaise and Glasnevin was great news for her. To cap it all, I told her I had won a scholarship to Ballyhaise Agricultural College.

I left the County Council and moved back home to spend some time with that cheeky young bunch before going to Ballyhaise in the Autumn. There was a great atmosphere at home. Mullahoran had won the County Championship in 1935 and were trying to repeat the performance. I got so many bits and pieces of jobs in auditing books that I actually stopped doing extra work in my last few months at home.

Yes, it was hard to leave that beautiful thatched house and its lovely garden of flowers and herbs. It would have been a nice place to tarry but time is forever moving on. My younger brothers and sisters would in time move out too. I hated leaving

Dublin. Now I hated to leave the place I would for ever associate with the Economic War. My godmother, Mrs Henry, had a farewell party for me. As usual she implied that I was altogether in her confidence. It may have been one of the last dances held in that farmhouse. The Dance Hall Act of the previous year in time was to put an end to such dances. This was a great pity. Dances in the farmhouses helped to keep alive Irish traditional music. The space available would for the most part only admit of traditional Irish dancing, while the bigger space of the public halls helped the spread of foreign dances. The waltz had been simplified after the First World War and was now a onestep. This could also be danced in the farmhouse kitchens. Anybody capable of walking could get on a dance floor.

The house we were in was built in 1806 by my great-grandfather Harry Rua Briody, who at the age of twenty three decided to build a new, two-storey, slated house. The house still stands and is comparable to any of the more modern farmhouses since built in the locality. In my time, it still had a large stone-flagged kitchen. In the centre was a dancing-stone, very smooth and measuring about four feet by four feet. Always during a night's dancing when the dancers were resting, a boy or a girl would step onto this stone and give a solo demonstration. Only an expert could venture onto that stone. Every dancer in the house was a critic. There was a large adjoining parlour where everybody got tea and cake.

This night remains in my mind for a special reason. The house we were dancing in was a distance of two miles from my Callanagh home and in between lay Clonoose National School. All the girls and boys at that party were from Ballymachugh parish. I had walked to school from the Mullarhoran area. I was dancing with the unknown. And what a sophisticated bunch they had become. Only a few were from my class. The rest were either older or younger. Most of them were now working in the local towns or in Dublin. Some of them had been to England and back. They all lived to come back to the local 'hop'. Their accents were more modulated than that which had obtained in our old national school at Clonoose. They made enquiries about their old class mates of yesteryear who had come from the

Mullahoran hills. I had to be very careful with my replies. On no account could I allow fun to be made of those wild Mullahoran girls. A problem of the night was that we were all under the watchful eye of Mrs Henry. She need not have worried. I was not going to let down those young girls I had walked with on the way to school. We had a few songs. Someone got onto the dancing stone and gave a solo performance. It was all-night dancing then and we only stopped when the morning sun came in the window. That was Clonloaghan 1936!

To say that I slept soundly the next morning would be to put it mildly. I would be going to Ballyhaise on the morrow and would need whatever rest I could snatch. Someone brought me in a cup of tea and I awoke with a start. It suddenly struck me that I had hardly seen my Shanvalla cousins since I came back from Dublin three years before. There was a time when they had been my very life. But the rush of things during the Economic War had cut them almost completely out of my life. I would have to make amends.

It would have been nice to slip along the Mass path to Shanvalla. All those little farmsteads along my route would expect me to call and say hello. I might even have to wait for a kettle to boil. No. I must take a bike and cycle along the three and a half miles of road. I had first travelled that road with Mama in a pony and trap before I learned how to cycle. I got a great welcome at Shanvalla. All the girls were there. Eddie, who had replaced Chassy, was now three years old. I was the man of travel. I was expected to tell the news. The girls had now become a very serious group and questions flew about Dublin. I was invited to go into the parlour but declined. I loved that old big kitchen in Shanvalla where I used practice speaking Irish with those girls. Aunt Kate seemed to sense that we were not at our ease. She took a small handball from the dresser. She told us to make ourselves scarce and to come back when she had a meal ready.

There was a rush for the door. In the yard were slated sheds with high walls, which lent themselves to handball. The girls were on familiar territory and I found myself slipping and falling. Luckily the ball got lost in the shrubbery and we had to

155

fall back on the game of 'tig'. This was a game where you tip someone on the shoulder and run away. That person becomes the 'tigger' and must tap somebody else. It is a game for the fleet of foot and I found myself in the exhaustive role of the tigger. In fact, I was only rescued by a call to tea.

I was the guest that day and was made to feel like one. It was a day of fun and banter. The girls excused themselves for pushing and shoving me around. However, I had only myself to blame. I had come across in the Twenties and taught them to play handball and football. They were a wonderful group of girls. They all could handle horses and they all did farm work in their turn. The farm-horses were very fond of them and on one occasion I saw one of them rub noses with a horse. The evening was one of song and music. All were great singers and had graced the *feiseanna* of the Twenties. At the time the revival of the spoken Irish language seemed only a few years away. Sadly, it never came.

I found I had to tear myself away as I hugged each one in turn. I would have loved to have had a chat with Charles about the Economic War, but time did not permit. In any event, he might not have wished to speak about it. It affected people in different ways. Many wished to put it at the back of their minds and to forget that it had been an uphill fight.

I suddenly realised that I was going to Ballyhaise on the morrow. I would like to chat with my family. So I hurried home. I was amazed as I neared the house to see a lot of bikes strewn along the hedge. The walkers of the Twenties had become the cyclists of the Thirties. There was a party in progress. The older people were in the parlour. The boys and girls of my school days were in the kitchen. Stories were being swapped when I arrived. I was too tired to talk. It was a time to sit and listen. The stories were racy and witty. Sometimes I was the hero of the piece. Sometimes I was the victim. Other times I was the unnamed rascal. It is important that we see ourselves as others see us.

Though employment outside agriculture improved during the Economic War due to Fianna Fáil's promotion of native industry, unemployment still remained a chronic problem throughout the Thirties. The numbers of unemployed were kept down by emigration. This in some respects was a blessing in disguise. The money sent back by the emigrants made a big difference in the running of the small farms. Fianna Fáil's social legislation during the Economic War helped improve working conditions and extend a degree of protection to the more vulnerable parts of society. For the first time small landholders, unemployed in all but name, and agricultural labourers enjoyed some relief. When valuation of the land was made in Cavan in the mid-nineteenth century, conditions were very bad. As a result of farm improvement and drainage, farms were in much better shape than in the previous century. In fact, the dole relief given by the Fianna Fáil Government to low-valuation holders took in more farmers that was intended. Quite a large amount of cut-away bog had been reclaimed and this had not been revalued. It was nice to know that something was in our favour.

The Economic war though eased, drifted along until April 1938. Truthfully, I thought it would never end. Some predicted the dispute would end in an economic abyss. This did not happen. The final settlement was very favourable to the South of Ireland. Britain lifted restrictions on Irish agricultural produce and in exchange British industrial exports were given preferential treatment. The Annuities question was resolved once and for all by the South paying Britain ten million pounds, only a fraction of the outstanding debt.

In a sense, for me the Economic War ended with my departure for Ballyhaise Agricultural College in the Autumn of 1936. I would be in Avondale Forestry School, home of Parnell, when the Economic War ended. I will recount below how I heard the news of the final settlement. The events I have recorded above happened over seventy years go and I am now in my mid-nineties. In recounting my experiences on the ground of the Economic War, I realise that I am to some extent following in my father's footsteps. Many of his stories were of another war, the Land War, and of his work with farmers in the years following. He also delighted in telling about the Great Exhibition held in Dublin in the early twentieth century. He had some great stories about the Exhibition – not of the actual exhibits, but of the people he saw there, who came from the four corners of

Ireland. It was always the past he spoke about, just as I am speaking about the past.

Dad and I had come very close together during the Economic War. It was now fifteen years since the War of Independence. He and I had not yet reached the stage when we could discuss politics. But then we had so many other wonderful things to talk about. I could listen for ever to his stories of the old days and the times he had lived through. While at home in Cavan during those difficult years I was often invited to join one of the local Fianna Fáil Cumainn. I always declined, out of consideration for Dad. He was a man to look up to. Mama was closer to me in my political thinking, but she said very little either. What she did say, said it all. She was a housewife, and farm manager, who had to deal with the nitty gritty of running a household and farm. She simply said: 'Politically we should be breaking away from Britain. Economically we should be nestling closer to other countries.' I was gradually moving over to that side of the road. The Economic War was for me a hard teacher. It was a fight against the odds.

Who really won the Economic War? I don't know. History has been kind to De Valera. His final triumph would appear to overshadow all else, like a last-minute winning goal in a football match. For me the jury is out. If it was a victory, it is to the people at the coalface who held each other up that credit should be given. The men and women who had to emigrate and leave their families on the little farms deserve a mention too.

Was I a casualty of the Economic war? My Dublin friends may have thought I was. At the time I may have felt likewise, but now I think I was not. I am glad to have been part of that fight. Glad to have been there to help Dad and Mama. Glad also to have been with a lovely family for a few years longer. I was only in Cavan twenty three years of my ninety five. Above all my experiences of the Economic War steeled me for the fight that lay ahead.

Next day Hugh P. brought me to Drumhawnagh Railway Station. I had two heavy cases, which contained mostly books. I had expected that the train would be joined by a number of students at Cavan. That did not happen and when I reached

Ballyhaise Railway Station, I was told that the students had arrived on the day previous. In those days a taxi was unheard of at a railway station. Luckily for me there was a young farmer who was going part of the way. He had a pony and cart. He put my two heavy cases on the cart and we sat up. The journey was easy and slow. When I told him I was from Mullahoran, he became alive. We had played against the local team. When we reached his house, he invited me in for a cup of tea, which I gladly accepted. His wife was equally friendly. I noticed that he did not take my cases off the cart. He told me that he would bring me all the way to the College. This I very much appreciated. It would have been nice to have met that farmer and his wife again.

Part III: The path to Forestry

Ballyhaise Agricultural College

It was four o'clock in the afternoon when I reached the College. To say that I was dwarfed by what I saw is to put it mildly. I had expected to see a small building with an experimental farm attached. Ballyhaise was a place where the past and the present were forever intertwining. It was a beautiful house once owned by a landed family with a large estate covering seven square miles. They must have been a family of great wealth. The big house and its courtyard with its many houses were expertly planned. So too were the farm yard, kitchen garden, Italian garden, sunken garden and orchard. Nearby, in a place called Dromhome, a sculpturer had made a collection of Roman and Greek gods and goddesses. It was all part of Ballyhaise's great past. It would be nice to be able to say that our studies in Ballyhaise included lectures in Roman and Greek culture. No. All our studies there were on an evolving agriculture, horticulture and sylviculture.

I found myself at the top of a flight of steps which led up to the front door. I rang the bell. A lady appeared. I told her who I was and that I should have come the day before. She took my cases and then directed me to where the students were threshing corn a quarter of a mile away. I had some difficulties getting there and had to make a few enquiries from farm workers along the way. I was dismayed when I saw the students. There were about twenty of them in all. They averaged from eighteen to twenty years of age. I was twenty three. This was a period of my life when I thought that a gap of three years was unbridgeable. They were all dressed in dungarees. Mine were in my case. I was wearing my Sunday best. I caused great activity when I arrived. Later I heard that the students thought I was one of the teachers. It was an afternoon in which I felt ill at ease. I was glad when the bell sounded and we came back to the house for the evening meal. Then I met my House Master. He seemed taken aback because of my age. He asked a few questions of me. Then he explained the method of working.

The House Master really was very kind. He asked me if I had any preferences. I replied that I would like to work with a boy much taller than myself. I felt this would conceal my age. He laughed at this and then introduced me to a six footer named Joe Hanahoe. Joe told me he was from County Mayo. I said I was glad of this as it would help me keep up my Irish. I concluded, being from the West he must know Irish. Imagine my surprise when he told me he had little of the language. He was hoping to get into Forestry but was afraid he might not pass the oral test in Irish. His face lit up when I told him that I would not speak a word of English to him until we said goodbye at the College gates the following Autumn. It was the beginning of a lifelong friendship. He was a man with opinions of his own. He was very practical. He had been to Mount Bellow Agricultural College, Co. Galway the previous year and he loved learning everything there was to learn about weeds and flowers. He supplied what I needed most, as I was aiming at Horticulture.

I would have liked to have shared the same dormitory with Joe. Because I was a latecomer, I had to share the smaller dormitory with five other students. The two larger dormitories accommodated around twelve each. I introduced myself to my five roommates. One was from Tipperary, two were from Clare and two from Donegal. All their accents were strange to me. Mine must have been strange to them, too. Before going to sleep the first night we talked for a while and then our conversations drifted into silence. We were on the top story of a large mansion. Down below we could hear water cascading over a waterfall. My nearest roommate, who was Dunne from Tipperary, told me that it was a waterfall on the River Annalee, a tributary of the Erne. I could not go to sleep with the noise of the water falling.

As usual in a strange place, I found myself wondering as to what took me here in the first place. All of my roommates had dropped off to sleep. To add to my misery two of them started snoring. How nice it would be to be at home and to slip down into the kitchen for a cup of tea. They say that you never miss the water until the well runs dry. I must have dropped off to sleep for I was awakened by the bell calling us to breakfast. The House Master entered and he proceeded to show me how to make up my bed. Apparently he had shown the other boys the 'modus operandi' the previous morning. I was a newcomer and had to be shown the ropes. I had made my bed on many occasions. I realised that a new perfection was being required of me. He told me that someone else would inspect the beds an hour later. If a bed was found to be 'undermade', its occupant would be sent for and stood over until a 'proper bed' emerged. Strangely enough, I was never called on to return to the dormitory. Stranger still, I never heard the water cascading over that waterfall again. I fell asleep when I hit the pillow.

The work and study at Ballyhaise were very well organised. When you reached the refectory in the morning, you went first towards a large sheet of paper hanging over the mantelpiece. There you found your initials and those of your partner. Opposite you would see where you should go and what you should work at for the day. I am not quite sure, but as far as I can remember, there would be fifteen pairs or thereabouts and a corresponding number of different locations: the dairy, the milking parlour, the feeding outlets, the carpentry shop, the stables with their horses, the poultry, the sheep pens, the vegetable-garden, and the harness room. Counting the various animals on the farm was another chore. There were several experiments being conducted and you could be sent to any one of these. There was only one tractor. I drove a tractor at twenty three years of age, I had to wait until my mid-thirties to drive a car. No big advance in farming seems to have been foreseen. We were all trained to be expert ploughmen with horse and plough.

On our first morning Joe and I found ourselves in the carpentry. It consisted of a very large room with smaller adjoining rooms. The carpenter made us feel at home. From the outset we knew that he was keen on imparting his knowledge to us. He was a teacher without a blackboard. Because of my agreement with Joe, I had brought a sheet of paper along with me. I asked the carpenter the names of all his tools, different types of timber, etc. I had actually to ask him for an extra sheet of paper to complete the list. Then I started to put the names in Irish on them. I was lucky that I had a pocket dictionary to help out. Otherwise I would have fallen at the first fence. In fact, I

instructions to the new students. She appeared puzzled that one student was doing all the work while his fellow-student was busy with pen and paper. To satisfy her curiosity I told her that I was teaching Joe to speak Irish and that he needed to know the Irish equivalents for everything in the place.

She was silent for a while and then she said: 'Would you teach me too? My Irish is only a faint memory.' 'No,' I replied. 'You are my teacher. I am your pupil.' She did not reply for a moment and then she enquired if it would be alright if she asked the Superintendent. I agreed to this. When she was gone Joe suggested that he be part of the class. It was a welcome suggestion and it would appear at the time to have solved a problem. Later I was to discover that two is company but three is a crowd. The situation was further complicated when I discovered that my new 'pupil' was also a Briody. I was hoping that my fellow-students would think that we were related, sharing such a rare surname. Most of the students hated the dairy and Joe and myself used often be called back there when an emergency arose. When a worker was absent, Joe did the separating of the milk and I did the butter-making. A special bonus for us was the opportunity of talking to the lady in white.

After a week of practical work we began classes. For most of us it was like going back to school. Supt. Delaney was an expert classroom teacher as well as being a great field man. He had a very stern exterior. Nevertheless he had a great understanding of the boys who passed through his hands. I was glad to have met him. I do not know what was the extent of his knowledge of Irish. He used the '*cúpla focal*' very effectively and later showed his sympathy towards the language in allowing me teach Miss Briody.

Our first day in class I still recall well because it was the first. The other classes I can only recall in general terms because of the span of almost seventy years. We were invited to ask questions and then we were asked to take a sheet of paper and to write down what should be the priorities of Irish farming. I had come to learn Horticulture not Agriculture in an effort to get to university. My contact with farming during the Economic War should have given me some fresh ideas but it did not. At any rate, it did not make me very optimistic about the future of agriculture. Nothing seemed to matter. The outlook appeared to me dreary and stark. Something of this must have come into my answer. In passing around the classroom, Mr Delaney glanced down at my page. He simply said: 'We will have another day.'

One aspect of farming that intrigued me was haymaking. If the weather came good it was a pleasure for everyone. If it came showery, there were nothing but scowling faces. Some farmers favoured cocking the hay as green as possible. Other farmers waited for the hay to rattle on the fork. It was either one extreme or the other. If it was too green, it fermented in the cocks. If it was too dry, it was less nutritious. There was always a breeze blowing in Callanagh and we were able to cock the hay on the following day. We had, however, a meadow of Mrs Lynch's in Clonoose, which lay along the river, a tributary of the Drumbricklis River. There was a line of high trees along the road which lifted the breeze. It was a difficult field to save. On one occasion we failed and had to cart the rotted hay to the manure heap.

Before going to Ballyhaise I had read in the newspapers that a process was being developed to convert grass to silage – a method which would bypass haymaking. Most farmers initially thought that this was not possible. When more became known of the method there was much debate as to whether animals would take to silage or not. It was hard to imagine that all the hay fields which dotted the countryside with their lovely roped cocks would be no more. I did not realise that such an attempt was also being made at Ballyhaise. An essay of mine on haymaking gave Mr Delaney his opportunity. They were conducting two experiments. In one the green grass was chopped to pieces and blown up into a silo. To this was added molasses. In the other experiment pits had been dug into the hillside. The mowed grass was thrown un-chopped into the pits and molasses added. The seeping of effluent from the bottom of these pits was unsightly. All this is a far cry from the modern method of making silage. Quite frankly, although I thought it might be an alternative to haymaking, at the time I did not think it would come to pass. It has been a marvellous breakthrough. When I think of all the times we waited for the clouds to lift and the sun to peep through. Haymaking was a pleasure with the Callanagh breeze blowing. Haymaking in Lynch's meadow along the river is best forgotten.

Gradually Ballyhaise grew on me and I found myself admiring its aims and ideals. At first I felt annoyed at what I thought was the excessive use of fertilisers that caused the disappearance of taste in the potato and turnip. I got to learn that soils varied from place to place. They could become depleted of potash, nitrogen and phosphates or they could become enriched by the application of those minerals. In my lifetime I saw the beautiful environment of organic living replaced by an inorganic way of life.

The common room in Ballyhaise deserves a special mention. It was a large well-lit room with an open-grate fireplace. The latter could take moderately-sized logs which were placed for use in a basket nearby. We were told that some accident or other had happened there the previous year. We were cautioned not to meddle with the fire. A kitchen boy called now and again and put on a log or two. We never questioned his prerogative. We had always a welcome fire during the autumn and winter months.

The common room was a place where I was taught to compromise. I was an Irish-Irelander. I had as yet only danced in the country kitchens and was very good at the traditional Irish dances. I had heard my new-found friend, Hanahoe, whistling a mixture of strange tunes as we went around the poultry runs. These tunes soon invaded the common room. Mayo was early with its dance halls. In the west because of all the immigrants coming back and forth from America they had jazz tunes earlier than we had in Cavan. At first amongst the students in Ballyhaise we had only one musical instrument, a melodeon. Gradually more instruments appeared. These varied from concertinas to tin whistles.

When *céilí* music was being played (usually by three or four together) we all got out and did the "Stack of Barley," the "Siege of Ennis," etc. The waltz was also a favourite, with all the musicians joining in. I got out on the floor and learned to dance

167

that too. The foxtrot was beyond me and I never descended to the one-step. The jazz music at first seemed crazy to me but gradually I began to appreciate that too. It was also common for men to dance together in Albert College, Glasnevin.

There were only four of us to begin with who spoke Irish in the common room. I was trying to get Joe going with bits and pieces of Irish. The two Longford boys, Dan McGuire and Terence Cronin, had tried for teaching but had failed because they could not sing. Their help was invaluable. From the ease they spoke Irish they must have been to the Gaeltacht. I had never been. My knowledge of Irish had been acquired from reading. We learned a lot from one another. It is difficult to know what really happened in that common room. None of the four of us ever pushed our Irish on the rest. They must have sensed that it was important to us. Maybe our circle was a nice one to join. I don't know. I only know that our circle widened until it embraced everyone. Of course, we used lots of English too, but Irish predominated.

We were almost a fortnight in Ballyhaise before Mr Delaney informed us that a national school teacher would come to teach us Irish for one hour per week. It would appear that Irish henceforth would be on the programme. I had not yet heard when I could start teaching Miss Briody and I was half hoping that she might be able to attend the Irish class. The Irish teacher was to arrive at four o'clock on a Friday evening. It was half past four before he came. He did not seem to see any of us at first. He was panting with the exertion of carrying a load of books. These he distributed, one for each student in the class. They were small readers concerning the antics of a dolphin. He asked us in English to have a look over the books during the weekend. He would call on the following Friday and would take us through the opening chapter.

I was very disturbed. I raised my hand. His eye caught mine. He came towards me. I informed him in Irish that Mr Delaney had promised us an hour of Irish and that we had only got a half hour from him. He seemed startled at my use of Irish. He asked for my name and he departed for the Superintendent's Office. We went for tea and later trooped back into the common room. Mr Delaney put his head in the door. He signalled that he wanted to speak to me. The boys must have thought that I was being sent home. I later learned that they had decided on a plan of action in that eventuality.

Life had been so full of twists and turns that I could have expected anything to happen when I entered that office. I was surprised when Mr Delaney shook hands with me. He then asked me to explain my side of the story. I explained that we had been expecting a higher standard of Irish from the teacher and that having come half an hour late he had given us a very simple text to read for the following week.

Then Mr Delaney unburdened himself to me. He had great trouble in arranging for Irish classes. A lot of it stemmed from the boys themselves. There were years when the majority hated the very sight of the language. He thought that it had been taught unevenly in the national schools. There also seemed to be a problem with the dialects. Referring to Miss Briody's request, he said that for a teacher to be asked to be taught by a pupil was something new. He then told me that he had arranged for me to start teaching Miss Briody the following week. A brief smile flitted across his face when he heard from me of the inclusion of Joe Hanahoe in the class.

On the following Tuesday we had our first class with Miss Briody, or Miss B. as she was known. It was in the kitchen of her flat. It was somewhat inconvenient that this class took place during our free time, which we would normally have spent in the common room. Miss Briody explained that it could not take place during working hours. We assured her that we did not mind and that it was a welcome break for us. We thoroughly enjoyed the tea she provided, but we declined her offer of biscuits. I had written up a piece of conversation about the work of the day in the dairy and poultry run. I had gone over this beforehand with Joe. We now went over it again. She seemed delighted with all the new names for the ordinary things. We then broke into English. I asked her what part of Westmeath she had come from. She was from Fore. I told her that I had read about the history of the abbey there but had never been that far afield.

The House Master informed us that we were having a new Irish teacher and that we would have a full hour this time. Friday arrived and we did not know what to expect. In fact, nobody came. A phone call to the House Master informed him that our new teacher could not come until the following Friday. However, we were allowed to spend the hour doing whatever study we chose to do. Then the House Master left abruptly. Generally he stayed there and kept 'the lid on things'. Dan McGuire was sitting in the desk next to me. As a language enthusiast, he must have felt that we were being thwarted. Then I saw him walk towards the blackboard. First he carefully cleaned it. Then he turned around and told us he was going to deal with the prepositional pronouns. Anyone who liked could join in. All he wanted was a few simple sentences from each student. I caught the mood and went around to each boy helping as best I could. It was a bit of fun at first with not everyone joining in. Gradually a more serious mood crept in with some boys showing off by contributing bits and pieces. Dan had started with the preposition 'ag', which is used to denote possession. Then he slipped along to 'ar' and 'le'. Soon we were all vying with one another. It is amazing how much idiomatic Irish involves the prepositions. It was an hour of fun and banter. Some of the boys tried to write the most crazy sentences imaginable.

The door opened and who appeared but Mr. Delaney himself. The House Master had told him of the nonappearance of the new teacher and he had come to apologise. What he saw changed his mind. I met him in later years and he spoke affectionately of that '36/'37 Irish class. Dan would have made an excellent teacher. His short sentences were the forerunners of those later used in the common room. And yet there are those who speak of Irish as a language that is hard acquired.

The following Friday came and so too came the new teacher. He introduced himself to the class. He had apparently a great welcome for himself. He was nevertheless a very nice man and soon put us at our ease. He told us he hated to teach a class where nobody asked questions but himself. He understood there were difficulties with the previous teacher and he would be glad to get any problem that existed out of the way. So he invited anybody with a problem to speak up. Dan McGuire took on the task. He told the teacher that nearly every county was represented and that there must be a clash of dialects. The teacher was glad to inform us that he had been dealing with that problem in various parts of the country.

The teacher grew on us as time went by and his classes were always lively and pleasant. He had the happy knack of not pretending to see or hear what was happening. Sometimes the Donegal boys in reading would try to imitate the Kerry or Cork boys. The latter in turn would try an imitate the Donegal boys. The teacher would look out the window as if nothing was happening. Yes, he was a good teacher and came into the common room on several occasions. He never disturbed us and he seemed to enjoy the crack and the music.

Joe Hanahoe and I were now in Miss Briody's flat every Tuesday evening. I had become friendly with Dan McGuire and was tempted to invite him with his lovely Irish to join us. It was probably his very good looks which prevented me from risking his inclusion. For the first time, I realised the importance of a third party in a conversation. Joe was a very good conversationalist in English and was gradually learning to express himself in Irish. Yes, it was a lovely, happy Winter in 1936.

I will have to write of Ballyhaise as I found it. I was aware that there were many boys who thought the place was boring and that the work was tedious. To me it was an oasis. The roads during the Economic War were long and windswept. Money was scarce and there was little to spare on many farms. On the road you either got many meals or too few, and far between. In contrast, the regularity of Ballyhaise was something new. I got up at a certain hour and had my meals at a fixed time. While on the farm you were always near some special shelter. Everything was taken care of. It was a completely new world, a world where only the past memories of fighting men, women and children imposed themselves upon the life of the College, which at times seemed unreal.

Our routine was varied. We might spend the morning in the dairy and the afternoon in the poultry runs. Then we spent a day in class. The first half of Saturday was usually taken up with study. I, however, availed of the time to write a letter home to Mama. Now and again I wrote a letter to my godmother, Mrs Henry. She was a woman who felt that she had a responsibility towards me. At times she was a burden to me. I liked her and only really appreciated her when she had passed on. My godfather, Michael Galligan, whom I used regularly correspond with, had died the year before.

On Sunday we went to Mass in the local church, which was only a short distance away in the village of Ballyhaise. There we purchased some Sunday newspapers. Miss Briody always retained the Irish-language section of *Scéala Éireann* (*The Irish Press*) for me. She would have these pages for me when we met in class. It brought my mind back to the time when I used contribute snippets of local news in Irish to the *Irish Press*. I went to Mass with Joe Hanahoe, Joe Munnelly, Dan McGuire, and John Mulligan. On the road to Mass, the tales of Cavan, Longford, Mayo and Monaghan intertwined. There was quite a competition.

It was in the milking parlour in Ballyhaise that I saw for the first time cows milked by milking machine. I was asked to finish by hand some pedigree cows who were high-yielders. I was complimented on my strong hands and found myself asked back on numerous occasions. The swilling of the milk stands was also a new operation to me and was another step forward in hygiene.

We were also often assigned to experiments. These were many and varied. In a sense, everything was being tested. It was a time when a big step forward was being taken in agriculture. The increased use of fertilisers was considered as the new weapon to feed the hungry millions on the planet. My generation had, for the most part, been reared on organic food. Imperceptibly we were being coaxed and lured away to another way of producing food. Although, we had beautifully-served meals, the tasty potato I had grown up with was missing. You either ate bread at dinner or partook of the watery cousin of the potato. A generation of people forgot the 'old faithful'.

Every pig in the station was a York pig. We still had the

large Ulster pig at home and I hated to see them replaced. The York pig was a thin lean animal. He was most wanted in the British market. Denmark had gone over to the York. We were expected to do likewise. The trouble for the Irish farmer lay in the fact that it took more food to feed the York. It also took more time to mature for market. The large Ulster pig was still common on farms. I found myself on hostile territory in Ballyhaise in advocating its retention. I withdrew my objections one by one.

We were also often sent to work in the gardens. It was for Horticulture that I had come to Ballyhaise. There was plenty of knowledge and lore to lap up from the gardener and garden workers and I took full advantage of it. There were a few bags of nitrogen, potash and phosphates in the shed. These were rarely availed of except to steal an odd handful for some hungry plant here and there. The gardener was organic-driven. He was a man after my own heart. He was skilled in compost making. The leaves of the beech trees when they fell were trapped by sunken trenches. They were left there until they were wanted for the compost heaps. The old men who worked the gardens may have come from the landlord days. There was 'something old and something new' about them. Horticulture and Agriculture owes a lot to the gardeners of the Big Houses.

The orchards were very interesting. There was a new area there where a lot of experiments were going on with tar-oil sprays, etc. Tar-oil sprays were used to control weeds. The trees there had been changed from a non-profitable variety to profitable ones. Some stocks had come all the way from Long Ashton Research Station in Somerset. There was a big effort to show what could be produced from these stocks. Apple trees were being grown there to satisfy various needs: a tree to accommodate the household with a small garden; a tree for early fruition; and one for late fruition.

The gardener seemed to sense that Joe and I were on his side. We found ourselves being asked back time and time again and always when there was something interesting going on. Both Joe and I had our sights on Glasnevin. Joe was also thinking of doing Forestry. His association with me initially seemed to have changed his mind. He was ideally suited for Horticulture. He had a great knowledge of wild flowers covering every part of the year. He went on to do Horticulture at Glasnevin after finishing in Ballyhaise. Dan McGuire did Agriculture at Glasnevin. Hanahoe and McGuire were both later responsible for my switching to Forestry. During our period of training in Avondale we were much together. Afterwards we rarely met. Both Hanahoe and McGuire ascended to the highest ranks in Forestry. We corresponded by letter and kept our friendship alive. Both would have more interesting stories to tell than mine. They gave their all to Forestry. Both died shortly after their retirement. My story should have been written twenty years ago. *Is fearr go mall ná go brách*!

There were times when Joe and I did not see eye to eye. On one occasion we were sent to one of the ploughmen. I'm not quite sure of his name. I think it was Tully. There were several ploughmen employed. This particular man was designated by Mr Delaney to teach the students how to plough. In our farm at home a plough called the Flood plough was being used. It was a very effective plough but required a highly skilled man to use it. It was without wheels. The type of plough at Ballyhaise was equipped with wheels. It was an easy plough for the amateur to handle. It enabled you to decide what breadth and depth of sod you wished to cut. An adjustment of another wheel at the coulter ensured that a uniform depth of ploughing was achieved.

At home, Hugh P., being the eldest of the family, was the ploughman. Oftentimes I would bring out tea in the evening where the ploughing was being done. John Galligan, our neighbour, would be there too with his horse. His animal and ours made a great team. Sometimes Hugh P. guided the horses. Other times John Galligan took over. Sometimes they would talk together as the green sward became brown. A line of seagulls would be twenty yard behind the plough. Hugh P. was very fond of reading. He always kept a newspaper in his pocket. When things were under control, he would seat himself on the headland and read to his heart's content, while John Galligan did the ploughing. It never crossed his mind that the boy who brought out the tea would love to plough too.

On the first occasion in Ballyhaise when we were being

instructed in the use of the plough, we were shown how to adjust the nuts and wheels in their proper positions. The reins to guide the horses were then handed to yours truly. It was a moment of intense excitement. The feeling of being in control of those two horses and turning over the sod was something I thought I would never experience. I heard myself shouting 'Hup! Hup!' to the lovely animals. It was an evening that could go on forever.

Joe Hanahoe was a realist. To him the days of the horse were numbered. He saw the tractor taking over. It did not come as quickly as he imagined it would. The War was to intervene. Six years later in the Golden Vale, I was to find myself teaching young farmers how to plough with horses. The area was mainly pastureland and many large farmers had given up tillage until forced to resume cultivation by wartime regulations. This I did in the evenings and at weekends. Joe never learned to plough. He acquired enough knowledge about it to enable him to answer a question on an examination paper.

We were having our usual Irish session with Miss Briody. When we broke into English I told her about my exciting day ploughing. Joe intervened to say that it was the most boring day in his whole life. He could have learned all he wanted to know in half an hour. On no account should a student be asked to plough. I was very fond of Joe and I knew that he was very fond of me. I switched the conversation. I said that maybe it was a mistake for me to learn to plough. Instead I should be learning how to drive a tractor. There was only one tractor in the station at the time and that was driven solely by the farm manager, Mr Hassett or by the assistant farm manager, Mr Maloney. There may have been other accessories for that tractor like ploughing equipment, but I was not aware of the existence of such. The only thing belonging to that tractor that I knew of was a small trailer, which served to bring fertilisers, tools, etc. from one area of the farm to another.

The Irish class with Miss B. was going well. Looking back it would appear that the Irish language itself was the sole winner. When we started in late Autumn I was glad to have Joe as camouflage. It was all very accommodating. Over the weeks something was occurring which was not altogether within our control. Joe and I were both growing fond of Miss B. She was aware of this and was careful to divide her attention equally between us.

We were becoming very proficient in the dairy and poultry runs, and knew what to do and what to avoid. One day when we were again assigned to work with Miss B., some time after the above discussion between the three of us on ploughing, she handed me a note and told me to deliver it to Mr Hassett in the farmyard. On reading the note, he told me that he had been asked to teach me how to drive the tractor. I was delighted. I sat up behind Mr Hassett and I watched him start the engine, change gears, etc. Then he stopped the engine. He got off and ushered me into the driving seat. He told me to turn the key. I did so. The engine responded and I found myself on the back of a shuddering monster. I wanted to go no further with the exercise. I got down from the tractor. Then Mr Hassett got up, changed gears and moved off. He stopped the engine and I got up again. I had got the message. This time I made no mistake and the monster moved off. Then I became brave and drove around the big yard to my heart's content. I was in seventh heaven. Mr Hassett signalled me to stop and I got down.

I was then told to hurry back to the poultry runs as quickly as possible. I was not on any account to mention to anyone that I had driven the tractor. He had only obliged Miss B., who was a friend of his. I had great difficulty keeping my newly acquired secret to myself. One of the greatest bonuses in life is to be able to tell good news. I should have thanked Miss B. when I met her. I don't know why I did not. I could not tell Joe. I realised that a girl had come between Joe and I, and that I had to treat the matter very delicately. I felt very bad about it as I could not afford to lose any of my friends. It seems a small thing now, but at the time it threatened to become a huge problem. I wanted both their friendships. Now I realise what kept us together was the fact that we three had a strong affection for one another. I was glad when the Spring came and the evenings grew brighter so that we finished up with the Irish class on a Tuesday. Ah dear!

I took a deep interest in the experiments that were being

carried out on the farm. Some of them may only have been replicas of experiments carried out elsewhere. One experiment stands out. It took place in October after we had arrived there. The Kerr's Pink was a lovely eating potato, which had replaced 'the Champion'. It started off as a great cropper. It was later attacked by scab and became unsightly. The experiment in question was a very effective one. It consisted of twelve drills of Kerr's Pinks approximately seventy yards long. The tubers had been planted 12 to 15 inches apart. A student and a farm worker were allotted one drill. The student tossed out a stalk of potatoes. Each potato was thoroughly examined. Only a potato that was scab-free and disease-free was permitted to go into the little carrier provided. Then the workman tossed out the second stalk and the examination began again. We did not appear to be getting anywhere. We had tossed out fifteen stalks before we found a stalk that had all its tubers scab- and disease-free. We had then only five disease-free tubers. Some of the diggers had got more. Some had none. Mr Delaney appeared when we were halfway through. I thought he would be disappointed. No. He quietly fingered the small quantity we had gathered in the carriers and departed.

When we finished we had not filled the carriers. The total amount for the twelve drills came to one and a half hundred weight. It was a small amount out of what was a heavy crop of potatoes. What we had salvaged was planted in the Spring. We were gone when the new students dug them out. I later wrote to Mr Hassett to find out how they fared. There had been a bumper crop. I have written about this experiment to show what painstaking methods obtained on these experiments.

Something occurred at this time which deserves special mention. The table I was sitting at was opposite to that occupied by the staff. In fact, Miss B. was sitting facing me. I made a special effort not to look at her. A boy beside me whispered to me that the entire staff was looking in my direction. I glanced across. I realised they were laughing at my expense. I concentrated on eating my dinner and left the situation to take care of itself. Next day I changed places with my friend Dan McGuire and I enjoyed the protection it afforded me.

A few days later I found myself again in the dairy. I was ignored by Miss B. for most of the time. I in turn acted as if she was not there. In the end she faced me down and demanded an explanation. I told her that I thought her table was having some joke or other at my expense and that I had changed places to protect my privacy. Then she told me she had got a lot of slagging because of my action. I felt sorry for her and in desperation asked her if I should resume my former seat. She declined my offer, saying it would make matters worse. We were friends again.

A feature of Ballyhaise was the number of clubs, both women's clubs and men's clubs who came to have a look around and to ask questions. A lot depended on what chore you were on. You could run into them or you could miss them altogether. On one occasion Joe and I were in the piggeries when a farming club arrived. It was having a look at the York pigs. There was a big resistance against the replacement of the large Ulster. Mr Delaney had a difficult job to fend off questions. Towards the end he was asked by one wit:

'When do the York pigs begin to wear spectacles?'

There was a great laugh. Then Mr Delaney asked me if I knew. I did not and I asked Joe. Joe caught the mood and he went off to find out. We got a great clap of applause from the crowd of farmers.

When visiting groups came Joe and I often found ourselves on call in the dairy and poultry runs. I think Miss B., who had been trained in England, did not feel at home with the country women. She left the explaining to the two of us. We were always careful to refer to her now and again. One day a club arrived from Grousehall. There are a number of Grousehalls in the country and I never heard of any club associated with the Grousehall in Mullahoran parish. I knew the townland in question well for that was where Paddy Lynch's shop was located. Joe was still in the dairy. I was in the poultry runs and I was given the job of talking to these women. I was startled when one of the women addressed me by my Christian name. I looked around and I recognised a certain brown hat which Mama was wont to wear. She was about fifty five years of age at this time and dressed always as a much younger woman. Shortly afterwards I noticed to my horror that she was conversing with Miss B, who was in full flight, talking to her. I had great difficulty in trying to answer all the questions I was asked. There were a few things we were trying to get across to the visiting clubs. On no account should fishmeal be used for poultry. Although it was very cheap meal and helped egg production, it left a trace in the taste of the egg. Some producers were adept at giving minute quantities which did not show up in the taste. We also emphasised how important it was to use clean bedding for poultry and to preserve the bloom on the eggs. There was to be no more washing of eggs. We were competing with Denmark.

There was a room adjacent to the poultry where visiting clubs got refreshments. I went in there too and I had a cup of tea and a sandwich with the woman in the brown hat. There was a glimmer of mirth in her eyes when she mentioned a lovely chat she had with the lady in charge. Afterwards when I met Miss B. I had to listen to an upbeat account of the day's proceedings. Then she mentioned her talk with the lady in the brown hat. I simply said: 'You were talking with my mother.' Miss B. put her hand to her mouth and exclaimed 'My God!', and ran out of the room.

In the Spring a slight flu hit the station. The fact that I got it myself precludes me from assuming that the students affected were only shamming. My friend Dan McGuire got it very bad and I was on hand in the ward to talk to him. I was now with a different set of boys from those of my dormitory. The House Master was wonderful. He it was who took our temperature and looked in on us to see if we were alright at night. The local doctor was not very helpful. He would appear to think that we should have got over the sickness on our feet instead of taking to the bed.

About one third of those laid up may have being pretending to be sick in order to enjoy a rest. More than half the students of the College were not affected. This included Joe Hanahoe, who was still on his feet. The kitchen boy brought me in a note from him to say that he was well and hoping that I would soon be out. I was wondering if he was talking to Miss B. I was relieved when I got a note from her. She said she missed me very much. It was a great lift for me. From that time forward I did not mind how much she talked with my friend Joe. While laid up in bed I had time to think things over. It was a time too when I began separating the beautiful present from the realities that lay ahead. Ballyhaise after all was only a moment in time for me. Dan McGuire turned out to be of great help to me. I found myself talking matters over with him.

Dan was in the next bed to me. Beyond him was a boy named Joe Munnelly. He had been with Joe Hanahoe in Mount Bellow and they were great friends too. Munnelly had a brother who was a forester. McGuire was very keen on Forestry and he could not hear enough about what was happening in the field. For the first time I heard mention of many of the forest centres scattered around the country, where a few pioneers were trying to get things going. Emo was mentioned as a school where young foresters were trained, but the name Avondale also cropped up in this connection.

I suddenly surprised myself by joining in. Dad had told me a lot about Parnell and Avondale. Munnelly had only heard of it as a place where beautiful trees from all over the world grew. To me it was the home of a great leader. I electrified them by telling of the man who had given his all for Ireland. Munnelly told us that his brother had brought him to Croke Park to witness a Railway Cup Football Final. There they had met a group of foresters who barely looked at the match. They spent the time talking about all the trees that they had planted. It all seemed so strange to me. Several years later I found myself at Croke Park listening to the same eternal tale of afforestation, which is ever new.

At the end of a fortnight in bed, I was feeling quite well. I was told I would have to remain another week there. I was glad because I was just barely able to walk. The Matron was exceptionally kind to us and we accepted every instruction that she gave. My appetite was still very poor and I appreciated the invalid meals she gave us. I was lucky. I became aware, however, that some of the boys in the ward were in a terrible state. Some who were supposed to be invalids were barely sick at all. They had been hoping for a few weeks' rest to break the monotony. They began to feel the pangs of hunger. To no avail. They would have to spend the required time in 'quarantine'.

Then one night one of the boys started telling what he had for Christmas dinner. This was excelled by another boy on the following night and so the pantomime went on. To the boys whose appetites were just improving, this was heavenly. The future looked bright. To those who were not sick it was a 'very Hell'. It was a time when strong men became meek and asked for half of another's dinner. It was a strange time. A truce would appeared to have been called and a little more food made its appearance.

In the last week of our convalescence we were allowed back to the common room. Several packs of cards were dished out and we were invited to play to our hearts' content. We played every game from Old Maid to Poker. The common room in the Winter and Spring was a heavenly place to spend a few hours and to speak Irish. Now, when we were recuperating, it was an ordeal. We were not allowed to go into the refectory for fear of contaminating the brave and the true. I felt an occasional pang of hunger during the last week of 'captivity'. What must have been the pangs of those who were not really sick at all? I considered myself a very good card player. I liked holding my own with the best. The last time I played cards was in that common room in Ballyhaise. I could not bear the sight of cards ever after.

I was glad to be on my feet again. I did not go as far as the 'Bo Meadow' to play football. I slipped into the ball alley and played against whoever I found there. I could feel renewed health surging up in my veins. The Irish lessons with Joe and Miss B. were over with the coming of the bright evenings. I still did my chores with Joe and was glad to meet the old faces again. I noticed that we were never called back to the dairy. I did not mind as I found the experiments very exciting. I seemed to be meeting Mr Delaney more often. In class I did my best to help him by asking some controversial questions. He in turn when we met outside class would sometimes ask me about the work I did with my father during the first few years of the Economic War, when times were exceptionally hard on the small farms.

Ballyhaise was an oasis after the ups and downs of the

Economic war. For me it was an introduction to how farming could be achieved in a working day from eight o'clock in the morning to six in the evening. It showed how work could be systematically completed in a set number of hours. Farming as I had known it had been from dawn to dusk.

We had given up making butter around 1925 and started going to the creamery. Consequently Ballyhaise was at first a complete enigma to me. Here, we were separating milk and making butter. A short distance away there was a creamery that could take the chore off our hands. Worse still, most of the pupils came from creamery areas where the art of butter-making no longer prevailed. Moreover, even where butter was still being made on farms, it was the girls of the household who did the butter-making. Hence teaching male students how to put in the correct amount of salt and water was no mean feat. This was very important as the salt and water could account for a considerable percentage in a hundred pounds of butter. It could be the difference between profit and loss.

Ballyhaise specialised in the breeding of prize bulls and heifers. The herd was pedigree. All calves when born were tagged and registered. A record of the progeny was kept. The same obtained for the herd of pigs. The retention of the new milk and the separation and churning thereof fitted in with this scheme of things. The young calves got their share of the new milk. One of the chores I did on my own was to feed the young calves. Each had its little pen. Each had to get its rightful share. I loved to feed and sometimes talk to the 'little rascals'. At times when there was no one around I would allow them suck my outstretched hand with their rough rasping tongues. Doing so brought me back to the days at home when I fed the calves before going to school.

I remember on one occasion there was a batch of young bulls to be walked out. A notice appeared in the refectory asking for volunteers. It was too difficult an operation for the College authorities to assign a boy to. It was better to look for volunteers. Most boys, including myself, would be afraid of bulls. My friend Joe had experience of handling bulls in Mount Bellow the previous year. He suggested to me that it would be an advantage to volunteer. Next day we both wrote our names on the blackboard. No one had associated either of us with bulls. The following day a half a dozen names appeared. Gradually, for fear of being accused of cowardice, everybody came on board. The House Master thanked us. He said it was the best roster for years. It was a test of the brave and the true.

Hanahoe became a source of information about how to deal with bulls. He had a great sense of humour and we had many a quiet laugh between ourselves. Hanahoe advised rubbing the animal's nose, taking care not to interfere with the ring or nozzle. Then when on your own, when out of earshot of anybody, it was important to have a small chat with the bull. Any subject would do, even football. You had to speak, however, in a coaxing manner. It was essential to make the bull feel important. Someone wrote on the blackboard: 'A soldier dies but once, a coward dies a hundred times!'

In fairness to the College authorities, let me say that all those young bulls were around two years' old. On no account were students asked to look after the older and more dangerous animals. It was an excellent training for any young man who went back farming and specialised in bull rearing. I enjoyed my walking out of the young bulls. I too rubbed their noses but my little chats with them are not for these pages. Little did I realise that I would one day become a bull rearer in very strange circumstances.

In 1937, Cavan and Mayo were in the Senior All-Ireland Football Semi-Final and it was arranged that it be played in Breffney Park in Cavan Town. Mayo had had a wonderful year. Hanahoe and Munnelly as well as myself asked for leave to see the match. Mulligan, from Monaghan, asked for leave, too. We were granted permission. A friend of Mr Delaney's, living in the village, was going there too and we were offered a lift. The snag was that he had later to go further afield after the match and would not be able to pick us up until ten o'clock at night. Not to worry! It would give me an opportunity to show my friends around the town and to bring them to my old digs where Mrs Cassidy would give us a good welcome.

We went to the match. It was crowded. I got nods of

recognition from old neighbours. Then I stood with my fellow-students to digest the game. It was a stylish display by Mayo. At times it would appear as if there were only one team on the field. Everything was going their way. Hanahoe and Munnelly smiled indulgently as they waited patiently for the game to end. It was a beautiful evening. The only problem was that the Cavan team were playing listlessly. I longed to hear the 'long whistle' and to repair to Mrs Cassidy for a cup of tea. Then something happened. It was like as if the entire Cavan team surged forward. Then there was a period of ball possession and 'wizardry'. Two goals were scored and the Mayo defence collapsed. Cavan went on to meet Kerry in the All-Ireland Final. Cavan won that game also but it was subsequently adjudged that the winning point scored by Cavan was palmed rather than boxed. The game was declared a draw. Kerry won on the replay.

It was an afternoon to enjoy. I was on familiar ground and my county team had won the Semi-Final. What better place to relax! The trouble lay in the fact that my friends thought they had been cheated. I noticed that the crowds were hurriedly leaving the pitch and rushing towards a nearby field where a meeting was being held. We decided to investigate. When we got there, we pushed through the milling crowd and came to within twenty yards of the platform where the speakers were getting ready to make their addresses. I was glad of the diversion as it took our minds off the match. A big banner was hoisted over the platform. It read 'Christian Front'. This was an organisation which was trying to get volunteers to go out to assist Franco in Spain in his fight to overturn the lawfully-elected Republican Government. He was being helped by Hitler and Mussolini. The Christian Front was trying to get the Catholic population of Ireland to help Franco out with funds and men.

The speakers spoke aggressively and were greeted with great applause. The fact that there were a dozen Guards close to the platform spoke volumes. Finally, a clergyman got up. He was an impressive orator. I recall he made reference to Owen Rua O'Neill in his speech. He seemed to be asking questions of those in the vicinity of the platform, and to be receiving answers which pleased him very much. Then, he looked in our direction and I thought he was addressing me.

'What would do?' he shouted.

'I'd shoot Franco!' I replied.

There was a great gasp from the crowd as if they could not comprehend what I had said. There were threatening shouts and then the crowd surged towards me. I was lucky that the band of Gardaí encircled our little group. The sergeant and his embattled circle edged their way towards the edge of the crowd. Then he turned to me and said.

'Who in Hell are you?'

'We are students from the Agricultural College,' I replied.

'Does your Superintendent know that you are here?' he asked.

'We got permission to attend the match and later found ourselves here,' I said.

'Well, I'll have to bring you all to the barracks where you will remain until I get orders for your release,' he thundered.

Then the sergeant arranged for eight or so of his men to go back to the crowd. He took the rest of his squad to shepherd us to the barracks and then marched us off to the applause of the crowd. It was a great day for democracy.

When we had gone a certain distance the sergeant took out his notebook and wrote down our names and addresses. Mine was the last to be recorded.

'By the way,' he said, 'there was a man of your name who worked as a clerk on the County Council.

'I am that man,' I replied.

'How were you expecting to get home?' he asked.

'We were to meet our lift at the Farnham Hotel at ten o'clock,' I replied.

The sergeant whispered something to his men and they went back towards the meeting. He walked in front and we followed until we reached the Farnham Hotel.

There he invited us in for a meal. When the order came, he told us to enjoy our meal. He then shook hands with all of us and departed. The meal was a hotel speciality. It consisted of fried rashers and eggs with a helping of boxty. Boxty, which has many varieties, is nowadays a rare item of food. I have described its preparation above. Its unique flavour of half-raw potatoes has haunted many an exile away from home down the years. My friends thought they had never eaten anything like it. They forgot the Mayo defeat and we had a great evening. They may have wondered at the changed attitude of the sergeant. They did not press me. I did not know why he acted so. It has always been a source of mystery to me.

I held my breath for a while after that outing at Cavan. I got the *Anglo-Celt* at the weekend. There was an account of a hostile group at the outskirts of the crowd at the Christian Front meeting. No mention, however, of where they had come from. The word 'student' would have given the game away. The friendly sergeant may have played a part.

I have sometimes been asked, because during my time as a forester I had dealt with workers from every province in Ireland, what were the workers in Ballyhaise like. Nobody ever asked me what were the members of the staff like. The workers were good. They kept to themselves to quite an extent. They were all skilled. The students in Ballyhaise had come from a variety of farms where workers were treated differently. Farm workers might live in their own cottages. If they did not have a family, they might stay in a loft or barn on the farm, getting their meals in the farmhouse. It was a period when most of the tillage and animal upkeep depended on manual labour. In contrast, the ordinary farmer nowadays does his own work. He may even have a part-time job in a local factory. Even though he sends milk to the creamery, he buys milk for his table in the supermarket. We only bought tea, sugar, flour and lamp oil. In respect of food, we were self-sufficient to a large extent, growing our own vegetables and rearing our own pigs and fowl for the table.

The workforce at Ballyhaise was reminiscent of the big squads I later encountered in Forestry. Unlike many agricultural labourers, they had to feed themselves. Whether they were paid more than the agricultural wage I cannot say. There were periods of overtime when they were probably paid more. They may have been able to buy food at a cheaper rate from the College farm and garden. I don't know. Or they may have tilled their half-acre cottage plots. They did not make friends with every student. They were very friendly to me. When working for my father during the Economic War it was terribly important to ask for all the members of the family. This happened here too but not as much as I would have liked. As the College farm derived from the old estate, which had been there for hundreds of years, some of the workers may have had links to that past, which I may not have comprehended. They were a friendly workforce.

One of my best memories of Ballyhaise is that of the haymaking. I was looking forward to see how the farm squad would manage the saving of the hay. We had a lot of wet summers in the late Twenties. Sometimes it was an uphill fight to save the hay. Our first task was to get the green sward off the ground. If the sun shone we just turned the sward and cocked it right away. There was always a welcoming breeze which helped matters. We considered that we were progressive farmers and saved our hay as green as possible. A few of our neighbours still waited until the hay 'rattled on the fork'. There was a constant fear of hay fermenting. We had one difficult hayfield, a rented meadow that lay along a river in Clonoose. There was always a heavy crop there. You had a feeling that rain would follow whenever the sound of the mowing machine was heard there. We had the misfortune to cut the five acres together on one occasion. We lost the entire lot.

We were taught a lesson. In after years we cut one acre at a time. Some of those acres found themselves making excellent hay. Others had to run the gauntlet and face rain and wind. How was hay saved in showery weather? Imagine an acre of heavy sward on the ground and a shower happening on the hour. What did we do? It would be nice to have six men on hand but four would do. The sward would be a yard wide and it would go around the entire field. The worker stooped down. He held one arm at right angles while he bundled two yards of sward around his arm. He placed this bundle on the ground. It was like a roll with an opening through the middle. This was called a lap. The following day, if the day came dry, you could turn this lap over with your foot and the bottom of the lap would now be on top. If the evening came dry, six of these laps were thrown together and were called a lapcock.

At this stage, the battle was considered won. You waited

for a good day and put the hay into large cocks. I was wondering what would happen on the hayfields of Ballyhaise. Nothing untoward happened. I should say that I was disappointed, but I was not. We had three weeks of brilliant sunshine. Everybody who could come onto the big hayfield came. Even the men in the garden came. I don't know the number of workers that Ballyhaise College employed. There appeared, however, to be a lot of strange faces on the hayfields. Extra hands were probably recruited for the haymaking. The workers acted as if there was rain in the offing. It was a real concentrated effort and the students helped. In spite of the mad rush the students were shown how to make hay ropes in the best possible way. The pace of work allowed for students, when convenient, to work with the horses. We were shown the skills of handling horses in more leisurely times.

I had a handy job. I was doing a bit of raking around the finished cocks. Something happened here which I found difficult to explain even to myself. I saw something which I thought was not quite right. I will not use his proper name here. There was a man of sixty who worked with me on the experiments. He was highly articulate. In fact, he had told me his life story. He came from a small farm. His wife was dead. His twelve children were either in England or America. He was living on his own. One of his boys was coming back to live with him when he retired. Now as I looked across I saw 'Neddy' doing something which he was not capable of. Ten years before the job in hand would have been an easy one. He was working a tumbling-rake with a very young horse. I realise that he would not last the hour. I went across to him and asked him to give me the horse and to take the rake instead. His eyes thanked me and I took over the horse. I realised I had a very flighty animal. Neddy had him making ten rows. I decided to make five. This meant that I was loading the horse to slow him down. The farm manager tipped me on the shoulder. He informed me that there were no students allowed to work horses during busy periods. He realised why I had done it. He said he would take over the horse himself.

Then the farm manager took out a bunch of keys. He told me to go back to the lower yard, take out the tractor and trailer, and to go up to the kitchen. I did as I was told. The girls there loaded the trailer with two creamery cans of lovely hot tea, a basket of cups and a hamper of sandwiches. I got a welcome cup of tea while waiting. I then sat up on the tractor and drove back. I had a great feeling as I drove along. I recalled being taken from the bench to assist the local football team in the last quarter of a particular game which ended in victory. I had that feeling again now.

Suddenly I became apprehensive: I should not be on the tractor. If it were not for the good nature of the farm manager in taking over from Neddy I would not now be driving it back towards the hayfield. I was doing the job that he should be doing. I had no alternative but to drive on. How was I to explain to my fellow-students how and when I had learned to drive? On no account could I let the farm manager down. No one must know where I had learned to drive. I would have to brazen it out and say I had been driving for years. As I was within two hundred yards of the hayfields I saw a tall figure approaching. Could it be Mr Delaney himself? In great fear, I stopped the engine and waited as the tall figure approached nearer and nearer. Then I realised who it was. It was no other than the farm manager, Mr Hassett. He had come to meet his wayward student. I got down and handed over the tractor to him. It was a welcome release. He was in high good humour. He talked of I getting him into trouble and of he getting me into trouble. I slipped into the trailer and in this way approached the hayfields. We got a great welcome. There was a cessation of work while tea and sandwiches were availed of by all. I helped to put the empty creamery cans, the basket of mugs and the empty hamper back into the trailer. Later at the end of the day's work I climbed into the trailer and stretched myself. I was on my way home to a much needed rest.

I enjoyed Ballyhaise in the Autumn. The reaper-and-binder had not yet arrived. There were two seats on the mowing machine which cut the corn. The man who drove the horses sat on one seat. I, in turn with other students, sat on the other seat. With a dividing fork we separated the falling corn into sheaves. These sheaves were tied by hand and stooked in batches of twelve. The stooks were protected by two sheaves turned upside-down and tied together at the top. These were called head-sheaves. Looking back, it appears tedious but we knew no better way and we were satisfied with what we were achieving. During the Emergency I spent several weekends cutting and sheaving corn in the Golden Vale and I thanked Ballyhaise for the skills it gave me. I had never used farm machinery before going to Ballyhaise

I could go on writing about Ballyhaise but I will condense the last two months of my sojourn there. I was enjoying the harvesting and the beautiful sunshine. I was tidying up a few bits and pieces connected with the experiments. Mr Delaney must have sensed that I was taking an extra interest for he allowed me to tabulate all the experiments. He was with me one day and I suddenly heard him addressing me as Thomas. That always foreboded trouble. 'Thomas', he said, 'you had a narrow shave at Cavan with the Christian Front. I phoned the Sergeant there to find out the details and I was glad for all of us that he took your part. He treated it as a joke.'

'I'm sorry that I created any trouble for the College,' I replied. 'I certainly did not intend to shoot anybody.' Mr Delaney laughed, shrugged his great shoulders and said: 'Water under the bridge.' Then he asked me to be more careful. Quite a number of people from Ballyhaise had been at the Christian Front meeting. They had been surprised at this protest by the College students. He had calmed the situation and had kept it out of the papers. I thanked him very sincerely. The last thing I wanted was publicity of the wrong order.

Something happened at this time which deserves special mention. I reminded my friend Joe that we had not been back to the dairy and poultry runs for a very long time. There was a time when we were there at least once a fortnight. Joe considered it was time to speak candidly to a friend. Now I realise that Joe, who was a good bit younger than me, was much older in the ways of the world. It must have been a problem to him, as it was to me, that we had fallen for the same girl. He was now in possession of a solution to the problem. He told me Miss B. was now doing a strong line with a member of the staff, a Mr

Hahessy, an accountant. I had done odd jobs for the same gentleman and liked him very much. I should have felt sad but I was strangely glad. It was nice to hear that she was with someone who could give her a good standard of living. Joe and I had yet to reach the stage when we could support ourselves. Yes, but it is so hard to let go!

When Joe and I arrived at the dairy we found the place empty. In the usual way we would have had some work to do to get things in their proper place. This was already done. We were looking at a fresh notice on the wall when Joe started speaking in Irish and I answered in that language. We were at the height of our fun when Mr Delaney, Miss B. and a senior official from the Department of Lands entered. He was on an inspection tour. He caught the mood when he heard us speaking in Irish. He told us that he could speak Irish with ease once. Now that he had no interaction with the language it was becoming a faint memory. I brought Miss B. into the conversation by referring a few problems to her.

It was a great morning's work and we were sorry when the inspector had gone. When we thought that we had finished with him, Mr Delaney returned and told us that we had been invited to join the inspector for the day. We accompanied him to all the different units of the farm. We were a big source of wonder to all the rest. We were also a big source of wonder to ourselves. The vocabulary lists Joe and I had compiled doubly served their purpose now. To our even greater surprise, we were invited to dine with the inspector. We found ourselves trying to eat. We overcame this when we saw that our host was putting down a hearty meal. In the silence, we all could eat. Then came the time for an after-dinner chat. It was an awkward situation with two students at the table. There were possibly things which Mr Delaney and the inspector would have liked to discuss if they were on their own. The conversation lagged and almost stopped. Then Mr. Delaney asked me to talk about the years I spent at home working for my father. I started talking of the men and women who had kept one another up during the Economic War on the little farms in Cavan, Longford and Leitrim. When I stopped talking, the inspector asked me to continue. That gave me an opportunity to talk more about those great people who were the salt of the earth.

My old friend Neddy whom I helped on the hayfield was often with me in experiments. On one occasion he asked me to help out a friend of his. To explain what I am going to relate I had better state a few simple facts. Money was very scarce in the wake of the War of independence and the Civil War. When the Civil War came to an end much of the very large Free State Army was disbanded. These soldiers had to be provided with pensions. The men in the IRA who backed the Treaty came under this umbrella. The anti-Treaty IRA were left out in the cold. When de Valera came to power he sought to look after the latter and where possible give them pensions.

At first it would appear as if there would be a flood of pensions coming down the line. As it turned out, however, each application had to be fought out on its own merits. In those days, many people were shy of putting pen to paper. Old Neddy's friend was one of these, although he was very verbal and had a world of stories to tell. I wrote on his behalf and got an application form from the Department of Defence. I decided to fill in the application form for him. It gave me an insight into another world, that of the Old-IRA. I discovered that he was not actually in the IRA. He was only fifteen years of age at the time. He had, however, been a dispatch-rider. The bicycle he rode was commandeered from someone who probably badly needed it. We needed the name of the officer who gave him the dispatches. However, all his contacts had been with the rank and file. Nowhere could we get the name of an officer who had dealt with him.

The applicant was sorely disappointed. I had to listen to him for hours before I hit on something which connected him with a real event. He related a story in which he lost his bike. He had been given what appeared to be an ordinary dispatch. As he cycled down hill, he saw the tailboard of a Black & Tan lorry turning a corner. He knew he would be intercepted, so he left his bike along the fence and crossed country to deliver the message to what was a sleeping IRA flying column. When he got back he saw that there were two Black & Tans waiting alongside his bike. He left the bike to them and went home.

I wrote up his story as best I could. At the end of the letter, I asked that the commanding officer of that flying column be asked to confirm that he received a message from the applicant on that particular day. We got a flattering response. The Department of Defence was not able to recommend him for a pension because he had not carried arms but it was hoped he and others like him could be accommodated in a future Bill. The man was in seventh heaven. He waved the letter on high. He had been recognised.

I could go on writing about Ballyhaise. The people I met there have long remained in my memory and so have those lovely drumlin hills. We were kept late in September 1937 to finish the harvest. To be candid we hated to leave. The classroom was becoming a memory. The common room had been vacated for the ball alley and the football pitch. It had been a satisfactory year in Ballyhaise. Quite a number of boys had applied for Forestry. They had all got through the written examination. The common room discussions saw them through the oral Irish examination. Of course, they had still to go through a stiff selection process where only twelve would survive out of a possible two thousand who had applied. I write this to show how difficult it was to get a job in the Thirties. I had no wish to go to Forestry, but I did the examination for the College's sake. Anyway, I was only five foot seven inches. I felt I had no chance. Most applicants were over five foot ten. It was an age when it was believed that a tall man could control a workforce better than a small man. We sat the Forestry exam some time before we left Ballyhaise in late September 1937. We would be in Albert College many months before we would hear the results.

Around this time also the Technical Branch of the Dept. of Education held an examination for prospective teachers. The employment offered was only a drop in the ocean. The numbers of posts advertised were twenty for rural science, twenty for carpentry, and twenty for domestic science. Thousands did the examination. The standard was high secondary-school honours. A surprising number of students from Ballyhaise got as far as the interview but only one got through. He was Dermot Dunne from

Tipperary.

Most counties had a follow-through scholarship to Glasnevin and the university. I had hoped that Cavan County Council would oblige but they did not do so. I would have to go to an estate garden like Mount Congrave, near Waterford City, to finish my education. It was becoming more difficult as I tried to reach my goal. Fortunately, there were five horticultural scholarships for Albert College. Hanahoe and I got two of these, which was another feather in Ballyhaise's cap. Joe was over the moon. Jokingly, he expressed the hope that there would not be another girl in Glasnevin to keep us apart. How very wrong he was.

Joe Hanahoe and I were in high good humour in that September of 1937. We would now be together in Glasnevin. There would be another year to think things out. Our friendship had been tested by the presence of a young woman and it had survived. By choosing someone else she had solved the problem for us. We were now in the last fortnight of the college year. We were already saying goodbye to the members of the staff we had met on our different chores. One of the students was a lovely chap from Sligo named John McGowan. He cut the hair for the students. Sometimes he was paid, and sometimes not. Joe and I made a collection for him. We asked permission to go to Cavan Town. There we bought a lovely watch. We decided to have a party and to make a presentation of the watch to McGowan. The rumour spread that a presentation was being made. It was something new in Ballyhaise.

Because Joe and I were in charge of the presentation some thought that the recipient would be none other than Miss Briody. We were very close to the gardener and spent a lot of time there. What better way to repay him. The House Master, the Matron, the teachers, even Mr Delaney himself were so much deserving of recognition. It was a relief to everybody when the presentation was made to John McGowan. In making the presentation I was careful to restrain from mentioning the recipient's name until the end. He was the most astonished man in the room. It was also an opportunity for me to thank everybody for a great year. As a stranger and a student I could say things in that room that none of the staff could say. Mr Delaney caught the mood. He gave us a very dramatic rendering of the song 'Bold Paud O'Donohoe'. He thanked me personally for promoting Irish in the College and then as an afterthought he said: 'We were lucky to have had you. We were lucky too that there was not another like you or we might have had to close the College.' I suppose he was referring to the incident with the Christian Front in Cavan Town.

On the evening before our departure, Joe and I went to say goodbye to the gardener. He had been wonderful to us. He had made two lovely bouquets of flowers for us. We thanked him and told him that we would endeavour to call back to see him again. I was about to go back to my room when Joe caught me by the arm and gently enquired if there was not someone whom we had to say goodbye to. I knew immediately whom he meant and appreciated the fact that he would not go there without me. I turned and kept in step with Joe.

Miss B. must have seen us approaching through her window. When we reached her door, it was wide open. We stepped inside. She was already putting cups on the table. It was as if she had been expecting us to call. When the tea was finished, we all sat back on the sofa. As usual she sat between us. Our flowers were on her table. We talked on into the night. There were so many bits and pieces of our different classes which surfaced and asked to be remembered. When we were leaving she handed us back our two bouquets. We remonstrated but she insisted and we did as we were told. We took our leave of Miss B. If there had not been three of us, we might have hugged, but we did not, alas! I never met her again, though I did meet a daughter of hers. She left a mark on me, however. In Co. Westmeath, where she was from, Briody is pronounced with the stress on the 'o', which is also pronounced long. In my home area our surname was pronounced as if written Briady (the vowels being pronounced as in diary). In Ballyhaise my fellow-students started pronouncing my surname after the Westmeath fashion and as some of them continued with me to Glasnevin and later to Avondale this is the way my name came to be pronounced in Forestry. In time I also adopted this pronunciation myself. Our surname is still pronounced as Briady in the Mullahoran area, but in more recent times some have added an extra 'r' and say 'Briardy'.

The morning we left Ballyhaise is better imagined than described. We were all full of fun, laughter and sadness. Most of us would never meet again. I had still the Mayo, Sligo, Donegal and Longford boys with me when I reach my local station at Drumhawnagh. I got great applause when I waved goodbye. My brother Edward was waiting to take me home. The guard in the rear van signalled that there was something to be collected there. We went to the van and found a small *banbh* (bonham pig), a progeny of Stanly James, a famous boar. It was a gift from Mr Delaney. I may have mentioned to him that we needed a change of pigs and he had taken this opportunity to do the needy. Also in the van was a crate with six Minorca pullets for Mama.

As usual, Edward's sole chat on the way home centred around football. The draw between our area and Kerry irritated him. He had been present at the match and was full sure that the winning point had been boxed not palmed. He was fearful of what would be the result of the forthcoming match. Dad and Mama were on hand to welcome me home. Dad was thrilled at the prospect of a young sow regenerating the pig herd again. Mama was very proud of her poultry but she realised it was a time to be generous, so she praised the visiting fowl. I mentioned that I had secured a place in the horticultural section of Albert College, Glasnevin. I told them there were five places there. Hanahoe, a friend of mine, had also secured a place. The news pleased my parents very much. The talk drifted towards events happening in the area. Mrs Dolan dropped in to welcome me back. Tommy 'a Park Smith came along. Soon I felt as if I had never left.

My brother Paul came in. He had been in Warrenstown Agricultural College, Co. Meath for the previous two years. It was a college run by the Salesian Order. Ballyhaise College, on the other hand, was directly under the Department of Agriculture. Paul was to choose Agriculture as a career and I was in time to choose Forestry. We both benefited by the interaction of those two professions. Foresters and agricultural inspectors often knew each other and in time people who knew Paul came to know me and vice versa. Paul shortly afterwards returned to Warrenstown to finish his studies. He became an agricultural inspector. We kept in touch and we were of immense help to one another.

There were a number of students from Cavan who had gone to various training centres. I was the first from the parish to have gone to Ballyhaise and now I was going to Albert College, Glasnevin. Nobody from the area had gone there before either. The word Glasnevin was linked to great leaders such as O'Connell, Parnell and O'Donovan Rossa who were buried in Glasnevin Cemetery.

We had been late leaving Ballyhaise on account of having to finish the harvest. As a result I had only a week at home. This had to be divided between seeing the Brady family at Shanvalla, calling on my godmother in Clonloaghan and spending as much time as I could chatting to my parents. Mama as usual was very attentive to my clothes. Dad reminded me of that day in 1931 when he had first brought me to Dublin. In his younger days he had gone regularly to Dublin, but had not been in Dublin since accompanying me there. I mentioned that maybe he might come to see me in Albert College. He would not promise but said maybe he might. He thanked me for all I had done for him during the Economic War. He was delighted that I had done so well in Ballyhaise. He may have been keeping more of an eye on my 'progress' there than I realised. He had lived in a changing Ireland. At the time I could not have known that I was to live through a period of much greater change.

A night or two before I left, tables and chairs were pushed back in the kitchen and we had an old country dance. Nobody seemed to care if it was against the law or not. I could not be let go without a sendoff. It is amazing what that little circle of neighbours meant to me. Most of the boys and girls I had gone to school with had already gone across to England and were employed in the munitions industry. My pal Pat 'a Park Smith was in the British Air Force. It was a relief to Mama that I was still in Ireland. It was accepted as a fact of life that the young people emigrated. I never visualised a time when young people would flock to our shores to avail of a better living here.

Albert College, Glasnevin

Albert College, Glasnevin catered for both Agriculture and Horticulture and was attached to University College Dublin. There were some fifty non-degree students in all. Forty of these were in Agriculture, the rest in Horticulture. Our numbers could be augmented by University students doing their practicals. We had our lectures with the University students. The Horticultural students worked in the gardens, while those studying Agriculture worked on the farm. There was only one female student doing Horticulture. She was a degree student. She was a daughter of Professor Drew, Professor of Agriculture. The gardener and his staff were excellent. There was plenty of lore to be picked up there. We also went regularly to the Botanic Gardens.

Our lectures on Horticulture were mostly given by the University staff and they were held in the Botanic Gardens. The lecturers made the flora of the Botanic Gardens their blackboard. They were of a high standard and I could listen to them for ever. We did not actually work in the Botanic Gardens, because they had apprentices and skilled workers of their own. There was always a spade, rake, or other implement handy and we found ourselves sometimes planting a shrub, sowing a seed or potting a plant under the eyes of a lecturer.

Sometimes instead of going down town on a Saturday we would stroll into the Botanic Gardens and mix with the visiting crowds. Joe Hanahoe had a special hobby of collecting leaves off trees. On the perimeters of the gardens where it borders the Glasnevin Cemetery there were a few lines of trees, some of which were rare. We were helped by an apprentice gardener whom Joe knew. He had a long clippers which reached up high. We used be like children enjoying the fun.

Only Hanahoe and I of the Horticulture students had an eye on the University. The rest were either seeking to work in the Botanic Gardens, the Dublin Corporation gardens, or the Big House gardens throughout Ireland. Hanahoe and I attended the Matriculation classes. They were also attended by the non-degree

198

Agriculture students, most of whom had scholarships from County Councils. After seventy years I have only fleeting memories of these classes. I remember that Irish was thought bilingually, with more English than Irish. I only remember the English classes because some of the boys were critical of John Ruskin's *Sesame and Lilies,* which was on the reading list. I have great memories of Hussey, the House Master. He was also a teacher. He interspersed his mathematics with great humour. I was shocked to hear that in later years he was confined to a wheelchair. I always think of Hussey and Glasnevin together. He was wonderful to get the debates going. Later we joined with UCD for debates and I enjoyed this immensely. Some of these debates were held in Albert College itself, others were in Earlsfort Terrace.

Once a week we used to go to the Corporation Market. There we got to know the prices of vegetables and fruit. As far as I can recall, we used go there on Thursdays. We enjoyed these outings very much. In those days the vegetables and fruit came to the market in horse-drawn carts. The produce was auctioned as it passed a certain point. I had often helped out with auctions at home. I was therefore on familiar ground.

What was most interesting were the women with their barrows of fish. I had heard of them in song and story and wondered what awaited me. We found them most courteous and helpful. Forty years later I had again occasion to visit the Dublin Corporation Market. I found that both horses and barrows had gone. In their place were mechanised vehicles. People I spoke to listened to me incredulously when I related my memories of the market. The past that was the late Thirties was completely wiped out.

While in Albert I received another type of instruction. In January 1938 students in Albert were given the opportunity to join the Pearse Regiment. Many of us joined. This was a reserve regiment of the Army. There were people in this regiment who were later to rise to national prominence such as Liam T. Cosgrave. We did a good bit of drilling, which reminded me of the drilling in the schoolyard during the War of Independence. This training was to stand me in good stead some years later.

The common room in Albert College was very different to that of Ballyhaise. In the latter, we had all got to know one another after a short period, and learned to accommodate one another. It became an area where we all spoke Irish or English as the occasion fitted. We had also quite an assortment of musical instruments, all borrowed from home. Here at Albert we had a large piano. Attached thereto was a notice board on which were instructions on how to treat the instrument. Joe Hanahoe could play the piano and when there was no one around he showed me how to play one tune only. It accompanied the song that went:
'They are tough mighty tough in the west,
And your trigger must be quicker than the rest.'
I practised when there were few present and in time became delighted with myself. I could not sing but had learned the staff-notation. My only acquaintance with playing music had been kettle drumming with the local Wolfe Tone fife and drum band. This was a step further. The Agricultural and Horticultural students shared the common room. At certain periods there could be upwards of forty there. About a third of them could play the piano. There would always be a dozen boys waiting their turn to play. It was a place to tarry. Everybody gave a short and sweet performance. That suited me as I had only one tune. Ah Dear!

There were about five different groups in the common room, all independent of one another. Eight had come from Ballyhaise and they had stayed together. Our group was known as the Forestry Group, because most of us had done the Forestry examination. We were joined by Jer Horgan and Dan Sullivan. Jer was from Coolavokig near Macroom and Dan from Com Ga, west Kerry. We were beginning to speak of forest centres as if we knew them. A year previous I did not know of the existence of such centres.

One of my great delights in being at Albert was that it gave me an opportunity to get to know Dublin again. I had left there in late 1932 to join my father in the Economic War effort and now in Autumn 1937 I was back. As we used say in Cavan long ago: 'It's hard to put a finger on it'. Dublin had changed. In Autumn 1931 I had been lucky to meet Eugene McGerty, a fellow lodger and a fellow Cavan boy. He had already been in

Dublin for a few years previous and had made himself acquainted with the greater part of the city. He knew a great deal about the history of Dublin as well as its geography. We both held the same political views. There was a General Election in the offing and together we attended all the Fianna Fáil election rallies, and canvassed for that party. It was a time when it was good to be alive: 'But to be young was very heaven!'

Now in late 1937 I was taking Joe Hanahoe around to see the city. We had half of Saturday and all of Sunday off. All the lore and history which Eugene had imparted to me slipped easily off my tongue. Joe was thirsty for knowledge. It is so nice when you have a good listener. At times I would stray away from Eugene's lore and tell of Uncle Pat's stories of the 1913 Lockout when children were imprisoned for stealing because they were hungry. I also augmented the lore I got from McGerty with other stories of Uncle Pat's about Dublin, concerning his time there from 1893 to 1920. Were it not for Joe I would probably have stayed in Albert at the weekends. I could have done a bit of study, read a book, or gone to the pictures in the evening. The task of showing Joe around gave me intense pleasure. Joe had the ability of asking the sort of questions which resurrected long, dormant memories in me.

Joe was especially keen to hear about the 1916 Rising and I brought him to all the places where the fighting had taken place. The G.P.O. took pride of place because of Pearse and Connolly. Joe lingered at the various places as if he could not get enough of the lore. As you can well imagine it took us a long time to get around. It was a sunny afternoon when we arrived at Mount Street Bridge. Here a handful of volunteers had held up a strong British force for hours as it made its way in from Dún Laoghaire.

I was explaining to Joe about the various vantage points taken up by the rebels when we were joined by an old man whom I thought was out of earshot. He had not been in the fight but had been a spectator. Better still, our circle of three soon became a small crowd. Some just listened but others had something to add to the old man's story. All seemed very proud of the part a few had played against the many. It later became one of Joe's great stories.

I brought Joe around to where all the big election rallies had been held during the 1932 General Election. In the years that intervened between the Civil War and that election, Republican men and women found themselves imprisoned for political offences. One of the slogans of the Fianna Fáil party in the 1932 election had been 'Release the prisoners!' After the election an amnesty was issued and the prisoners were released. McGerty had brought me to Arbour Hill when the prisoners were being freed. It was a night of intense excitement. The Gardaí Síochána were in an unenviable position. They had helped to put the prisoners behind bars. Now they had to listen to catcalls from the triumphant crowd. McGerty and I were at the prison gates. We were intrigued by the many friends welcoming their loved ones out. Madame Despard and Maude Gonne came along. They may have thought that McGerty and I were two prisoners who had nobody to welcome them. We found ourselves tapped on the shoulders by the two ladies and thanked for our efforts. They told us they were expecting trouble from the police and to get away as quickly as possible. This we did.

On another Sunday evening Joe and I were sitting on a seat in Foster Place near Trinity College. I was imparting to Joe all the lore I had acquired of the place. McGerty had often brought me there to hear various small parties talk to their followers. There was nobody there now and it brought home in a strange way how different was the Dublin of 1931/32 to that of the Dublin of 1937/38. My mind was crowded with memories of the past and I may have lapsed into silence. Joe finished his cigarette, got up and enquired if I was going to stay there for the night. I got up too and as I did so a gentleman crossed over from a seat opposite. Apparently, he had been observing us for some time. He excused himself for abruptly intruding on our conversation. He was curious to know who we were. I told him that we were Horticultural students from Albert College. He said that he was impressed by Hanahoe's fine stature. He was in a position to get him into the Irish Guards. This regiment was attached to Buckingham Palace.

Hanahoe thanked him. He said that he would like to have

a talk with his people at home. I explained that we had been together studying for upwards of a year and a half and were hoping to successfully complete the course in Horticulture. We had also done an examination for Forestry and that was another option. We would like to stick together. That brought the fire down on me.

I suddenly sensed that he might be about to offer me a job, too. He asked me if I had any clerical experience. I outlined what I had. Then he asked me if I would like to work on the clerical staff of the British Air Force. He gave me a brief summary of pay and conditions there. On no account would I be asked to join the Air Force itself. I thanked him for the offer and told him I would think it over. For the first time in my life I was being offered a job with a comfortable life-style. In my subconscious mind I was trying to hang on to Joe. If Joe went to London, then I would go too. I found myself telling this recruiting agent that I knew someone in the British Air force. He enquired whom and I told him of Pat Smith of bygone days. To cap it all, he knew Pat Smith, he said. We would have application forms by return of post. He pressed us to join him for lunch. We thanked him but said we were stuck for time and had to get back to the College. After a few days we received our application forms. Attached to each was a personal note of recommendation. It was time for Joe and me to examine the ins and outs of our situation. Our mutual desire to achieve a niche in Horticulture seemed years away. Was the bird in the hand worth two in the bush? Joe would settle for Forestry if he got it. My stature would, most likely, preclude me from getting Forestry. After a deep discussion we decided to part if that was the only way forward.

We wrote to our 'benefactor' telling him we were waiting for the results of an examination and that we would delay a decision until then. He acknowledged our letter. We realised that he was holding on to us. Joe and I decided to keep the matter to ourselves. It is said that 'a watched kettle takes a long time to boil.' And so it was with the results of the Forestry examination. The days passed into weeks and were set to become months. Then one morning I received a note to undergo a medical examination for Forestry. I was the only one at the College who had been called. The big men were astonished. I should have been ruled out on account of my height and now I had been given pride of place. Thankfully, Hanahoe, McGuire, Horgan and Sullivan were called within a day or two and we all had a great handshake. We felt in a strong position. We would be a group of five in a class of twelve.

I was sorry to leave the prospect of a life in Horticulture behind me. Why did I abandon this career? I had been hoping to get a scholarship to the University from the Cavan County Council, but it did not materialise. I would therefore have to spend a long time working through the various big gardens of Ireland, such as Mount Congrave, Co. Waterford or Powerscourt, Co. Dublin. I would have to depend on recommendations from all these gardens in order to become a County Instructor. What had seemed within by grasp was receding bit by bit. Doing the rounds of the big gardens of Ireland would not have paved my way to University, but it would have given me a secure job.

The advantage of having four comrades with me buoyed me up. They, however, were more suitable for Forestry than I was. The fact that there was a national effort to re-afforestate the country nevertheless fitted in with my political way of thinking. As the years passed I became more enthusiastic and the happiest days of my life were spent among trees.

I left behind me an Albert of many memories. Principal among these were the debates. For some reason or other I seemed to find myself placed always with the team who were opposing the motion. I often had to defend positions which were totally opposite to those which I dearly held. My preparation and research for those debates took me into hitherto unfamiliar areas. It was a training which helped me in later life when I was often up against what seemed the insurmountable. Among other things' it helped me to look at myself and to understand some of the people I encountered down the years who had different views to mine.

I had a week to wait until the day of my medical examination arrived. I had no fear of the medical test as I felt physically fit. I began to get lonesome for Dublin. I had just got accustomed to the city again and was accommodating myself to the many changes that had occurred there since I first saw it in 1931. Long before hearing about the history of Dublin from Eugene McGerty and getting to know the city, I had been listening to my Uncle Pat talk of his experiences working there as a policeman. Woven into some of Dad's stories were things he had witnessed in Dublin in the Great Exhibition of 1902. Mama had also gone to the Exhibition and often spoke of Dublin. In fact, Dublin seemed to belong to me and now I was leaving it for Avondale, Co. Wicklow. It would be nice if I could tarry.

I loved working in the gardens at Albert College. It was very relaxing. Joe and I worked together at the different jobs ascribed to us. When we were out of hearing of the other students we would lapse into Irish. On one occasion we had Professor Drew's daughter with us. We were actually seed-sowing. Joe and I were credited with having 'green fingers'. For us it was just another chore. For Miss Drew it was a nightmare. She had tried seed-sowing on a few occasions with disastrous results. Three of the twenty boxes were for her sowing.

I whispered to her that I would sow the boxes for her and that she should watch carefully what I was doing. Everything depended on detail. She was delighted. She said that she could hardly wait for the little seeds to make their appearance. It would be a great thrill to show off to all and sundry. She was about to give me a hug when Joe intervened. He told her that his friendship for me had been almost shipwrecked in Ballyhaise where we both fell for the same woman. She was fascinated listening to this story and mildly asked if we were fearful it might happen again. Joe said that we were taking all precautions against such an eventuality. Like Miss Briody, Miss Drew was a beautiful girl.

The day for my medical examination came and I was delighted to hear the doctor exercising his Irish. I rose to the occasion and all 'went merry as a marriage ball'. Suddenly he asked me to put one leg across the other. I did so. He gave me a sharp tap on the shin. I jumped outright. I got a fright and asked him if I had failed the test. He laughed. Then he showed me my result. For the first time in my life I had scored 100% in a test. I was delighted and told the good news to the others when I got back.

The following morning the House Master tapped me on the shoulder. He told me the Matron had asked to see me. I was to call at 10 o'clock a.m. on the following day. I assumed that she was going to congratulate me. One of my chores had been to flood the tomato glasshouse at five o'clock in the morning. It was a procedure at that time to water growing plants at night and has long been superseded. There was a good depth of oaten straw beneath the plants to absorb the water. On one occasion in the darkness I had cut my hand on the heavy iron doors. The nurse attached to the College bandaged it up for me. I had then to report the matter to the Matron. She had to compile a case history for it. Among other things I mentioned the Economic War. Her family had suffered from it, too. We had a great chat and I found myself going back to show her my hand long after it had been cured. I had not seen her for a good while. I was delighted to know that she had remembered me and looked forward to seeing her.

I knocked at her door. On entering, I noticed that her usual smile was missing. Her face implied that she was dealing with someone who had misbehaved. I decided to open the conversation. I merely said:
'I am leaving for Forestry.'
She stamped her feet on the ground. Then she opened up.
'You are leaving for nowhere,' she shouted. 'Listen to my story first and then you will not want to go.'

I was dumbfounded. I knew that it was beyond her brief to tell me what to do. I realised at the same time that she was trying to help me. Her face told of pain and anguish. She began the telling of her story. The boy she began speaking about was one identical to me with a great love of country. She did not say if he had been her boyfriend, brother or cousin. He was someone she had cared for, and he had been thrown to the wolves. She was trying to ensure that I would not suffer the same fate.

The boy in question had gone to the University and had come away with singular honours. He was nationally-orientated and decided to attach himself to the emerging Forestry Division.

He became a paymaster. On one occasion he found that his books did not balance. There was a gap of twelve pounds. He could have got the money from home. He decided that the money would show up sooner or later. He let the matter run. There was a snap inspection. He was sacked and brought to court. He escaped being jailed by paying the money. The departmental officer giving evidence said that the defendant had achieved rapid promotion during his short period of service. The judge asked what was the difference between his salary at entrance and his salary at departure. The answer was one pound. The judge threw up his hands in disgust.

At this stage I knew that the Matron had exhausted herself. I thanked her and quietly left the room. I did not know what to do with the information. I assumed that the man who did the snap inspection had to go by the book. He had to report the matter. The small sum involved suggested that this young man had been shafted. I had no way of knowing the truth of the matter. I decided not to tell the other Forestry boys for a day or two. The matter was decided for me. The House Master again tapped me on the shoulder. I went again to the Matron's office. I met a different person. She apologised for her behaviour. She told me to do what I felt was best. I thanked her again for telling me her story. I told her it would place me on the alert and might come in handy if any 'wolf' came my way.

I was the only boy who got a clean bill of health. The others, who were stronger than me, had problems with their teeth, which had to be attended to. They got a bit of banter from the rest of the students about this. The rumour spread that they would have a mixture of leaves and timber for their meals. I was called to go on the morrow but I hated to go on my own. I asked the House Master if I could wait until one of my comrades was ready. I had become friendly with him during the debates and he supplied me with an excuse for delaying.

Dan McGuire, who had been with me in Ballyhaise, and was now an Agricultural student in Albert, was the next to be ready. I was delighted. Dan was a great *Gaeilgeoir* and had acquired an amount of knowledge about the various forest centres around the country. He was very articulate. His manner of joining any group who were having a discussion was famous. His formula was 'Who, What, Where and When?' He was very good-looking. He was around the six foot and his massive black wiry hair gave him a few inches extra. He certainly caught the eye. Dan and I would be the first of the new junior trainees to enter Avondale. There we would be meeting third-year students. The second-year students were already dispersed to various forest centres throughout the country for their practical year.

Our group would appear to have been a special group. We should have been recruited the previous October and now it was the month of March. We would only have to do a six-months course for our first year of training. The entry age had been eighteen to twenty one years. Now, it had been extended to twenty five. This was done to attract students who might have been in agricultural schemes and who had acquired expertise that might be useful in Forestry. I myself was twenty four and a half years. I was still wondering how I got in. The fact that I had horticultural, agricultural and clerical experience must have seen me through. I had yet to accommodate myself to Forestry. I had yet to acquire 'the feel for Forestry' which consumed me later on.

We had a bit of a singsong in the common room the night before we left. Only students were there. There was plenty of banter and teasing. Miss Drew was conspicuous by her absence. I was delighted that I was able to contribute to the entertainment on the piano. One of the speakers jokingly forecasted that I would never see a piano again. The mood was light and frivolous.

My life had taken a strange turn. When I was first notified that I had acquired a place in Forestry I realised that I would have a difficult job explaining my action to Mama. She it was who had initially helped me to identify the various farm and bog weeds. She had taught me the magic of seed-sowing. She it was who had taught me the wizardry of matching the various colours in the flower-garden. Now I would have to attempt to explain to her my desertion. I spent hours trying to write something that would appear plausible. On finishing a page, I would re-read it, only to tear it up and write it again. In the end I

208

decided to write a simple note. I told Mama that it was a bread and butter decision. The road to Horticulture had become bleak and unfunded for me. For the present I would have to shelter under the mantle of Forestry. In the future, God willing, I would join the ranks of Horticulture again. It was usual to get a letter from Mama by return post, but no letter came. Instead I got a letter from Dad on the day before my going to Avondale. It was one of the few letters I ever got from him. He was over the moon about my going to Avondale. Mama had been upset, but he had got her laughing again. He told me that he would love to be with me and to show me around Lovers' Leap and the Battery Road.

I said goodbye to all in the garden and common room. The House Master said goodbye to us in the morning. Joe Hanahoe arrived with a bouquet of flowers from someone who wished me well. He did not say whether it was from the Matron or Miss Drew. He left me thanking them both in my mind. Hanahoe was in a strange position. He was walking down to the tramway to see us off. In a few days, he, Jer Horgan and Dan Sullivan would join us. Until he arrived in Avondale, he would not know what befell us. He was half-inclined to come with us. We had managed to arrange to be together for a couple of years more, and he was reluctant to part even temporarily. I was glad when my tram came. What a lovely fellow Joe was. Had he not got Forestry, he would have joined the Irish Guards and I would have been with him in the British Air Force. And now I was wending my way towards the Wicklow Hills. How strange life is.

For a while Dan and I closed our eyes and pretended that we were asleep. How nice it is to be able to be alone with one's thoughts. I was saying my morning prayers and I said them for Mama. It is so difficult at times to fathom who steers the boat. I have a feeling that there is someone who rows with us. I was glad when we left Dublin behind. I had to forget Dublin when I was helping out at home during the early years of the Economic War. Now I would have to forget it again in the Wicklow Hills. Who knows but that one day I would live in Dublin again. When we left the tram we got on a bus for Rathdrum. It must have been a tourist bus for the conductor gave us a running commentary as we passed along. It was very entertaining and it answered most of the questions we might have asked. We were soon conscious that the terrain had become hilly and that there were lots of trees around. We had been told to alight at the crossroads beyond Rathdrum. We asked the conductor to help us out.

Part IV: Forestry trainee

Avondale Forestry School/First year

We had been told that Avondale House was a mile or so from where the bus would stop. We were wondering how we would get there. Dan said that it would be very significant if the Superintendent came and brought us back by car. It would be less significant if he sent a car to collect us in and then interviewed us in the office. The bus stopped and the conductor signalled to us to alight. We got out and looked around. There was no car in sight. In fact there was nobody there except ourselves. There was no cause for worry. We were probably a bit early and a car would come for us in due course. We waited for half an hour. The pangs of hunger told us that it was time to seek refreshments. We decided to go into Rathdrum, which was about two hundred yards, off.

We wended our way there. Dan drew on his store of information. He had heard that the students frequented Barry's Hotel. Accordingly, we went there. We were amazed at the welcoming reception we got. There we met a local character, whose name I think was Tom Dickson. He had a saying: 'Never a dull moment.' Afterwards we heard students refer to him as 'Mr Never a Dull Moment' and so his original name got lost. Anyway, he was very nice to us and gave us a free lunch. He confirmed Dan's report that Avondale students spent a lot of their free time and money there. Afterwards he brought us to a garage where bicycles were sold. He informed us that we would need a bicycle to get around Avondale. He whispered to the man in charge. We were given two machines on an installment plan. We were delighted that we would not have to start paying until the following month. The bicycles cost £12 each and we undertook to pay this sum back before we left Avondale.

We were now approaching Avondale on bicycle. They could keep their old cars! We were independent. The lovely Avondale House came into view but there was nobody in sight. Where was everybody? It was a beautiful day. In fact, it was the first of March. Everywhere, shrubs abounded and some of them were already in bloom. We rang the bell at the hall door. A maid appeared and we informed her who we were. She told us that the House Master and students were four miles away planting trees. The Superintendent was at a conference in Dublin and the Matron had the day off. The students had brought packed lunches and dinner would be at six. She advised us to go into the common room and to listen to the radio until someone came along. It was all such an anticlimax. We were both glad of one another's company to absorb the shock of our rough landing. We went into the common room and set about listening to the radio. After a while my thoughts were interrupted by the sound of snoring. I realised that Dan had fallen asleep. I turned off the radio and tried to join him but to no avail. Sleep would not come. My thoughts were long, long thoughts.

The sound of a door opening broke my stream of thought. A well-groomed lady in her late thirties appeared. I nudged Dan and he was soon awake trying to interpret the new situation. She informed us that she was the Matron. It was her day off. She had been golfing down at Woodenbridge. She apologised that there had been no one to meet us. She was about to have a cup of tea and she invited us to join her. We were glad of the invitation and followed her to her room. There we got tea and sandwiches. She was obviously struck by Dan's good looks and his mine of information on Forestry. She had been three years in her job. She was now learning more of Forestry from Dan than she had ever heard before. She began to impart her own store of knowledge. They were hoping to have a special class this time. The age limit had been extended to admit of older and more seasoned applicants. She had been told that there were two Horticultural students coming. Dan introduced me to her as one of these. She seemed taken aback.

She turned her attention to me. She appeared stuck for words. For some reason she was on the defensive. She became cagy and enquired if I would be suggesting any changes in the lay-out of the lawn. I replied that I considered that it was expertly done. She was glad that I thought so. She told me that she awaited the blooming of each shrub in turn. I told her that I had heard a lot about Avondale and had been looking forward to seeing it. Her face relaxed into a smile, and we started talking as if we had known each other for ages. A knock came to the door and the House Master came in. She introduced Paddy Verling to us and soon we were seated comfortably in his office.

He first asked us our ages. On hearing mine, he said that he was a year younger than I was. He had been in the service since 1932 and had studied in Emo, Co Laois. His class and the classes that followed, he informed us, regarded themselves as the pioneers of Irish Forestry. The present was difficult but they were hoping for a better future when Forestry would be given its due share of the national cake.

The House Master had been talking all this time to Dan. This was due to the fact that Dan was such an enthusiastic disciple for Forestry and could not get enough answers for his questions. He turned to me and asked why I was so late joining Forestry. I replied that I was being educated at Dublin but had been recalled home by my father to help out in the Economic War. He told me he had great sympathy for me. He had seen the effects of the Economic War in the different areas he had been in. In fact, the Forestry Division had been starved of funds on account of it. He asked me why I had left Horticulture. I told him that the prospects had become bleak and that I had come into Forestry for a living. He then told me that he had a big interest in horticulture. He was from Great Island, near Cobh, and had grown up close to the lovely Fota Gardens.

The little knowledge he had picked up from visiting these gardens had been of immense benefit to him in Forestry. When he came to Avondale nobody had to tell him the names of the various shrubs. He knew every one of them. Better still he had been able to discern whether they benefited from their then habitat or not. 'A fellow feeling makes us wondrous kind' and from that day forward I regarded the House Master as a man to look up to. He was to become a great counsellor and friend to me in Avondale. We parted company in the Autumn of 1938. I was not to meet Paddy Verling again for a number of years until we found ourselves married to two sisters. What surprises life brings!

I knew on our first meeting that I could ask him any

question I liked. I began that day in his office by asking him what the workforce was like in Avondale. He astonished me by saying that there was no workforce there at all. That is, if you did not take into account one old gardener (a Mr Breen) who had been there since the time of Parnell. He was the connection between the two periods. Later I was to meet and appreciate that old man. The House Master told me that the senior students had met the different working squads throughout the country. They were capable of instructing the incoming students about the 'know how' in Forestry. We in turn would go out next year. We would be sent to four different centres, spending three months in each. At present the second-years were in centres around the country. The system appeared to be working quite well.

I also recall asking him why Forestry workers had only the pay of agricultural workers. The latter had at times the benefit of meals provided. They also sometimes got several drills from the farmer to grow vegetables for themselves. Moreover, forestry workers had to work in out-of-the-way locations. The House Master said that was all due to political pressure. Not exceeding the agricultural wage had become a sort of principle. It would in time be addressed. I then asked him if workers had to work in the rain. He told us that most foresters were humane. They had an agreement with their workers whereby a balance was maintained by working a bit harder during dry periods. There was no official agreement on 'wet weather'. It was left up to the serving foresters to decide what to do.

He then told us that we would meet with foresters with different ideas. In fact there was a small minority who did not believe in a permanent workforce. They saw men as people to be taken on during rush periods and let go during slack periods. Fortunately, as the forests grew in size, a permanent workforce would have to be the norm.

I also asked the House Master about something that has hounded Forestry down the years. I had heard that Forestry always insisted on proper title to land they bought. This puzzled me, seeing that nobody could easily contest the state's title to land of this sort it acquired. I asked the House Master if this was indeed the case. He replied that this way of doing things had come from England. Then he told me that Head Office were fully behind the policy and did not want it discussed at all by foresters. He said it was one of the sore points in Forestry. In time we might get around it. During his time he had seen large tracts of land let slip because of the insistence on a proper title. During the Forties and Fifties, I myself was to see a great deal of land turned down for want of a proper title. The legal cost of obtaining a title was prohibitive for the farmer as he would have nothing left after paying the solicitors. The idea of a proper title for purchased lands prevailed during my period in Forestry.

In hindsight there are many other things I would have liked to have discussed with the House Master that day. For example, that farmers who sold land to Forestry should have been able to retain a 30% stake in their holding. Moreover, they should have been guaranteed employment on their former land once it was planted with trees.

The House Master stirred uneasily in his seat. He seemed exhausted after all the talking he had done in explaining the ropes of Forestry to us. Dan looked across at me. He was very articulate and words slipped easily off his tongue. He began by thanking our host for all his useful information and the many helpful suggestions he had made. He stopped and we were both getting up to go when the House Master raised his hand.

We sat down again wondering what was coming. Our host seemed at a loss as to how to introduce his subject. Then it came in a torrent of words. He did not know if he had any right to interfere in our private affairs. The common good was his sole excuse. The lecture which followed became Dan McGuire's party piece for many a gathering. He could imitate Paddy Verling's Cork accent to perfection. His usual smile would give way to a terrified look of foreboding disaster. Dan's performance usually brought down the house.

The House Master began by telling us of his early days in Emo in 1932. There he was one of a small class of boys who worked among the trees during the week and emerged on a Sunday to go to Mass. Nobody seemed to notice them. They were considered as ordinary workers. All that was to change. In the years that followed, Forestry was to become known as 'The

Coming Job'. The young foresters were all good-looking. Many of them were six-footers. They had mostly come from middle-class farming families who could afford to keep their sons dressed like gentlemen. This would pay off later when their boys would come into their own. Young foresters were now competing in the dance hall with the teachers and doctors. Young girls seemed to favour the foresters.

The House Master rambled on. We realised we were fortunate to have such a steering hand. He warned us against getting into undesirable company and to remember that the good name of Forestry was in our keeping. Later when Dan McGuire used tease Paddy Verling about his sermon to us that day, he would laugh. He passed it off by saying it was part of his job.

At this stage I looked out the window. There I saw a group of men cycling around a bend in the drive. They were coming in single file. The 'front runners' were approaching the College. I could see the end of the line. The middle part of the line had disappeared at a dip in the road and were beginning to appear behind the 'front runners'. Most of these wonderful men are now forgotten and it gives me great pleasure to record them here. They were among the pioneers of Irish forestry. I will now try to recall them to my mind's eye as they came towards us on that March evening of 1938. They all got down as they reached the Big House. They then walked with their bicycles to the left of the house to store their machines in a shed in the farmyard for the night.

The first were a group of three Corkmen. One of those was Denis Hayes. He is still alive at 95. He left teaching for the open life and never looked back. He rose rapidly in the ranks. He was also very active in trying to get better conditions for foresters. A son of his, like one of my sons, became a Army cadet. I have remained close to him down through the years. He and I joined forces in obtaining pensions for a section of foresters who had none. He was a man to admire. The next was named Joseph Deasy. He was a clever, colourful young man. At the end of the year he was awarded a travelling scholarship to Germany. He was a man who caught the imagination of everybody. He was especially kind to me. When I was stationed in Castleblaney in the mid-Fifties I would seem to have been a forgotten man. On his way from Dublin to a big gathering of foresters on the Shane Leslie Estate he called in order to bring me along with him. I very much appreciated his coming to take me there. He went out of his way to help me. He probably would have reached the top of the Division but death intervened. *Ar dheis Dé go raibh a anam!*

The third man, Donal Keohane, was from Bantry. He had a fund of stories. I never spent any time in Bantry but I have the feeling that I could make my way around there from his descriptive tales. He never allowed me to go near a barber in town. He insisted on doing the job himself. He had a cultured Cork accent. In the first half of the twentieth century accents were sharper and more distinctive than they are now. In fact, each of those three Corkmen had different accents. Nowadays due to radio and television all our accents have changed.

The next in line was Mick McNamara. He is still alive at 96 years. He too rose in the ranks. He did Trojan work for Forestry. He spent all his free time trying to get better conditions for foresters. He was a cultured man and came from Clare. The man beside him was Mick McCarthy from Cork. He was a deep thoughtful man of few words. He was a brother of Tim McCarthy, who was one of the great inspectors in Forestry in the early years. Mick is also still alive at 95 years of age. He is the father of Seoirse McCarthy who played a big part in the Coillte era of Forestry. My late friend Jimmy Donoghue of Portlaw forest was forever talking of Mick. They had both worked in Wicklow forests.

The next bunch that came into view were from Mayo. Their names were Frank Gennings, Bill Barrett and Patrick Kelly. They were all from the same Christian Brothers school in Ballinrobe. They certainly attracted our attention. They were Honours Leaving Cert students. They should in the ordinary way have gone for the civil service or teaching. The fact that they had come into Forestry augured well for the future. They were the first group of students from a Christian Brothers school, outside of Dublin, I had encountered. They were crazy about sylviculture. Patrick Kelly was a great violinist or, should I say, he was forever playing the violin in the common room. I was very fond of music myself and had a secret ambition one day to learn the art of fiddle playing. Our townland of Callanagh was where the renowned Belfast traditional musician Sean McGuire's father came from.

I became very great with Patrick Kelly. He loved to play classical music. If I was around he permitted himself to descend into traditional Irish music. One of the things he dreaded most in Forestry was loneliness. He envisaged that when our training ended we would find ourselves among the hills with nobody to talk to other than the workforce. How right he was. I myself had the privilege to work in four mountain areas: the Slieve Aughty Mountains in Galway, the Slieve Blooms in Laois/Offaly, the Comeraghs in Waterford and Slievenamon in Tipperary. On occasions I often found myself miles away from anybody. In fact, there were times of my life when I said more prayers on mountains than in church.

The next group consisted of two Donegal men, John Boyce and Con Curran. They came from Diocesan Schools. They were very interested in the Cavan style of football. They asked me more questions than I had answers for. They were very skilled and later imparted to me a lot of Forestry lore they had learned when on their year around the country. They may have felt isolated, seeing that Donegal is so far away from the rest of the country. Their accents seemed to cut the air.

The last two cyclists were Nick Devereux, a local man, and Mike Dooley from Galway. They were both very interesting characters. Mike had a fund of stories of what befell him when he was on his second year around the country. Nobody listening to him seemed to believe him. Nowadays I am not quite sure whether to believe him or not. His tales could have happened. Nick Devereux came from a mile or so away from Avondale. He never invited anybody to his home, keeping his Forestry life and his home life in different compartments. His mother ran a guesthouse. I got married during the War years and found it difficult to get a hotel to honeymoon in. Nick came to my rescue and I have great memories of him and his family.

The above is a brief glance at the men I met on that

March evening in 1938, which is more than seventy years ago. They each deserve a book. Unfortunately, I have left it too late. I must finish my own book first.

Dan and I thanked the House Master for his information and kindness. We moved towards the refectory. The pangs of pent-up hunger were asking to be assuaged. There were two sections: one for the seniors and one for the juniors. The House Master had a table to himself at the top. The seniors had already filled their seats. They were ravenous for food after an afternoon of planting trees. Although hungry, their eyes were upon the new recruits. Dan was conscious of their stares. He seated himself with his back towards them and he indicated to me to do the same. Dan told me that he had heard great stories of where seniors had interviewed juniors for the fun of it. He said we would probably be assailed after dinner. He asked me to leave the matter to him. Several of the seniors approached me after dinner for an interview. I told them that they would have to go through Dan. He in turn informed them that our leaders had not yet turned up. He asked them to await till they came. All their plans for fun and enslavement had gone awry. Instead of going to the common room, Dan and I went for a walk among the beautiful shrubs that were everywhere.

Parnell had adorned his estate with every tree and shrub that could grow there. One wondered how he could ever leave such an enchanting place. But then his country called! Dan usually did the talking but he was a keen listener on that March evening in 1938. All that Dad had told me about Parnell and Avondale rose in my throat and asked to be remembered. In fact, I almost forgot that Dan was by my side. We lost track of time. The ringing of a bell indicated that it was time to go to bed. Accordingly, we returned to the house. We were assigned one of the rooms reserved for the juniors.

We were down early next morning to get our breakfast. The senior group were already there. These were all fitted out in their working clothes. Apparently they were going out planting trees again. What we did not know at the time was that they had to be at their posts at a certain time. We were to hear that later on. The House Master told Dan and me that we were to sow seeds for the Matron. The rest of the juniors were coming on the morrow. We were glad to hear this as it included Jer Horgan, Joe Hanahoe and Dan Sullivan from Albert College. In fact we were longing to see our friends.

We had a very relaxing day with the Matron. She loved flowers. She had not a flower-garden as such. Her flowers were scattered in odd corners here and there. This had a charm all of its own. She lamented that her plants were not all together. I assured her that the present arrangement had a lot to recommend it. She allowed us to do as we pleased. I asked her to remain and she did for a while. It was a great day. I cannot remember how many cups of tea were brought out to revive us. It was a day that sticks out in my mind.

We had a lunch in the middle of the day in the refectory. The senior students were planting in Connery, which was four miles away. The place was very quiet. You could hear a pin drop there. We were never to be afforded the pleasure again. Our memories of the refectory were of loud noise and laughter. After we finished working for the Matron we had to await the arrival of the seniors. On passing by the bicycle shed, Dan remarked that he could not see our new bikes. I had never visualised that our bikes could be stolen. I looked at Dan and I saw him point to two decrepit machines that had seen many a Winter. I slowly realised that our machines were out at the planting area. Not to bother! They would come home and all would be well again.

Dan, however, had other ideas. He saw that we had to take a stand on the matter. He asked me to leave things in his hands. To me it was a trifling offence and I had decided not to record the incident in my book. Because of what ensued, I have to. I will, however, take the liberty of not mentioning names. We waited at the bicycle shed. I saw the first half-dozen riders coming towards us. Right enough, two new machines were in front and were glistening in the evening sun. One of the riders had taken his hands off the handlebars and was behaving as if he was in a circus. He was in seventh heaven when a bloodcurdling yell rent the air: 'Get off my bloody bike!'

I realised that I had to support Dan, so I walked up to the rider of the machine and asked for an explanation. It is very hard to relate what happened. The remainder of the riders had now come on the scene. One of them, who appeared to be the leader, asked us if we had given permission to anybody to take our bikes. We retorted that we had not. Then we heard him say: 'This is an internal matter.'

At first it was only the leader who was doing the 'tongue thrashing'. He was then joined by all and sundry. In no uncertain terms they all implied that they had been greatly let down. In fact, I was beginning to feel sorry for the poor devils who had stepped out of line. I was about to say that it did not really matter when I caught Dan's eye. He signalled to me that we should move towards the refectory, which we did. The incident expresses more than anything else the Forestry of the period. We closed ranks against outsiders and stood up for one another, but Devil take the man for whom we had to tell lies! He found himself on his own.

Dan and I took our seats in the refectory. This time we did not bother to sit with our backs to the seniors. As the seniors came in, they each in turn came to us and apologised for the misuse of our bikes. Dan whispered to me that he was sorry that he had bothered. The incident showed that there was a strict code there. We ourselves would need 'to watch our step'. It was an evening to remember. The seniors did one of their plays for us. They said they looked forward to our group doing something similar. I mentioned that we had not attempted drama in Albert but that we had had several debates. It gave us an interaction with the University. We would like to do something similar in Avondale. I was astonished at the cool reception that my suggestion got. I was later to learn the reason.

Next morning we found ourselves in the classroom. Dan and I felt ourselves dwarfed by all the sylviculture around us. Every British colony was represented. Each colony had a separate press. Apparently, forestry had been a special care of the colonisers. I could well understand that the extensive forests in the colonies were waiting to be exploited. They were a gift from Heaven, one of the fruits of conquest to be plucked. The cleared land could then be used for other purposes. It was one of my first insights into one of the motivating factors that went to make the

Empire.

The door opened and our Superintendent made his entry. He was a Scotsman, very good-looking, with a becoming moustache and his eyes met ours in turn as he introduced himself. He was carrying a file. He asked us our names as he checked the details. Obviously, he knew more about us than we did about ourselves. He then told us that he was Alistair Grant. He had seen service in Scotland, England and the colonies. You very quickly got to know that his love was for Scotland. Instead of using the word 'Yes' he would say 'Ach aye'. In fact, in later years we were to hear of him spoken of as 'Mr Ach Aye'. He was a very good teacher and did his best for his students. He was also a Catholic, which was rare among the foreigners who helped us in the early years in Forestry. He asked us to leave our seats and accompany him around the various colonial presses. These contained immense detail of Britain's effort to promote and exploit forestry in the different countries of the Empire.

He then brought us to the press representing Ireland. Here, the tale was woeful. Most of our big estates had been gutted to supply material for the trenches in the Great War. Many estates had already been divided among surrounding farmers. Portions of these estates had been allotted to Forestry. It was on these former estate lands that re-afforestation was taking place. We then went outdoors. I suppose he was trying to find out what knowledge we had acquired of Forestry. We already had the names of the trees and most of the shrubs. We listened avidly to the details he filled in.

He then told us that he was detailing us to meet the remainder of the junior students who would be alighting off the bus at Rathdrum in the afternoon. He had already phoned Barry's Hotel. We were to take the students there. Afterwards Mr Dickson would accompany us to the garage where each would be fitted out with a bicycle. We felt very important in being asked to carry out this task. We went towards the refectory. There we met the Matron who told us that preparation had to be made for a dinner for twenty five.

We were at the Rathdrum cross ten minutes before the arrival of the Dublin bus. Naturally we were anxious to meet

Hanahoe, Horgan and Sullivan and to give them the 'lie of the land'. There would be other students bound for Avondale travelling on the same bus whom we did not know. We felt a thrill of excitement as we awaited the arrival of the bus.

The bus came and Hanahoe, Horgan and Sullivan hopped out. With the help of the driver they extracted their luggage, which in those days used be stored on a roof-rack at the rear of the bus. Three other men alighted, got their cases, and went over to sit on an earthen ditch. They were evidently waiting for some car to come along to take them to their destination. They would appear not to have noticed one another in the bus. Now they were in close proximity to one another. It was only a question of time before they would discover that they had a common purpose. Two of them were already talking. The third was looking in their direction. He appeared to have difficulty in making up his mind if they were also Avondale students. Dan suggested to me that I go across to the two men. He would look after the loner. Accordingly, I went across. I said: 'I am from Avondale Forestry School. Are you Forestry students?' They were both big men and seemed delighted with the question. One of them said:

'Yes. Are you one of the staff?'

'No,' I replied. 'I am a student. I came two days ago.'

I was taken aback when one of them remarked:

'Are you not too old to be a student?'

'Maybe,' I replied. 'I am twenty four and a half years of age. I am within the limit.'

At this stage we all shook hands. Dan came across with his captive and introduced him as the 'Man from Emo'. I was taken aback when the Emo recruit asked me: 'How is Paddy?' I had no idea of whom he was speaking. Dan came to my rescue. He explained to me that he was referring to the House Master, Paddy Verling. This boy had known him in Emo four years before. We only knew him as Mr Verling and we would like to keep it that way. Dan got the message across to our Emo friend. He told us that his name was Mick Rigney. He had met the House Master four years before and had great memories of him. He had become very interested in Forestry and had signed on as

223

a forestry worker. He was eventually put in control of a forest squad. He was about my own height. As he spoke, he was getting bigger and bigger by the minute. He appeared to be a nice fellow. His acquaintance was certainly worth cultivating. When he heard I was from Cavan he became very excited. Cavan was one of the great football teams of the period. He was an admirer of Cavan football. He told me he was also a footballer and looked forward to playing inter-county.

Both my men were from Clare. One was Peadar O'Grady, who was to become a lifelong friend. The other was Joe Conway, with whom I had many a great day. While we were all getting to know one another, the Dublin bus from Gorey pulled in and two young men alighted. Ten of the junior students had now arrived. The two men on the Gorey-Dublin bus had evidently got to know one another. They were helping each other with their cases in a comradely, friendly kind of way. Suddenly, one of them rushed across and hugged Jer Horgan as if he was a lifelong friend. In fact they were from the same parish of Ballyvourney. Jer introduced us to him. His name was Cal (Ceallachán) McCarthy. Cal put flesh on the bones by telling us that he had been working for the Department of Agriculture. He had come into Forestry to see if he could better his position. He then introduced us to his fellow passenger, Dan Nyhan. Dan was a very good-looking man with a cultured Cork accent. He whistled softly to himself as he looked around. He appeared to be trying to accommodate himself to this strange group of Forestry students. He asked me my name a couple of times. Mine was not the only strange name for him in the group. He might have been pardoned for thinking that we had been chosen because of our strange names. He was a lovely, interesting young man.

We were short two students. We waited for half an hour hoping that they would come from somewhere. Dan McGuire and Jer Horgan started walking towards the town and we all followed. I was questioned as to why we were walking in that direction instead of towards Avondale. When I mentioned that we had been invited to Barry's Hotel there was a noticeable increase in our pace forward. The cases which seemed so heavy as they were tugged along had strangely now become light. They were now carried on the shoulders of the marching men.

We arrived at Barry's Hotel and got a great welcome. Tom Dickson was giving his best performance. Cal McCarthy remarked that it was better than he had ever hoped for. Never before had he got such red-carpet treatment. Tom asked us for our choice of drinks. His face fell when only three opted for pints of porter. The rest would appear to have been teetotallers. Worse still, four of the group had actually asked for water. When we had finished lunch, we were shepherded by Mr Dickson down to the garage where the newcomers were given new bicycles. They were delighted when they heard that their first monthly repayment would not be until the first of the following month. Cal thought that this was a bit over the top. Nobody agreed with him, but said nothing.

When we reached the big entrance gates of the Avondale Estate, McGuire and Horgan took control. They informed us that instead of riding in a haphazard fashion, we should go two abreast. This would give a more trained-like appearance if we chanced to meet the Superintendent. This we agreed to do, leaving about four yards between pairs. We must have appeared very orderly as we careered along. As we approached Avondale House, we noticed that the senior students were already dressed for dinner and were standing in the porch to vet the new arrivals as they passed by. They appeared to be enjoying the situation. They had their hands in raised position as we passed by to give us a welcoming salute. They saluted us and we saluted them.

After housing our bicycles, we brought our new friends into the washroom where we all gave ourselves 'a freshening up'. Imagine our surprise on entering the refectory to find two strangers sitting at the junior table. The 'missing two'. Somehow they had got there unaided. I introduced myself. They were Mick Higgins from Galway and John Ryan from Tullow, Co. Carlow. I welcomed them and told them that we would bring them to town on the following day where they would be fitted out with bikes. Soon everybody knew everybody else. Dan informed them that the seniors would attempt to give them a 'false interview'. We had a lot of fun and banter during the meal. The seniors put up a great wall of silence. When the time came later to interrogate us, we took it all in our stride. Even though the seniors saw fit to make fun of us, we gave them back as good as we got. The battle that night was the last battle. As a group, we stood up to our seniors.

The House Master informed us juniors that we would be in class the following day where we would meet our Superintendent. He told us that the latter was an exact man. He advised us to be on our best behaviour. Dan and I had already met him. The other students were anxious to know what he was like. We tried to fill in the details. We entered the classroom the next morning. To say that the students were awed by the their surroundings is to put it mildly. The big presses, each representing a colony of the British Empire, were very impressive. Each was overflowing with hundreds of books and pamphlets. Each colony in turn shrieked for attention.

Dan and I tried to tell them what the Superintendent had told us. We felt ourselves unequal to the task. The door opened and Mr Grant entered. He had his file with him. As he called out the names, the student named responded. He read out the details in his file. He asked each student in turn if there was anything to be added or subtracted from the file. We were all glad to leave things as they were. Then he asked us each in turn what part of the 'island' had we come from. The question awed us. We realised that we were in the company of a man with colonial experience, who may also have roamed the world.

His opening remarks took us by surprise. He thanked us for having chosen Forestry and for having come to Avondale. We were in a challenging situation. The country was ripe for re-afforestation with estates being broken up. We were starved for funds. The Economic War had not helped matters. There were a dozen projects, Agriculture in particular, which had a call on funds before Forestry. In fact we were trying to sell Forestry to the Government and the public. There was a great sympathy for us out there, but there was a feeling too that Agriculture should be given immediate priority. Mr Grant, however, stressed that now was the opportune time. The dust would settle down in a few years and our chance would not come again.

Alistair Grant was a good teacher and motivator. We

were all much indebted to him for the detailed knowledge he gave us of Forestry. The fact that he had retained his Scotch accent after all his colonial travelling was an added incentive to our liking him. We enjoyed his friendly eye while in class. We had to get used, to and understand, how that friendly gaze became a militaristic steely one in the field. We had to separate and understand the two compartments into which he divided his work. We liked him.

The next day, found us juniors out in Connary planting trees. We had four of our seniors to show us the ropes. The rest of them were in class. It was our first day at the coalface of Forestry. It was also one of the days that persisted in our memories. The House Master planted the first tree. He was a skilled operator, adept at using a spade. All the elements of planting were carefully explained. First of all there was the digging of the pit. The depth of this pit was determined by the nursery mark (i.e. how deep the seedling had been in the soil) on the young plant. When planted, the soil should be just one inch above the nursery mark – no more no less. The back of the pit on which the plant should rest was to be perpendicular to the bottom of the pit. The plant should be pulled under the spade and the roots stretched out at the bottom of the pit. Half a spade-full of clay was then thrown in. The foot was then inserted to press down the roots and press the young plant against the perpendicular cut. It was impressed upon us that this procedure was crucial in the life of a tree and was where success or failure began.

Our four seniors started planting lines that were forty yards apart. These were known as 'pole lines' and were indicated by stakes at each end. We were given the task of planting the in-between spaces. We all had five-foot measuring rods. There were seven lines to be filled in. Then we took a measurement from one plant to the next. We were planting five by five. When finished, the area would have to look perfect. You should be able to shoot an arrow along the lines uphill. You should also be able to shoot an arrow along the lines that crossed. I am afraid that did not happen on that bright sunny day in March 1938.

For most of the group it was their first brush with a

227

spade. I first heard that articulate man, Dan McGuire, using the phrase 'my first brush with a spade'. I have heard countless foresters since use that phrase in their opening remarks on their first days in Forestry. The House Master was on hand to help each student over this obstacle. Joe Hanahoe was measuring from the other pole line. The plough had long superceded the spade. Joe and I had been privileged to have met two Donegal Boys in Ballyhaise who had imparted the art to us. To them the spade was like a friend from home. No area, however big, was incapable of being controlled by the spade. It was a delight to see them use a spade. Gradually, I learned to use the spade likewise. Demonstrating to squads down the years the art of spadework has given me great confidence.

One of our seniors slipped from the planting crowd. We soon saw smoke issuing. Then we saw a blazing fire. Later we heard the sound of a whistle and we all moved towards the fire. There we saw half a dozen cans bubbling over with boiling water. Then we saw the senior students putting spoons of tea and sugar into each waiting can. It looked for all the world like a travellers' camp on a country roadside. Milk was then added to the brew. We were each given a large mug. The senior student had a larger mug still and he inserted this into a can of tea and filled each one of our mugs. The junior students looked at one another as if they were about to be poisoned, far away from home. Someone drank first and we all did likewise. The tea seemed strangely sweet. To hungry men it was a beautiful nectar which tasted like nothing else on earth. We had packed lunches, which were enjoyed immensely. We were having a well-earned rest when the shrill sound of a whistle told us that we had to take up our cross again. We got back to our posts and the work began once more. As we were all beginners it was not expected we would learn the skill of planting immediately. Attention to detail was the over-riding element in our instruction.

In planting, each planter keeps to his line and is always moving forward. In fact, this is a big factor in successful planting. On this particular day, however, all this was waved aside. It was a day when we were all learning the ropes. We showed what we were doing to one another. The House Master was on hand to settle all matters. In fact, it was a day on which he was able to illustrate how the selection of tree species could best be achieved by noting the weeds and grasses growing there as well as the texture of the soil. Some of us had a good knowledge of the various weeds and grasses. We were all inspired by the House Master's explanations. This amounted to a classroom lesson held outdoors. He took a fistful of soil and let the grains slip through his fingers. A worm slipped out. This put the icing on the cake for the House Master. We were planting European larch. In fact, this soil could grow anything. We were really impressed. It was a day when we all learned something new.

For me that worm falling through the House Master's fingers triggered some inner recesses of my memory. I had always been impressed by the amount of work worms do in activating the soil. This time, however, something startling obtruded itself. In many Cavan, Longford and Leitrim farms there are certain fields that are very difficult to plough. Using a procedure, common to all three counties, such fields can be prepared for ploughing over a period. We had one such field. It was known as the Sheep Field. I don't remember seeing sheep there. It was our highest field. It was from there that we and our neighbours saw Granard burning in November 1920. To begin with, the soil could range from three inches to eighteen inches in depth with a rock peeping out here and there. How was it managed? It all began in the farmyard. There outside the piggery, where a pool of liquid manure collected, a few loads of peat from the bog was thrown. This dried up the liquid. The resulting mixture was added to pig manure. The Sheep Field got an annual dressing of this. This was applied in wet weather in order to encourage grasses and especially worms. After a dozen years this became the best grazing area on the farm.

I recognised the area we were planting in Connary as similar to the Sheep Field in Callanagh. The pits we were digging were about nine inches in depth. In places we had the nine inches of topsoil when digging pits. In digging other pits there was only five inches of topsoil, the remaining four were subsoil. In the latter pits the roots stretched out at the bottom of the pit were in subsoil. The farmer dreads the mixing of subsoil with topsoil. The subsoil eats up whatever amount of farmyard manure is applied. I realised that the planting area had never been ploughed. Where possible in former times most areas of the country had been cultivated. Connary would appear to me to have been a place that was top–dressed in wet weather and only grazed in the summer months. Horses and goats would not have been allowed there as they would bite the grasses too close. The area had been 'nursed'. The worms had got working and there was an abundant crop of grasses to conceal what lay below.

I was wondering what I should do. I knew that the terrain would not carry European larch. I could not say so. The area had probably been selected by an expert. I was only a student, on my first week in Avondale. I noticed the House Master was moving along the line inspecting the work of each student. I hit on a plan. I dug out five inches of topsoil and put it on the right bank. I then dug up four inches of subsoil and put it on the left bank. The two soil types stood out in sharp contrast to one another. I had dug out four pits in this manner when the House Master reached me. He enquired as to why I was not planting the plants as I went along. I told him that I was in a dilemma. I had separated the subsoil from the topsoil. If I now spread the roots at the bottom of the pit, they would be lying in the subsoil. I was at a loss as to whether I should throw the top soil on to the roots and get other top soil to finish the filling of the pit.

The House Master was taken aback. No words came out and he seemed to be shaking his head as if he was trying to convince himself that he was not dreaming. After a few moments, the House Master seemed to have got hold of himself. He called the students together and told them what I had done in separating the topsoil from the subsoil. For the remainder of the day every student should do the same. We would then get an idea of where the topsoil rose and fell. The result looked more like a laboratory exercise than a field exercise. The House Master had realised that the area would not carry European larch. There were some ugly looks in my direction. It was a different ball game now. The separating of the two soils meant that there was a clean empty pit. No chance now that a tired student could slip his plant down at the back of the spade and go forward. It was so unkind to hungry men thinking of that dinner in Avondale five miles away.

To increase the mystery, the House Master rode alongside myself and Hanahoe on the way back. This was unusual. He generally rode by himself. 'What in Hell was up?' We were later asked what we were talking about. Our reply that it was mostly about football cut no ice. All was forgotten when we reached the refectory. We had one thing in common. We were all ravenously hungry. The House Master's table was empty. I surmised that he had gone to see the Superintendent. He came in towards the end of the meal. He told us that we were being given a break from the planting for one day. We were to spend the first half of the following day among the trees and shrubs. He himself would supervise the tour. In the evening we would repair to the study and write some notes on what we had seen. It was a welcome break and everyone enjoyed and appreciated it.

The day following our 'siesta' we were back in Connary again. This time we were planting a mixture of Sitka spruce and pine. Mr Grant must have gone out and checked. We were finished planting there a week later. I would have liked to have seen the results of our planting. I left Avondale in the last week of September 1938, and although I returned in October 1939 for another year, I was never to see this plantation in Connary again. It would be so nice to know how the two different selections fared. There have been so many surprises that I will not call this one.

We got a surprise a week later. Half of the students were being sent down to a forestry centre named Baunreagh in the Slieve Bloom Mountains for six weeks or so. Some of the senior students had been there two years before. They had hilarious tales of what happened there. We were all anxious to partake of the fun. I was not one of those sent to Baunreagh. Later I learned that the selection was made on the basis of the football team. Those who would be useful for the team were kept in Avondale. Those who were not were sent to Baunreagh.

The seniors appeared to keep to themselves. Perhaps, it is

not fair to criticise them for doing so. When we became seniors, we did likewise. When we went out the country during the following year we wrote and kept in touch with one another. They most likely did the same. This helped to foster bonds. We juniors in time became lifelong friends. The seniors either went to town in the evenings or stayed studying in the classroom. We became aware of an intense rivalry between them. They were a brainy bunch and all highly motivated. They were equally talented. There was a scholarship to Germany, which anyone of them could have aimed for. When our turn came, we had no such inducement. The War had intervened.

Soon after we went to Avondale the House Master brought us out to see harvested European larch that was piled up along a ride line. It looked lovely timber. Dan McGuire asked the House Master what they were charging for it. He informed us they could not sell it. If someone were to get it for free and have it milled locally, the price of having it sawn up into planks would be more than what he would pay for a similar quantity of sawn foreign timber. We were taken aback. Dan McGuire asked: 'What are we doing here if we can't sell our timber?' Paddy Verling replied: 'You have a country!' Foreign timber was at the time of better quality and more seasoned. The War changed all that. People had to make do with Irish timber. In time also we were able to produce good quality seasoned timber of our own.

We were paid thirty shillings a week. Out of this we had to pay for our food. Every week, one of the seniors went into town and shopped around to provide the food. On a Friday he collected the bills. Under the supervision of the Matron he totted up the bills and arrived at a total. This was divided by the number of students. On Saturday, each student paid his share. We had only been in Avondale for a couple of weeks when our seniors decided that they had done their bit. It was time for the junior students to learn the art of housekeeping. Alphabetically, I came first. So I was elected to do the shopping. I would be assisted by a senior, John Boyce. He was one of the seniors with whom I was very friendly. He remarked to me that it was an opportunity to break new ground. I informed him that I had been shopping since I was seven years of age and was amenable to any suggestions.

The first problems involved the eggs. The number of students requiring an egg for breakfast every morning would amount to fourteen dozen per week. With two each, twenty eight dozen would be required. We had to get twenty dozen at the very least. John informed me that meant going to several shops. There were times of the year when there were no eggs available at all. I suggested to John that we go to some farm and get a contract from them to supply eggs. This excited him greatly. He got a list of egg-farms from his fellow-student Nick Devereux, who lived a mile away. We went to one farm and were received with open arms. They were delighted to get better prices than those obtaining in the shops. They were glad that they had the future secured for them. Sadly, however, the order was too big for them. They would have to get the help of their neighbour. We agreed and the contract was signed. Then John enquired if they were capable of supplying us with potatoes. We would require twenty stone per week. This they were glad to do. They would also like to bring in their neighbour on board. I enquired if they used farmyard manure in growing potatoes. Their reply gladdened my heart. As yet they were not subservient to the bag of artificial fertiliser. Even the hens on the free-range farm looked happy. John told me that he could not wait until he informed the seniors of the events of the morning.

When we went to the dairy farmer, we had to step gingerly. He was already supplying us with twenty gallons of milk. He was generous with the measure and may have been giving us a gallon extra. I was tempted to ask for some buttermilk to supply a private craving. John did not seem to favour the suggestion, so I did not insist. We then went to the butcher. There we got a great reception. It was clear that we were his best customer. Everything was so clean and neat that it was out of the question to ask for a tilly. However, I suggested that we would like some bones to make soup. He was delighted with the suggestion and gave us a good supply free. We called on the baker next. He had never dealt with us before. Our bread had been bought in several shops which he supplied. We contracted at six dozen for a lesser price. He appeared to like the contract and threw in a dozen extra loaves in case we were hungry.

Then there were a lot of miscellaneous odds and ends, which the Matron bought herself. She provided us with a bill for these when we were making up the weekly accounts. She always came along and lent a hand. The previous week the costs had amounted to 8/6 per student. That week they were only 6/-. The Matron suggested that we make it 6/6 and keep a little money for a possible rainy day. This we agreed to. The students were more than delighted with this reduction in their weekly expenses. I shared the credit with Boyce. When someone said that only a man with a Cavan upbringing could do it, I began not to like the turn of the conversation. There are so many jokes about Cavan thrift. However, as the year progressed and some other students got the opportunity to learn the art of housekeeping, I was able to take a rest until my turn came around again. In the lean years which followed for foresters, the lessons in housekeeping in Avondale may have helped us to survive.

In Albert College, Dan Sullivan and I had been invited to play football for the University during the summer months. However, we had left for Avondale in March. We were now invited by the Wicklow GAA to play on their county team. The fact that Dan was from Kerry and I was from Cavan may have helped. With Kerry wisdom, Dan said to me that he would first like to see the Wicklow county team play. Accordingly, we attended two games: one was against Carlow, the other against Wexford. He was not impressed. To be fair, perhaps I had better state the case for Wicklow. Many of its clubs like Clash and Laragh had as high a quality of football as I have seen in Ulster. There were clubs such as Rathnew who could play physical and quality football as the occasion demanded. It should have been easy to develop a good county team from the material available. This did not happen. It was a county in a province of twelve, where there were some of the best teams in the country. They were therefore constantly experimenting with new players. Time did not permit of holding onto a given set of players until they matured to fit into a perfect team. In fact, the club teams played with real craft and teamwork; the county team did not. Dan and I decided that we would not fit in. In the event, we only played one or two games with the county team. We told them that as we had only a few months before being sent around the country, it would not be worth our while to continue. Perhaps when seniors, we might think the matter over again. We were satisfied. Life was too crowded as it was. Moreover, our great fear was of getting hurt.

As we came in the Spring of 1938 to Avondale, we did not spend so much time in the common room. We used often go into Rathdrum in the evenings but we also spent much of our free time on the playing field. On rainy days we would be in the common room. When people were confined indoors cards were played a lot. No plays were performed in our time there.

We did not have enough hurlers to form a team, but we had sufficient numbers for a football team. Mr Grant's house was close by. He had a great interest in shinty, which he had played in Scotland. In former years when there was a hurling team at Avondale, he would take his chair out to the pitch and enjoy the play. Now when we were playing football he would just walk around and go home again. We had plenty of material for a football team. The problem was what to do with it. We had great difficulty in stopping sensational hand-to-toe runs, which more often than not ended in disaster. Everyone seemed to be playing on their own. They were all so individualistic. In Avondale we did not play as a team, not initially at any rate.

I was appointed captain. Gradually, I got the players who were to be our forwards to learn where it was possible to score from. I myself could only score from a certain side and from a certain distance. I was a place-kicker and I knew where the ball should be to get a score. If it was not a scoreable spot, I left the kick to someone else. From sheer practice I got them to learn the basic techniques of scoring points and goals. I had to teach them how to get in range. It is so sad to see a forward movement end by kicking the ball into the goalie's hands. Nowadays a young player looking at television can pick up useful tips. It was so different in 1938. Then it was considered spectacular to pick the ball out of the sky and kick it up-field as far as it could go. It did not seem to matter if your opposite number got possession at the other end.

Those first months in Avondale were happy and satisfying. The juniors and seniors were two great bunches to work with. The House Master kept things rolling. A junior and a senior found themselves paired in doing the various tasks. The seniors were supposed to be teaching us, but sometimes it was the other way around. In Ballyhaise and Albert, I had got great pleasure from the debating societies. I was to learn that debating was taboo in Avondale. On no account would our seniors have a debating society. We were now in Forestry. Now we were working in a government job. Our duty lay in carrying out the orders that were handed down to us from Head Office. Private views about the rights of workers or the proper title of lands purchased were not to get in the way of promotion. Many already had ambitions of getting posted to Head Office. When speaking on such matters I found that the conversation abruptly changed to a less controversial subject. Very few, if any, of these students had the same conception of farm and country life as I had. Working on the Economic War coalface had given me values and insights which shrieked to be expressed. I found myself almost alone.

Also of great concern to me was the treatment of the Irish language. In Ballyhaise our common room was a place where Irish was spoken generally. In Albert, the Irish language was muted, but very active among a small section. Avondale promised a lot. Irish was prominent in the both the examination and interview for Forestry. Some of us were hoping that we would be able to do our work with Head Office through the medium of Irish. It was so disappointing. Many were well disposed towards the language, but in a very busy life as Forestry was it was better to put the language on the back burner. I found it hard to get anyone to discuss the matter with. The older foresters out in the country had no Irish and we had to accommodate them. The Agricultural and Horticultural Colleges employed teachers who taught Irish. Had Avondale done likewise, we would have been able to realise our full potential in Irish. It did not happen. Neither did it happen when the service grew bigger. There were big classes in the Fifties and Sixties. I am not sure if anyone complained except myself. Moreover, in the first year there was a Conradh na Gaeilge *timire* (travelling teacher) in the area. I saw him speak to one of our seniors, but he was never introduced to me or to anyone of my class. We sometimes went to some of the *céilí* dances he organised in schools at Laragh and Avoca, but never to classes. I had a lot of contact with the Conradh in Carrick-on-Suir in the Sixties. I would dearly love to have made contact with it in the Forties and Fifties. It might have made a difference.

I was like a fish out of water for the first two months in Avondale. After that the place and my classmates grew on me. They were an interesting bunch. They had all come from different backgrounds. Each had a separate life story. The Juniors were in two dormitories. I was along with Hanahoe, McGuire, Horgan and Sullivan. In the field we met with the seniors. It was thought that by pairing a junior with a senior for the different forestry chores that the skills required could best be imparted that way. In hindsight I realise that the fear of a possible accident also entered into the reckoning. In my years as a forester-in-charge I never allowed a man to work alone. There was always a big element of danger in the various chores.

Avondale House was a substantial house, but not a very big house as Big Houses go. We also had chores to do indoors. Mine was to light and quench the twenty one oil lamps throughout the house. These were double-wick lamps and one was expected to be very safety-conscious in handling them. When we returned to Avondale after our year out the country, electricity had been installed.

While the seniors 'hibernated' more and more in the classroom, we juniors often found ourselves walking into town in twos and threes of an evening. There was a time when I thought I could not do without my friends Hanahoe and McGuire. Now I realised I could manage just that. I began to make new friends. On certain summer nights we would find ourselves invited by Barry's Hotel to dance with their invading busloads of tourists. We were beginning to see a part of life that we had not seen before. There was no cinema in Rathdrum. There was a very good one in Arklow. They kept abreast with the latest films. We often went there. To do so, one had to get a late-night pass from the House Master. In these days when television and video have almost replaced cinema, it is necessary for me to state the difference between today and those far off days in the Thirties.

In the Thirties and Forties you dressed up in your best suit to go to the cinema. There you saw and met all the people of your neighbourhood. Cinema-going was a new phenomenon after the First World War. It put new life into rural and urban communities. Television would appear to have the opposite effect. Nowadays people stay at home and choose between the different stations. We are even losing the art of natural conversation. In those days in Avondale, students vied with one another in recounting the number of films they had seen. If you were not in that category, you kept quiet. There was a big difference of opinion as to who were the best actors. The male actors got little notice; the adulation was reserved for the ladies.

Some of our students must have been subsidised from home. They were able to pay for taxies to and from Arklow and Wicklow Town. The majority of us had to rely on our bicycles to get us there and back. We enjoyed these outings. We could always rely on the House Master to give the necessary permission to come home late. We generally needed an hour extra to accomplish the journey. Usually everything went well and we found that we had ample time. Then came the night when everything seemed to go wrong for Sullivan, Nyhan and myself. But that was not until our last year in Avondale. More of that later.

That Spring and early Summer at Avondale was one of the happiest periods of my life. I enjoyed walking with Hanahoe through the lovely rides. All the exotic trees and shrubs were out in open ground. The names of the less common trees and shrubs, as well as the country of origin, were given on a metal plaque stuck in the ground alongside. To me it was like being in another world and being introduced to new friends.

It was while I was in Avondale that the Economic War ended in April 1938. Its effects had been easing off for a number of years, but it still drifted along. I thought it would never actually end. I had read news of the agreement between the Irish and British Governments in the morning paper. Later that day I was entering Avondale House and I met the Superintendent, Mr Grant, going out. I generally saluted him and passed on. I stopped and said: 'You have won the Economic War'. 'How? When?' he replied. His face grew solemn and he said: 'We have lost our ports to you and we have thrown one hundred million at you.' He laughed and then we had a long chat. On leaving me he said: 'Ach aye! You certainly must have read the newspapers.' I was to remember that remark of his when much of the detail of Forestry he had taught me had faded.

I got another letter from Dad. He was delighted that the Economic War had ended. He had lost a lot during the years of its duration. He would have great difficulty in getting back to where he stood in 1932/33 and would have to start building up the business again. The last years had been helped by the young men working in the munition factories in Britain. The money that they sent home worked wonders in the neighbourhood. People were hoping that the deserted pig farms around Lough Sheelin would take off again.

He asked me to send him a map of Avondale, so that he could walk around in spirit and relive the old days. It was great that a man of his age who had been through the Land War and the Economic War could lift the flag again. We owe a lot to his generation. They had held on against the odds. I also got a letter from Mama. She was glad to know that I was doing well. She said that she often thought of the surprise visit she had paid to Ballyhaise. Avondale was that bit too far away for a visit but then miracles do sometimes happen. I felt that I would henceforth have to be on the alert.

Time seemed to fly in that Summer/Autumn of 1938. Our field work was a pleasure and our classwork was not too arduous. We could enjoy a dance at Barry's Hotel. We could go to a film in Arklow or Wicklow Town. Playing football became manageable too because we knew we had not to play to win. We knew that we had not the potential to reach the top. We were playing football for the game's sake, and had a great rapport with the surrounding teams. In fact, when I think of Wicklow, it is the faces of some of those local players that come to mind.

This particular weekend, we were to play Rathnew. We

had played them once before. We knew that we could not match their capability. They were a team who could play delightfully. When pushed, they could also be physical. In fact, that was what the Wicklow county team lacked. Rathnew could be physical but never dirty. We did a bit of running around the roads on the Saturday before the match. Sometimes when you know that you cannot win, you play your best football. We had planned that ours was to be more defensive than offensive.

Sunday came and we found ourselves on the playing field. We had our Superintendent and our Matron among the spectators. I hoped that they were not expecting too much. The game started and the first half will always rank among the strangest I have ever played. We managed to get three points but Rathnew got eight. There were no goals scored. We had a talk among ourselves at half time. The trouble was that Rathnew had a strange new player. He may have been a Guard who had recently been posted to the area. We had no player to match him. In fact it was hard to know in what position he was actually playing. Sometimes he appeared to be on the defence. Other times he was to be found at centre-field. Neither was he above playing in the forward line. We had a good goalie, who had saved repeatedly in the first half. We were fearful of what might happen in the second half.

I was approached by a Mr Brady at half time. He kept a shop in Rathdrum and had sold us a number of bikes. He had a great interest in our team. He told me that he had noticed that the Rathnew players were forever passing the ball to their new 'hero'. He suggested that we get our best player to intercept the passes. We selected Pat Kelly from Mayo. He was always long-kicking the ball. In fact, he specialised in drop-kicking. This was very important. When he had intercepted a ball, as he was a fast runner, he would be free of an adversary in kicking the ball to the desired position.

The opening of the second half was a dream start for us. With Kelly intercepting the ball, we got past the back line. Rigney scored three points. The game took on a new look. We were attacking instead of defending. We were only two points behind. We sensed that we might win. Our man Kelly intercepted a ball and sent it down towards the goal. One of our players was away this weekend and his place had been taken by our House Master. He was a good hurler but I had never seen him kick a ball. This time Kelly had sent the ball in his direction. The ball was rolling when Paddy Verling reached it. If he could get it into his hands he might score a point. Instead he kicked the ball with all his might and it flew across the goalmouth for about twenty yards. It was now running towards the end line. I was coming up on the opposite line and I had to make a big effort to reach the ball. I succeeded only just and tipped the ball back a few yards. At this point I realised that the goalie had left the goal and was rushing towards me. From the angle he was coming he had his goalmouth covered. To get past him, I could try toeing up the ball, obtain possession and try and slip past him. I had, however, left toeing-up behind me in my Cavan days. Instead, I edged the ball to the right and then kicked hard for the far corner of the net. The ball hit the post and was coming back towards us with the goalie and I trying to gain possession. I slipped and fell on the wet goalmouth. Something hit my head and I lost consciousness. I was later told that there had been a stampede in the Rathnew goalmouth. A goal had been avoided by conceding a fifty. Nothing resulted from the free. When I awoke, I was in Rathdrum Hospital with two nuns bending over me. I was in terrible pain. I had been trampled on. My right leg was excruciatingly painful. The kick to my head was only superficial in comparison. It was the second time in my life I had experienced real pain. I had as a boy been knocked unconscious in the school yard at home while playing football.

It should be said, however, being trampled in Rathdrum that day was not the only injury I sustained playing football on the pitch. Gaelic football can be very physical and rough. When kicking the ball with my right foot, I would often get a violent kick on the heel of my left foot. This was only once noticed by the referee. Years later when I was seventy years of age I was getting a hip replacement, I asked the consultant if he could take away the big prominent lump on my left heel. He jokingly replied: 'It took some kicking to put that lump there. Bring it with you when you are going. It might help you to get the sympathy of St Peter.' 'You cannot win them all,' I replied.

The hospital in Rathdrum was the first time that I had any contact with nuns. To me they will always remain as angels of light. Their soothing hands seemed to alleviate the aching pain. Present also when I came to were Peadar O'Grady, Joe Hanahoe and the Matron, Miss Devane. She it was who had brought me there with her car. I was told that the doctor had come and gone. I had no bones broken but the muscles of my right leg were in a terrible state. It would take some considerable amount of massaging before the muscles of my badly injured leg could be brought back to normal.

I was looking forward to a long stretch in hospital. I got a fright when O'Grady told me that the team had not been insured. I had always played under the protection of insurance. I was now told by O'Grady that I would have to go back to Avondale. He asked the nuns to show him how to massage. This they did. The nuns told us to come back once a week and they would be able to tell if progress was being made. I was given a pair of crutches to get around but O'Grady had to carry me on his back to the car. Later he carried me up to my bedroom. I owe a lot to Peadar O'Grady. It was easier to get down the stairs on crutches, but I had to be helped up for quite some time.

The House Master and Matron were aware of what was going on. The Superintendent had been apprised of the situation but the severity of my injuries were played down. I would have to spend a few days working in the office. He did not mind this as I was an ex-clerical worker. For him it may have been a blessing in disguise. He hated office work. He loved all that pertained to outdoor Forestry. After a few days he became a nuisance. He wanted to inform my parents. I asked him not to do so as they might be unduly worried. The House Master came to the rescue. He made a job for me in the nursery, moss-balling tiny eucalyptus plants. This was better, because I got many a cup of tea from the kitchen that was close by.

The Matron brought me to the hospital once a week. O'Grady always came, too. He had always some questions to ask the nuns and they in turn had some questions to ask of him. I loved the conversation which sometimes evolved into banter.

There was always a cup of tea to ease the throat. What delightful interesting women those nuns were!

I said my own prayers in the bedroom on the first Sunday. For the following six Sundays I was brought by the Matron to Mass in Laragh parish, where her brother was a priest. I would go into the sacristy there and through an open door I would hear Fr Devane say Mass. At first the alter boys were curious and they kept looking at me. I used shake my fist at them. On the second Sunday, they behaved themselves. I was no longer of interest to them. I had been a nine day wonder. After Mass I was given a lovely cup of tea and a ham sandwich, which the priest's housekeeper brought in to me. Many acts of kindness have been shown me down the years.

I left my pair of crutches in my room when we had class. I was trying to make as good an impression as possible. I knew that the Superintendent was considering what to do with me. After a month, I tried to cycle but to no avail. I heard that Mr Grant used still take a turn around the playing pitch. I imagined he was on the look-out for my return there. I decided to go there. He did not turn up for a week or so. I had never played in goal. That was where I now went. In fact, I could not have played anywhere else. At first the ball used slip past me on every side. Gradually, my knowledge of forward play came to my rescue. I began to anticipate the play of the incoming forward. From then on very few balls got through. Of course, I was helped by a number of eagle-eyed backs who took few prisoners. It was on one of those evenings that I found the Superintendent standing behind me. He told me that he had not expected to see such madness. I was to take things easy and do a bit of reading in my spare time. This I was glad to do.

I got a severe jolt during a conversation I had with Peadar O'Grady. He was a realist. He considered it unlikely that I would ever be able to walk the hills and mountains of Forestry. The fact that I was as yet poorly able to cycle augured badly for the future. Peadar suggested that I contact the Air Force in Britain. I should inform the gentleman I had met in Foster Place, I had told him about, of my present predicament. Peadar considered that I should keep this line open as an escape route. It was nice to know that I had a friend over there to help me. Accordingly, I dropped a line to London. I did not say that I was very disabled. I just said that I would not be able to do a lot of walking and cycling. The result was a surprise: I was being made welcome. In fact, I also got a special note from Pat 'a Park Smith. He would dearly love to have me on the plane with him. I thanked both of them and said that I was awaiting developments.

The last month at Avondale saw me improve very much. It is said that it is good to have more than one string in your bow. And so it was with me in that last month of our first year at Avondale. I appreciated having an alternative; a back door to escape if necessary. I came first in the final examination and I began questioning the seniors about the possible forestry centres to which I might be sent. I learned that some foresters out in the country were nice, and others not so nice. The day came when the big envelope came from Head Office detailing the places where both juniors and seniors would be sent. Soon after the House Master informed me that the Superintendent wished to see me in his office. I had a hunch that he might have bad news for me and took my letter from the British Air Force with me. Mr Grant was most charming. He wished me well on my holiday break, but he told me that I was not going out the country. Instead, I would be staying on in Avondale for the Winter and Spring. I could go out the country during the following Summer and Autumn.

The Superintendent appeared to be satisfied that he had solved a big problem. He may have expected me to thank him. He looked towards the door as if intimating that the discussion was over. I took the letter out of my pocket and handed it to him. I merely said: 'I am not coming back after my holiday. I am crossing the Irish Sea.' I walked towards the door. I did not look back. He did not stop me. I assumed that I was finished with Forestry. I would only tell O'Grady, Hanahoe and McGuire. I would quietly take my leave. I felt a little sorry for I had built up a great camaraderie with both juniors and seniors. This was another crossroads. I could expect more crossroads down the line.

I told the news to O'Grady first. He consoled me. In my

then physical condition I would be unfit for Forestry. I might have to leave eventually if I stayed. In his opinion it was better to grasp the nettle now. Hanahoe was devastated. He had looked forward to the time when we both would be foresters. We would always be in a position to visit one another. I was afraid that he might even come across to London and join the Irish Guards. I remembered that he had still an open invitation. I held my breath.

My encounter with Dan McGuire was still more disturbing. He reminded me of the great days in Ballyhaise when we had raised the flag for the Irish language. He had hoped that we might be able to do the same in Forestry. On no account was I to go among 'the Gentiles'. There were plenty of Irish people in London at the moment. There was no need to add an extra. I realised that there was two to one against my going. I had a big problem on my hands.

I got a lovely letter from Mama. It was a cheery optimistic one. The Economic War was becoming a memory. For the first time in a good many years farmhouses and outbuildings had been whitewashed. It made such a difference. Furthermore, the local boys and girls who were working in munition factories in Britain were coming back for short visits. It reminded her of the mid-Twenties when the comings and goings were from America. In spite of the Dance Hall Act of 1935, dances were being held in the farmhouse kitchens. In fact, she was planning to have one for me when I had concluded my holiday visit. How was I to tell Mama that I was quitting Avondale and heading for England and a job in the RAF. I knew that if I mentioned Pat 'a Park Smith, she would assume that I would soon be climbing into the cockpit of a fighter plane. My sky had become very dark indeed. I began wondering if I should go home at all.

I was wont in my spare time to do a bit of caring for Miss Devane's scattered garden. I owed so much to her. I set about removing all the withered flowers and uninvited weeds. Miss Devane must have seen me through one of the open windows but she did not appear until I had finished. She invited me in for a cup of tea. I was glad of the offer. While working, it flashed across my mind that maybe I should talk to her about my dilemma. It is said that if you have to cry on somebody's shoulder that it is best done on a woman's. It was so difficult to know where to start. I was really tongue-tied. Then I saw her smile and break into a gentle laugh. She merely said: 'You have not to tell me anything. I know your entire story. I cannot open my mouth. You are being taken care of.' I could only say: 'Thank you very much.'

I enjoyed that cup of tea and I partook of a second one. She was politically orientated and we spoke of all the goings-on in the Dáil and Seanad. She had a great sense of humour and she enjoyed the Mullahoran-Cavan lingo. In fact, we spoke about everything else except what was uppermost on my mind. She thanked me for my work in the garden and I thanked her for her kindness to me. I felt an urge to hug her. I did not. I was afraid that she might not understand. Now I think that I should have.

Both seniors and juniors were after their examinations. It was a time for fun and banter. Everybody was wondering about the places they were being sent to. The seniors between them already knew most of the centres throughout the country. The juniors had to rely on the seniors for their information. Then the dreaded day came. Both seniors and juniors walked into the classroom. High on the blackboard were chalked the places where each one was to go. I thought that my name would not be there. Hanahoe tugged at my sleeve. He said:
'Isn't that amazing! You are going to Kilsheelan and I am going to Portlaw, Co. Waterford. We will only be fifteen miles or so apart. We will be able to meet once a week.'
I found it hard to take it in. For me the best part of it was that I would not have to tell Mama that I was going abroad.

Everyone felt very friendly towards one another. All little rows and misunderstandings were forgotten. There was, however, one fly in the ointment. Since coming to Avondale I had been caring for two beautiful multicoloured brooms. I thought at first that they would not survive. I really had to nurse them. The House Master was elated that I had got them through. He would take one himself and give the other one to me. I was very pleased. The evening before the breakup the House Master and I went to pack the brooms into boxes. They had disappeared. He was crestfallen. It was customary for the House Master to make a small speech on the last evening. He did not appear at all. Someone had stolen his beautiful brooms.

I was sorry for Paddy Verling. He was so fond of those beautiful plants. He told me that he was going to give it to his brother. Every time he would return home, he would be looking forward to seeing its growth year after year. I was sorry that I had not mine to give him. It would have been less hard to bear if only one had been stolen. Everybody was so outraged by what happened that we began to think that it must have been some outsider who had committed the felony.

It was a joyous breakup but it was a joy tinged with sadness for our homeward journey. We all hoped that we would meet again. We were all together until we reached Dublin. Then the southern boys went south and the western boys went west. I headed for Mullingar with the two Donegal boys. I was particularly friendly with them. They admired Cavan football and that was a common bond. When we were about to part, one of them gave me a present. It was in a long thin covering. I was told to wait until I got home to open it. We parted.

I was met at Drumhawnagh Railway Station and was conveyed home by horse and trap. The neighbours as well as my family were waiting to welcome me. After a while I looked around for my mysterious parcel. It too had disappeared. I consoled myself by saying, 'what I had never had, I had never lost.'

Next morning I took a stroll into Mama's beautiful garden. There was always something new to see there. A surprise awaited me. Occupying a place of honour in the garden was none other than my missing broom. Mama came behind me. She said she could not resist opening the parcel. She had got up early and planted the broom. She was delighted. The story I told to her was a simple one: of a kind House Master rewarding me with a priceless broom. There was no mention of the felony. Had it not been stolen, it would still have ended up in Mama's garden.

It was nice to be home again. The newly whitewashed farmhouses made everyplace look good. I had a feeling that the country was pulling itself up again. Dances in the farmhouses were still being held in spite of being outlawed. The local dance hall was also doing well. It could cater for bigger crowds. Accordingly, I went there one night. There were quite a number of boys and girls back from London for a short spell. Amongst others, some of my former school pals were there. I hardly recognised them. They had become so sophisticated and confident. In Ballyhaise, Dublin and Wicklow I had learned to dance the foreign dances, too. I recognised one girl with whom I had shared secrets on the road to school. I went across to her and asked her out to dance. She accepted. She looked at me in a strange sort of way as if she was amazed at how much I had changed. She relaxed for I had become a good ballroom dancer. Maybe I was showing off to the locals. We had been dancing away in silence when I suddenly became conscious that she was talking to me. She said:

'On the road to school, we used to talk of meeting each other in Boston or New York when we grew up. Now I am in London and you are in Wicklow.'

I could only murmur, 'Ah Dear!' We danced on but suddenly I realised that she was a little angry. Then it all came out in a torrent of words:

'The whole locality is talking about you,' she said. 'You are an educated man. Are you only planting trees?'

'I am working for my country,' I replied.

'You did your bit when you came back from Dublin to help your dad. Why not do something for yourself now?'

I closed my eyes. I could not think of any answers. Then she held me a little closer and I heard her say:

'Don't mind a silly girl. We are all fond and proud of you.'

I could only say: 'Thank you.'

I spent the rest of the week with Dad and Mama. Dad was now in his mid-seventies but had the attitude of a man of fifty. He was still working in the auctioneering business but more and more delegating duties to Hugh P. He had survived the Economic War and he was proud of that. I made a short visit to my godmother in Clonloaghan and another to see the Brady family in Shanvalla. Mama was arranging a party and dance for me on my last night at home. She and Dad were very excited. It would only be the second dance in the house since the great monster dance before the 1918 General Election. He had probably hoped in vain that somehow that dance would be a prelude to victory for the Irish Parliamentary Party nationwide. Instead it represented the end of a great era. My parents may have been on opposite sides but for them that dance of 1918 was to come up time and time again in conversation. Something new would be told each time. On that memorable night, the yard helped out to accommodate the dancers. The barn was no longer adequate. The road gate had been locked and already Sinn Féiners were dancing outside on the road. Somebody had unlocked the gate around midnight. From then on both Sinn Féiners and Hibernians danced together in the moonlight. The fact that the two political factions could mingle and dance is part of the folklore of Mullahoran.

It was all-night dancing in those days and my send-off party was no exception. In fact, it did not last long enough. I was sorry to say goodbye to my kind neighbours and relatives. I did not go to bed, but slept by the fireside. Mama awakened me in the morning for a cup of tea. It was a prelude to a hearty breakfast, which was meant to get me through to Dublin and beyond. The household got up to see me off as I was catching an early train. The goodbyes were cheerful. I was glad that Dad and Mama thought I was in a good job.

Hugh P. had the horse and trap ready and soon we were in Drumhawnagh Railway Station. He was also quite cheerful as we said goodbye. Afforestation had been started in east Cavan. Maybe some day I might work in one of those centres. He spoke as if Callanagh was the centre of the universe. I slept all the way to Dublin. There I met my first cousin Harry Briody and we had a pleasant afternoon together. My train south was not until evening. When saying goodbye to me, Harry appeared worried as if he would never lay eyes on me again.

A practical year:
Kilsheelan

It was already dark when I reached Clonmel. I went to where the forester, Mr McCool, was living. Meeting him made an enormous difference to me. He was the perfect gentleman. Without deliberately attempting to do so, he motivated everybody he came in contact with. His wife was a friendly welcoming woman. After a meal Mr McCool informed me that my digs were at Kilsheelan, which was five miles away. Kilsheelan was the next station after Clonmel, but it was too late to get a train there. Unfortunately the River Anner was in flood and I could not cycle there on the flooded road. Mr McCool took me by car across the River Suir at Two-Mile Bridge and back again over the bridge at Kilsheelan. I seemed to be in a forest throughout the journey.

Mrs Dempsey was about to go to bed when we arrived. I thanked Mr McCool and he told me where I would meet the workforce next morning and that I should get there after a few inquiries. He departed after telling me he would contact me in a few days. Mrs Dempsey insisted on making me a meal. Then I went to bed for a good night's sleep. I was up early. After breakfast Mick Dempsey took me by car to where the workforce were. This was a once-off favour. Tomorrow I would have to cycle. Everybody seemed to be kind to me.

When I was leaving Callanagh, all the flowers in the garden had been blasted by an early severe frost. Here the sun was shining with no appearance of frost anywhere. It reminded me of Summers in Cavan. I found the men clearing a fire-trench. It was an operation that was new to me and I took special interest in the procedure. Lunch time came and we all sat out on the grass. I was truly amazed at the men's clothing. It was difficult to know what was the original cloth of their clothes, especially the trousers. They were a mass of patches. Many of the men were six-footers. They did not speak to me at first. Later they became very friendly. I got the first mug of tea from the 'black can'. I was hungry. I opened my lunch pack. It consisted of lovely ham sandwiches. I glanced at the man next to me. His lunch consisted of home-baked bread and jam, which was probably made from wild fruit. I offered one of my sandwiches to him. He politely refused, telling me that he would enjoy his dinner when he would get home. I respected his pride. I managed afterwards to eat most of my lunch furtively before lunchtime, leaving only one sandwich for the 'black can'.

Mr McCool called the following day. He had a special job for me to do. About five hundred acres had recently been acquired. He had got paths cut through it in order to assess its potentiality. My job was to go through the area and try to make a selection of species. He would call from time to time and inspect what I was doing.

Mama had taught me the names of the common weeds and I had improved my knowledge in Ballyhaise, Albert and Avondale. I felt fairly confident in tackling the job. There were also some trees growing here and there which helped my selection. I brought a book with me to check new weeds I would come across. I did not think that there was any permanence in what I was doing. I thought it was simply an exercise in my training. Mr McCool came the following day. He seemed pleased with what I was doing. He disagreed with me on some of my selections. When I asked him if I should substitute his species for mine, he said not to but to ask the man who was cutting paths through the area for me to dig a pit wherever we had disagreed. I did so and as a result came around to his opinion. From that day forward I found digging pits a great help when I was in doubt. Mr McCool came every second day and I was glad to discover that our points of disagreement were becoming less and less.

I went to the nursery in Cooliseal to facilitate Mr McCool in paying the men. There I found myself with a very large squad. I took an interest in the men and also in the welfare of their wives and children. The knowledge I learned in this way was to get me over many a stile. I liked the appearance of the nursery and I complemented Larry Whelan, the foreman, on how it was kept. He seemed surprised. He was not used to being complimented on his work.

After six weeks I had finished the selection of species. Mr McCool found me another chore. The Shannon Electricity Supply Board had been faced with a problem. A creature called the muskrat had been burrowing at the embankments and had caused considerable damage. An expert named Wade from Wales was recruited to solve the problem. He succeeded so well that there was not a muskrat left. He might have made a job for life for himself if he had been less efficient. The state had then to provide another job for him to do.

Deer were a proud feature of the estates in the old days. Now they were being poached wholesale. The Department of Lands decided to do something for the herds that were on the estates that fell to them. The problem lay in the fact that the poachers were only taking out the younger and more edible animals. This, if allowed to continue, would mean the disappearance of the herd after some time. The Department decided to cull the undesirables, the aged, as well as the unhealthy and the maimed.

When Wade ended the muskrat menace, he was assigned the care of deer in Kilsheelan. I was sent along for two reasons. Firstly, Wade was carrying a high-velocity rifle and must at all times be made to shoot into hill country, to avoid shooting people or farm animals by accident. Secondly, there was considerable local opposition to Wade's presence in the forest. The locals considered that the Department were interfering in an area in which they had previously poached. Wade might require a certain protection. The presence of a Forestry trainee might prevent him from being attacked.

Wade was a very interesting man with a fund of stories. He may have had military service. I don't know. For me working with him constituted part of my education, which I might otherwise never have acquired. He taught me how to recognise the foot-prints of the different animals. He always went to where there was a drinking-place. The poachers, who were shooting the younger animals, were not experts shots. There was a lot of inaccurate shooting. Some of the animals who got away were badly maimed and were in agony. Wade was an expert shot and could shoot from a considerable distance. He shot to kill instantly.

I was delighted to be assigned to Wade and I was looking forward to shooting with a high-velocity rifle. I had previously had experience of shooting with a shotgun. I was disappointed when I was told that I was not under any circumstance to handle the rifle. Wade was a man coming into his sixties and I offered to carry the rifle. He informed me that it was against the rules. Now and again he had to sit down and rest. I felt sorry for him. On pay day we were to meet our paymaster, Mr McCool, at a certain gate at a certain time. I suggested to Mr McCool that he send one of the men to carry the rifle for Wade now and again. McCool had a talk with Wade. Next day Wade told me that he had decided to let me carry the rifle provided it was not loaded.

I was delighted at first in being allowed to carry the rifle. Then my disappointment grew in not being shown how to use it. Weeks passed and I had become used to my job. I noted carefully how Wade used the sights. While he was examining the footprints of the various animals, I would practise looking through the sights. Then one day a strange thing happened. I saw Wade fix a small tin canister on a tree. Then he unloaded the rifle until there was only one bullet left. He brought me back the road until we could barely see the tin canister. Then Wade handed the rifle to me and invited me to hit the target. He knew that I had been practising. Now it was my turn to fire. I could hardly see the target, but I hit it dead on. My mind went back to that place on the Longford road when my friend Pat 'a Park Smith had hit bull's-eyes consecutively at a roadside show. How nice if I could be with him again.

Those were happy days with Wade until one day Mrs Dempsey told me that a woman living outside the village had buried a piece of bacon to stop Wade. This was an old pagan custom to bring harm to an opponent. Wade laughed at the idea when I told him. Maybe I laughed too. One morning we were both tracing the imprints of animals. I had got quite good in doing this. We were about one hundred yards from one another. Wade was in the forest. I was along a forest path. A shot rang out. This was followed by a very weak blow of a whistle. I sensed danger. Wade always carried a whistle. There was another very weak blow, and I went hurriedly in the direction of the call. When I found Wade he was lying on the ground and his eyes were closed. I thought that he was unconscious. I took his whistle and blew a shrill blast. Thereupon he opened his eyes. He had been trying to bear the pain of the wound inflicted by the rifle. He indicated that the shot had got him below the knee. I rolled up his trousers and used my necktie as a tourniquet to staunch the blood.

Four of the forest squad arrived. I sent one of them back to Mick Dempsey with a request for his car. The men made a rough makeshift stretcher of strong branches. We carried Wade to the main road where we met Mick Dempsey with his car. We went straight to old Dr White's house in Kilsheelan. He had been through the Troubles and made light of the affair. No need to go to hospital. It was a flesh wound. The bullet had gone through at the back of the bone. In a couple of days Wade would be able to walk again with the aid of a walking stick. I did not share the doctor's optimism, but I had to submit to medical opinion.

Wade did hobble around on the job after a few days but a lot was due to his heroic stamina. Another man might have stayed in a hospital bed for a week or so. I was glad to have met Wade and to have learned so much from him. I was sorry to say goodbye when I left the Kilsheelan forest to go to Aughrim, Co. Wicklow.

At this stage I think I should refer to the private side of my life. I had been doing a lot of walking over rough terrain and was beginning to develop a limp on my right leg. This disturbed me because of its possible implications for my career as a forester. I went to a doctor in Clonmel. He told me that an inflamation had developed from a past injury. He advised me to get on the dance floor and do as much dancing as possible. He gave me anti-inflammatory tablets to take, two per day. I took his advice on dancing. It was hard at first. It became a pleasure as time went by.

As well as running a lodging house, Mrs Dempsey also had a small shop. The Dempsey household consisted of Mrs Dempsey, her son Mick and daughter Josie, or Jo as she was more often known. Both Mick and Jo were a few years older than me. Jo had been to America and back. Mick had a poultry business. He was also a big exporter of rabbits. Jo helped her mother in the shop and in the lodging house. Their first cousins were the Prendergast sisters. Kathleen Prendergast ran the local post office. May Prendergast helped her mother in another poultry business. Kathleen and May were very kind to me, especially May. Kilsheelan was than a small village of one hundred and fifty people. The village itself was in Co Tipperary but the Kilsheelan forest was across the river in Co Waterford, on the foothills of the Comeragh Mountains. Now seventy years later there are 2000 residents in Kilsheelan. I was also friendly with the O'Sullivan and Ormond families. I cannot speak too highly of them. All my friends in Kilsheelan made me feel at home. I was also besieged by the local and Clonmel teams to play Gaelic football. I stood firm. My football days were over. I could never play again.

The famous Mick Delahunty band was on the road at this time. It would have been about three years in being. It is the best dance band I have ever danced to. The pity for me was that the dancing which I had learned in Wicklow was no longer adequate. Delahunty's band had inculcated high standards among its dancers. The Kilsheelan girls helped me reach a passable standard. The competition on the floor also helped me. At first I thought that it was beyond my reach. It was my introduction to proper ballroom dancing. I learned slowly but I learned well. In so doing I forgot all about the limp in my right leg. We followed Delahunty's band to all its venues. We danced twice a week and sometimes three times. To those who have danced to Delahunty's band no explanation is necessary. To those who have not no explanation is possible. It was a dance band to remember. I have many fond memories of Kilsheelan, of a friendly forester and a friendly people. My next forest would be a complete change. I worked with the men during the day and used fall into bed in the evening from sheer exhaustion. I did not have time even to dream of my former dancing nights.

Aughrim

I received a letter from Head Office to transfer to Aughrim forest, Co. Wicklow, on the 1st January, 1939. A letter from Dan McGuire, who had been in Aughrim for the previous three months, forewarned me that work there was a little difficult. He had been in digs in the forester's house but had only seen the forester on pay days. However, his treatment in comparison with the previous trainee was quite good. It was a forest in which I would have to mind my step. Each day could be completely different from that which went before.

Perhaps I should better state what effect the second year's work experience had on trainees. It would appear that foresters were very much conditioned by their second year out the country where they were meeting with different foresters with different ideas. The four foresters I met with could have come from four different countries instead of four different counties. Each dominated the forest in their charge. This may have been noticed by the people at Head Office. Later their advice to us was that in taking over a new forest as a forester-in-charge we should not change anything for a few months. Even then, change should be gradual. I have followed this advice and have seen hostility change to friendliness.

I travelled to Aughrim as directed. I had expected to meet the forester at the bus stop. Instead, I met Dan McGuire, who was leaving. He informed me that my new digs would be at Ballymanus House. This was situated three miles away. I had acquired extra luggage, which consisted mostly of books. I had therefore to engage a taxi. Thankfully, this was covered by my transfer expenses. The cash I had left over after my sojourn at Kilsheelan was in coins not notes.

The digs at Ballymanus House were excellent. Moreover, there was a forest foreman staying there named Jimmy Donoghue with whom I developed a lifelong friendship. Sadly, I was not to be working under him. He directed me to the nursery itself, which was personally surpervised by Mr Alfie Leonard, the forester-in-charge. Accordingly, I went to the big nursery, where I introduced myself to the foreman-in-charge. He informed me that I had been allocated to a lining-out operation. I was familiar with lining-out from Avondale. I had not to be shown what to do.

I was with a gang of ten. I was in the middle with five men on my right and five on my left. Stretched along the area to be lined out was a rope three hundred yards long. This rope had to be kept taut to enable the men to cut a straight trench along it. The men at either end of the rope were responsible for re-fixing it after a line of seedlings had been planted. To compensate them for their work they were given four yards less to line out. They lined out twenty four yards while the rest of us did twenty eight yards. I considered myself skilled in digging and shovelling soil after Ballyhaise, Albert and Avondale. I was looking forward to holding my end up. However, I was surprised by the pace of work which developed. The men on either side of me had to help me.

The man on my right did four yards for me while the man on my left did four more. This left me with only twenty yards to do. The pace was fast and furious and I found it hard to achieve even that much. Worse still, I realised that the quality of my work was slipping. I looked to my left and right. The quality there was in marked contrast to mine. We were trained to evaluate quality of work in Avondale. I was fearful lest the forester whom I saw through the office window might come out and chastise me. I had not met him yet. Half past eleven came and one of our squad slipped away to boil the kettles for the midday lunch. Simultaneously, the forester emerged from his office and took this man's place. He nodded to me as he passed me by. I was relieved that he did not look at my efforts. Now and again I glanced in his direction. He was very skilled. He had finished before the rest of the squad and was on his way back to the office. The man on my right, who was helping me out, looked at me and muttered: 'The forester thinks we are having the time of Reilly.'

Perhaps, I had better explain to the reader who is unacquainted with forestry methods what we were doing. The rope was stretched along an earthen bank. Our lots were pegged twenty eight yards apart, with the man on top and bottom having twenty four yards each. Along the stretched taut rope we now cut a trench a foot deep. This trench had a vertical bank. We each had a padded bag to kneel on. In our left hands were handfuls of fifty seedlings. With our right hands we selected one plant from the bunch, placed it against the vertical bank of the trench with the roots outspreading at the bottom of the trench. We now covered the roots with a handful of soil while pressing the seedlings against the vertical part of the trench.

I had been the fastest 'liner out' in Avondale. I was

ambidextrous, being both left- and right-handed. Instead of holding on to a bunch of seedlings with my left hand, I could scatter them along the top of the bank. I could then use my left hand to place the seedlings in the allotted space. My right hand I used only for applying the fistful of soil. To compensate my two fellow-workers for their digging on my behalf, I was able to help them with their 'lining out'. For me it was still an uphill struggle.

The reception I received from the workers at lunch time compensated for the inhospitality of the forester. I was given the first mug of tea from the 'black can'. While in Avondale I had played football in Aughrim. Some of the men had recognised me. It was common knowledge in Wicklow that I had been invalided without insurance cover whilst playing football. My chief difficulty in Kilsheelan had been to eat my ham sandwiches before lunch so as not to let the men see them. Now I had no such escape. I got another surprise when I saw the men open their lunch packs. I had not realised that the pace the men were working at could not be maintained with insubstantial lunches. Instead of bread and jam, they had several slices of home-baked bread, well buttered, and with what appeared like boiled bacon. When I opened up my lunch pack, I discovered that Mrs Lynch had also included boiled bacon. It was to be a feature of my stay in Aughrim. One of the men told me that the lining out would be finished in three weeks' time. It seemed like an eternity.

In a short time, however, I began to get used to my situation. Two weeks passed and I was now entering my third week. I was beginning to like the men. Better still, it appeared they liked me. They were not used to one of the staff enquiring after the welfare of their families. I like to think I was the better for doing so. The men told me very few trainees were able for twenty yards. One of them could only achieve eight yards. He had not been used to the spade and shovel. Irrespective, of what a trainee was capable of, he had to be helped. The men had to achieve a certain number of lines per day. Any trainee, however good, was a hindrance in the operation. He had to be carried, no matter how good.

This brings me to something which seems to have gone unnoticed by certain foresters. The pay of the forestry worker was so small, and his working conditions such that he could not afford to take a day off. He had to come out to work except when he was very ill. Sick men were carried by the rest of the gang. It could be one man's turn the one day; the next day it could be another man's turn. Even when 'time and motion' obtained and gangs were reduced to six's, it was still achieved against the odds. Six was a small number to carry a man on; it was easier for a bigger squad. I was very conscious of this. When work and workers were studied and values (i.e. the length of time it took a certain number of men to do a certain operation) were applied, we discovered how some workers had been wronged. The work of the men who were 'lining out' in Aughrim – who were barely thanked for their efforts – could thirty years later have been assessed at 130%.

I used barely be able to limp home in the evenings. I used fall into bed and wake when called. In my third week in Aughrim I was called into the office. I did not know what to expect. I found a distraught forester there. He would appear to have been at the end of his tether trying to get a grand total right. The amount of paper scattered on the floor indicated to me that his skill in 'lining out' was not matched by his office skills. I recognised the document in his hand. It was a summary of the total insurance stamps he had used for the year just ended. In fact, I had completed such a summary for Mr McCool before I left Kilsheelan. Now, almost three weeks later, Mr Leonard was trying to come to grips with a similar problem. I mentioned that I was familiar with what he was doing and had completed such a form in Kilsheelan.

His face lit up. He said that he would check on what the men were doing outside and that I could look over the accounts. I asked him what was missing. He said that the cash was right but that he was sixty stamps short. He departed and I could hear him give a bellow at some of the men as he made his check. I straightened up all his threes and fives and checked. There was still a shortage of sixty stamps. Most of the older foresters did not put a stroke on the middle of their sevens. You had to rely on the top of the seven to identify it. Sometimes there was barely a wing there and you had to rely on the context to know whether it was a one or a seven. I found one such 'invalid' and it was in the 'tens'. I had found the missing sixty. I was tempted to take all the papers off the floor and to order them. I put the thought aside and called in the forester instead. He came in. I asked him to tot up the total again. He did so and found that everything was correct. He put the document into an envelope and departed for the post office. I resumed my lining out and was glad when the day ended. I was nice to have my boss say 'Thank you'.

The next day saw me switched from the lining out area to that of the seed-beds. These had been sown the previous year. Seed-sowing is a very skilled operation and it is generally left to the forester or to a seasoned worker. Those beds had been very successful. This meant that they were very uniform: each square yard of bed containing as many seedlings as the next square yard. The forester had already got an estimation of the total number. In Forestry, we were allowed a 5% leeway. The men also knew the approximate number in the seed-beds.

They divided a sixty-foot bed into five sections of twelve feet each. An older man raised the seedlings with his fork. He then tossed them back to an adjoining piece of ground. The rest of the men were all young fellows like myself with nimble fingers for counting. A heap of dug-up seedlings was picked up in the right hand and tossed over the palm of the left. The soil fell through the fingers, leaving the seedlings ready for counting. The men started counting and told me to do likewise. When they reached a hundred, they stopped counting. For a moment they held the bundles in their hands as if they were estimating the exact size of the bundles. The older man took his bundle and placed it in my hands. He asked me to get used to the size of one hundred seedlings. The men then started making bundles without counting. One man expertly tied them.

When they reached the end of a twelve-foot stretch of bed, they stopped. They checked to see that it tallied with what they were supposed to have. They then proceeded to the next section. As we were no longer counting any more, we had plenty of time to chat. I told them that we had counted every seedling in Avondale. They gave me two bundles to count. One had 102, the other 98. I had to concede that this method would give the average of 100%.

They were nice young fellows and had plenty to say. I listened to them. They were different to the men down in Kilsheelan. There the men were Republicans and were rather proud that the anti-Free State IRA had made their last stand in the Comeragh Mountains in 1923. They also spoke well of Germany. Here in Aughrim, the talk was different. Wicklow had a Labour T.D, named Everett, who looked after their interests, and many of them voted for him. They were also more in favour of England. Many men in the area were in the British Army. There also seemed to be a long-standing connection with Wales, going back to the mining days in Avoca and Aughrim. I liked listening to them. They were something new.

Later in the Fifties when work study and bonuses became the norm in Forestry the working methods of these young men were vindicated. I am not sure if Mr Leonard knew of their strategy in not counting every bundle. The fact that it speeded up the work might have found his approval. In the early days of Forestry, foresters would appear to have expected too much from the workforce. The art of knowing what a man is capable of doing per day is not easily learned. There were foresters who were forever letting go older men and taking on younger men. They apparently forgot that they would one day be old themselves. Thankfully, most foresters thought otherwise and remembered that men had children and wives. One thing that work study did was to show up the 'slave drivers'.

The Wicklow of Spring 1939 was very different from the place I had known in the Summer and Autumn of 1938. Then, there were a lot of tourists around with plenty of football, dancing, and swimming along the coast. Now the roads were empty. There was a depressed air about everything and everybody. I cycled down to Mass on my first Sunday in Aughrim. The following Sunday, I went to Mass in a village called Assingap. This was a little mountain village consisting of a chapel, a schoolhouse and a shop. It was only two miles from my digs but the going there was tough uphill riding. The return journey was a freewheel ride. I was glad I went there and continued going there during my three months' stay. In contrast to the people around Aughrim, the people were very friendly. The people around Aughrim village minded their own business. The mountain people were more open.

I was surprised that so many men saluted me on the way to Mass. Later, I was to learn that they were the same men who worked with me in the nursery. I barely recognised them out of their old working duds and clean-shaven. They only wore battered hats in the nursery. When you met a worker on his way to Mass, his shoes were so well polished and shined that you could see yourself in them. The older men still wore caps and hats to Mass. The young fellows of the seed-beds were 'going in their hair'. In fact, it was there that I first saw hair split in the middle.

The girls and boys wore every conceivable type of garment. It was evident that many of their clothes came from America, Britain, Australia and elsewhere. The little church was bursting at the seams, but there was always a seat for me. I must have been a complete mystery to them. I must have also been a puzzle to my boss down at Aughrim when he didn't see me at Mass there. In the gallery was a large harmonium. There seemed to be a different person playing there each Sunday. Everyone in the church sang to their heart's delight.

It was only by chance I began going to Mass in Assinagap. I was privileged to see and hear those mountain people. While in their church I was imagining that I was back in one of those little thatched churches of the pre-Famine days. After the Famine the people regrouped and built those big churches that are to be seen all over the country. A teacher who was detailed to go to Assinagap thought to improve her address by calling the place 'Donkeyinagap'.

Ballymanus House was a nice place to stay in. It was a large house. There had been a few priests in the family a generation before. There were many rooms, each crowded with surplus furniture from bygone days. The owner of the place was a Mr Lynch. He was about forty years of age and his wife was about thirty. She had brought her father to live with her. He made a great contribution to the place. He was good to talk to the guests and he helped with the chores. He was an very interesting man. An elderly teacher, who taught in Assinagap, stayed in Ballymanus House. She spoke to me now and again. She was very interested in national politics. I would have loved to hear her talk of her pupils at Assinagap. The subject never came up. This teacher, Jimmy Donoghue and myself were the only people regularly staying there. The Summer and Autumn would see up to thirty staying there.

I was in Aughrim for twelve weeks. During the first three, while I was 'lining out' I used be so tired that I used just fall into bed and get up again next morning when called. When I was transferred to the seed-beds, I began to enjoy my surroundings, especially the digs. On my fourth Saturday I cycled to Arklow with Jimmy Donoghue. I was to come across Jimmy at various places during my career in Forestry. Eventually he became head-forester at Portlaw, Co. Waterford. I ended up at Carrick-on-Suir just nine miles away. He had a famous saying: 'In an argument there are two sides: "Your side and my side and somewhere between lies the truth."' We had plans to establish a nursery together in our retirement. We were both of the same age. Sadly he died before retiring and I never saw that nursery.

There was a big garden attached to the house. It took a lot of vegetables to cater for the heavy influx of visitors. I happened to stroll into it on a Saturday. I found Mrs Lynch there about to sow the seeds for the year. Seeds are sown mostly in the Spring. They are planted out in the late Spring and early Summer as required. She was delighted when I took over the chore from her. She dreaded the task of seed-sowing. I spent a number of Saturdays planting them out.

Easter that year caught me napping at my post. Cards were arriving every day. I was amazed to find how many friends I had made in a couple of years, and I had not yet begun to answer them. I noticed that the house was getting a facelift. There were a few girls pulling the place together. Jimmy told me that there was a crowd of visitors coming for Easter. He had an invitation to dinner from a friend for Easter Sunday. He would bring me with him and we would get out of the way. Some of the visitors came on Good Friday. They were coming all day on Saturday in dribs and drabs. Every room had been filled.

Suddenly, sixty boys arrived on bicycles. I wondered where they would be put up. Jimmy told me they came every Easter. They would sleep in the hayshed at night. They had brought provisions with them. They ate their meals at a big table in the barn. For them Ballymanus House was at the end of their ride from Dublin through lovely Wicklow – a rest on the hay before returning.

I was sorry to go off with Jimmy. It would have been nice to stop and talk with those young boys. Dublin haunted me. Early on Easter Sunday, Jimmy and I set out for Aghavannagh. We reached there about noon. Our hosts, the people Mick McCarthy stayed with, gave us a hearty welcome. Mick had been my senior in Avondale. Jimmy would be two classes ahead. I was in good company. We had a lovely meal. We then set out on what was to be a cycle tour of all the Wicklow forests. We came back to Mick's digs in Aghavannagh and slept soundly. Most of the conversation was about their trainee days. In fact, in later life I found that foresters looked back nostalgically to those days when they had met the men who created Forestry. We seemed to be remembering the sunny days and forgetting the ice and snow.

Jimmy and Mick were two interesting men. By reason of the fact that foresters came from different counties and from various backgrounds, it would be difficult to pin down what characterised a typical forester. When I joined forestry, I was told that I was the second Cavan man to do so. The first was Tom Prior. Prior had served in the National Army and was a stickler for discipline. In later years, he and I were supposed to represent the two extremes. He was the terror of young trainees. If a 'first year' stepped out of line in Avondale he was told that unless he mended his ways, he would be chastised during his second year by a Cavan man.

Jokingly, some said that my county mate had written a book called 'My New Trainee'. Until then I knew him only be repute. Later he will come into my story. Forestry looked different in those days to many men for whom it was an attraction. At this distance from 1939, I now realise that Jimmy and Mick were now trying to show me another side to Mr Leonard's view of forestry.

I had played a lot of football in Wicklow and was now

meeting friends and opponents on our tour. I was not good enough to play for Cavan. In Wicklow I managed to get by. Jimmy treated us to a meal in Glendalough and we then went our separate ways, Jimmy and myself back to Ballymanus House and Mick to Aghavannagh. By the time we got to Ballymanus House, all the guests had gone.

I had to go back to the seedling plots next day. I found light at the end of the tunnel. Head Office Informed me that I was going to Kinnity, Co Offaly, at the end of the month. I had heard great accounts of the place from the trainee whom I would be replacing, no other than Dan McGuire. I was hoping earnestly that things would turn out all right. I had never been in the centre of Ireland before. This should be an experience. Moreover, it would be a handy place from which to slip back to Callanagh during a bank holiday weekend.

My last day at Aughrim came. Generally, it was the custom to give the trainee the last day off. In some forests it was only a half-day. I wondered which would it be. I said goodbye to the men at lunch time. I was expecting to be let off. Nothing happened. An hour later I realise that the men were whispering to one another. Then the forester emerged from his office and called me over. He informed me that I had to catch an early bus and that I could come down and stay at his place for the night. I thanked him. I informed him that there was a farewell party for me in Ballymanus House and that it would be more convenient to stay there. We said goodbye to each other. I was surprised that he gave me a surprisingly firm handclasp. As I walked out of the gate, I waved back towards the men. I got a great handclap. I don't know if it was the first handclap ever heard there, but I'm sure it irked the disciplinarian in the office.

We had a lovely party at Ballymanus House that night. The boys and girls of the neighbourhood came in. Because it was a guesthouse they had until then kept out of the way. It was the first time I had seen them. It was also the first time they had seen me because of my going to Mass in the mountains. I don't know who got the best of the banter. I was certainly in high good humour. It was a pity that the party had to end. I promised to come back some day. I never did. There were so many places that I never got back to.

I was at the bus stop early the following morning. There was a well-dressed woman waiting there, too. She looked at me in a friendly sort of way. I was looking forward to a nice chat to while away the time on the way to Dublin. Then I saw a friendly-looking woman coming across towards me. When she reached me she stretched out her hand. She introduced herself as the forester's wife. She had heard so much about me and had come to say goodbye and to wish me good luck. I was tongue-tied. I found it hard to associate her with the recluse in the nursery office. I listened to her as she chattered on. Apparently, I was the first trainee who had prayed with the mountain folk. I like to think I was remembered in Aughrim.

Later, when I was a forester at Mount Bellow, Co Galway, Alfie Leonard's father, who lived locally, used call on me on his way to the bank. He was a lovely old man with a store of forest lore. I would dearly love to have recorded some of his stories.

I got to Dublin only to be told that I would have to wait four hours for a bus to Kinnity. It would be nice to re-visit Dublin. I had great memories of the Eucharistic Congress, of the General Election of 1932 before my return to Cavan, and later during my stay in Albert College of the Botanic Gardens, the Corporation Market and the Teachers Hall where we 'danced the light fantastic'.

Kinnity

A strange feeling came over me. I could not bring myself to go back to visit those places. Instead I had a meal somewhere in O'Connell Street and slipped into a church to pray. By the time I got my bus it was getting late. I realised it would be dark before I reached Kinnity. I would not be able to see the countryside I had never seen before. I stowed my cases on the roof-rack and got in. I soon dropped off to sleep. Tomorrow would be another day. The conductor wakened me before I reached Kinnity. A friendly forester was waiting to welcome me off the bus. That was my first introduction to Kinnity.

After Mr Joe Egan and I exchanged greetings he told me that I would be staying up in the mountains with the Mooney family. Beyond the Mooney farm was a small nursery where I would be working on the morrow. The man in charge there had full instructions as to what I had to do. Mr Egan invited me in for a meal. I thanked him but said I would prefer to get to my digs. He brought me across the road to where there was a taxi. Soon I was up in the mountains. There was a man waiting for me at a nicely-painted gate. He introduced himself as John Mooney. He brought me into his little mountain home. The holding consisted of just a few acres. The middle room of the house, into which we entered, was the kitchen. It had a back door. On each side of the kitchen was a bedroom. Over each of these was a loft which was ascended to by a small ladder. At the top of the ladder was a door. A window in the gable let light into the loft.

At that time in the Slieve Blooms most of the farmhouses were thatched. This house was slated. I learned later that the house belonged to the Bernards of Kinnity Castle. The man I met at the gate was still working at the Castle. Twenty years later that castle was to become a Forestry School.

The Mooney family consisted of a man of over eighty years of age; his daughter, a woman of sixty; a son, a man of fifty (whom I had met at the gate); and a niece aged twelve. I introduced myself to this friendly family. I was given a nice meal and after a short conversation, I begged leave to go to bed. John Mooney escorted me up the ladder and showed me my room. That loft was like Heaven to me because I was completely exhausted. I was dropping off to sleep when I heard the Mooney family reciting the rosary. Next night I would join them. It brought back Cavan memories. I woke up early next morning. I looked out through my window. It had a lovely view of the road and forest below. When I descended the ladder I was greeted with a blazing turf fire. I had not got the smell of turf since I had left Cavan. Suddenly, I felt at home again.

The man in charge of the nursery was named John Connors. I was surprised that there was such a large number of seed-beds for such a small nursery. Later I was to realise that trainees were sent to Kinnity to learn the art of growing seedlings, and this explains the intense cultivation practised there. John told me that he had been instructed to show trainees the ropes. He was such a knowledgeable man that I accepted everything he told me. For someone with little formal education he was extraordinarily well-up. He had developed a craze for forestry literature. A trainee, none other than my friend Peadar O'Grady, had given him some books. I was in good company. I listened and learned. My stay in Kinnity was to prove very fruitful. I was given every chance to improve myself.

If a gate was being erected at a certain place, I was sent there to assist the skilled worker. Most important of all, I was taught the art of sharpening tools. It was of immense help to me in later life. I always insisted that men had the best tools available and that they were kept sharpened. This stood me in good stead during World War Two when I had large gangs procuring firewood to keep trains running and to heat hospitals and government offices. Most of those gangs were unskilled and I had to keep a man continuously looking after the sharpening of tools.

At this stage I had better write about what I remember most about Kinnity or better still why Kinnity should remember me. Kinnity was once described as the prettiest village in Ireland. I would have too many competitors if I attempted a description. All the big estates had either a town or village in their shadow. The landlords if they resided at home took a special pride in keeping their showpieces looking good. The village or town dwellers had to play their part. Kinnity was no exception. Even when the Bernards, the local landlords, left the area the people of Kinnity excelled in keeping the place trim and tidy.

I was leaving the church in my Sunday best when the local priest caught up with me. He had a problem. He was repairing the church. He had a drama group going, playing and raising funds. He had seen me in the distance. He asked if I would join the group. He told me that they were rehearsing two plays. One was called 'Cough Water' and the other 'Lawsey Me'. Maybe, he suggested, I could coax them to do such uplifting plays as 'The Merchant of Venice' or 'She Stoops to Conquer'. I replied that I was not even a novice but that I would do my bit. He introduced me to the group the next evening. He spoke of me as one having a perfect knowledge of the work in hand. I began feeling that I had gifts of which I was previously unaware.

I was careful to wait until the clergyman had left. Then I asked them to show me the scripts of the plays. Perhaps they might perform the plays for me on the following night. The plays were very witty and good comedy. Each play had sufficient dialogue to last for half an hour. The group had taken the liberty to intersperse here and there in the scripts bits of their own. This involved the mentioning of local characters, something which would bring down the house. The weakest character in 'Cough Water' was the doctor. The groom in 'Lawsey Me' was also weak. I was asked to play both parts. I had no previous acting experience.

I had known an alcoholic doctor, who also had the reputation of being a good doctor. He was a single man and highly eccentric. Perhaps I could imitate him. I also knew a fellow in the old days who might do the groom. He was known as 'The Smiler'. He was a do-gooder who was forever helping people but instead of helping the situation his advice was constantly getting them into trouble.

We rehearsed the plays for about a week. What were originally plays of half an hour had lengthened to an hour and a quarter. I had to embellish the speech and character of my doctor and each actor had to do the same to allow for the extra time. I hoped that nobody would recognise me. I was a doctor with an Oxford accent, stammering and searching for words.

When the time came for my stage entry into the clinic, my first patient was already coming in. As I walked towards him I stumbled and fell. My patient assisted me up and seated my on the patients' couch. He asked me if he could help me in any way. I told him that I had had a very good week. Now things had changed. Today I was seeing rats all over the place: red rats, brown rats and grey rats. If I could get rid of the red and the brown rats, I could put up with the grey ones. I asked for a drink and he gave me a cup of 'Cough Water'. Everything changed and I was myself again.

I examined my first patient and told him that he was suffering from an inhalation of Sambucus Nigra, the botanical name for elder. I gave him a bottle of 'Cough Water' and sent him home. I found that my next patient was suffering from Thuja Plicata (red cedar). He was delighted. Other doctors had treated him with contempt and told him his problem was all in the imagination. The magic cure for all ailments was a bottle of 'Cough Water' and a walk in the wood before sunset. Ah Dear!

In 'Lawsey Me' my imitation of 'The Smiler' went down well. I portrayed him as a man who was forever forgetting to get, or rather slipping away from getting, married. I gave him a rich Cavan brogue with all the Hiberno-Irish phrases for which the county is famous. I was complimented later in having created two different characters in the doctor and 'The Smiler'. We took the plays to all the villages and towns around. The plays lengthened as we went along and we were asked to include titbits from the audiences for the next performance. It was my brief brush with the stage.

I associate Kinnity with a particular event, the memory of which has remained vividly in my mind. I was coming home from a dance. It was early in the morning. To my east I saw a large fire engulfing an entire block of forest. I was completely stunned. There was no fire-trench because there was no terrain of furze adjoining, which would have posed a fire hazzard. The fire must have started in the middle of the forest. I had been trained in forest fire-fighting. There was no help at hand. I was at a loss as to what to do. For want of doing something, I knocked at a nearby house. After an long interval a sleepy man emerged. It was easy to see that he was furious at being disturbed. The urgency of my chattering was the last straw. He looked at me far a long time. Then he inquired if I was drunk. He pointed towards the forest. There arising out of the trees was the morning sun.

Mr Egan switched me around to the places where different operations were in progress. This was fifteen years before 'Work Study/Time and Motion' and Bonuses became part of the working life of foresters and forest workers. He would come along at mid-week and would ask me to estimate the position the squad would have reached by Friday. I would do so and he would indicate his own estimation. On Friday we would check on our different calculations again. As I neared the end of my stay time in Kinnity, I knew that we were speaking the same language.

I developed a great friendship with Mr Egan. However, something happened to cause friction between us which was not of my making. I got a letter from Pat 'a Park Smith in the British Air Force telling me that war was inevitable before the end of the year. He asked me to keep an eye on his folks at home. He was fearful of what might happen. The fact that Britain had ceded the ports to the South of Ireland was now being regretted over there. London was belatedly realising that the retention of those ports was vital to their own defence. He was afraid that they might have to take them back by force. He never envisaged that he might have to fight his own country. I wrote him an upbeat letter in which I stated my opinion that Britain would not take back the ports for to do so they would have to declare war on Ireland. I also assured him that his brother and two sisters were very capable people and were well able to look after his parents.

As the days passed, I became unsettled. I began to look at myself. Here I was with only minimal military training if my country called. I decided to ask Forestry to allow me to serve in the Irish Army for a few years. I would like to come back to Forestry when peace returned. I went to the local Garda barracks to enquire where I might enlist. I met a Sergeant there who told me I would have to go to Athlone. In his opinion, however, I would serve my country better as a forester than as a soldier. I don't know how it happened. Within a few days I saw several people looking strangely at me. The news had got out.

I was working with John Connors in the nursery. We had a difficult job on the seed-beds. When tree seeds are sown they lie dormant for some time before they germinate. In the mean time, the exceptionally well-cultivated ground is an ideal place for weeds to take off. These must be got rid of before the tree seeds come up. Otherwise, some of the tree seeds might come away with the weeds. It was an operation that had to be carefully watched. By the time I became a forester, tar-oil sprays had arrived. These were applied after the tree seeds were sown. The weeds were thus held in check until the tree seeds were over ground. This was an important factor in reducing the cost of producing forest plants.

John Connors and his squad were trying to get rid of the weeds. I was helping out. Suddenly, Mr Egan appeared. He was not due for a couple of days. He called me over. As it was nearing the end of my term, he said he would like to show me how the existing plantations were doing. They were not in the same area. It promised to be an interesting evening. As I sat into his car, I knew that something else was on his mind. We visited a few plantations. I knew that it was beyond his brief to tell me what to do with my life. So I saw no harm in opening up. I told him that I had decided to write to Forestry telling them that I was going to enlist. He asked me what qualifications I had for soldiering. I replied that I had been a member of the Pearse Regiment while in Glasnevin and that I had as a result a certain knowledge of the art of soldiering. He seemed taken aback and relapsed into silence. I was in no mood to break into his thoughts. Then he said: 'Your resigning from Forestry concerns me. As a forester, I have to advise you to wait until you reach Avondale. There, some of your class may join you. You will probably be accepted as officers.'

I liked Mr Egan. I realised that he was trying to help me and told him I would accept his advice. We shook hands. Then he started talking and I realised that he was one of the real pioneers of Forestry. It was a long time before anyone paid much attention to his generation of foresters, he said. Even now those early pioneers are under-appreciated. Afforestation was so long-term that it was impossible for most people to comprehend and accept it. People wanted the money spent on agriculture and industry. Joe Egan was a man to look up to and imitate.

In 1942 when I was sent to Cloneslea as forester-in-charge, I was unaware that I was so near Kinnity. People would come across from Kinnity to Cloneslea. On meeting me again they found it hard to reconcile the trainee of '39 with the forester of '42. I had changed so much. It was, of course, hard to reconcile an alcoholic doctor with a hardworking forester.

The days flew and I found myself saying goodbye to Mr

Egan, the workers and the friendly Mooney family. I was being transferred to Woodford in south-east Galway. There was no direct way to get there.

Woodford

After changing busses a few times, I managed to reach my destination. My new boss was a Mr Dungan. I was surprised to find that no other trainee had been there before me. The fact that he was an elderly forester made me wonder for a time if I was being groomed to take over from him on completing my training.

Mr Dungan enquired if I drank. I told him I was a member of the Pioneer Association. This news delighted him for my digs were to be in a public house, owned by a Mrs Coughlan. I was aware that Forestry would have preferred to have me living by the edge of a wood. I noticed that Mr Dungan was very agitated and I asked him if I could help. Mr Dungan brought me into his office. He showed me a letter which he had drafted out. He was going to resign and was handing over the forest to me. I felt that I had to help him. I took a memo pad and asked him to give me the facts of the case. He started off. He was a Dublin man who had accommodated himself to rural Ireland. I gathered from him that he was a man who had achieved a lot without much recognition from Head Office.

I drafted a letter covering all the points he had raised. He was astonished when I read it over to him. I asked him to sign it. No. It was too drastic. Then I told him to rewrite it in his own words, which he did. I knew that he was really in love with the job. I asked him to throw his letter into the fire. This he did. He seemed very relieved. Then I asked him to write a letter to his District Inspector telling him that I had arrived and that there were a few matters he would like to discuss.

The District Inspector came in a few days and everything calmed down. My forester was a happy man again. My landlady, Mrs Coughlan, told me that there was another forester living across the road, who was in charge of the Loughrea forest. I went across and met Joe Mahon. He was to become a great friend of mine. I wrote to him on many an occasion. He had risen from the ranks of the workers. He had been recognised early and had been promoted. There were other men like him throughout the country. Some of the men trained at Avondale, and later at Kinnity and Shelton, did not recognise them. The more mature foresters did.

Of all the forests I have been in, Woodford has special significance. It was during my period there that war was declared by Churchill on Germany. I remember being at a dance when the news came over the airways. There was a mixed reaction, and it was received with boos and handclaps. There was considerable anti-British feeling in Woodford, but people did not know until later in the War of the horrors of the Holocaust. I can still feel the booming voice of Churchill as it came over the radio. Listening to him that evening I had no idea that the War would last so long, but like many at the time I felt Germany would come out victorious, as her war-machine appeared indomitable.

Mr Dungan brought me to his squads operating in the Slieve Aughty Mountains. He had considerable trouble with the workforce there. The area had been planted in the first years of native government with Scots pine and had done surprisingly well until recently. At the time, Scots pine was not regarded as a crop that pays for the cost of planting it. In Scotland, only plants that were raised within a radius of eight miles were accepted for planting. Adopting a similar procedure might have been the solution here. To make matters worse, this crop had been planted on a previous crop of Scots pine followed by another crop of Scots pine. Thus there had been three generations of the same species. This was a recipe for disaster. The young crop was being attacked by aphis. Maybe I could do something to help.

I told Mr Dungan that I considered that the battle was lost. However, in Forestry we were told never to run away. I advised trapping the weevils as he had being doing. I said it would be advisable to drag all the old tops onto a ride line and to burn them there. Where there had been failure, he could plant some spruces. We had to learn a lot of lessons the hard way in the early days of Forestry.

The work force in Slieve Aughty had been very

troublesome. All that was to change. I found to my amazement that the squad had a lot of familiar names like McCabe, O'Reilly, Tierney, and McKiernan. The people in Woodford called the mountain inhabitants the 'Ultachs' or Ulstermen. There were none of my name there. The name Ultach was applied to people whose ancestors had been transplanted form Ulster in earlier centuries.

I was not treated as a trainee by Mr Dungan. I was given full foreman status and I enjoyed it. Because of my Ultach credentials the troublesome mountain squads became the best in the Woodford forest. I found that my forester was really in love with Forestry. He was one of the older men who had been passed over in the search for inspectorial material. His success in field work was possibly lost sight of because of non-attention to office routine.

In normal Forestry work, foresters did not come into contact with the families of the workforce. Some of us did concern ourselves with the welfare of our workers and their families. For some foresters and inspectors the families of the workforce were non-existent. In fact, I once heard a forester on being promoted inspector say that it gave him a chance to get away from what he called 'the labourers'. This, of course, was certainly not true of all inspectors. Most of them realised that the proper treatment of men and their families was essential to the drive for afforestation. For a long time Head Office used the term 'labourer' and 'head labourer' in their time-books. Daringly, some foresters crossed out these headings, which were hated by the men, who wanted to be called 'workers' and 'working foremen'. The term 'labourer's cottage' was of that era. In fact, these cottages were so alike that they were readily identifiable.

I found myself dropping in and visiting the homes of the forestry workers in the Slieve Aughty Mountains. They all had bits of land, most of which had stone-wall fences. I expected to hear some Irish spoken here. Sadly it had gone just some years before. It had been a battle against the odds. It is heart-rendering to come across a place where a language has died. Everybody regreted its passing but nobody seemed able to keep it from slipping away. They all spoke of the language their grandparents spoke as the 'ould seanteanga', not to be confused with the modern book Irish. As I passed from one farmstead to another, I was conscious of another period in my life when I had roamed the countryside in similar fashion. It was during the Economic War when I had to leave Dublin to help out my father. The homes of Cavan, Longford and Leitrim helped me to reach out to the homes in Slieve Aughty.

Grass-cleaning in Slieve Aughty stands out very clearly in my memory. It was an opportunity for me to refresh my knowledge of the weeds and wild flowers which I had been taught in Ballyhaise and Albert. I was astonished to learn that there were many more than I had previously known. I took the specimens back to my digs and identified them with my book on weeds. I was surprised that the men had local names for them all. Each was associated with a cure for some disease or other.

The time keeper in Slieve Aughty was Pat Power. If there were days I could not reach the squad, he would always have a collection of weeds ready to be identified. One day when I came along he was very excited. He had discovered a grass with a blue flower. I thought that I had learned all the grasses in Ballyhaise. This one was new. I was delighted, but I was disappointed that he had not got the roots of the grass. I sent the blue-eyed grass to Avondale. They were equally excited there. I was asked to search for more specimens. Sadly I could find none. Then one day I got a note from Mr Grant. There had been a blue-eyed grass discovered and recorded by Lynam in 1880. It was now 1939. It has always remained a mystery to me that a grass could have remained so long in obscurity and with so few samples. For good measure the specimen recorded by Lynam was only a mile away from where we found ours.

After spending six weeks in Slieve Aughty, I was switched over to another squad working at Derrybrien East. The squad were felling oak trees, cutting them into five- or six-foot lengths and then splitting them into stakes. It was a highly-skilled workforce and the forester was very proud of the operation. He was supplying his own forest with stakes as well as local farmers. He was also catering for many of the forests west of the River Shannon. I did not say anything and he looked at me surprised. He may have expected to be congratulated. He deserved to be. I asked him what he intended planting on the cleared ground. He said that it would be mostly planted with Norway spruce. I asked him why not plant oak again. He said that oak would take too long to reach maturity. He asked me for my opinion. I gave it to him for what it was worth. I said it would be better to leave one hundred of the better trees per acre. He could take out the rest and make stakes of them. There would then be a good oak forest one hundred years hence. He took my advice. Ten years later I heard that some forester who had succeed Mr Dungan had cut down this oak wood leaving just shelter belts here and there.

This was a squad very different to that of Slieve Aughty. They were all big strong men. They never spoke while working. At lunchtime they were certainly worth listening to. Half a dozen of them had been on the erection of the Shannon Electricity Scheme. They had picked up a lot of German words from the engineers who were working there. Some of the words would not be suitable for these pages. There was one ex-Army man. It was he who was put in charge of boiling the 'billy cans', i.e. black cans. We all gave him six pence per week. Out of that he provided tea and sugar. It was an illustration of how money has depreciated in value. At that time there were two hundred and forty pence in the pound. There were items that could be bought for one penny.

Lunchtime lasted for one hour. Nobody spoke while eating. There was always a dog waiting for the scraps. The animals would appear at lunchtime and disappear again. They would appear to have been perfect time-keepers. Perhaps it was the smell of the fire which enticed them to come along. When the lunches had been disposed of, the men sat back and talked. Some of them smoked pipes. Others smoked cigarettes. A minority did not smoke at all. The chat was of a general nature with everyone joining in. It would appear that there was a strong tendency to disagree with one another for the sake of doing so. I did not take part and I realised they were putting on a special show for me.

One of the many things I missed on leaving Dublin were the debates between Albert and the University. If I had to give my verdict on the debating skills of the students at Dublin and those of the workers at Derrybrien, I would have to vote in favour of the latter. They were more seasoned debaters, and this made the difference. They may not have read many books but they certainly read the newspapers. I remember on one occasion there was a witty debate on marriage.

Woodford stands out as the forest where I made most friends on my year around the country. I was approached by a boy (a young unmarried man) who asked me if I was a brother of a Paul Briody whom he had met in Warrenstown College. I replied that I was. He then invited me up to his father's house in Ballinakill. The famous Ballinakill Céilí Band rehearsed in a nearby hall. I had spent so many happy hours listening to *céilí* music at the Cairn O'Reillys in the Twenties that this seemed like a gift from Heaven. It was a nice refresher course. The band rehearsed on Wednesday and Saturday nights. The trouble was that there was a very steep hill to climb to get to Ballinakill. I must have been crazy to hear the music for I found myself buying an auto-cycle. This was a great investment. Sadly I had to discard it in the War years when petrol was reserved for essential services.

Joe Mahon lived across the road. He had a small farm outside the town where he grew some vegetables, mostly potatoes. He had also a cow or two. His father and mother were still alive. The old man managed the little farm. They all lived in the house across the road. There was an open hearth in the kitchen with a blazing turf fire. When I reached Woodford, the dry turf was being brought back from the bog. The shopkeepers bought their supply of turf. Most of the townspeople cut and saved their own during the summer months. The week after I arrived in Woodford saw a constant stream of carts bringing the turf home to be stored in ricks or sheds for the Winter.

In the evenings, after my dinner at Mrs Coughlan's, I often crossed over to Joe Mahon's house. I was at this time of my life a strict teetotaller. I steered away from drinking folk. Joe Mahon was a busy man with his forest and would be late in coming home. The old man and his wife would be there. They were both interesting people and lovely to talk to. He had an immense lore about landlord days in Loughrea. I have forgotten the details of the stories. It is one of my regrets. His wife had not been in America but some of her sisters had. She was very articulate and spoke of the streets of Boston as if she had been there. I swapped stories of my American aunts with her. I surprised her when I said that I had intended to finish my education over there but for the Wall Street Crash. By this time I rarely spoke of my earlier intention of going to America. I remember one night when she was in full flight telling one of her stories. She was sitting on my right. Suddenly news came over the radio that the Athena had been torpedoed by a German submarine in Galway Bay. She jumped past me to take refuge on a little seat in the corner. I always recall this incident whenever the Second World War comes up in conversation.

War had been declared. There were fears that Woodford might be mistaken for Ardnacrusha and become the target of German bombers. The Ardncrusha power station was the centre of the Shannon Electricity Scheme. A strict 'black out' was enforced in Woodford. On one occasion a man was walking down the main street. It was dark and he struck a match to light a cigarette. He was pounced upon by two Gardaí who accused him of giving the town away.

On a Sunday, Joe Mahon and his wife would go for a stroll in the country. They would go out of town one road and come in another. I used join them. Joe had a great fund of tales about events which had happened in his time or in that of his father. I loved listening to him. I used throw in an odd bit of my own. Mrs Mahon was adept at pointing out little loopholes in our stories. She was a very exacting listener. To satisfy her a tale had to be consistent. Of course, when she told a story, we both accepted it as gospel truth.

Now and again I would go down to the hurling field. I had stopped playing football. It was not played locally. It was all hurling. There would appear to have been about fifty men and boys on the playing-pitch from goal to goal. They were not actually playing a match. They were just practising, with the ball more in the air than we see nowadays. The men used *comán*s similar to nowadays. These were made from ash. The boys used *cománs* made from furze roots. The latter were ideal for ground hurling but useless for lifting or hitting the ball in the air. There were three balls being played at the same time. The players had to be on the alert. Very rarely did the balls come near one another. I was advised to stay on the edge of the playing-pitch. It was not safe to be even there. It was such place of humour and banter that I found myself drawn to the playing-pitch ever so often.

Sometimes Joe Mahon would ask Mr Dungan for what he would describe as 'the loan of me'. It would be half in jest and whole in earnest. Joe was very proud of his work over the years and he liked to know what others thought of it. What he liked about my judgement was that I based it on an estimation of what the future growth of the crop might be. I used like to visualise what a newly-planted crop would look like fifteen years hence. Conversely, I liked to visualise what a crop of twenty years' standing looked like three years after it was planted.

Joe was lucky that he grew up with his forest and was left there to watch it battle through its many vicissitudes. The plantations I planted in Slievenamon and Mount Bellow remained but memories. By chance, I happened later to see some of the fruits of what I planted in Cloneslea, Castleblaney and Foxford. Some turned out as I had visualised. Others turned out differently. Joe saw tree selections imposed on him on ground which he considered should be planted otherwise. He was in a position to see who was right and who was wrong. He conceded that he might have been wrong at times. He was an unique man. He had not the background of the men of Avondale, Kinnity or Shelton. He was a real forester without any *cur i gcéill* ('pretence').

In 2002 my daughter Anne and her husband, Tom, were taking me to Galway. We had to pass through Woodford. I never imagined that anybody I met there would recognise me. Sixty three years had come and gone. I enquired in a shop whether Joe Mahon was alive. To my surprise he was and still living in the same house. I went straight to the place where Joe had lived. I knocked at the door. A middle-aged daughter answered the knock. He recognised me instantly and we found each other in one another's arms. He was deaf but as good to speak as ever. He could not hear me and I found myself writing note after note. He said that he had 'been watching the papers for years wondering if I was alive or dead.' He was ninety five and I was eighty nine. Joe was living with a daughter who was looking after him. His grandson was living a door away with a young family. Joe's family had done well and he could talk forever about them. I surprised him when I told him I had a family of eight. He had thought I would never marry. We had something sad in common. Both our wives had died. We had been left to carry on without them.

On one occasion, Joe and I were cycling along a road which bordered on the grounds of the Loughrea County Home. Joe alighted and asked me to listen. There were four old men sitting on a bench with their backs to us. They were speaking in Irish. Up to that time, I had never been in the Gaeltacht but I had met people from there. I had never heard the language spoken so slowly by native speakers anywhere else. I suppose these men had all the time in the world to have their little chat. They were not in any hurry. I would have loved to cross that wall and talk to them in Irish. That was the only Irish I heard spoken in south-east Galway. My son Mícheál informs that in fact there was some Irish spoken in the area for a decade or so after I was there. I should have met it in the Slieve Aughty Mountains and in Ballinakill. Sometimes the stranger fails to hear the spoken tongue just because he is a stranger.

On a hill near Loughrea a small stream crossed the road. There was no more than a trickle of water. Joe told me that the folklore of the area had it that if you washed your hands there you would be able to solve any problem. We found it hard to find enough water to wash our hands. Joe took the good out of it when he said that it only applied to other peoples' problems. The years which followed proved him right.

I will always remember my last week in Woodford. It was also the last week in September. For some reason which I cannot explain I hated to leave Woodford. There was an attitude there which instilled peace of mind. Mr Dungan gave me the last few days off to visit the various squads to say goodbye. I made it easy by telling all and sundry that I would see them all again. If I had been given a forest at or near Woodford, I would not have minded. By strange coincidence, twenty one years later when I was appointed forester-in-charge of Carrick-on-Suir forest, I was to discover that the Crehanagh property, adjacent to the house I have lived in ever since, had been planted by none other than Mr Dungan in 1933. *Ar dheis Dé go raibh a anam!*

One of the youngest of the men at Derrybrien was missing when I called there. He was a promising young man and I had many a chat with him. I asked the man in charge where he lived. It was in a small village on the other side of the hill. On a Sunday afternoon I cycled there. I had been told that it was a house with a green painted door. It was easy to locate. There was only a dozen houses in the village. I knocked on the door. It was opened by a small attractive girl of about twenty two years. It was easy to see that she was a sister of the young man I had come to see. She smiled enquiringly at me. I introduced myself by saying:

'I am from Forestry. I have come to say goodbye to Jim.'

She stepped outside pulling the door after her. Her eyes when they met mine told me that she was prepared to tear me asunder. She was probably the first and most angry woman I have ever met. I saw her hand turn into a clenched fist. She shouted:

'Are you from the Government?'

'Yes and No.' I replied. 'I am from the Department of Lands.'

'Are you a follower of Dev and Fianna Fáil?'

'Yes.' I said.

'Do you realise they're ruining the country.'

'In what way?' I asked

'They've taken away our dignity with the dole, and instead of a loaf they've given us a slice of bread.'

I endeavoured to counter this as best I could.

'Why doesn't Dev,' she says 'fit out our boys and girls who have to emigrate with the skills to obtain better jobs, instead of loading them with the useless Irish language?'

I felt sad. I had not come across such an attitude before. In Cavan I had grown up with a love for the language.

'Have you no idea how Irish girls are treated in England?

'No,' I replied 'I have met girls who have worked in the munitions factories and they have been very well treated.'

This drove her mad altogether and she flew into a rage. What she was saying was for me an eye-opener. I thought of the little girls I went to school with, whose ambition was to emigrate and to send a few pounds back to their mothers. Was this the reality I was listening to? Were some of my school chums being maltreated in domestic service? Worse still were they being preyed upon? As she raged on, I decided to coax her out of her tantrum. I said: 'I have come here to see your brother. Where is he?' She quietened down. She really had exhausted herself.

She then told me that her brother had taken her mother, who was in a wheelchair, up to see her aunt who lived a half a mile away. She said that she would go up and fetch him over. I asked her if she could give me a chair to sit on while I waited. She looked at me for a moment or two and then she opened the door and invited me in. I was glad to sit down. She disappeared out the door. I pulled a chair over to a table and rested my head on it. I was shattered to hear that something like this could still be happening after seventeen years of native Government. I found it hard to keep back the tears. It would have been a relief to have cried.

After ten minutes I felt a hand on my shoulder. She had come back. She had seen her mother and brother coming back in the distance. She seemed like a person about to say something but could not find words to say it. My eyes met hers and I asked if she could get me a cup of tea. She did so. She said she was sorry to have upset me. Was it possible that I did not know what was happening in England? I told her that I also had seen how people had suffered at home here in Ireland during the Economic War, and how people had to emigrate, and how these emigrants helped those left behind. I spoke at length and this had a soothing effect on her.

At this stage, Jim and her mother came in. She was not exactly confined to a wheelchair and with the aid of a stick could hobble into an armchair. She only used the chair when visiting. She was a delightful old woman with a charm of her own. The atmosphere changed. Jim had told her about the debates during

the forestry lunchbreaks, especially my enjoyment of them. The young woman began frying rashers and sausages. I asked her if she was going back to England. No. She was marrying a boy down the road. If she had children she would not let them cross the Irish Sea
. Her mother raised her eyebrows and smiled at me, as if saying when the time comes she'll change her mind. It was an evening that was to haunt me down the years, especially my initial encounter with Jim's sister. In the years that followed, I would have loved to have met that girl again.

I left Woodford on the 1st October 1939. We had a little party the night before at Joe Mahon's. I had not got home from any of the forest centres. I had been twelve months away. I was looking forward to seeing my old parents again, but had no inkling of what awaited me at home. On the way home from the railway station Edward broke the news to me:
'Tosty,' he said. 'we're building a new house.'
I merely said: 'I don't mind, so long as you leave the beautiful thatched house where it is.'
'The thatched house has been knocked down. Only your room remains,' he replied.
I was devastated. Edward tried to console me:
'Like you, Paul was born in that house. The old house meant a lot to him also but he has put the past behind him. Hugh P. and I were born in Capragh, which was a slated house. When Dad bought the farm and brought Mama to live there, he promised her that he would in time build a slated house for her. He has kept his word.'
I had no answer to this. As we approached my old home from the Callanagh crossroads the sight I saw looked to me like a war-torn strip from 'no man's land'. The three beautiful cypress trees which sheltered a shack for our childhood frolics were no more. The beautiful flower-garden had become a dumping ground for all sorts of building materials. Of the old house, only my room at the road remained. The yard and the flower-garden had merged. It seemed like nothing would ever be the same again.

Dad and Mama were on hand to ease the pain of their wounded son. We went into the kitchen of the new house. Where

I was used to seeing an open hearth, there was a gleaming white range. It all seemed so much part of a new world. I would never again have the opportunity of looking into the blazing fire and to dream my dreams. Although it was small consolation, I was still able to sleep in my old room along with Hugh P. and Edward for the rest of my stay at home. It was a strange sensation to be sleeping in the ruins of the old house which I had left secure a year before. After I left again for Avondale, it too was demolished. In the meantime I had to get used to the new reality and in order to distract myself began talking about my year around the country at the various forest centres.

My godmother came to see me. I had sent her many a newspaper from the different areas I was in. I heard her talking outside to Mama. She was enquiring about me:

'Has Tosty any strange news?'

'He has not come around to news yet. He is still talking about trees.'

That remark gives you some idea of the change that my parents saw in me. Not alone was I seeking to afforestate the country, I was becoming quite afforestated myself. Something else was happening. I began to sense the absence of trees in my home place. A lot of change seemed to have occurred during my two years' absence in Forestry. My sisters and brothers, whom I had helped with their homework four years before, had grown taller and more self-assured. I was glad that they hadn't forgotten their Irish. Soon they would all be drifting apart. My parents would then be very lonely. I was the first to break the family circle. Soon others would follow. Everybody has at some time of their lives felt the pangs of the family breaking up, so there is no need to describe my feelings on the matter here.

Ever present at Callanagh were thoughts of Pat 'a Park Smith. I had not been in the Smiths' house for years. I dreaded to call. What a lovely reception I got when I did! Mrs Smith was so thankful for all my care of Pat during his motor-cycling days. I merely said: 'Pat looked after me and I looked after him.' Pat's uncle, known as 'My Dear Man', was there. He was anxious about the recently-declared war. Obviously, Pat was uppermost in his mind. He said: 'I hope he survives.' Mrs 'a Park replied:

'He's in God's keeping.' It is the mothers who keep all the vigils!

They were a lovely family to know. They were in Dad's Hibernian circle. However, Pat's mother had Republican tendencies. Another of Pat's uncles had joined the RIC. As I have related above, he was killed in an accident when a police station was attacked during the War of Independence. The Black and Tans fired shots over his grave. That drew attention to the family they could have done without. The Smiths were glad that I had kept in touch with Pat. I secretly hoped Mrs 'a Park had not told Mama all she knew.

My Shanvalla cousins had a party for me. Mrs Henry had another. They were all delighted that I was in a job and could come to see them more often.

Avondale, final year

I went back to Avondale after a fortnight at home. I had mixed feelings when I reached there. It seemed so different from the Avondale I left twelve months before. My fellow-students had earlier looked like a band of young boys. Now after a year out the country, they had come back seasoned men. They seemed slow to engage in conversation. When you asked one of them a question, he would think for a while before replying.

After a day or two a flood of stories began circulating. Every forest seemed to be a kingdom of its own. Where a senior forester had been in charge for upwards of twelve years, the atmosphere was most noticeable. The centre reflected the personality of the forester. Most foresters were nationally-minded and they gave their services free to the surrounding community. They had built up a bank of goodwill. There were other foresters who closed their office sharp on time and let the public take care of themselves. The treatment of the workforce also differed from forest to forest. The trainees were quick to notice if there was a degree of tension in the centre. Every trainee during their year out would appear to have got a taste of the 'benign' and the 'malign'. Human nature being what it is, you can take it that reports of both kindness and rough treatment were exaggerated. There may have been wisdom in Head Office's decision to let us have the rough with the smooth.

Our new House Master was a Mr Bill Breslin. He was a footballer and we had much in common. I had been elected captain of the football team in my first year in Avondale. Because of my injury in the Summer of 1938, I felt that I could not give of my best to the game any longer. I asked Mr Breslin to take over the captaincy. He was delighted and our friendship deepened. I was set for an interesting third year. One never knows what is around the corner. Events were to push the House Master and myself apart for a time. This happened unexpectedly. I was working on my own in the nursery when Mr Grant came in. He enquired about my stay in the various centres. He was at a loss as to how to read the situation. He had come across from Scotland, where one centre was an exact duplicate of another. In Ireland every forest centre and its forester were different. He was anxious to hear my verbal account as distinct from my written report. I thought it a good time to mention Mr Egan's advice to me about not joining the Army. I also said that Mr Egan had suggested that trainee foresters in Avondale could be trained in civil defence.

Mr Grant may have been in the British Army. His face lit up. He told me that I had made his day. We would have a class the following day and he would set things in motion. I did not mention a word about this to anyone. I was fearful of the reaction. When Mr Grant entered the classroom next day, he was accompanied by the House Master. We had never seen the latter in the classroom before. The House Master's smile was missing. Instead his face had lengthened and we wondered what catastrophe was about to unfold. In contrast, the Superintendent. was beaming from ear to ear. He came to the point quickly. He had met one of the students who told him that he had been advised by his forester not to join the Army. Instead, the forester had hoped that there would be a Local Defence Force (LDF) unit set up in Avondale. He was now about to realise the wish of that forester. I was thankful that he did not mention my name. The Superintendent asked for volunteers. Everyone put up their hand except for the House Master. When Mr Grant looked enquiringly at him, he too put up his hand.

Mr Breslin came to me after a day or two. He probably had done a bit of enquiring and had stumbled on the fact that it was I who had been about to join the Army. He asked me if it was true. I told him it was so. He then revealed his private view, which came as a shock to me. He believed that the auxiliary defence force should be recruited from the unemployed and the lowly- paid. People like the students of Avondale should have a different, and more demanding role to play. He felt that it was a step backwards. I simply said that I would feel privileged to serve in the Local Defence Force. He was silent. I realised that our friendship was under strain.

The captaincy of the football team in our third year was far more difficult than during our first year. My injury in our first year cast a shadow over the then team. They had not foreseen the need for insurance. The Superintendent was horrified that such an omission could have occurred. He was forever telling the juniors to be careful. There was not the same enthusiasm for football among our juniors. This was in marked contrast to our seniors in 1938. Each one of the latter felt that he had his county's prestige to uphold. In 1938, we could after a while put up a decent showing against any of the local Wicklow teams. Now we could not even do that. At times, we had to get a few players from Rathdrum to help out. We were glad to help them out in return.

I tried my best to get on the right side of the House Master. I offered to play in any position in which his team was weak. I had hitherto played in every position on the field. He utilised my suggestion to the full and I found myself marking the best players. I must have looked helpless at times. It was a strange experience but I enjoyed it. Moreover, my friendship with the House Master was rekindled. In after years the House Master and I used laugh at the events of our Avondale days.

Joining the Local Defence Force made a big difference at Avondale. To accommodate it, our classwork and fieldwork must have suffered. At first it was done in our free time. Our drilling was taken care of by those of us who had served in the Pearse Regiment at Glasnevin. We also joined up with the

Rathdrum LDF unit. Henceforth we had to train and go on manoeuvres with them. This sometimes occurred at night. On one occasion one of our students was guarding a flank position. He heard frogs croaking in a pond. He fired a shot and raised the alarm. He thought it was a German invasion. Later in Forestry he was nicknamed 'Croak Croak'.

On another occasion lights were seen in the sea beyond Arklow. We were called out along with other units in Wicklow. It was a night to remember. The weather was nice, dry and warm. It was a lovely night to be out except that we were facing possible death. As the tension grew and as the lights became more pronounced, it was decided to withdraw to Rathdrum, leaving a skeleton number to take rearguard action on the beach. We found ourselves in that unit. We were reinforced by tea, soup and sandwiches. Nothing happened and we were allowed home. When we reached Avondale in the morning, we were told to go to class after breakfast. We did so. There was no sign of Mr Grant nor the House Master that morning. We quietly slipped up to our beds for a well earned rest. We do not seem to have been missed.

Our involvement with the LDF in Avondale helped lift our minds from the present. The fact that we were training to defend our country may have helped some of us to remain in Forestry. This was great excitement for our juniors. However, they did not seem to be able to manage on the same amount of money as we had. In fact, they wrote a letter to Head Office asking for a raise. They did not get it. Foresters and Forestry workers were to bedevilled down the years by poor salaries.

Dan Sullivan and I were working together one day. We were putting up a fence. This consisted of strainers dug well into the ground at a distance of about fifty yards apart. About twenty stakes were driven in-between. There was a strand of barbed wire attached four inches from the top of the stakes. Further down the stakes was another strand of barbed wire to which was affixed lettuce-wire. The latter was to prevent the encroachment of rabbits. There was a trench a foot wide at the bottom. When the lettuce-wire was affixed, the bottom part was covered with soil. Approximately fifteen inches of lettuce-wire lay at the bottom of the trench. When rabbits burrowed to get under the fence, they were met by the lettuce-wire under the ground. It was very effective.

It was an easy chore for Dan and I. The trouble for us was that we had a junior with us who had never worked on fencing. Affixing the lettuce-wire required putting one hand behind the barbed wire and receiving the lettuce-wire from the other hand. If you were right-handed you followed the fence-line to the right or left. If you were left-handed, you worked back from about fifty yards further up. It was a common procedure. Accordingly, I asked our junior if he was right-handed or left-handed. He seemed confused, as if he did not know which he was. I asked him which hand he wrote with and he raised his left-hand. This was helpful as he would be coming after us. I showed him how to affix the wire. I waited until he had done a yard of the fence and then I left him. I went back after a half-hour to see how he was getting on. His hands were covered with blood. I presumed that he had torn his hands on the barbed wire. No. He had had a heavy nosebleed. I called Dan. We got him to lie on an earthen bank with a cold stone under his head. We then got our overcoats and made him comfortable. The bleeding had stopped. We asked him to go asleep if possible. He was very anxious to know who was to do his chore. We told him that we would, and that this was common practice. Sometime he might have to do the same for someone.

When I went back to see him he was fast asleep. This young man was unskilled. Later he became skilled and rose in the ranks to hold the post of Inspector of Time and Motion Incentive Schemes. He was very proficient at this work.

Years later I was doing a refresher course at Avondale. When I went into the classroom I saw the names of the participants including my own on the individual desks. I recognised none of them. Dan Sullivan entered the room and slipped behind a desk which bore the name Dónal Ó Súilleabháin. I went over to him. He greeted me in Irish. After further conversation, I gathered that his oldest was then doing the Leaving Certificate.

My thoughts went back to our time in Avondale. He

often worked with me. He was from the Gaeltacht, from west Kerry. He wanted me to teach him better English, but I would have wished him to teach me better Irish. He used often ask me the English equivalent of Irish phrases. Nevertheless he was not so willing to speak Irish. Now the pendulum had swung in the opposite direction. Dan Sullivan had disappeared and had been replaced by Dónal Ó Súilleabháin. I was careful to speak to him in Irish. Dan had met them all at breakfast. I had been late for breakfast. He was able to introduce me to all and sundry in his best Irish.

A silence fell on the room as our teacher entered. It was none other than J. J. Thornhill. He was the boy under whose head we had placed a cold stone many years before. He smiled at my puzzled face and then looked out the window as if he was recalling a scene from the past. I looked at Dan. He nodded. I contented myself with getting out my notebook for the coming lecture. Then I heard the teacher say: 'Before I begin my lecture, permit me to thank two of my seniors at Avondale who are present here today. I was working with them erecting a fence-line. I got a heavy nosebleed. They came and lay me on an earthen bank. They placed a cold stone under my head and made me comfortable with their topcoats. Moreover, they did my chore for me.' Mr Thornhill continued: 'We are now at a stage when all work has to be governed by work studies. Will there be place for the kindness which was shown to me? Workers who were not feeling too well were carried by the rest of the gang in the past. It was their bad day today, it could be yours tomorrow. Now work study and the resulting bonus operates in gangs of six. Is the gang too small to admit of somebody being carried? Only time will tell. What I do know is that the two men present will find a solution.'

As juniors we had been in two big dormitories. The seniors were accommodated in smaller rooms. Then I had all my old friends, Hanahoe, McGuire, Horgan and Sullivan as room-mates. This gave us a sense of strength and security. Now we were separated because we were in the smaller rooms. I was along with Peadar O'Grady and Cal McCarthy. I had hardly spoken to McCarthy in my first year, but I knew O'Grady quite well. Peadar O'Grady had been a trainee in Kinnity while I was in Kilsheelan. He had kept up a correspondence with someone in the area and had been kept abreast of my strange 'goings on' during my period there. The ingenuity of O'Grady in telling stories lay in the fact that he only unfolded one episode at a time. Cal McCarthy, my other roommate, listened and asked for more details.

Once I found O'Grady in a distraught condition. We were alone. He had discovered that Cal closed his eyes and pretended to be asleep while listening to our conversation. I told him that Jer Horgan, who was a friend of mine, was from the same general area as Cal in west Cork. They had known each other to see before coming to Avondale. I promised that I would find out from him how serious was the situation. Horgan broke his sides laughing when I apprised him about Cal. No! Cal was a genuine person but a little curious. The trouble was that we were not telling him enough about ourselves. We were advised to let him keep his eyes closed while telling stories that would raise the hair on his head.

There followed a very funny part of my life. O'Grady was a past-master at storytelling. At a critical part of the story, he would drop his voice down to a whisper. Cal would be halfway out of his bed trying to catch the end of the story. We pretended not to notice. The end came one evening. O'Grady was speaking of a row which broke out in Barry's Hotel on the night before. It was a graphic description of food being scattered off tables and jugs being broken. I glanced at Cal. His eyes were wide open and his ears were strained to hear every word. He was concentrating on O'Grady and did not notice me enjoying the situation.

At this point O'Grady was unable to contain his laughter. He walked out the door and signalled me to follow him. We were scarcely outside the door when Cal burst out upon us. He shouted:

'Who in Hell was fighting?'

'Barry's tomcat was fighting with Brady's tomcat.'

Cal McCarthy did not speak to us for upwards of a week. I got Horgan to come in to make the peace and in a day or two we were as good friends as ever. In fact, Cal contributed to our conversation. His idea was that although Forestry was a lovely life to lead, there was no money in it. We asked him what he thought of the foresters he met out the country. He replied: 'They were all pure mad and they treated me as if I was a lunatic.'

When Cal was a year or so a forester, he joined Agriculture. He was very competent. He later worked with my brother Paul in Roscommon on land improvement. Paul did not recognise me in his stories about Avondale. O'Grady and I figured better than we deserved. I would have loved to have met him again and to have heard more of the boys who were 'pure mad'.

To make up for falling out with us, Cal began reciting long folktales for us in our bedroom about the 'Son of the King of Ireland' and such like. I was completely unfamiliar with this sort of story. Uncle Henry's stories were about historical events and much shorter. I had also heard ghost stories. Cal's long tales were new to me. He had probably heard them told in Irish in his native district.

The senior students in the class of 1939/40 were Joseph Conway (Clare), Peadar O'Grady (Clare), Dan McGuire (Longford), Joseph Hanahoe (Mayo), Jer Horgan (Cork), Cal McCarthy (Cork), Michael Rigney (Offaly), Dan Nyhan (Cork), Dan Sullivan (Kerry), John Ryan (Carlow) and myself. We had twelve originally but one student left after joining.

Our junior students came in the first week and served for the full term. We only served in our first year from March to September. The names of our junior students were: Tim Collins (Cork), Moss Collins (Cork), Tom Mahony (Cork), Pat Finnerty (Mayo), Jim Heverin (Mayo), J. Flanagan (Monaghan), Patrick Flynn (Clare), J. Guilfoyle (Clare), Brendan Hester (Roscommon), and J.J. Thornhill (Cork). There were originally twelve but two left after joining.

On arriving in Avondale as juniors Dan McGuire and I resisted an attempt by the seniors to interview us. Our juniors were not so fortunate and had to undergo mock interviews. They arrived in Avondale in twos and threes. This left them in a position to be preyed upon. It was great fun for the interviewers but not so for those running the gauntlet. This practice persisted down the years. The gems extracted from these 'victims' became many a party piece. It formed part of the lighter side of Forestry.

I found our juniors very interesting people. They were mostly honours-Leaving-Certificate students and came from local Diocesan Colleges and Christian Brothers Schools. Our year had come mainly via Agricultural and Horticultural Colleges. A few had come from Technical Schools. To a certain extent, the two classes were poles apart because of our Agricultural and Horticultural background. About four in each class were *Gaeilgeoirs*. The rest were in favour of Irish but did not want it to interfere with their work. Two of our seniors were from the Gaeltacht: Dan Sullivan from west Kerry, and Cal McCarthy from Cúil Aodha in west Cork. Jer Horgan was from a Breac-Ghaeltacht area and had a lot of Irish.

I was friendly with Peadar O'Grady during my first year in Avondale. During our third year our friendship blossomed even further. I was gradually getting away from my old friends Hanahoe and McGuire. I often found myself walking to town of an evening with O'Grady. I felt Peadar was lonely and in need of companionship. He was very well read and had a great fund of quotations and 'put downs'. We began talking about personal matters to one another. After some time I found myself talking about my disappointment with Forestry not acquiring lands without proper title. He listened carefully to my idea of leaving the sellers with 30% possession. My idea of creating a forestry tradition among farmers did not seem to impress him. He said that he was very glad that I had brought up the subject. He had been endeavouring to broach it himself. He reminded me that we were two small insignificant players on a very large stage. Head Office had got this idea from England. They were determined to build up a 'title empire' here where they would own every acre of ground under trees themselves. We could never change things unless we got to the top. Even if we got there, we might leave things as they were. Then he explained to me what was historically the case.

No one had really a proper title. The people who had right titles owned plundered lands which had been torn from the original owners. The descendants of the latter were now in hill country with untitled land. Only a revolution could change the situation. He believed that this state of affairs had been left unchanged for so long that a change was no longer possible. He advised me not to talk about it for the present, especially to the juniors. Most of them were unsure of themselves as they were. There was no need to encumber them with ideas that might get them into trouble.

The Winter of 1939 and the Spring of 1940 was taken up with fieldwork, classes and participating in manoeuvres with the LDF. The censored media kept us, to quite an extent, in the dark about the War. The massing German forces were sheltering behind the Siegfried Line. Some thought it was only a question of time before their bluff would be called as the combined English/French forces were ensconced behind the well-fortified Maginot Line. As it happened, the Maginot Line was to prove no protection as the Germans in early May 1940, without warning, attacked through Holland and Belgium and surprised the Allies. About this time I got a letter from Pat 'a Park Smith. He did not say anything about the War because his letter was censored. He just asked me to pray for him. That I did. The rosary beads, which were usually kept in my Sunday coat pocket, now found themselves in my working clothes.

Then there followed the retreat to Dunkirk. I got a letter from Mrs 'a Park Smith. Pat had survived. She did not know for how long. A German attempt at invading Britain seemed inevitable. It was an unbearably hot Summer. We had to throw off our blankets in trying to get to sleep. One night I could not sleep. I had to get out for a walk in the forest. O'Grady followed me outside and I told him about my friend Pat 'a Park. He was afraid that I might come to harm.

Then came the Battle of Britain later that Summer. I got a letter from Mama. She told me she met Pat's mother every day. Mrs 'a Park would have liked if I had been with Pat in order to keep him safe. I wrote back to Mama telling her that my rosary beads were forever in my hands. Pat was one of the heroes of the Blitz. He was shot down and invalided out. He was sent to Canada as one of the instructors to help train the Canadian Air Force. This must have been a great relief for his family, as it was to me. I always felt a deep debt of gratitude to O'Grady for his council during those tortuous weeks. It is a period which I have tried to forget.

An incident occurred sometime in late July, I think, which was to have long-lasting repercussions for me. The film 'The Wizard of Oz' had come to Arklow and everybody had to get to see it. On this particular weekend the House Master, Mr. Breslin, had to go home to Donegal. Dan McGuire was appointed by the Superintendent to fill the office for the weekend. Dan Sullivan and Dan Nyhan and myself were going to Arklow. We got ample extra time from the temporary House Master. In fact, we would have time to spare or so we thought. 'The Wizard of Oz' had been flagged, in other words advertised in advance. To say that we enjoyed the film would be an understatement. The lovely Judy Garland fuelled our imagination. That night she was all our idol.

We had coffee after the film. As yet, we were all teetotallers. In those days you attempted to whistle the principal tune of the film. That night I had two very good competitors. I felt that I was falling behind. I had to be satisfied with my own efforts. Their renderings caused me to lapse into silence. It was at this point that disaster struck. We were about a mile from Arklow. The back tyre of Dan Sullivan's bicycle burst with a loud bang. We had material with us to mend a puncture, but Dan would require a new tyre. All shops were closed at that hour of night. We were not beaten yet. I wheeled Dan's machine alongside while riding my own. Dan Nyhan took the other Dan on the bar of his bike and we all moved forward but at a slower pace. After a while Dan Sullivan took my bike and wheeled the patient. I sat on the bar and Nyhan did the cycling. It was slow work. We were encountering small hills which we had never noticed before.

Eventually we reached Avondale. We were only ten minutes late. The place was in darkness. We hated ringing the bell. Nyhan suggested that we go around and throw pebbles at some of the dormitory windows. The night was so dark that it was impossible to find a suitable pebble. Then Sullivan noticed that the common room window was slightly open. It was a very big window with the lower half raised for about a foot and a half. I climbed up on Dan Sullivan's back and pulled myself on to the windowsill. I pushed the window up another foot and pulled myself in. Dan Nyhan had now got on top of Sullivan's shoulders and I pulled him in. Nyhan and I now reached down, each searching for a different hand of Dan's. After a big effort we had Sullivan inside the common room.

We were congratulating ourselves. In fact we were actually laughing. At this point the room was flooded with light. There in the middle of the room was none other than the Superintendent. He was standing erect with a book and pencil in hand. Gone was the charming smile of the classroom. Instead, we were treated to a steely militaristic gaze. Although he knew our names, he persisted in asking our names, each one in turn. He stopped short of asking us to spell them. He then told us to appear in our walking-out suits with our cases packed at ten a.m. the following morning. He did not utter another word, but departed in his best military stride. It was a sad ending to a lovely evening. We went to our respective rooms and fell into bed. We left the morning to take care of itself.

Next morning we arrived at the office. We did not have our cases with us, hoping we would not be dismissed. We were, however, cleanly shaven and had polished our shoes. We knocked at the door of the office. The table on which accounts were done was now pushed to the centre of the room. Behind it were three chairs. On one sat the House Master, who had just returned. In the Middle sat the Superintendent. To his left sat the 'Deputy House Master', Dan McGuire. The House Master and his Deputy looked very uncomfortable. They would appear to be wishing themselves one hundred miles away from the place of execution. The three condemned stood in front of the table. I was in the centre with a Dan on either side.

We each acknowledged our name as it was called out in turn. Then the Superintendent read out the charge:
'That you T. Briody, D. Sullivan and D. Nyhan did get permission for a late night. The times thereto were specifically stated. Ample time was allowed. You deliberately stayed out ten minutes extra, thus putting your fellow-student, Dan McGuire, in

an embarrassing position. Have you anything to say?'

Dan Nyhan was on my right and he pressed a foot on mine. Dan Sullivan was on my left and he pressed a foot on my other foot. I did not know whether they had this prearranged or not. Looking back I prefer to think it was just coincidental. I cleared my throat. I thanked the Superintendent for giving me a chance to give the explanation that really should have been asked for the previous night. In fact, we had nothing to apologize for. If things had gone as we had planned we would have been the first home. Events, however, dictated otherwise. We should have rung the bell and have got entry by so doing. Instead, we had gone around and entered the common room through a window that had been left open. We had only been a mile from Arklow when disaster struck. We got a puncture which we were unable to fix because of the lateness of the hour. We could have left the man with the punctured tyre to complete the journey on his own. Instead, we waited and helped out our fellow-student. I described how one of us wheeled the incapacitated bicycle alongside his own, while the other carried the other student on the bar. We had actually exceeded our expectations. Instead of being a half an hour late, we were only ten minutes late.

All this time I had been looking out the window in my search for words. My debating training stood to me. As I was pressing the last point home, I looked straight at the eyes of the Superintendent. What I saw there astonished me. He was completely dumbfounded. He looked at his watch and signalled to the House Master that it was time for class. We walked out the door. Nothing else was said.

As we entered the classroom we were conscious of a hushed silence. Sorrowful faces looked up as if all had prepared themselves to say a last goodbye. Suddenly Dan Sullivan started giggling to himself and he was joined by Dan Nyhan. I was asked to give an explanation. I replied that I had done all the talking inside and it was the turn of one of the Dans to do the talking now. Dan Nyhan took up the task. They say that every tale increases with the extra telling and Dan's telling was no exception. He had the advantage of looking at the Superintendent's puzzled face while I was looking out the window. He was able to paint a picture in words of the changing features of Mr Grant's face. I had only said once that we had no apology to offer. Dan said it a few times for me. In fact, my explanation became his party piece. Years later when I had forgotten the incident, I would come across some younger forester who would ask me if I was the man who had bested the Superintendent at Avondale.

And yet I was sorry the incident had ever occurred. I admired Mr Grant and all the qualities he stood for. I was aware that the rapport which had grown between us had vanished and that things would never be the same again. He would appear subsequently to be choosing his words with me. He was more kind to me than ever but he spoke as little as possible to me. I had to live with the situation. To illustrate the point, Mr Grant generally read his lecture to us. If his prepared lecture was short, he read slowly and filled in with minor details. If it was long, he read very fast, almost nonstop. I had learned shorthand and this stood me in good stead. I would take down the lecture in a jotter and transcribe it later into a proper notebook. On one occasion, towards the end of a lecture, Mr Grant came across to me. He may have noticed that I was at times waiting for him to continue. He glanced at my jotter. I explained to him that I had taken down the lecture in shorthand and would transcribe it later. He simply nodded his head.

The next time we had a class, the House Master came into the classroom, something he rarely did. This time he informed my classmates that my lectures were taken down in shorthand and transcribed into a more legible form later. It would be of help if they compared their lecture notes with mine. This they had already being doing. How nice it would have been if Mr Grant had made the suggestion instead of the House Master!

The Autumn of 1940 passed quickly enough. There were plenty of football matches, but I was careful that I did not get hurt. There might be miles and miles of cycling in my future forest – better be careful! To lesson the danger of injury, I did not do any football training or practice. I got on well with my juniors. Two or three of them would ask me to go for a walk through the Avondale grounds in the evenings. I mixed history with silviculture as I talked to them. They liked it that way. I had all the lore from Gardener Breen about Lovers' Leap and the Battery Road. Sometimes I would take them as far as Connary and we would walk in as far as possible into the disused mine shafts. It was part of the famous vale of Avoca. The students made a parody on the famous song. I must say this did not get my complete approval:

> 'Oh the Vale of Avoca, Thomas Moore calls you sweet,
> But if he had to plant trees through its valleys and glens
> He would not care a damn about the place where the bright waters meet.'

I forget the rest of the parody, but perhaps it is best that way.

Later when I would meet those students, who had now become foresters, they would talk of Battery Road. Perhaps it was the only classroom in which I was permitted to talk about horticulture and silviculture. For me those walks were an occasion to revive old forgotten things. Strangely enough, I learned as much from those students as I taught them.

The War was beginning to grip. Rationing was in the offing but not yet implemented. Letters from home were filled with war news. Some of the casualties had been local. I began longing to get home. The burning topic was the War. Everybody would listen avidly to the radio news in the common room. Of course, it was all filtered and censored. Even so the main events could not be camouflaged. Sometimes Hanahoe, McGuire, Sullivan and Horgan would pay us a visit in our little room. O'Grady was always good to listen to. Cal McCarthy regarded the War as extreme madness. He would have loved to knock all their heads together. McGuire and Hanahoe could not be satisfied except with an Allied victory. O'Grady and myself felt the restoration of peace would be best for everyone. Germany had been dealt with unfairly after the First World War. Their treatment had contributed to the present outbreak of hostilities. However, we felt a German victory would make matters worse. Of course, we knew nothing of German atrocities at that juncture.

An event occurred in the last few weeks of our stay in Avondale which deserves to be mentioned. I was on my usual walk to town with O'Grady. As we passed the Convent gates, he turned to me and asked: 'Who paid your hospital expenses when you were injured?' It was like a bolt from the blue. In fact, the matter had never crossed my mind. I suddenly felt very bad about it and told O'Grady so. The following evening I drafted a letter to the Convent, thanking the nuns for their kindness and asking them for a bill to cover my injury. I got a letter back in reply. I would have to pay nothing. They realised I was near losing my job without any compensation. They were glad to have been able to help me during my hour of need. They would be glad if I would call on a certain evening and at a certain time.

So on the following Thursday at seven p.m. we called at the Convent. I had asked O'Grady to come along. I thought it might be hard to persuade him. No. He was delighted and I was, too. I hated the idea of going on my own. We found ourselves seated at a table on which was a lovely meal. The Reverend Mother was there and the two nuns who had been so kind to me during that awful period. When we had partaken of the meal, we all sat back. One of the nuns produced a violin and played a delightful piece of music. Although my Aunt Rose was a nun in America, before being injured two years before I had never had any contact with nuns. I was amazed how natural they all were. In fact, on this occasion I amazed myself and gave a few recitations. Peadar told a few safe jokes about the nuns in his own town. The nun with the violin sang a few songs for us. One of them was for me, 'Come Back Paddy Reilly to Ballyjamesduff'. The other was for Peadar, 'The Girl from Clare'. We promised to call again, which we did.

Peadar and I were the talk of Avondale over our visits to the Convent. We were fit for anything. Cal McCarthy was annoyed that he was not invited too. Maybe it was just as well. Cal would have considered them 'pure mad'. I took a few weeds out of the Matron's garden and I took the opportunity of telling her of the generosity of the nuns towards me. I also thanked her for the many lifts she gave me to Mass while recuperating from my injury. All this kindness helped to soften the bitter pill of that unfortunate accident on the pitch.

The last weeks in Avondale slipped quickly away. Some

of us would never meet again. The juniors were hoping that they might be in the same forest as a senior they knew. We had a last homily from Superintendent Grant. We owed him a lot. I never met him again. I had become a problem to him, a problem that was not of my making. I was sorry to say goodbye to Hanahoe, McGuire, Horgan and Sullivan. They had been with me from Ballyhaise and Albert. I said a special goodbye to my roommates O'Grady and McCarthy. Before leaving Avondale I was informed that I was being sent to Clonmel/Kilsheelan forest. It was normal in Forestry for the forester-in-charge of the forest where a junior forester was being sent to welcome him by letter. I expected to receive such a letter in due course.

I came home and I enjoyed the rest immensely. Dad and Mama seemed to be happy. The auctioneering business was doing well. Mama was in good form and the tales she and Dad reminisced over were pre-First-World-War ones. The in-between years were safely put to bed. I was the third in the family. The fourth, fifth and sixth had died. Paul was the seventh. After studying Agriculture for two years in Warrenstown he was looking for a job. My brother Austin was also to train in Agriculture and Horticulture during the War and in time, like Paul, become an Agricultural Inspector. Austin was a good footballer and played at County level for Cork, Sligo and Donegal.

I made a special visit to Shanvalla. Charles and Aunt Kate were still hale and hearty. There was nobody left at home except Eddie. Four of the girls, who were living in the locality, came back to Shanvalla to give me a party. I would have had a great story to tell them about being injured, but I refrained from doing so. Instead, I listened to their recital of stories. I realised how out on a limb I had become because I was a forester. For the first time I felt very lonely. I had another party in Clonloaghan. My godmother was at her best. She could not understand how I had not a girl somewhere. To relieve her curiosity, I was tempted to invent one, but I knew she would torture Mama with her special news. I had to be careful.

Dad only wanted to hear about Avondale. I was glad that I had taken such an interest in the house itself and its beautiful surroundings. He was sorry to hear how the Forestry Division was so structured. It seemed so different from what his generation had fought for in the Land War. He had seen countless farmers sell portion of their farms in order to hang on to the rest. He had seen strong men cry as they signed on the dotted line when selling their farms. How nice it would have been if farmers had been able to retain a partial claim on the lands they had sold to Forestry. He could not understand how a native government could stand over it. Neither could I.

Mama was anxious that I look after myself. She was very particular about the airing of clothes. Dampness had to be avoided at all costs. I promised that I would bring her to one of my forests when in charge. She kept me to my promise when I was in Mount Bellow six years later.

My holidays at home had slipped away and only two days remained. They would be taken up with going to my many friends to say goodbye. I had as yet not received any notification from Clonmel. When word eventually did come, its tone was not what I expected and the contents of the letter were to remain forever in my memory.

One day the postman arrived with a strange envelope. On top was written one word, 'Briody'. Underneath was a manipulation of an address. To my humiliation, Dad had already opened the letter. It read: 'Briody come ahead. You were here before. I would prefer if you were not coming. Let me see if I can fit you in.' Dad came to my rescue. He told me not to tell Mama. He said that I could come back home any time I chose. He proclaimed: 'Better to be a collector of bottles and to be your own boss!' He told the rest of the family that I had been to the place I was being sent to before under a different forester. It was a time when I had to pull myself together. I wrote a letter to Head Office. I enclosed the offending envelope and letter. I said that the postman did not know what to make of the address and that my father, who had the same Christian name as me, had opened the letter to find out what it contained. I had the humiliation of hearing it read out to me. I said that the man who wrote it owed me an apology.

I left home. Only God knew what was in my thoughts. I

was travelling on an early train and had a few hours to spend in Dublin. I had finished my traineeship. Britain was at war. Perhaps I would be a more welcome guest over there than at Clonmel. My making a hasty decision on the matter was averted by my meeting with my cousin Harry. He got two tickets for us to visit Guinness's Brewery. We went there. I was now twenty seven years of age. I was a Pioneer and had never drank. We were part of a large crowd. We were offered several kinds of brewed ale. I broke my pledge. The fact that I was a little drunk may have influenced me in boarding the train for Clonmel.

Part V: A qualified forester

Clonmel-Kilsheelan/ forest foreman

When I reached Dempsey's in Kilsheelan, where I had stayed as a trainee, I was told that Mrs Dempsey was in poor health. The Slievenamon forester, Jack McCarthy, was staying there. He informed me that we might have to look elsewhere for new digs. Because of the War and the rationing of supplies, he said, there were few digs available. We could, however, hang on for the present. All this came as somewhat of a shock to me. Some of my old acquaintances heard I was returning and were in the house before me when I arrived; others soon dropped in. In no time I was my old self again.

I slept soundly. Next morning I went out to where my former gang had been. It was nice to feel those warm handshakes again. I was having a look around when I heard a call, 'Hoy! Hoy!', on my left. I kept looking to my right. Then I heard a whistle. I looked in the direction of the whistling. Then I saw a bulky figure rushing towards me. Finally he reached me. 'Briody', he said, 'did you not hear me whistling?' 'Crammond', I replied, 'I only use a whistle for calling a dog.'

He seemed taken aback. Then I opened up. I told him I was sent there as forest foreman. I would be available to carry out any orders that he might give. I would prefer to get those in writing. He did not reply. He went down to where Larry Whelan was with the forest gang. He probably had never had to deal with a situation like this before. He came back and told me that I would have all instructions from him on the morrow. In the meantime, he asked me what aspect of forestry was I most interested in. I told him that I had heard that there was a Emergency Fuel Scheme in the offing. He said that he had heard that too but that he would have to wait for concrete instructions.

I asked him if there was any scrub area available for the scheme. He told me that there was a hundred acres of scrub at Glen. He intended planting the area in the next three years. I then said that I knew the area well and that it would require shelter belts for wind protection. He agreed and then asked me if I had any experience of such work. I told him that I had been working on shelter belts in south-east Galway. He seemed anxious to get away from me. Then he left. He had gone only one hundred yards from me when he returned. He said abruptly: 'You have solved a problem for me. I have two trainees coming tomorrow. I have failed to get digs for them. Wait in until they arrive. Try and persuade Mrs Dempsey to accept them. If you succeed, give them a day to recover. You can go shelter-belting with them on the following day.

Jack McCarthy had been a schoolteacher. He was one of those who felt that Ireland needed reafforestation. He had left a comfortable teaching post to become a forester. Before coming to Slievenamon he had been a forester in Ashford Castle and had experience of dealing with large gangs of workers. He was an interesting man to talk to. I was glad to have met him. I was later to go to Slievenamon as forester-in-charge and benefited very much from having got the 'low down' from him.

Jack was able to get Mrs Dempsey to take the two trainees who were coming on the morrow. He told her that he would ask them to be as useful about the place as possible. They would be leaving after three months. The trainees duly arrived next day. They had been my juniors in Avondale. Pat Flynn from Clare was an impressive good-looking chap. He was a very intelligent fellow and rose rapidly to inspectorial rank. John Flanagan was from Monaghan. He was a gifted footballer and was quickly availed of by the local team. They were both relieved to have got digs and promised to be as accommodating as possible. The following day I brought them out to the scrub area. They had no experience of planting shelter belts.

The scrub area was a very tricky one. The hill rose from the south-west for the first four hundred yards and then dropped gradually on the other side. I explained to the two boys that we had to leave a buffer shelter belt on the north-west edge of the scrub area. The next shelter belt would have to be positioned to the left of the wind over the hill. Mr Crammond arrived. He had come from estates where wind protection was a must. He knew where every shelter belt should go to a yard. As he worked, he

306

became a boy again. Whistling is an art which has gone out of fashion. He entertained us by whistling the latest hit. Listening to him whistle, I wondered how he could have written that awful letter. He even clapped me on the shoulder on one occasion. I again asked him what preparations he had made for the forthcoming fuel scheme. He repeated that he had to wait for instructions before laying the ground. I informed him that there might be a shortage of employable young men in Carrick-on-Suir, some six miles away, as I had heard many had already left to work in munitions factories in England. We would also need horses to extract the timber, which would then have to be carted to the railway station. The next day Crammond went to the Carrick-on-Suir Labour Exchange. There were no suitable men there. There were none in Clonmel either.

We had the shelter belts completed in a fortnight and I took the trainees back to the planting area and left them there. I began recruiting horses. I worked late into the night. I knew a lot of men in their fifties and sixties who had worked preparing pit-props for the trenches of the First World War. I went to Tracey Park in Carrick-on-Suir and recruited twenty young boys who could work with bush saws at the roadside preparing cords for carting to the railway station. By this time I had persuaded my boss to start felling, hauling, and cutting firewood up into cords. A cord was a forestry measure. The firewood was cut into four-feet lengths. A cord was four foot high, four foot wide and four foot long.

When the word came to begin operations, we were already sending supplies to the railway station at Kilsheelan. From there it could be sent to wherever it was required. The fuel was like old gold. My boss at Clonmel was getting a similar operation going. He came to me one day in a very agitated state. Some civil servant had asked him who had given instructions to him to go ahead with the operation. He told me I could claim ignorance but that he might have to take the boat to England. I advised him to do nothing for the present. It gave me a jolt. I had taken the initiative. I had set a scheme in motion. For the first time I realised that I was not working for Ireland but for a government department. Worse still, I had got my boss into a mess which was not of his making. My boss had now become the 'white-haired boy' instead of 'an old tyrant'.

I did not see Mr Crammond again until pay day. I was dreading what might be in store. When he came he was in high good humour. He told me that we had won the day. All the inspectors claimed to have hinted to him to begin operating the fuel scheme. He had never heard any such thing. They were now all trying to take credit for the operation. Our little scheme had only been a pilot one, it would appear. This affair was the best thing that ever happened to me. Henceforth, I resolved only to carry out orders which were given to me by a superior officer. The only orders I could give were to the men under me. I was to learn slowly.

Nothing in my training in Avondale prepared me for what I was about to experience. I watched in sheer amazement at those men of another generation working. One of the horsemen had a number of pulleys. He had a small pony. With these pulleys he was able to get timber over rocks and out of difficult crevices. Chainsaws had not yet arrived on the scene. Crosscuts were kept razor-sharp. These men were able to achieve as much as forest workers of thirty years later who were equipped with chainsaws and tractors for hauling.

The boys with their bush saws worked in pairs along the roadside where a horse and cart could reach. The daily quota for two boys was four cords, which they easily achieved. This meant that we had ten pairs operating. The number of horses drawing firewood to the boys depended on the distance the timber had to be hauled. This was decided by the man in charge of the boys. Sometimes a horseman would suffice for a pair. At times he might be able to supply two pairs. Sometimes it might take two horsemen to supply a pair. It was an ongoing situation. The more- seasoned staff were engaged in felling the firewood and they had to keep the supply flowing.

The operation seemed to progress on oiled wheels. The work was very systematic. There was an additional factor. The men sensed that they were working for the country. They were waiting for fresh 'orders to advance'. It was a part of my life of which I am very proud. I realised that I was doing more for

Ireland than if I was in the Army. Furthermore, men were still asking to join the scheme and soon we had sixty in the operation.

We had areas around Mission Cross and the Charity House which had not been thinned to their full capacity. At this point in Forestry development only straight trees were saleable. It was a big leap forward, in later years, when crooked timber was converted into composite timber. We availed of the opportunity to take out the undesirables. This material was to prove a godsend in helping to fire the trains. Spruce and Scots pine were very inflammable, even when fresh. So too was ash, but other deciduous trees such as oak and beech would take about two months to dry out. Initially, some unsuitable timber had to be burned fresh, but in time this was no longer necessary as we built up stores of all sorts of timber. My two trainees were sorry to leave after their three months' stay. They would have preferred to finish their second year in the Clonmel-Kilsheelan forest. They pretended to me that they had learned more with me than in their first year in Avondale. I was not aware that I was teaching them anything. I hoped that they might find their next forest to their satisfaction.

Mr Crammond asked me to help out at Clonmel. Five miles beyond Clonmel lay Russellstown where the chief supply of fuel was to be found. I left Kilsheelan with sixty men in the care of Larry Whelan. Larry had been a working foreman for a long time. He had two time-keepers to help him. The situation was such that I knew that things would go on there as if I had been present. I went over to Russellstown and stayed there for a few weeks. We had a small gang of twenty. When I was leaving we had sixty. They would appear to have come out of nowhere. In passing I should say that ninety pounds paid sixty men at thirty shillings per man per week. The majority of those men had families. They must have had small gardens to help out. How was it done? And yet they were a cheerful group and always thanked me when getting their pay.

At Kilsheelan, we were near the railway station. At Clonmel, we were five miles away. It was too far for a horse and cart. Mr Crammond was tired from asking Head Office to provide lorries to transport the fuel. Getting petrol was the problem. We decided to concentrate on Kilsheelan. Then Head Office woke up and gave us the petrol we needed. I must have left Russellstown running on oiled wheels, for Mr Crammond spent every second day with me. He was really a very interesting man. He came to Forestry from an estate and may have got his education in a boarding school. He appeared to know more about trees than about men. We were one day walking among large oak trees. It was wintertime. I always hated this season when trees are devoid of their leaves and I must have said so to him. He looked at me in amazement. Then I saw his eye travel along the gnarled branch of an oak tree. He paused and looked back at me. I nodded. Then his eyes travelled on to a place where it had stopped and gone upright. Then he went on to another tree, remarking that he had never found two trees alike. I had an agricultural, horticultural and silvicultural training, but that was the first time I had seen the beauty of those naked oak trees.

Mr Crammond gave me the gift of a lifetime that day. When I was retired, my successor in Carrick-on-Suir forest, John Healy, gave me the present of an oak tree that had been battered by the wind. It was supposed to be for my winter fuel. My daughter Anne, who is environmentally conscious, has persuaded me not to touch it. She would like to see the old tree finish its days a habitat for bacteria as it rots away. She may have heard me talking about trees to myself. Maybe we never die. There is always someone to hand on the torch to.

I had been getting the usual weekly letter from Mama. I was happy with how things were at home. She seemed to like the stories I told her of Kilsheelan. Suddenly I realised that Dad was also reading my letters too and must be wondering what on earth was really happening. I wrote to him telling him of my meeting with Harry in Dublin and how I had nearly crossed the Irish Sea. Then I went on to describe my first meeting with Mr Crammond and of his subsequent climb-down. There had been a conversion on both sides. Now he seemed to be doing everything to please me and I was doing my best for him. I sent the letter to Dad's office in Granard. Mama still did not know anything about Crammond's abusive letter to me. I got a letter back in reply. He had spent an anxious time since, and told me he had included me in his prayers. He suggested that my sending this strange letter of Crammond's to Head Office may have tipped the balance in my favour. He told me to watch my step as a leopard never changes his spots. I wrote back and thanked him for his advice. His was the wisdom of the years.

Things went so well for us that there was a possibility that we might run out of scrub. Mr Crammond told me to examine an area off Carney's Road on the other side of the Glasha River. It was mid-February. I went up there. There had been heavy frost on the previous night. I had to walk and push my bike uphill. To get across the Glasha River there was a plank two feet wide and ten feet long. About a yard above the plank there was a strong wire stretching from one bank to the other for the person crossing to hold on to. This makeshift footbridge was used by the people of Toor on the far side of the river. They had erected a small hut near the road where they kept their bicycles. Coming from work in the evenings, they left their bicycles in the hut, they then crossed the plank and went home through the wood. On examining the site, I saw many difficulties there and decided that extracting scrub from the area would be too troublesome.

I must have been still pondering the matter. As I walked back across the plank, my foot slipped and I fell into the river. It was in full spate. I was carried on for a few yards. I caught on to a projecting rock and pulled myself up. I was in a cold, frozen state. I knew that there was no house within three miles of me except for a gamekeeper's lodge above on the far side of the road. I did not know if it was occupied. I had never seem anyone come out of that house. Nevertheless I made my way towards the lodge in a sodden, half-frozen state. A girl came out and locked the door behind her. Then she saw me. She turned and unlocked the door. She invited me in. My drenched clothes told their own story.

She turned the wheel of the bellows and the fire blazed up. She rummaged in an old trunk and brought out an old nightdress, more suitable for a woman. She gave it me along with a towel. She told me she was on her way to Kilsheelan village, which was three miles away. I told her that I was a forester and asked her go to Mick Dempsey and get him to come and collect me. She left for the village. I took off my clothes. I dried myself as best I could and I put on the nightdress. The fire was warm but without the nightdress on me I might have got a chill in the draft. My shirt was the first to dry. Bit by bit I got clothed. Maybe I might make myself a cup of tea. Luckily enough, there was water in the kettle. Soon I had it boiling. I searched for a teapot, a cup and a few leaves of tea. Best of all, I came across a jug of goat's milk. I had not tasted any since my time in Kinnity. It was a cup of tea to remember. The door opened. Mick Dempsey and the girl of the house came in. She had not found him at home and had to go further to fetch him. In recent years I discovered the girl in question was the aunt of one of the drivers of the taxi service I avail of here in Carrick. Burns was her maiden name; Mrs Creed was her married name. She lived into her nineties.

My escape from the Glasha River was the talk of the neighbourhood. I got several letters from foresters advising me to take the pledge. It was about this time that Mr Crammond and I seemed to edge further towards one another. We discovered that we were both Ulstermen. He was from Donegal. We began talking about horticulture as well as sylviculture. I was invited to his home where I met his wife and children. They were nice cultured people.

Gradually I discovered the cause of his behaviour on our first meeting. Someone had told him that I was a semi-revolutionary and might influence the workforce. Getting me working on the shelter belts for the first three weeks was to keep me away from the workforce. Something else was happening. Mr Crammond was promoted inspector. He told me that I was partly responsible for his good luck. Jokingly, he said that I might, if things had gone badly, have been the cause of him being sacked. My premature starting of the fuel scheme got the blessings of his superiors because it had succeeded. Now he thanked me for getting him promoted. That was not true. He was a hard worker and deserved all he got.

Another cloud appeared on the horizon. Mr Tom Prior was being promoted to head-forester and would take over the

Clonmel Forest. He was the terror of every forest squad who had come into contact with him. He had served in the national Army during the Civil War. He had subdued many a troublesome trainee. As I have already said above, when a trainee stepped out of line in Avondale, he was threatened with a spell under Mr Prior. His reputation had gone before him and the forest squads at Kilsheelan and Clonmel were closing down the hatches and preparing for the coming storm. All Forestry were watching. Mr prior was coming to Clonmel. He was a Cavan man and a keen disciplinarian. I too was a Cavan man with a different philosophy. Mr Crammond jokingly remarked: 'When Greek meets Greek then comes the tide of battle!'

The forester in charge of the Clonmel-Kilsheelan forest had always stayed at Clonmel. Mr Prior, however, was to rent a house nearer Kilsheelan to be closer to the work on hand. Everyone was anxiously awaiting what might happen. Mr Crammond left and Mr Prior arrived. I remember my first meeting with him. He was accompanied by Mr Petrie, our Divisional Inspector, who introduced us to one another. Prior looked at me as if he was expecting to see someone else. He took me in with a wide sweeping glance. Then his stern face relaxed into a smile. He extended a very big hand.

'I expected to meet a tough Mullahoran man,' he said.

'I would have been that if I had remained,' I replied

'Are you sorry you left?' he queried.

'I don't like to think too much about it,' I replied.

'Maybe we both should have stayed.' he said in a low voice.

I congratulated him on his recent marriage, especially as he had married a Monaghan girl. Then the Divisional Inspector asked us to discuss the work in hand together. It was all business-like. Mr Petrie took his leave and we were left together. Prior informed me that he was getting a forest foreman fresh from Avondale and that I was being promoted to take over the Slievenamon forest. The Emergency Fuel Scheme was new to him and he would like for it to be a success. He would have preferred if I would have been left a few weeks with him. The rest of our conversation was about Cavan football. He would have made an excellent football coach but I would not like to have had to take instructions from him. I had the feeling that he would expect a high scoring tally. I had not much to do with him after that. Instead of informing Prior of the ins and outs of the fuel scheme, I imparted the knowledge required to his new foreman, Denis (Dinny) O' Sullivan when he arrived.

Slievenamon/forester-in-charge

I had been forest foreman in Kilsheelan. I would now be forester-in-charge in Slievenamon. Although being transferred to Slievenamon forest avoided a possible confrontation with Tom Prior, it presented me with another problem. The Slievenamon forest had often been serviced by a junior inspector from the District Office who had a car at his disposal. My journey on pay day would in all amount to forty eight miles. This I would have to do by bicycle as it was rare in those days for Head Office to sanction the use of a hired car for paying the workforce.

Slievenamon was a difficult forest to concentrate on. The Killurney property was on the west of the mountain; Kilcash was in the middle facing south; Glenbower was at the east; and the Boherboy property was in the middle at the back of the mountain facing north. Later the Slievenamon forest was converted into two distinct forests. At the time I could only concentrate on one property a day. I used have to spend a second day a week in Boherboy. Some years before I arrived in Slievenamon there had been a very serious fire in Boherboy. A lot of Douglas fir was destroyed. It was very charred but we managed to salvage it. It was very dirty work. There had been an attempt to replant the area but the scorched soil did not respond well. It would have needed a dressing of phosphates. This practice did not come into Forestry until years later. In the meantime, I could do nothing except think of possible solutions and suggest them to Head Office. It was a new experience for me and I had nothing in my notes to guide me.

When I first went to Slievenamon I spent a period extracting poles in Killurney, where we had a pole depot. This was my first experience of such work and I was not to have much to do again with poles until I returned to the area in 1960. I could

314

have spent more time extracting poles at this juncture but the Emergency Fuel Scheme demanded my attention.

I remember Killurney for two reasons. One time I was dreaming that I was at Killurney. As I reached Killurney one of my men said: 'There is someone dead over there. Maybe you recognise him.' So I went across and I looked in and it was myself who was lying there. I woke up immediately with the shock. It was the biggest shock I ever got.

On another occasion I was going to Cavan on a holiday a few days hence. On this particular morning I went into Clonmel before going out to the forest. There I bought a new suitcase and also an alarm clock, which I put in the suitcase. When I came as far as Killurney there was a lorry waiting to load poles. As we did not have the type of poles required, I said to the driver; 'I'll go along with you to Boherboy and we can get some poles there.' Then I went back to this cottage and told the woman of the house that I would be back, leaving my bicycle there and giving her my case to mind inside.

I went around the mountain with the driver maybe five or six miles or more to Boherboy and we loaded the poles there. After we had loaded the poles I got the idea that maybe I would go uphill and cross over the top to Killurney. It was a lovely morning and I got up on top without much difficulty. It was then I realised that I was about eight miles from my destination. I had to make the most of it. There was very heavy foliage at times, which was hard to get through. Fortunately there were other bare patches. Eventually I reached Killurney and I went straight to the cottage where my bicycle was only to find that a crowd had gathered. Somebody said: 'Oh there he is.' I knew I was the object of some curiosity. My alarm clock had gone off and the woman of the house had thrown my case out into the cabbage-garden, thinking it was a bomb. The neighbours had been alerted and were waiting further developments.

While in the Clonmel-Kilsheelan forest, Mr Crammond and I had felled and railed 10,000 tons of firewood to help run the trains and heat the hospitals. Another 10,000 tons had been felled at Slievenamon but it remained in the wood because the right-of-ways were such that they did not allow access by horse and cart. Somebody at Head Office had decided to leave the firewood as it was until the following Summer when conditions would be dry and extraction easier. I was not made aware of this. Instead I got a memo from the Emergency Fuel Scheme telling me that they were running short of fuel and to rail the felled firewood as soon as possible.

Suddenly Mrs Dempsey took ill and I had only a week to find alternative lodgings. I failed to do so because rationing was too severe. Dinny O'Sullivan, Mr Prior's forest foreman, and I decided to try to rent a house between us. We started looking at vacant houses. It was an uphill battle. Finally we moved into a house at Ballydine, roughly equidistant between the Kilsheelan and Slievenamon forests. It had advantages. Our landlady, Mrs Kehoe, was sympathetic to Forestry. The rent was nominal and our milk was supplied. Not having to pay lodgings, we had more money in our pockets than ever before. A local woman did our washing and even starched our shirts. Dinny was an expert cook and I did my best to help him.

Our rented house was only four miles from the firewood in Slievenamon waiting to be railed. I went to the site and concluded that there was only one way to extract the firewood. There was a field between the firewood and the road which would allow for the firewood to be extracted if we got a period of hard frost. I had to approach the owner. I was not long speaking to him when I realised that I had caught a Tartar. He had great contempt for Forestry, and regarded us as the curse of the country. I kept listening. His kind wife intervened by giving me a much needed cup of tea. The owner left and his wife informed me that he was the 'nicest man in the world' actually. Forestry was one of the bees in his bonnet. He was satisfied when he had tongue-thrashed me. She had her own troubles. There were trees which were endangering the house, but her husband pretended there was no danger. This was an opportunity for me. I would come out the following Saturday with a helper and together we would lop off the offending branches and fell the trees. I asked her not to tell her husband we were coming until an hour before we arrived. Better still, she said she would send him on a message.

My helper and I arrived on the evening of the following Saturday. We had two climbing belts, two sharp handsaws and an equally sharp crosscut. There was no sign of the man of the house about. The woman of the house was not the cheerful person I had met on the previous occasion. In fact, she was a little tense. She confided in me that she thought she had bitten off more than she could chew. She was afraid that some of the branches might fall on the roof. She was sorry that she had sent her husband away. I asked her to allow me to cut the lowest branch off one of the trees.

I climbed the tree. I made a slight cut on the under surface of the branch. To those who have not done such an operation perhaps a little explanation is necessary. When you start cutting on the top surface of a branch, for the first third of the operation you will find it normal cutting. After that the weight of the branch causes the cut to yawn open and the rest is easy. There are those who when dealing with a very heavy branch would often speed things up by sitting out on the branch for a while, adding their weight thereto. I always considered this practice too dangerous and never allowed it under my charge.

The woman watched the operation from a safe distance. When the first branch fell harmlessly by the bole of the tree instead of on the roof of the house, she retreated indoors. The first part of the job had been safely accomplished. After that it was a friendly competition between my helper and me: he debranched one tree and I another one. When we had the house-side of the trees debranched, we took our sharpened crosscut and felled the boles. It was then that we saw the man of the house approaching. It was a difficult situation to find oneself in. He solved our problem by turning around and wheeling his bicycle towards the road again. My friend suggested that he might be going to the local Garda Station. We were then called in to a lovely well-deserved meal.

After some time the farmer arrived back with a boxful of stout. It was a joyous occasion. I drank two bottles. My friend made up for me by accounting for four. Our host was in high good humour. He took out a check book, signed it and handed it across to me to fill in. I handed it back to him without writing

317

any sum on it, and assured him that as foresters we were always there to help the public. I was careful not to give any hint to him that I might have something else at the back of my mind. We left the crosscut with him. With the help of a neighbour he was able to cut enough firewood to last them both for two years.

We were leaving when he turned and said: 'You can cart the firewood across my field. You need not wait for a hard frost.' I thanked him. I told him that he was doing a service for the country by helping to feed the trains. I had made a great friend. He told me to call in for a cup of tea when passing. This was an added bonus. Bicycling in fine weather can be lovely exercise. It was different when there was rain and wind. You always had to bring rain gear. At times, this did not suffice and you had to take shelter in a friendly farmhouse. You learned which were the friendly farmhouses over a period of time. You could often meet inhospitality as well as hospitality. You had to be careful.

I waited. A week elapsed. There came a period of cold weather and the field to be crossed was well frozen. I put all the carts at my disposal hauling the timber and over a period of time we got it onto the roadside. I had earlier been railing from Kilsheelan Railway Station but had been changed to Carrick-on-Suir to admit Mr Prior railing his firewood from Kilsheelan. There had in fact been an altercation between us. I used sometimes meet Tom Prior at Kilsheelan Railway Station while loading. He was loading five wagons and drawing from just four miles away. I was only loading two wagons because I was six miles away. On one occasion I arrived to find that he had thrown some firewood into all the wagons. He was thus trying to commandeer all seven wagons. After this I switched my gang to new time, although it was still the depth of Winter. In this way I commandeered five of the wagons, leaving him two. The inspector must have sensed that there was a row in the offing. I was switched to Carrick-on-Suir Railway Station, and Prior was left in Kilsheelan. The arrangement made for peace. I was now seven to eight miles from my loading place.

Dowley's (the grain merchants) lorries in Carrick had been grounded during the War. I was able to get petrol coupons for them and employ two of their lorries to transport our material. The roads in those days were narrow and we had great difficulty keeping falling logs from obstructing the traffic. We made sure that the roads at least were safe at night. This did not placate the County Council for they wrote to Head Office complaining of the chaos on the roads. Head Office could not understand the situation. It had decided to leave the cords of firewood on Slievenamon where they were until the following Summer. They were unaware of what I had initiated. They had not sold timber in the area to any of the timber merchants. Where did the material on the roads come from? It is difficult to serve two masters at any one time!

Mr Crammond was now my inspector. When I told him what I had accomplished, he threw up his hands in horror. He told me of the Department's decision to leave this timber where it was until the following Summer. He asked me to think deeply and try to find some excuse for my action. I was never asked for an explanation. Once again I had taken an initiative without consulting my superiors. In fairness to myself, I have to say I was not made aware of this departmental decision.

In admonishing me, Mr Crammond may also have been thinking of another unauthorised action of mine. This involved a parcel of land sold by a Mr St. John to Forestry. When measured the area sold was two acres short. Forestry attempted to take in an extra two acres from one of his fields. He objected and took down the fence. That was the position when I arrived in Slievenamon. I met Mr St. John accidentally in a public house. He was very furious at first, but I calmed him down. I suggested to him that he buy back the two acres at the same price he got per acre. I reminded him that he had got paid for two acres extra. I drafted out a note in my field book. He signed it. He gave me ten pounds and I gave him a receipt for it. I forwarded the note and money to District Office. I got back a note of thanks. Everyone was satisfied that the matter had been satisfactorily settled. Everyone, that is, except the Section of Head Office who bought the land. I got a curt note from them informing me that I was not trained to buy and sell land. All further transactions must be through their hands. I would like to say that I replied belligerently. I did not. I ignored the letter.

A terrible tragedy occurred some time after I switched sending firewood from Kilsheelan to Carrick-on-Suir Railway Station. A young man called Lonergan, aged twenty two from Ballyneill, worked on one of my squads in Slievenamon. It was pay day and he had been to Carrick with a load of timber. He stayed on in the station to get a lift home with one of the lorries. He and two others were travelling on the open lorry and at some stage he fell off and was killed. He had his full wage packet in his pocket so there was no question of him being drinking. The various forests around made a collection for his family. We wrote to Head Office for them to contribute. They were very sympathetic but gave us nothing. The accident had happened after working hours. I had £20 pounds saved at the time and I gave that to his family.

I had kept in touch with the LDF since leaving Avondale, but I did not rejoin as I did not feel as free to do so now that I was a forester-in-charge. Nevertheless, I attended many of their training sessions but did not participate in manoeuvres. I noticed that some of the men from my four squads were also members. This helped me establish a rapport with them in my forest work. I used often hear the men say 'rough weather' at times when the sun was shining. Could it possible be an IRA password? I had to be careful. I tried 'rough weather' with different men. The result was amazing. It was the cause of bringing everyone to life. The men were eager to cater for my every whim. I had little difficulty in motivating the squads after that. There had been a big IRA presence in the Slievenmon area but it had been quite dormant for some time. There was a lot of dissatisfaction among Republicans with the Government whom they believed were putting national issues on the long finger. Removing the border and achieving a Republic had become too aspirational. I had heard this from an officer in the local LDF. I had heard similar talk in the pubs. The IRA was now quite active in the area.

In response to this renewed activity, an old RIC barracks at Glenbower, where the Dublin-Clonmel road forks for Carrick-on-Suir was occupied by upwards of a dozen detectives. This was close to the Glenbower property, which was divided between two forests. What lay to the west of the Dublin-Clonmel road belonged to Slievenamon forest. What lay to the east of the road belonged to the Carrick-on-Suir forest. One day while cycling past the barracks, the detective sergeant waved me down. He was anxious that his men would be able in their spare time to obtain firewood for the barracks. He would like if his men could work alongside the Kilcash squad. In this way they would be killing two birds with the one stone. He was very disarming. His face fell when I told him that this would not be possible. Instead, I would get firewood for him beyond the hill opposite the barracks. It was very light material. His men could easily shoulder the timber down the hill to the barracks. The area would be cleared for planting later. He thanked me and volunteered to burn the tops. I asked him for a pound and gave him a receipt to show anyone who came across his men working there that everything was in order. Subsequently, I avoided cycling past the barracks. Instead I went to the Boherboy property by going through Kilcash village.

Kilcash is a lovely village situated high up the southern slope of Slievenamon. At night its lights shine out over the Golden Vale. Its friendly people are proud of the area's history. Nearby are the ruins of Kilcash Castle, about which the famous song 'Cill Chaise' was composed, which begins '*Cad a dhéanfaimid feasta gan adhmad?*' ('What will we do henceforth for the timber?'). Kilcash was a very small village when I first went there in the early 1940s. It has grown a lot since. Even then a lot of people used to go there for a drink. To get to the village from the Kilsheelan side there was a very steep climb. For this reason when working in Boherboy, before the above incident with the detective sergeant, I used cycle there via Grangemokler, but I would come back along the flank of the mountain through Kilcash. The people of the village and area were very friendly towards me. I could stop in many farmhouses along the way for a cup of tea or out of the rain. Further down from Kilcash was another small village, Ballypatrick. Here there was a creamery and farmers' coop where I was able to get meat very cheaply.

We had a small planting programme above Kilcash village in 1942. Because of the Emergency Fuel Scheme we did not get there until late in the season. In fact, it was the first time I

321

had been to this actual spot. I noticed that all the drains were running to the centre of the area. There the water disappeared down an iron grating. I asked Jacky Flynn, who was the time-keeper, for an explanation. He pointed to Kilcash Castle, which was three quarters of a mile away. We were about fifty feet higher than the top of the castle. There was an underground conduit from the grating to a reservoir, which in the old days supplied the castle with water.

I took the initiative. I told Jacky Flynn to take his squad back to the fuel scheme. On no account could I plant the area, because of its historical importance. Jacky Flynn told me the local people would be relieved and thankful. The District Office agreed with me. However, it was planted six years later.

Something that happened in the Kilcash area reminded me of my days working with hard-pressed farmers during the Economic War. Farming on the foothills of Slievenamon (the high country from Kilcash to Ninemilehouse and further on to Atheny) in 2009 bears no resemblance to that of the year 1942. There are now spacious sheds to house cattle in Winter. That did not pertain back then. There was also far less winter feeding and cattle had to be wintered on the hills to graze on the sparse grass. The area was also windswept. The hungry faces of the animals as they waited at gates along the roads and lanes for hay to arrive was a very sad sight to see. I had about a dozen men with horses who were hauling firewood. They were farmers who were trying to make ends meet. They worked for three pounds a week: 30/- for themselves and 30/- for the horse. The rest of the forest workers got only half their wage. These farmers had not to be motivated. They turned in a good week's work.

One of them asked me if he could buy some of the firewood to build a cattle shelter. He told me he did not mind how crooked the material was. He gave me the specifications. At first I was getting nowhere. However, by suggesting eight standing posts instead of six I was able to avail of shorter pieces of timber to be used as crossbeams for the roof. In the fuel scheme we utilised everything from 6 inches in diameter upwards. The lop and top (i.e. branches and top) was super fluous. This came in handy for the sheds.

More orders followed this initial request. Soon one of the buyers got choosey and said he would wait for a better lot. So we made a list and put his name at the end. Everyone had to take what was offered. The roofs of these sheds were covered with straw, which was roped down. Many of them were cut into the hillside and this required less timber for their construction.

My inspector approved of the scheme, but told me we had to sell it as firewood (not timber). Helping the farmers was a blessing in disguise. When a farmer came with his hay-shifter to take off lop and top for his shed he generally took a bit more of this waste material for fencing, etc. We got rid of our lop and top in this way. There were forests where getting rid of the lop and top was a problem. It had either to be burned or let rot. I was transferred sometime after and I am not able to tell how this business concluded. When I came back to the area eighteen years later, I was to find myself recognised as 'the man who gave shelter to the cattle on the hills.'

Dinny O'Sullivan was promoted to another forest. I was sorry to see Dinny go. He had been of immense help to me after I changed from Mrs Dempsey's. We had surplus cash. Goods were still quite cheap. Under Dinny's guidance I acquired an amount of shoes, shirts and other clothing which saw me through the War years. To occupy myself after Dinny left I began painting the house in Ballydine. I made an office out of part of the kitchen. I kept the fire-machine for getting the firewood to light. It was a far remove from my Cavan turf-days. I became a happy busy man again. Henceforth I was on my own except for some weeks when a young forester named John O'Connell, working on a survey of natural woodland, stayed with me. His boss, Divisional Inspector Petrie, used collect him in the morning and drop him off again in the evening. They might cover twenty miles or more together in the day. Although no other forester lodged with me after that, the house in Ballydine was a handy place to drop into. Quite a lot of foresters knew of its existence. Many a forester broke his journey by calling in and even staying the night. This kept me abreast of the forest gossip. I was alone but not lonely. I had other social outlets as well.

There was a Nelson Eddie/Janette McDonald musical

show at the Castle Cinema in Carrick-on-Suir. It was difficult to obtain a ticket. An officer in the local LDF unit got me one. It was there I met my future wife, Nora O'Hickey. She was with her boyfriend. I was sitting beside them and during the interval I managed to get talking to them both. All went well until the Pathe News came on. It showed none other than de Valera asking us to hold on. When he finished the crowd erupted and I heard Nora say 'Up Dev! Up Dev!', I had lost faith in de Valera partly because of the Economic War. I should have said nothing. Instead I found myself saying: 'It's time to kick him out!'

I don't know what happened next. This young woman and I were shouting at one another. The lights came on and the manager arrived. We were both pushed out into Castle Street where we continued shouting at one another. A crowd gathered. It was then that we realised how foolish it all was. We went our separate ways. My bicycle was in Carrickbeg across the river. As I crossed the New Bridge to fetch it, I chanced upon this strange young woman again at end of the bridge. We were both apologetic about what had happened between us a short time before, and she invited me for a cup of tea back to her friend's house nearby, where she was staying. I accepted the invitation. Everything was going well until she discovered that I was a forester. Forestry was in her black books because of all the beautiful rhododendrons which had been cut down in the forests above her native town of Portlaw. She continued her attack: 'Are you one of those fellows going around planting trees. Don't you understand that our farmers need help and our roads mending?' I realised that it was time to leave and I made my escape as soon as I could. The winds of adversity were blowing and I was a stranger in the place. I was unprepared when my District Inspector asked me for details of the cinema incident. His laughing face disarmed me.

That strange woman I had met at the Carrick cinema crossed my mind for a week or two. Then the image faded away. One evening an officer in the local unit LDF called. He was on his way to Portlaw to give out certificates to those who had acquired first aid skills. He asked me to come along and say a few words, as he knew me to be a good public speaker. I agreed to do so. A dance was just finishing up when we arrived at the hall. It was to be a pleasant chore. As I looked down from the rostrum, I saw that there were quite a number of boys and girls waiting to get their certificates. At the end of the queue was that woman who was the cause of my humiliation at the pictures. The officer told me she was the local artist who had adorned the certificates. He requested me to say a special word of thanks to her. I decided that I would speak as if I had never seen her before. I did so and I presented her with a bouquet of flowers. She merely said: 'Thank you. Have we not met somewhere else?' 'Yes,' I said. 'Can I see you home?'

I was living on my own in Ballydine when I met Nora. I was banking on remaining about four or five years in the Slievenamon forest. I was twenty eight years of age. I would wait until I was in my thirties to get married. Our Superintendent, Alistair Grant, in Avondale had been worried about the adverse publicity that Forestry had been getting. He felt that we had a battle on our hands and were against the odds. He had asked us to wait until we were in our thirties before getting married. I was a great admirer of his. I was the first to break ranks. Circumstances gave me no choice.

Visiting foresters would sometimes pin pictures of some of their film-star idols on the walls in Ballydine. On the first occasion Nora called to see me she congratulated me on my choice of 'holy pictures'. Nora loved the house. On no account should the fire machine be got rid of. Nora called on two occasions. There was never to be a third.

A whole new world opened up to me. I had met someone whom I thought I would like to marry. I was little over a year in Slievenamon. According to normal practice at the time, I would have still four years or so to serve there. It was a challenging forest and I felt equal to it. Four years hence I would marry and settle down. Everything seemed to be going my way. My inspector called. He had a small problem for me to solve. He had been informed that the Cloneslea forest workers were drifting away to work on turf-cutting schemes in the Bog of Allen and had refused to go up the Slieve Bloom Mountains to plant. They had worked for Forestry on the mountain the previous year. The tyres of their bikes had got worn on the mountain roads leeched by the rain. It would be impossible for them to work there for another year as they would have no tyres. I was told that I would only be there for a short time. I went there not knowing how to solve the problem.

The forest map of Cloneslea revealed that there was a back road to Cadamstown. Leading off this road was a mountain path, which almost reached the planting area. I got permission from the mountain farmers to open and widen this path. I then extended it for about 500 yards to meet the planting area. I erected a small bridge over a stream. I then constructed a few shelters along the path. Unknowingly I had stumbled across an area where there was a willing workforce. We required twenty men. We could have got forty. I was complemented on all sides. It had, however an unforeseen ending. I was told by Head Office that I was being made forester-in-charge of Cloneslea. If I had not met Nora, I would have taken the transfer in my stride. I felt I could not let Nora go.

I had to go back to hand over Slievenamon to Batt Crowley. I did not go out to the forest. Instead I gave him all my notes. We spend two days pouring over maps. It was as if I was leaving somebody behind me. It was never understood by Head Office how attached a forester becomes to his forest. Even after he leaves, it still remains in his mind. I have gone back to some of mine. It comes as a shock to see that the little trees you left at one and a half feet high have now become giants of the forest. It gives you an eerie feeling that time has moved on. The men who toiled to plant those trees deserve to be remembered. They had wives and children too!

After I left Slievenamon my house in Ballydine was availed of by several foresters. I expect each would have a different tale to tell. The house still stands. It is a lovely home owned by someone. The place abounds with flowers which have crept onto the roadside. Even the gate which is always half open has a friendly appeal. Every time I pass I am tempted to go in and knock on the door. No. I will never go in. For me it must remain as it was: a place where I dreamed some of my dreams! In different circumstances it might have been Nora's and my first home. How nice it would have been for Nora to enjoy the near proximity of her mother during the latter's evening of life. As it was, once married, she was only to see her mother at rare intervals. We were to have many homes all over Ireland. Nora is gone these past nine years. Now on a Summer's evening when I sit out for a spell in my garden in North Crehanagh, near Carrickbeg, I can see Slievenamon across the River Suir in County Tipperary where I was first forester-in-charge almost seventy years ago.

In late 1942, I returned from the Slieve Blooms a bewildered man. I had to arrange with Nora to marry at the end of the following year instead of at the end of four years. I had myself to pay for the transfer of my furniture. I was a householder but I was not married, and as a result I did not qualify for transfer expenses. I had no idea of the immensity of the fight that lay ahead.

My next book will be an account of my life with Nora and of my years as a forester in the service of the State and our struggle together to cope against the odds and to win through.

Map 1: Location of author's home area

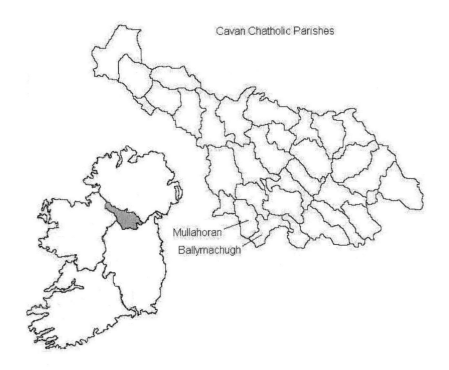

Mullahoran and Ballymachugh Catholic Parishes, Co. Cavan, by Tuomas Briody

Map 2: Briody Farm, Callanagh Middle, Mullahoran

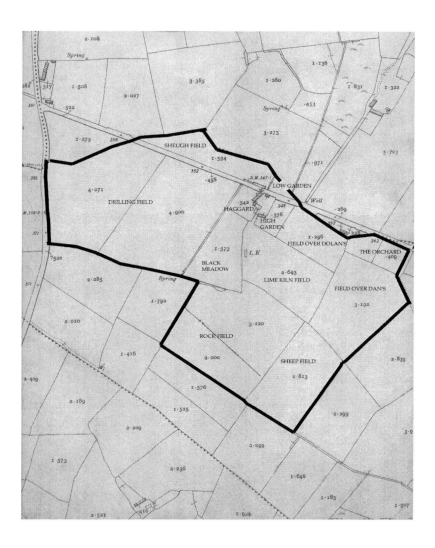

Adapted from the 1912 Ordnance Survey Map of Ireland by Tuula Sakaranaho

Appendix
'Like snow off the ditches': the decline of Irish in south-west
Cavan
Mícheál Briody

There are many references in my father's memoirs to the Irish
language: among others the teaching of Irish in the national
school, his own interest in Irish from an early age, the stiff oral
Irish exam to get into Forestry, and its subsequent neglect during
his training. In his text my father tells how his own father
attended an Irish language class for a time in his youth, taught by
a curate in Ballynarry. He also surmises that his father must have
come across traces of the Irish language as it disappeared. It is
most likely that he did, but he did not speak of coming across
Irish-speakers, or if he did, his son did not remember. It is not
surprising that he might not have told of such encounters. In
many areas Irish died out with little or no attention being paid it.
It also disappeared in many areas in a very short space of time,
even within a generation.

Charles McGlichey (born 1861), speaking of the decline
of Irish in his lifetime in Urris on the Inishowen Peninsula in
Donegal, says:

> Down to my young days there was nothing spoken in this
> parish at fair or chapel or gathering of any kind but Irish.
> A lot of people in my father's time had some English and
> a few of them could read it. The English language came
> in greatly in my own time and in one generation Irish
> went away like snow off the ditches. But with the old
> people it was all Irish you would hear spoken.[1]

My father remembers that when he was a boy there was
an old woman in Boston (Callanagh Lower) who used say her
prayers in Irish. She was known as 'Mary Jockie'. When
occasionally Canon Egan would use a few words of Irish in
church, people could be heard remark: 'That's not the same as

---

[1]McGlinchey 1986, p. 7.

Mary Jockie's Irish.' My father's brother Paul (born 1920) remembers hearing of two sisters in the locality, still alive while he was attending national school, who used converse together in Irish. They were Katie O'Reilly of Glascarrick and Mrs Kirwan of Killydream. The fact that Mary Jockie said her prayers in Irish does not in itself mean that she would have been conversant in Irish. She may indeed have been, or she may have forgotten most of her Irish for want of practice. One could also have to ask did the two sisters, referred to above, always speak together in Irish, or did they do so to exclude others, particularly children. Even after Irish had been abandoned for normal communication, it was common practice to speak about certain matters in Irish where children were present.

Nevertheless, these vestiges of Irish indicate that Irish had a presence in the area in the not too distant past, as do the numerous Irish words and even some phrases in the English of the area when my father was growing up.

How far back does one have to go to find Irish spoken extensively in south-west Cavan, particularly in my father's native parish, Mullahoran, and also in his parents' native parish, Ballymachugh? This is a difficult question to answer. The first census that asked about a knowledge of Irish was not taken until 1851. It is generally accepted that this census underestimated the number of Irish speakers, for a variety of reasons. Garret Fitzgerald, working back from the later census of 1881 (that is considered to be more accurate in respect of enumerating Irish-speakers) estimates the 'minimum level of Irish-speaking' for the whole of Ireland for the previous hundred years, barony by barony. His estimates for the barony of Clanmahon (in south-west Cavan) and the adjacent barony of Granard in County Longford are as follows:

Decennial Cohort	Clanmahon	Granard
1771– 1781	40–49%	40–49%
1781–1791	40–49%	30–39%
1791–1801	30–39%	20–29%
1801–1811	30–39%	10–19%

1811–1821	20–29%	3–9%
1821–1831	10–19%	3–9%
1831–1941	3–9%	0–2%
1841–1851	3–9%	0–2%
1851–1861	0–2%	0–2%
1861–1871	0–2%	0–2%[2]

It is interesting to note how Irish declined much more rapidly in the barony of Granard, after 1781, than in Clanmahon. This most likely in time had an effect on the position of Irish in parishes such as Mullahoran and Ballymachugh that bordered the barony of Granard.

In respect of the figures given above, Fitzgerald stresses that these are minimal estimates and have to be treated with a degree of caution. One problem is that baronies can be very extensive, and while the number of Irish-speakers for the whole barony might be quite small, areas within the barony might have high percentages of Irish-speaking. For this reason it is not possible to estimate with any exactitude what the percentage of Irish-speaking for, say, the Catholic parishes of Mullahoran and Ballymachugh was over this period. Fitzgerald sought to address some of these problems in a further study based on the census returns for 1911, particularly that posed by large territorial units. In this latter study, he produces numerous charts and maps showing Irish-speaking levels by Dispensary Districts (of which there were 789 in the whole country) and by District Electoral Divisions (3915) for people aged over 60. The intention was to derive at some sort of minimal estimates for Irish-speaking in the period immediately preceding the Famine for territorial units significantly smaller than the barony. In this study the areas comprising the Catholic parishes of Mullahoran and Ballymachugh (as well as the rest of the barony of Clanmahon) are recorded as having less than 3% Irish-speaking in the period immediately preceding the Famine.[3] Garret Fitzgerald's two

[2]Fitzgerald 1984. Above statistics compiled from maps appended to this work.

[3]Fitzgerald 2003.

studies into the decline of Irish, invaluable as they are, are purely statistical studies, and do not tell the whole story. They need to be supplemented from other sources. One such source is the 1901 census. Before looking at this census, a word of warning about Fitzgerald's research. It is easy to interpret his findings wrongly. His 1984 study should not be interpreted as charting levels of Irish-speaking in particular baronies, but rather of Irish-language acquisition among successive generations of young people.[4] In respect of his 2003 study, Máire Ní Chiosáin has pointed out that the fact that many people claimed to be older than they were in the 1911 census as a result of the 1908 Old Age Pension Act, in an effort to bring forward their eligibility for the old-age pension, somewhat distorts Fitzgerald's findings.[5]

To take a case in point in respect of Fitzgerald's 1984 study, he estimates that the minimum level of Irish-speaking in the barony of Clanmahon in south-west Cavan was 10-19% for the cohort of people born between 1821 and 1831. This should not be interpreted as the percentage of people in the barony who knew Irish in this period. Many Irish-speakers had already taken the decision not to pass on Irish to their children. Thus, the level of Irish-speaking would be higher, and possibly substantially higher, than the level of children who were raised with Irish or acquired Irish otherwise. When the level of Irish-speaking was high in an area, many children not brought up in Irish would probably have acquired it anyway from the surrounding community. In certain areas, however, use of the tally stick (see below) would have been a huge incentive for children not to acquire Irish from their surroundings, or to forget what they had inadvertently acquired later in life. There may also have been other factors that encouraged 'linguistic amnesia', which I will touch on below. Of course, as Irish weakened significantly in an area, the likelihood of children not spoken to in Irish by their parents or grandparents acquiring Irish became much less.

The 1901 census is the earliest census for which returns

---

[4]It should be said that Fitzgerald sees many of the shortcomings in his method-ology. See Fitzgerald 1984, pp. 120-123.

[5]Ní Chiosáin, 2006, p. 86.

for individual households are extant. In this census some 120 people are listed as knowing Irish and English in the Catholic parishes of Mullahoran and Ballymachugh, among others an Andrew Briody of Clonloaghan. This Andrew Briody was a son of Harry Rua Briody and a granduncle of my father's. His brother, Hugh, my father's grandfather, died in 1899, some two years before this census was taken. Should we assume that Hugh also knew Irish? Unfortunately, no other member of Harry Rua's children apart from Andrew survived Hugh, so we have no way of knowing if the other siblings knew Irish. As Hugh was born in 1819 and was some two years older than his brother Andrew, there is a high probability that he knew Irish. I will return to this question below.

Time does not allowed me to make a thorough study of the 1901 census returns for these two parishes. Some general comments must suffice at this juncture.

In this census the ages of the people in Mullahoran and Ballymachugh listed as Irish-speakers range from age two to a hundred and two:

Age	No of persons
1-9	2
10-19	19
20-29	8
30-29	6
40-49	11
50-59	17
60-69	30
70-79	15
80-89	8
90-99	2
100-110	1

What do these figures tell us? Some nineteen people in their teens, as well as two children under ten, are listed as knowing Irish and English. It is certain that some of these learned Irish at national school or from a parent who was a learner of Irish and an enthusiast of the Irish revival; others would appear to have learned Irish from a native speaker of Irish, most likely a grandparent. Even though the Gaelic League, founded in 1893, had not yet had time to affect language teaching in the national schools to any appreciable extent by 1901, it would appear that Irish may have been taught as an extra subject in a number of schools in the parish of Mullahoran. However, Irish acquired at school would not appear to be involved in the case of some of those under twenty years of age who are recorded as knowing Irish. Moreover, people over twenty are unlikely to have acquired Irish through schooling. However, we cannot be certain of this: a precursor of the Gaelic League, the Society for the Preservation of the Irish Language (founded in 1876) managed to have Irish taught as an extra subject after teaching-hours from 1878 onwards. Although it was estimated that some 2,000 National School teachers knew Irish at the time, most of them being native speakers, the fact that teachers had to pass a stiff examination in order to qualify to teach Irish greatly limited the number of schools where Irish was taught as an extra subject.[6]

Almost half of those listed in the two parishes as knowing Irish and English in the 1901 census (some 30 persons) were born in the 1840s (the decade of the Famine) or before. Another substantial group were born in 1850s, the decade immediately following the famine (17 persons). Eleven persons born in the same decade as my father's father (1860s) are listed as Irish-speaking. The fact that fractionally more people born in the 1880s were listed as Irish-speaking than in the 1870s may possibly be explained through emigration and death.

What is fairly certain is that people in the area who were acquiring Irish after 1860, and possibly well before, were not being brought up in Irish by their parents but were learning Irish from a grandparent, or some other old person with a poor knowledge of English. In such a situation, parents may also have occasionally spoken to their children in Irish in the presence of the grandparent. However, once the old person passed from the scene, no more Irish would have been spoken to children in the house, though parents, in some cases, may have continued to use

---

[6] Ó Murchú 2001, pp. 157-161.

it among themselves. This phenomenon is well illustrated by the case of a particular family in Gortrasna (Ballymachugh): the father, aged 74, had Irish; his wife (60) also had Irish; their eldest son, aged 35, is recorded as knowing Irish; but the other siblings, aged 29, 27, 25 and 22, knew only English. We can surmise from this that Irish ceased to be spoken in that household circa 1866, most likely with the death of a grandparent. Another family from Legwee (Mullahoran) is more difficult to interpret. Both father (aged 65) and mother (42) knew Irish. The eldest of the family, a son aged 25, knew only English. Three other siblings, aged 19, 14 and 10, also knew only English, but a son aged 16 had Irish and English. It is most likely that this boy acquired a certain knowledge of Irish at school, but we cannot rule out the possibility that he had been exposed to some old person with a poor knowledge of English, possibly by living under their roof for a time. This is, of course, only conjecture. Another case that is difficult to interpret is that of a family in Drumshowragh (Mullahoran). The father, aged 60, and the mother, aged 50, both know Irish. A son aged 30 and another aged 21 also knew Irish. A daughter aged 25 had Irish, but two other sons aged 23 and 19 had only English. Again one has to ask why a twenty-one-year-old son would know Irish while his twenty-three-year-old brother did not.

This is not the only question one has to ask. One also has to ask how well did many of those under forty years of age know Irish. Those who had acquired Irish at school, most likely had only a smattering of Irish in many cases. Those who learned Irish from a grandparent or other old person would probably have ceased to speak Irish once that person passed from the scene. Moreover, in most cases it is unlikely that children spoken to by elderly people acquired anything like a full mastery of the language. One does not simply learn a language from one's elders, one also acquires much of it from one's peers. It is unlikely that any of these people under 40 years of age spoke Irish with their peers growing up.

It is interesting to note that very many of these younger people recorded as knowing Irish in the 1901 census are not recorded as knowing Irish in 1911. Research done by Aodh Ó

Canainn in the Sperrin Mountains in south Co. Derry would suggest that when parents in certain areas put down children as Irish-speaking in the 1901 census what was being recorded in many cases was not that these children definitely knew Irish, but that they had been spoken to in Irish as children, either by themselves or most likely by a grandparent. In the meantime Irish had ceased to be spoken in the household. The parents may have concluded that their children's knowledge of Irish, like their own, was reasonably intact, when it may not have been.[7] Many of these young people by the time of the 1911 census were now adults or heads of household in their own right and when they came to record their own knowledge of Irish, they did not consider it such as to warrant mention. Moreover, some who most likely acquired Irish at school would also seem to have forgotten their Irish by the time of the 1911 census.

It would appear that many of the older people with a knowledge of Irish in 1901 were no longer alive in 1911. This, in addition to what I have related above, would account for my father (born in 1913) coming across so few traces of Irish in the area as he grew up. However, it was not just the case of some of the above-mentioned under-forty-year-olds no longer being recorded as Irish-speaking; some older people, that one would expect to have kept a command of Irish are no longer recorded as Irish-speaking in the 1911 census. For instance, an eighty-five-year-old from the townland of Killykeen Lower (Ballymachugh) is recorded in 1901 as knowing both Irish and English. Although still alive in 1911, he is not recorded as knowing Irish. There are other examples of this sort. It could be, given his advanced age, that he took no part in filling out the census form on this occasion. His son, who appears not to have known Irish, and who may never have heard his father speak Irish, may have concluded his father did not know Irish. There may, of course, be some other reason for this omission.

Irish had long gone underground in Mullahoran and Ballymachugh. It was not the case, say around 1900, that when old people who knew Irish gathered together they invariably

---

[7] Ó Canainn 2006, pp. 26-27.

spoke Irish, as happened in other areas.[8] The vast majority of those over seventy, i.e. those born in the 1830s, are recorded as knowing English only. Indeed a majority of those in their eighties are also recorded as knowing only English. This might appear to support Garret Fitzgerald's research that Irish was in a very weak state in the area well before the famine. However, certain other sources suggest that Irish was in a somewhat stronger position in the decade or so before the Great Famine than the returns for the 1911 census indicate.

For instance, the fact that an elegy on the death in 1825 of Rev. Patrick O'Reilly of Crosserlough was composed in Irish would suggest that Irish was not in such a week position in the general area in the period. Séamas P. Ó Mordha, who has edited and translated this elegy, says of Fr. O'Reilly:

> It is generally believed that he was murdered – a victim to the unhappy sectarian strife of the day. His dead body was discovered on the roadside in the townland of Aghawee, between Kilnaleck and Drumkilly. The author of this eligy was a Patrick Coyle of Moynagh in the parish of Ballymachugh.[9]

This elegy was not composed simply for the poet to express his own personal grief and anger, but it was most likely addressed to a wider local audience who could understand and sympathise with what he said. There is, of course, the possibility that it was an antiquarian exercise. However, I think this unlikely.

Moreover, among the manuscripts of James Coyle (Séamas Mac Giolla Chomhghaill) of Dungimmon, Mount Nugent, Co. Cavan in the early twentieth century was an address in Irish 'to Daniel O'Connell in prison from the people and clergy of Mullahoran'.[10] The whereabouts of the manuscript in which this address was contained is not now known, but Séamas P. Ó Mordha dates the address to the release of O'Connell from

---

[8]See Murphy 1973, pp. 33-34.

[9]S.P. Ó Mordha 1985, p. 95. See also his edition of elegy in S.P. Ó Mordha 1958.

[10]Ó Muirgheasa 1905, p. 837.

prison in 1843.[11] This address to Daniel O'Connell, if genuine, would again indicate quite a strong presence of Irish in the area at this time.

James Coyle was the son of Patrick Coyle, author of the above-mentioned elegy for Rev. Patrick O'Reilly. His father was a schoolteacher and Irish-language scribe. He taught his son to read and write Irish, and his son carried on compiling and copying Irish-language manuscripts until the early twentieth century. Like his father, he was also a schoolteacher.[12] Although a native of Ballymachugh, by the early 1880s, James Coyle was teaching at Garrysalagh National School, Mount Nugent. It is not certain if he taught Irish in his school, but he had links with the Society for the Preservation of the Irish Language and in 1882 informed the society that he had been 'for some time busy copying decaying MSS in the Irish tongue.'[13] Séamas P. Ó Mordha describes Coyle as 'the last scribe of the South Ulster-North Leinster region. With him there died a Bréifne scribal tradition that spanned almost fourteen centuries.'[14] Elsewhere, his brother, Brian G. Ó Mórdha, says: 'Mountnugent can boast of having had the last traditional scribe or writer of Irish manuscripts in the whole country in the person of James Coyle – Séamas Mac Giolla Chomhghaill as he called himself–of Dungimmon who died in 1916.' This fact in itself, he suggests, would be ample reason for someone to 'make a study of the decay of Irish in that area!'[15]

The fate of many of Coyle's manuscripts is not clear. Seven of his manuscripts, then in his possession, were examined by Énrí Ó Muirgheasa/Henry Morris in the early twentieth century. A description of these manuscripts was subsequently published by Ó Muirgheasa.[16] It would appear that Coyle presented these selfsame manuscripts to the Gaelic League in

---

[11] S.P. Ó Mordha 1982, p. 54.

[12] Ibid., p. 54.

[13] *Report of the Proceedings.*, p. 9.

[14] S.P. Ó Mordha 1982, p. 54.

[15] B.G. Ó Mordha 1979, p. 58.

[16] Ó Muirgheasa 1905.

1903.[17] One of these manuscripts was still in Gaelic League possession in 1954 and was later presented to the Franciscan Library, Killiney.[18] Nothing is known of the whereabouts of the six other manuscripts examined by Ó Muirgheasa. They may have been lost or destroyed during the 1916 Rising or during the troubled years that followed. A number of other manuscripts of his have also survived.[19] In 1903, Coyle published a ghost story in Irish in the *Gaelic Journal* that he had written down from the dictation of his brother in Ballymachugh in the 1860s.[20] We are fortunate that he published this story for the whereabouts of the manuscript in which it was contained is not now known. This is one of the earliest examples of this genre collected in Irish and is also very illustrative of the Irish as spoken in south-west Cavan before it disappeared off the face of the map.

Breandán Ó Buachalla has noted that spoken Irish (as well as the literary tradition in Irish) declined more suddenly in Breffney in the first half of the nineteenth century than in other areas, and states that the main cause of this sudden decline was the activity of Protestant proselytisers and the rancour they caused.[21] Here he is referring to the activities of organisations such as the London Irish Society, which sought to convert native speakers of Irish by teaching them the scriptures through Irish. The London Irish Society had it Irish headquarters in Kingscourt, Co. Cavan and had a school in Ballymachugh for a short period in the 1820s.[22] Many hundreds of Catholic teachers taught for the Irish Society, not necessarily out of sympathy with the ultimate aim of the Society, which was to convert the Catholic population to Protestantism, but in order to help put bread on the table. Of course, the presence of the Irish Society in the area does not in itself indicate that Irish was still spoken extensively, but it would

---

[17]Ó Súilleabháin 1984, p. 186.

[18]Mooney 1959, pp.113-117.

[19]See S.P. Ó Mordha 1955.

[20]Coyle 1903.

[21]Ó Buachalla 1975, p. 31.

[22]For the Society's activities in Ballymachugh, see Pádraig de Brún 1983, pp. 292-293 and de Brún 1987, pp. 70-72.

341

suggest that the language was not exactly in its death throes in the area.

Ó Buachalla quotes the Irish-language scholar, John O'Donnovan, who was employed by the Ordnance Survey: 'the teachers of the Bible through the medium of Irish have created in the minds of the peasantry, a hatred of everything written in that language.'[23] Séamas P. Ó Mordha also suggests that where communities were already bilingual, the rancour caused by proselytising societies may have made speakers of Irish abandon the language altogether in Cavan.[24]

There is no disputing the rancour these proselytising societies caused, and that their activities impacted negatively on Irish.[25] It has to be noted, however, that Irish was losing ground before they came on the scene. Although there had been sporadic attempts to proselytise the Irish through the medium of Irish in the seventeenth and eighteenth centuries, it was not until the early nineteenth century that systematic efforts were made to use Irish for this purpose.[26] The Hibernian Society, founded in London in 1806, used Irish to some extent in its proselytising work.[27] The Baptist Society, founded in 1814, also used Irish[28], but it was not, however, until the London Irish Society, founded in 1819, began operating that Irish was used on a large scale to proselytise Catholics.[29] This is not to argue that attempts to proselytise Catholics and the reaction of Catholic priests to such activity did not play a significant part in the decline of Irish as many Catholic priests turned against the language when it began

---

[23] Ó Buachalla 1975, pp. 31-32.

[24] S.P. Ó Mordha 1962, p. 82.

[25] The activities of these societies in Breffney are dealt with in detail in O'Connell 1942, pp. 477-581. For a more recent, and less emotional, treatment of the activities of these societies in Cavan, see Wheelan 2005, pp. 172-182.

[26] The first serious attempt to use Irish to convert Catholics to Protestantism in the Cavan area was made in the early eighteenth century by Rev. John Richardson, Anglican Rector of Belturbot. See O'Connell, 1942, pp. 228-245.

[27] Ibid., p. 514.

[28] Ibid., p. 516. This society mainly operated in Connaught.

[29] Ibid., pp. 540 ff.

to be used as an agent of proselytism. It may also have contributed to the destruction of Irish-language manuscripts and the disparagement of Irish-language tradition.[30] In Cavan, as elsewhere, in the change-over from Irish to English, very many Irish-language manuscripts were to end up in the fire, on the dung heap, in the river, or left to rot in damp conditions. Others were fortunate to be purchased by collectors of manuscripts or acquired by various institutions. Some are still in private possession, but it is estimated 'that only a fraction of the manuscripts once in existence now survive.'[31]

There is no doubt that the roots of the decline of Irish in south-west Cavan, as elsewhere in the region, are complex. Brian G. Ó Mórdha lists the reason for the decline of Irish in Tullaghgarvey barony in north–east Cavan in the 19th century as follows:

(a) English was the language of the ruling classes and of all aspects of administration.

(b) English was the language of commerce in its widest sense, buying and selling at fairs and markets, shopping, etc.

(c) English was the language through which such education as was available could be obtained.

(d) English was increasingly becoming the language of the Catholic Church for many reasons one of which, but not the most significant, was the use made of Irish for proselytising by Protestant sects.

(e) English was the language of politics and because of the struggle for Emancipation–and because of the success of that struggle–many of the ordinary Catholic people were beginning to take a keen interest in politics.

(f) English in the popular mind was linked with prosperity and was seen to be a sine qua non for success in the world while Irish was linked with poverty and hardship.

---

[30]For the ill-effects of this proselytising work on the Irish language in south-east Ulster, see Ní Uallacháin 2003, pp. 22-28.

[31]See de Brún 1969, pp. 560-561.

(g) Although emigration was but starting in the area at this time there can be no doubt but many people were beginning to consider it as a way to escape from destitution and, of course, if one left Ireland English was necessary.[32]

To this Ó Mórdha adds the effect of the Great Famine, which 'greatly accelerated the growth in the use of English both because it linked more firmly than ever in the folk mind Irish and poverty and because it also brought many people into greater contact with Government agencies of all kinds. English was the language of the various relief organisations and of the workhouse...'[33]

There is little doubt that education played a major role in the decline of Irish in south-west Cavan, as elsewhere in the county and indeed in other counties. Long before the establishment of the National Schools, the hedge-schools played an important role in the acquisition of English in Breffney. To quote Philip O'Connell: 'Irish still remained the language of the home and the tongue in which prayers were recited; but early in the nineteenth century English had become the principal medium of instruction in the Breiffne schools.' He adds: 'After 1800 the Irish language appears to have gradually fallen into disuse as a literary medium in Breiffne, although it still remained the spoken language of the home.'[34]

Another instrument in language change was the tally stick (the *bata scóir*) by which children had a stick hung around their necks and each time a parent or adult heard them speak Irish a notch was etched on it and they were accordingly punished by the teacher (or parent). Philip O'Connell downplays the effect of this system and also attributes it a somewhat late origin: 'Despite the "Tally System," which was adopted in particular districts for the purpose of counteracting the vicious activities of the proselytising societies, the Irish language

[32]B.G. Ó Mordha 1979, pp. 61-62.

[33]Ibid., p. 63.

[34]See O'Connell 1942, pp. 380-381.

survived.'[35] It is certain that use of the tally stick predated extensive proselytising in Cavan as elsewhere. Its origins go back into the eighteenth century, and was often resorted to out of desperation by parents whose own knowledge of English may have been meagre enough but who fervently wished their children to learn English.[36]

As I have said above, Irish declined in many areas with little or no comment, so it is difficult to chart its decline over time, particularly in the eighteenth century. By the beginning of the nineteenth century a knowledge of English had spread to areas that had been strongly Irish-speaking in the eighteenth century. While Garret Fitzgerald's estimates for minimum levels of Irish-speaking for the period 1771-1871 have, as he himself admits, to be interpreted with a degree of caution, it is nonetheless remarkable that for the period 1771-1781 he estimates that the minimum level of Irish-speaking for the Barony on Clanmahon was only 40–49%. Even if these are minimum estimates, and although they may give a somewhat distorted picture of the position of Irish in the barony, there is little doubt that English had gained a strong foothold in the barony and in Cavan generally by the last quarter of the eighteenth century. How did this come about? There is no doubt that conquest, settlement and religion played a major role.

Speaking of the religious and linguistic situation in Ireland as a whole in the early eighteenth century, William J. Smyth says:

> By the early 1730's the Protestant population constituted around 27 per cent of the total population of the island. For the greater part, one can assume that this is an English-speaking population. Between 1660 and 1730, Ulster English had clearly gained significant ground. Ulster Protestants then constituted nearly 60 per cent of the population of the province, utterly triumphant in the northeast, where it is likely that some Irish-speaking populations had been assimilated.... But there is also a

---

[35]Ibid., p. 371.

[36]For more on this cruel method of punishment, see Crowley 2005, pp. 122-123.

dramatic and aggressive pushing southwards of settlement and speechways into south Armagh and Cavan and the establishment of secondary cores for expansion in Longford and Sligo.[37]

Even though Cavan experienced less settlement as a result of the Ulster Plantation than some of the other counties involved, from the early seventeenth century the English language had a presence in the county, and in some areas a strong and long-lasting presence. By 1861 Protestants amounted to twenty per cent of the population of Cavan. This was not evenly-spread over the whole county. Some parts of the north-west, north and north-east had protestant-populations of 30-40% or more. Protestants were far less numerous in the south-west, south and south-east. The only civil parish in the south-west of the county with a relatively high percentage of Protestants was Ballymachugh, with a Protestant population of 20-30%. The civil parish of Drumluman (comprising the Catholic parish of Mullahoran and the western part of the present Catholic parish of Ballymachugh) had a Protestant population of only 0-10%.[38] How much of this Protestant population was long-established in Cavan and how much the result of proselytism in the previous few decades is difficult to determine. It is interesting to note that many areas of the county which had high percentages of Protestants in 1861 are also recorded as having low levels of Irish-speaking in the 1851 census.[39] This would appear to indicate Protestant communities of long-standing.

Although the introduction of Protestant settlers in the seventeenth century also resulted in the introduction of English speech to many areas where previously it had been virtually non-existent, it took some generations for this to effect a significant decline in levels of Irish-speaking amongst the Catholic population. Nor was it a simple one-way process. Speaking of the effects of extensive settlement in Ireland during the first half

---

[37]Smyth 2006, p. 408.

[38]Duffy, 1995, pp. 32-33.

[39]Compare map given in Duffy (ibid., p. 33) with map appended to Ó Cuív 1971.

of the seventeenth century, William J. Smyth says:

> If we assume that only settler families and their offspring spoke English or Ulster English, these 1660 patterns confirm that at the very least 22 per cent of the population knew and spoke these languages. However, if we add the many families of Old English descent who knew and spoke these languages, as well as the increasing number of Irish-speakers who for reasons of proximity to large settler speech-regions, for reasons of trade, social advancement and/or dealing with the writ-governed world of the courts and landlordism and/or assimilation to the Established or Nonconformist Churches, it is likely that the number of English-speakers in the country in 1660 constituted, at the minimum, one-third of the total population. Likewise, assuming a minimum level of bilingualism amongst the families of settlers or settler descendants, the total number on the island who understood and spoke Irish constituted well over four-fifths of the population.[40]

Although some Protestants in Ulster in the eighteenth century had Irish as their first language, it is safe to assume that most Protestants who knew Irish had acquired a knowledge of Irish, among other things, to facilitate communication with their Catholic neighbours or servants/workers. In areas such as Cavan, a level of relatively stable bilingualism probably continued into the late eighteenth century, with Irish remaining the dominant language among Catholics, but with increasing numbers of Catholics having a knowledge of English. This type of bilingualism was not destined to last. As the century advanced Irish became more and more associated with poverty and backwardness, and at least some better-off Catholics may have switched to rearing their children in English.

The State did not accord any status to Irish, and it was without any institution to support it. One might have expected the Catholic Church to have been a mainstay of Irish, but such

---

[40]Smyth 2006, pp. 407-408.

was not the case. While the Catholic Church during the Penal Days tried to provide sufficient numbers of priests with a knowledge of Irish from its seminaries on the Continent, it did not always succeed in doing so. Niall Ó Ciosáin says: 'The extent to which English-speaking priests ministered to Irish-speaking congregations had been a continuing problem for the Catholic hierarchy in the eighteenth century'.[41] While the Church may have done its best to provide Irish-speaking congregations with Irish-speaking priests, despite the loyalty of certain bishops and many priests to the language, as an institution it did not seek to promote the Irish language. However, the extent to which the Catholic Church neglected Irish is difficult to access, particularly in the eighteenth century, and there is not space to do it justice here. However, by the early nineteenth century, the Church may have been led by the people as much as giving a lead in such matters, for there is no doubt that many of their congregations by this time were trying to shed themselves of what they saw as the shackles of Irish. Nevertheless, it should be noted that in other matters, such as politics, the Catholic Church, sought to lead its flocks rather than be led by them.

Religion also influenced the decline of Irish on another front. The fact that the Catholic Church, unlike Protestant Churches, did not emphasise the importance of literacy among its faithful, particularly the ability to read the Bible, weakened the language at a time when people were striving to become literate. During the course of the eighteenth century only a handful of Catholic religious texts were published in Irish. Philip O'Connell in his study of Breffney notes 'The absence of printed books hastened the decay of Irish.' He says, 'Dr. O'Reilly's Gaelic Catechism does not appear to have been used in Breiffne after 1830.'[42] By this time all Catholic children in Cavan were presumably at least bilingual. O'Reilly's Gaelic Catechism was one of the few Catholic publications in Irish produced in the eighteenth century. Its author, Michael O'Reilly was a native of

---

[41]See Ó Ciosáin 1990, p. 53.

[42]O'Connell 1942, p. 381.

Cavan.[43] A vibrant religious print literature in Irish might have helped the Irish language maintain its position better in an age when literacy was being emphasised more and more. However, this failure to provide religious printed material in Irish to any extent has to be set against the failure of a print culture to develop in Irish, even though a vigorous manuscript tradition existed in certain areas well into the nineteenth century.[44]

Despite the decline in the fortunes of the language, due to the explosion of population in the first few decades of the nineteenth century, the number of Irish-speakers in the country as a whole increased, but Irish-speakers were becoming more and more marginalised, and lack of knowledge of English a social stigma. Thus, the early nineteenth century saw the expansion of the Irish language demographically in many western-areas in particular, but geographic contraction in other areas, amongst others south-west Ulster.

The early nineteenth century also saw the first questions on language use in Ireland being asked. The Royal Irish Academy began to commission a series of statistical county surveys and one of the questions asked of compilers concerned the use of the Irish language in the county in question. These surveys are not as informative of the Irish language as one might expect. As Brian Ó Cuív notes: 'The information obtained depended largely on the individual who had undertaken the county survey, and so it varied in quality. Some authors seem to have endeavoured to get accurate information, while others are vague or silent on the subject.'[45] The statistical survey of Co. Cavan only speaks of the state of Irish in the barony on Tullygarvey, in the north-east of the county, and is silent on the other baronies. The compiler says of Tullygarvey: 'All speak English; very few understand Irish.'[46] This can hardly have been the case. Garret Fitzgerald in his 1984 study gives a minimum

---

[43]For more on this catechism and its significance, see Tynan 1985, pp. 22 ff.

[44]For some of the reasons why a print culture did not develop in Irish, see Cullen 1990, pp. 38-40.

[45]Ó Cuív 1971, p. 20.

[46]Ibid. p. 82.

level of Irish-speaking for Tullygarvey of between 10 -19% for the period 1801-1811 and 20-29% for the period 1791-1801.[47]

The civil parish of Drumluman, which comprises the Catholic parish of Mullahoran and part of the parish of Ballymachugh, is one of the few civil parishes in Co. Cavan to have had a Ordnance Survey memoir compiled for it. The compiler was Lieutenant Andrew Beatty and the memoir is dated 1835. Although this memoir contains a wealth of information about the parish, apart from referring to the Irish-language origin of Drumluman, it does not refer to the Irish language at all.[48] Under 'Schools', Beatty writes: 'Schools have not long been established in the parish to enable us to see any improvement in them. Their effect will be more plainly seen in the rising generation. The people are very anxious to have their children instructed and afford them every facility.'[49] By improvement, among other things, he may well have meant the disappearance of Irish.

There is little doubt that Beatty came across Irish in the parish, although he did not care to mention it. Stiofán Ó Cadhla says of those who complied these memoirs: 'Most memoir-writers valorized [i.e. assigned a value to] the use of English and their reports tried to reassure where possible that it was in fact spoken in a particular area.'[50] One could say the same of those who compiled the statistical surveys a generation earlier. This silence on the part of certain statistical survey and Ordnance Survey writers in respect of Irish was not simply due to attitude or prejudice. Irish-speakers may well have had the habit of switching to speaking English in the presence of strangers, officials or their 'betters'. Such people would also have been greeted in English by Irish-speakers. This situation could be interpreted by some outsiders as evidence for Irish being next to non-existent in certain areas, when that may not have been the case.

---

[47]Fitzgerald 1984, Maps 3 and 4.

[48]Day and McWilliams 1998, pp. 12-18.

[49]Ibid., p. 15.

[50]Ó Cadhla 2007, p. 105.

Some of those who compiled statistical surveys and such like were more sympathetic towards Irish and more informed about the language. Speaking of the spread of English vis à vis Irish at the turn of the eighteenth and nineteenth centuries, Philip O'Connell quotes from such a source:

The following paragraph in Thompson's Statistical Survey of County Meath may be accepted as applying equally as well to Breiffne at the same period:—

The English language is pretty generally in use throughout the county, and we very seldom meet with any person who is not capable of speaking it with some degree of fluency; yet, when together, the peasants all converse, and if they have a story to tell, or a complaint to make, *they still wish to be heard in Irish; understanding the idioms of that language better than they possibly can those of the English*; their story can be conveyed more expressively and, of course, work more on the feelings of their auditors; indeed there is no language more copiously supplied with pathetic expressions or more calculated to touch the feelings, than those of Irish.[51]

Irish was a good deal stronger in Meath, north Meath in particular, at this period (early nineteenth century) than in the barony of Clanmahon in south-west Cavan, nevertheless the above, to a lesser or greater extent, probably describes the situation on the ground at the time in the civil parish of Drumluman (Mullahoran and Ballymachugh) in respect of the Catholic population. English would appear to have been known by most and had come to dominate more and more of the public sphere, such as school, chapel, political meeting, etc., but Irish still prevailed in many homes around the fires. There is no doubt, however, that the language was losing its grip on the community.

If still spoken around the fires, as the nineteenth century advanced it was being spoken less and less by parents to children. This does not mean that many children spoken to in

---

[51]See O'Connell 1942, pp. 380-381. Italics in original.

English would not have acquired Irish from older relatives or from the community at large.

This brings me back to my father's family. We know from the 1901 census that his grand-uncle, Andrew Briody, knew Irish. I surmise above that his grandfather, Hugh, who was a few years older than Andrew, probably also knew Irish. Presuming that Hugh knew Irish, we might ask did he and his brother learn Irish from their parents, or did they pick it up from a grandparent or from the community. Would a young progressive farmer such as Harry Rua Briody in the drumlin area of south-west Cavan, who built a slated, two-storey house for himself and his young bride in 1806, have raised his children in Irish? Many a strong farmer in Munster might well have done so, but Irish was much stronger over much of Munster at the time. We have no way of answering this.

Most of Andrew Briody's age-group who survived until the census of 1901 are not recorded as knowing Irish. It is hard to believe that many of these when children were completely ignorant of Irish. Even if not raised with Irish by parents, many would have at least acquired an understanding of Irish, if not an ability to speak the language. If I am correct in assuming so, most of these would appear to have forgotten their Irish as the language declined and went under. Be that as it may, Andrew Briody's age-group (those born in the 1820s) would certainly have heard a lot of Irish spoken while growing up, irrespective of how much of it they understood. However, it would appear that even people brought up in Irish in the area in time ceased to speak it not just to their children but also among themselves. What made them do so? We know that the activities of proselytisers caused friction in Ballymachugh in the late 1820s.[52] Further research would need to be done to ascertain if religious friction of this sort played a significant part in making people in the area abandon Irish altogether. If Irish-speakers ceased speaking Irish among themselves because it became linked in their minds with efforts to convert Catholics to Protestantism, or more particularly if they were made to feel guilty at their own

---

[52]O'Connell 1942, pp, 499 ff.

association, or that of relatives or neighbours, with 'Protestant schools', this, as well as lack of practice speaking Irish over time, might explain why so many over-eighty-year-olds in the area (that one would expect to have some knowledge of Irish) in the census of 1901 are returned as not knowing Irish at all. The Famine is also likely to have contributed to silencing Irish in the community and wiping it from people's minds.

Some Irish-speakers resolutely clung to Irish, for whatever reason, and this explains why there were still children in Mullahoran and Ballymachugh acquiring a knowledge of Irish from native Irish-speakers into the 1860s and 1870s and possibly even later. As late as the 1920s there were still native speakers of the language in the area. Pádraigín Ní Uallacháin, speaking of south-east Ulster, has said:

> There are many reasons why spoken Irish was abandoned in a relatively short period of time and within living memory in southeast Ulster, not least the effects of the Great famine (1845-7), leaving entire communities with only a vague memory of the language and traditions of their grandparents, and causing a breakdown of communication between generations, often between parent and child, and with it a significant loss of ancestral memory.[53]

My father's paternal grandfather, as I have said, probably knew Irish, like his younger brother Andrew. For all we know they may both have been raised with Irish. If so, when did they last speak it together? No tradition has come down in the family of them conversing in Irish, or indeed of the older generation knowing Irish. There was an understanding, however, that Irish was spoken in the area in pre-Famine times.

Irish has long roots in south-west Cavan, yet in the first half of the nineteenth century it was torn up by the roots. That is now a long time ago, and in the meantime English has put down deep roots. When my father was born in October 1913 those roots were already well established. Irish was still very near him

---

[53]Ní Uallacháin 2003, p. 28.

(nearer than he realised) as he became conscious of the world around him, but yet so very far away!

The above account of the decline of Irish in south-west Cavan is not meant to be definitive, and admittedly involves a degree of conjecture. My main purpose in including it in this book is the hope that more of those engaged in local studies and family research, who very often ignore the question of language change, may be encouraged to investigate the decline of Irish in their own areas and take Irish into consideration in their research. I also hope that what I have written above may pinpoint some of the pitfalls in interpreting census returns and studies based on them in respect of language use and language change. Another reason for including this appendix in this book, is that my father asked me to do so, as it is a subject near his heart. I hope to complete a more comprehensive study on the decline of Irish in south-west Cavan at some future date.

Bibliography

Crowley, Tony, *Wars of Words. The Politics of Language in Ireland 1537–2004* (Oxford University Press; 2005).

Coyle, James ('Druim Luamáin'), 'Sgéal Shéamais a' Réisidhe', *Irisleabhar na Gaedhilge/The Gaelic Journal* 13/154 (1903), pp. 357-359 and 374-375.

Cullen, L.M., 'Patrons, Teachers and Literacy in Irish : 1700-1850' in Daly and Dickson 1990, pp. 15-44.

Daly, Mary and David Dickson (eds), *The Origins of Popular Literacy in Ireland. Language Change and Educational Development 1700 — 1920* (Dublin 1990).

Day, Angélique and Patrick McWilliams (eds), *Ordnance Survey Memoirs of Ireland. Counties of South Ulster 1834-8* (Institute of Irish Studies, The Queen's University Belfast; 1998), pp. 12-18.

de Brún, Pádraig, 'Some Irish MSS. with Breifne Associations'. *Breifne* iii/12 (1969), pp. 552-561.

de Brún, Pádraig, 'The Irish Society's Bible Teachers 1818-27' (part i), *Éigse* 19 (1983), pp. 281-332.

de Brún, Pádraig, 'The Irish Society's Bible Teachers 1818-27' (part iv), *Éigse* 22 (1987), pp. 54-106.

Duffy, P.J., 'Perspectives on the Making of the Cavan Landscape', in Raymond Gillespie (ed.) *Cavan. Essays on the History of an Irish County* (Irish Academic Press; Dublin 1995 [2005]), pp. 14-36.

Fitzgerald, Garret, 'Estimates for baronies of minimum level of Irish-speaking amongst the successive decennial cohorts, 1771–1781 to 1861–1871', *Proceedings of the Royal Irish Academy* 84, C, no 3 (1984), pp. 117–155.

Fitzgerald, Garret, 'Irish-Speaking in the pre-Famine period: a study based on the 1911 census data for people born before 1951 and still alive in 1911', *Proceedings of the Royal Irish Academy* 103, C, no 5 (2003), pp. 191-283.

McGlinchey, Charles, *The Last of the Name* (The Blackstaff Press; Belfast 1986).

Mooney O.F.M., Father Canice, 'An Irish MS. from Mount Nugent', *Breifne* i/2 (1959), pp.113-117.

Murphy, Michael J., *Tyrone Folk Quest* (Blackstaff Press; Belfast 1973).

Ó Buachalla, Breandán, *Cathal Buí: Amhráin* (An Clóchomhar Tta; Baile Átha Cliath 1975).

Ó Cadhla, Stiofán, *Civilizing Ireland. Ordnance Survey 1824-1842. Ethnography, Cartography, Translation* (Irish Academic Press; Dublin 2007)

Ó Canainn, Aodh, *Teacht den tSliabh Tráthnóna* (Coiscéim; Baile Átha Cliath 2006).

Ó Ciosáin, Niall, 'Printed popular Literature in Irish 1750-1850', in Daly and Dickson 1990, pp. 45-57.

O'Connell, Philip, *The Schools and Scholars of Breiffne* (Browne and Nolan Ltd.; Dublin 1942).

Ó Cuív, Brian, *Irish Dialects and Irish-Speaking Districts* (Dublin Institute for Advance Studies; Dublin 1971 [1951]).

Ó Mordha, Brian G., 'Meath na Gaeilge i dTeaghlach Ghairbheith/The Decay of Irish in Tullaghgarvey in the 19th Century', *The Heart of Breifne/I gCeartlár Breifne* (1979), pp. 58-67.

Ó Mordha, Séamas P. (Séamas P. Moore), 'Two manuscripts from South Cavan', *Éigse* vii/iv (1955), pp. 275-277.

Ó Mordha, Séamas P., 'Tuireamh ó Chondae an Chabháin', in *Celtica* iv (1958), pp. 273-278.

Ó Mordha, Séamas P., 'An Ghaeilge i gContae an Chabháin, i gContae Longphuirt agus i gContae na hIarmhí san Bhliain 1823', *Breifne* ii/5 (1962), pp. 80-83.

Ó Mordha, Séamas P., 'A Lament for Father Patrick O'Reilly' *The Heart of Breifne/I gCeartlár Breifne* (1985), pp. 95-102.

Ó Mordha, Séamas P., 'Some Aspects of the Literary Tradition of Bréifne-Fermanagh', *Breifne* vi/21 (1982), pp. 18-56.

Ó Muirgheasa, Énri (Henry Morris), 'MSS belonging to James Coyle', *Irisleabhar na Gaedhilge/The Gaelic Journal* 14/177 (6/1905) pp. 808-809 and 14/178 (7/1905), pp. 835-837.

Ó Murchú, Máirtín, *Cumann Buan-Choimeádta na Gaeilge. Tús an Athréimnithe* (Cois Life Teoranta; Baile Átha Cliath 2001).

Ó Súilleabháin, Donncha, *Scéal an Oireachtais 1897-1924* (An Clóchomhar Tta; Baile Átha Cliath 1984).

Ní Chiosáin, Máire, 'Meath na Gaeilge i gCléire', in Aidan Doyle and Siobhán Ní Laoire (eds) *Aistí ar an Nua-Ghaeilge in ómós do Bhreandán Ó Buachalla* (Cois Life; Baile Átha Cliath 2006).

Ní Uallacháin, Pádraigín, *A Hidden Ulster. People, songs and traditions of Oriel* (Four Courts Press; Dublin 2003).

Smyth, William J., *Map-making, Landscapes and Memory. A Geography of Colonial and Early Modern Ireland c. 1530–1750* (Cork University Press; 2006).

Report of the Proceedings of the Congress held in Dublin on the 15th, 16th and 17th of August1882 (Society for the Preservation of the Irish Language; Dublin 1884).

Tynan, Michael, *Catholic Instruction in Ireland 1720-1950* (Four Courts Press; Dublin 1985).

Whelan, Irene, *The Bible War in Ireland. The 'Second Reformation' and the Polarization of Protestant-Catholic Relations, 1800–1940* (The Lilliput Press; Dublin 2005).

Photo Gallery

1

Author's father, Thomas Briody
(1864-1950)

2

From left: author's Aunt
Kate (1889-1973), his
maternal grandfather,
Edward O'Reilly (1846-
1916), and mother, Annie
O'Reilly (1882-1974)

3

Author's Aunt Kate (left) and mother, Annie

Three eldest of Briody family: from left, Edward (1912-2003), Tosty (author),
and Hugh P. (1910-1999)

5

Author's mother, Annie, and
younger brother Paul
(early 1920's)

6

Author and mother
(back row) with his
younger siblings:
from left, Anna
Celia, Austen,
Gerald, Rosetta and
Paul

7

Author's Uncle – Patrick Briody
(1868-1937)

8

Author's wife, Nora O'Hickey
(1916-2000)

9

Tosty outside the
house Harry Rua built
in 1806

10

Tosty's and Nora's wedding photograph

11

Paddy Verling – Avondale House Master
1936-39

12

Avondale Forestry School, class 1937-40
Standing (from left): W.J. Breslin (Forester-in-Charge & House Master),
J.F. Ryan, J.A. Conway, D.J. McGuire, A.J. Hanahoe, P.P.O'Grady, D.J.
O'Sullivan, A. Grant (Superintendent)
Seated (from left): T.J. Briody, M.C. Rigney, Miss M. Devane (Matron),
D.J. Nyhan, J. Horgan (Photograph courtesy of Avondale House)

13

Junior (j) and seniors (s) forestry trainees, Avondale 1938.
Standing (from left): D. Keohane(s), J. Horgan(j), C. McCarthy(j). M.
Rigney(j), M. McNamara(s), T. Briody(j), D. McGuire(j), M. McCarthy(s),
J. Hanahoe(j), P.O'Grady(j), J. Ryan(j), D.O'Sullivan(j), J. Conway(j), P.
Kelly(s)
Seated (from left): J. Boyce(s), M. Dooley(s), J. Deasy(s), C. Curran(s), D.
Hayes(s), W. Barrett(s)

Index of Names

This index includes personal names, placenames, and field
names on the Briody farm, Callanagh, as well as the names of
schools and various educational institutions. The index covers
only the text of the *Road to Avondale*. The relationship of the
author to relatives, neighbours and close associates is indicated
in round brackets. Members of the staff of Ballyhaise
Agricultural College, Albert College, Glasnevin and Avondale
Forestry School are indicated by '(Ballyhaise)', '(Albert)' and
'(Avondale)' respectively. Foresters, Forestry Inspectors, and
other Forestry staff are indicated by '(forest.)'.

A
Aghavannagh 264
Albert College 152, 168, 193–207 passim, 220, 221, 234, 236, 251, 257, 266, 276, 277, 302
America, United States of 3, 5, 7–8, 17, 21–3, 31–4, 37–8, 47, 49, 55–7, 71–2, 89, 94–5, 98, 100–1, 105–6, 109–11, 113, 118, 131, 146, 152, 164, 167, 188, 245, 254, 262, 279, 301
Annalee, River 161
Anner, River 250
'a Park Smith (see Smith, 'a Park)
Apple-Garden 28
Arbour Hill Prison 121, 202
Ardkill Mountain 3
Ardnacrusha 279
Arklow 237–9, 263, 289, 296, 298
Armagh, County 73–4
Ashford Castle 306
Assinagap 261–3
Atheny 322
Aughrim 254–66
Australia 3, 7, 10, 37, 49, 58, 262
Avoca 237, 261, 300
Avondale 11, 148, 157,174, 180, 195, 205, 208–46 passim, 251, 256–60, 264, 272–4, 276, 280, 285–302 passim, 306, 308–9, 313, 320, 325

B
Ballinagh 132
Ballinakill 278, 281
Ballinamuck 99
Ballinrobe 217
Ballintemple 88, 90, 101
Ballydine 316, 323–6
Ballyhaise Agricultural College 152–3, 155–7, 159–198 passim, 200, 205, 207, 228, 236, 239, 245, 248, 251, 257, 276, 302
Ballymachugh 2, 7, 9, 12, 44, 51, 53, 82–3, 90, 128, 148, 154
Ballymanus House 256, 262–5
Ballynarry 12
Ballyneill 320
Ballypatrick 321

Ballyvourney 224
Ballywillan 16
Bantry 78, 217
Barrett, Bill (forest.) 217
Barry's Hotel 211, 222, 224–5, 237, 239, 292
Baskinagh 4–5
Battery Road 209, 300
Baunreagh 231
Baxter, Mr 53
Bealnablath 68
Belfast 21, 52, 62–3, 83, 110–11, 218
Belgium 295
Bernard family 267–8
Blackrock 125
Black Meadow/Well Field 28, 40, 58, 116
Blind Lake 38
Bog of Allen 113, 325
Boherboy 314–5, 321
Bo Meadow 181
'Boston'/Callanagh Lower 3, 14, 18, 25, 29, 69, 88–9, 140
Boston (USA) 90, 248, 279
Botanic Gardens 198, 266
Boyce, John (forest.) 218, 232–4
Boylan, Philip (schoolboy) 53
Brady, Charles 59, 95–6, 98, 156, 302
Brady, Charles/Chassy (first cousin) 95, 155
Brady, Eddie (first cousin) 95, 155, 302
Ballyvourney 224
Ballywillan 16
Bantry 78, 217
Barrett, Bill (forest.) 217
Barry's Hotel 211, 222, 224–5, 237, 239, 292
Baskinagh 4–5
Battery Road 209, 300
Baunreagh 231
Baxter, Mr 53
Bealnablath 68
Belfast 21, 52, 62–3, 83, 110–11, 218
Belgium 295
Bernard family 267–8
Blackrock 125
Black Meadow/Well Field 28, 40, 58, 116
Blind Lake 38

Bog of Allen 113, 325
Boherboy 314–5, 321
Bo Meadow 181
'Boston'/Callanagh Lower 3, 14, 18, 25, 29, 69, 88–9, 140
Boston (USA) 90, 248, 279
Botanic Gardens 198, 266
Boyce, John (forest.) 218, 232–4
Boylan, Philip (schoolboy) 53
Brady, Charles 59, 95–6, 98, 156, 302
Brady, Charles/Chassy (first cousin) 95, 155
Brady, Eddie (first cousin) 95, 155, 302
Brady, Elizabeth/Bal (first cousin) 96
Brady family (first cousins) 29, 59, 95–8, 155–6, 197, 248, 302
Brady, Kate (née O'Reilly, aunt) 1, 2, 6–7, 34–5, 37, 59, 96, 98, 116, 155, 302
Brady, Mary Francis (first cousin) 96
Brady, Margaret 10 (see also Briody, Margaret)
Brady, Mr (Rathdrum) 240, 292
Breen, Mr (Avondale) 214, 300
Breffney Park 146, 183
Breifne hills 25
Breslin, Bill (Avondale/forest.) 287–9, 296
Briody & O'Reilly (auctioneers) 10, 21, 106, 112, 129, 132
Briody, Anna (aunt) 10
Briody, Andrew (granduncle) 9
Briody, Anna Celia (sister) 95, 135
Briody, Annie (mother) 1–42 passim, 48, 50, 52–3, 58–60, 62–5, 68–71, 73–5, 92, 94–6, 100–3, 110–2, 128, 130–1, 133, 135, 137–8, 152–3, 155, 158, 172, 178,196–7, 205, 208–9, 239, 245–9, 251, 284–6, 295, 302–3, 310
Briody, Austin (brother) 21, 95, 135, 302
Briody, Edward (brother) 1–2, 12, 14, 23–5, 35, 42–8, 53, 58, 60, 63, 68–71, 95, 133–41, 196, 284–5
Briody, Elizabeth (sister) 16, 39, 41–3, 58–9, 71, 96
Briody, Gerald (brother) 71, 135

Briody, Harry (first cousin) 128, 249, 304, 310
Briody, Harry Cruise (second cousin) 84
Briody, Harry Rua (great-grandfather) 9–10, 15, 41, 154
Briody, Henry (uncle) 10, 13–4, 17, 68, 71, 102, 136, 293
Briody, Hugh (grandfather) 15
Briody, Hugh (uncle) 10, 58
Briody, Hugh (first cousin) 71
Briody, Hugh P. (brother) 1–2, 12, 14, 23–5, 30, 42–8, 53, 58–71 passim, 86, 95, 98, 102, 112, 135–7, 141–8, 158, 174, 248–9, 284–5
Briody, John James (brother) 58–9
Briody, Margaret/Mrs Henry (godmother) 6, 10, 17, 23, 113, 154–5, 172, 286, 197, 248, 285, 302
Briody, Matt (second cousin) 84
Briody, Mícheál (son) 281
Briody, Miss/Miss B. (Ballyhaise) 165, 168–72, 175–81, 191, 194–5, 205
Briody, Patrick (uncle) 10–11, 12–3, 39–43, 58–9, 63–4, 68, 72, 100, 114, 136, 201, 205
Briody, Patrick Vincent (brother) 43, 58–9
Briody, Paul (brother) 25, 71, 135, 196–7, 278, 284, 293, 302
Briody, Peter (first cousin) 71, 148
Briody, Rosetta (sister) 71, 135
Briody, Sammy (second cousin) 148
Briody, 'The Smiler' 38–9, 269–70
Briody, Thomas (father) 1, 5, 8–12, 14–8, 21–2, 30, 34, 36, 38, 40, 44, 48, 50–53, 58–60, 62–9, 71, 74, 82–3, 86–7, 93, 95, 98, 100–3, 106–7, 110–4 129–33, 135, 137–8, 140–1,153, 158, 180, 196–7, 205, 209, 219, 239, 248–9, 284, 286, 302–3, 310
Broadstone Rail Terminus 113
Bruse Hill 3
Bruskey 88
Burns, Miss 312

C

Cadamstown 326
Caffrey's College 106, 113–6, 119, 129
Caffrey family (neighbours) 56, 97
Caffrey, Mr 115–6
Callanagh Lower (see also 'Boston') 3,
13–4, 46, 88, 140
Callanagh (Middle) 1, 11, 14, 16, 21,
32, 43–5, 59, 68–9, 82, 135–6, 154,
166–7, 218, 229, 249–50, 265, 284–5
Callanagh Upper 3, 30, 140
Canada 49, 295
Capragh 43–4, 284
Capragh House 12, 21
Caragh chapel 64
Carlow, County 234, 255, 293
Carnaross 4–5
Carney's Road 311
Carrick (Cavan) 2, 4, 7–8, 12, 51
Carrickbeg 324, 327
Carricknabrick 87
Carrick-on-Suir/Carrick 84, 130, 237,
263, 282, 307, 310, 312, 318–21, 323–
4
Cassidy, Mrs (landlady) 152, 183
Castleblaney 216, 280
Cavan, County 1–5, 10, 13–5, 17, 20–1,
42–44, 56, 62–3, 65, 70, 76–7, 84–5,
88–9, 92, 101–2, 105, 109, 114, 118,
126–158 passim, 167, 172, 183–4, 191,
194, 197, 200, 204, 218, 224, 229, 234,
241, 246–50, 264, 265–7, 276, 282,
313, 315, 323
Cavan Town 2, 24–5, 35–6, 44, 48, 70,
73, 93, 105, 132, 146, 152, 183, 186,
190, 194–5
Chambers, Mr 51
Charity House 309
Chicago 6, 96
Churchill, Winston 274
Clare, County 161, 217, 224, 293, 301,
306
Clarke, Pat 69
Clash 234
Cloneslea 272, 280, 325–6

Clonloaghan 3, 9, 13, 15, 23, 44, 51,
68–9, 102, 110, 113, 132, 136, 140,
148, 155, 197, 248, 302
Clonmel 249–50, 254–5, 302–3, 304–7,
309, 312–3, 315, 320
Clonoose 44, 166, 187
Clonoose School 31–2, 45, 52, 57, 69,
90–2, 96, 101, 106, 133, 148, 154
Cobh 213
College Green 116, 121–3
Colley, Harry 120
Collins, Michael 68, 122
Collins, Moss (forest.) 293
Collins, Tim (forest.) 293
Collins-O'Driscoll, Mrs 122
Comeragh Mountains 3, 218, 255, 261
Com Ga 200
Connary 227, 229–31, 300
Connemara 96, 134
Connolly, James 200
Connors, John (forest.) 267, 271–2
Conway, Joe (forest.) 224, 293
Coolavokig 200
Coolishal 251
Cork, County 68, 128, 171, 215–7, 224,
292–4, 302
Cosgrave, Liam T. 199
Cosgrave, William T. 111, 113, 117,
121–24
Coughlan, Mrs (landlady) 273, 278
County Bridge 65
Coyle, family (neighbours) Mr 31
Coyle, Maggie 6, 14, 30–2, 34, 39, 46,
53, 58, 60–1, 64, 71, 100
Crammond, George (forest.) 305–15,
319, 323, 325
Cranwhinche, The 53
Creed (see Burns)
Creevy 14–6, 43
Crehanagh 282, 327
Creighton's mill 33
Croke Park 145, 180
Cronin. Terence 168
Crowley, Batt (forest.) 326
Cruise, Tom 84
Cúil Aodha 294
Curran, Con (forest.) 218

D
Daly's (public house) 33–4
Dalymount Park 118–9
Daniel, Pat 87
Dawson Street 129
Dease family (relatives) 4, 12
Dease, Major (relative) 138
Deasy, Joseph/Joe (forest.) 216
Delahunty, Mick 255
Delaney, Denis (Ballyhaise) 165–6, 168–70, 174, 177–8, 181, 183, 189–91, 194–6
Dempsey, Josie/Jo 254
Dempsey, Mick 250, 253–4, 311–2
Dempsey, Mrs (landlady) 250, 254, 305–6, 316, 323
Denmark 123, 173, 179
Derry City 73
Derrybrien East 276, 278, 282
Despard, Madame 121, 202
Devane, Fr 243
Devane, Miss M. (Avondale) 212, 220, 222, 232, 234, 240, 242–3, 245, 301
Devereux, Nick (forest.) 218, 233
de Valera, Éamon 67, 77, 117, 120, 122–8, 132–3, 142–3, 158, 192, 282, 324
Dickson, Tom 211, 222, 225
Dolan family (neighbours) 19, 43, 56, 65, 69, 71, 196
Dolans' Hill 69
Donegal, County 62 , 74, 134, 161, 171, 196, 218, 228, 247, 296, 302, 312
Donoghue, Jimmy (forest.) 217, 256, 263–5
Donohoe's (forge) 29, 98–9
Dooley, Mike (forest.) 218
Dorset Street 114, 116
Dowleys (grain merchants) 318
Drew, Miss 198, 205, 208–9
Drew, Professor (Albert)198, 205
Drilling Field 29, 40–1, 102
Dromhome 160
Drumbrucklis 4
Drumbrucklis River 89, 90, 101
Drumension Hill 13
Drumhawnagh 13, 21, 30, 35, 44, 70, 93, 158, 196, 247, 249

Drumluman 51
Dublin City 10–3, 26, 43–4, 62, 67, 86, 106, 112–32 passim, 137, 141, 143, 148, 153–8, 197–213 passim, 217, 222, 224, 247–9, 264, 266, 273, 276–8, 304, 310, 320
Dublin Corporation Market 199
Dublin, County 52, 125
Dundavan Bridge 35–6
Dungan, Bill (forest.) 273–5, 277, 280–2
Dungarvan 85–6
Dunkirk 105, 295
Dún Laoghaire 201
Dunne, Anne (née Briody, daughter) 280, 310
Dunne, Dermot 161, 193
Dunne, Tom (son-in-law) 280

E
Earlsfort Terrace 199
Edgeworthstown 105
Egan, Fr (Canon) Robert 49–50, 91–2
Egan, Joe (forest.) 267, 270–3, 287
Emo 180, 213, 215, 223
England 7, 9, 54, 81, 106, 110, 113, 128, 133, 152, 154, 178, 188, 197, 215, 222, 245, 261, 282–4, 294
Erne, River 89, 161
Europe 11, 106
Everett, Mr (TD) 261

F
'Fagan, Patsy' 86
Farnham, Lord 9
Farnham Hotel 185
Farrelly's (sand pit) 99
Feetham, Mr Justice 73
Fifteen Acres 119, 124
Figgis, Darrel 6
Finlay, Fr Tom 127
Finnea 2, 5–6, 11, 143, 149
Finnerty, Pat (forest.) 293
Fitzmaurice, Master (schoolteacher) 96
Flanagan, John. (forest.) 293, 306
Flanders 138
Flynn, Jacky (forest.) 322

Flynn, Patrick (forest.) 293, 306
Fore 169
Foster Place 121, 202, 243
Foxford 280
Foyle, River 74
Franco, General 184–5

G
Galligan, Charles (neighbour) 21
Galligan, Con/Conny (neighbour) 44, 82
Galligan family (neighbours) 19–22, 25, 29–30, 40, 54, 97
Galligan, John (neighbour) 20, 174
Galligan, Mary (neighbour) 20
Galligan, Michael (godfather) 17, 72, 101, 109, 172
Galligan's Fort 65
Galway Bay 279
Galway, County 3, 146–7, 150, 161, 218, 225, 266, 273, 280–1, 306
Gardiner Street 116–7, 127
Garland, Judy 296
Gennings, Frank (forest.) 217
George, Lloyd 67
George, Pat 87
Germany 216, 232, 261, 274, 300
Glasha River 311–2
Glasnevin 152–3, 168, 173–4, 194–9, 272, 288
Glen (Cavan) 29, 32, 34, 87, 98
Glen (Waterford) 305
Glen River 38
Glenbower 314, 320
Glendalough 265
Golden Vale 175, 190, 321
Gonne, Maude 121, 202
Gowna 67
Grafton Street 116
Granard 1, 4, 5–6, 8, 10, 14–6, 45, 47–8, 63–70, 95, 100, 129–30, 164, 229, 310
Grangemokler 321
Grant, Alistair (Avondale) 222, 225–7, 231, 235, 239–40, 242–4, 276, 287–9, 296–9, 302, 325
Greaney, Master (schoolteacher) 79, 81

Great Britain 68, 78, 104–6, 111, 127, 131, 142–3, 148, 157–8, 222, 239, 243, 245, 262, 271, 295, 304
Great Island 213
Gregory, Lady Augusta 16
Greville Arms Hotel 64
Griffith, Arthur 13–4
Grousehall 13, 32, 99, 178
Guilfoyle, J. (forest.) 293

H
Hahessy, Mr (Ballyhaise) 191
Hanahoe, Joe (forest.) 161–84 passim, 190–1, 194–205, 208–9, 220, 223, 228, 231, 237–8, 242, 245–6, 291, 293–4, 300, 302
Harcourt Street 115
Hassett, Mr (Ballyhaise)175–7, 189
Hayes, Dennis/Dinny (forest.) 216
Healy, John (forest.) 310
Hester, Brendan (forest.) 293
Heverin, Jim (forest.) 293
Higgins, Mick (forest.) 225
High Garden 29
Hitler, Adolf 184
Hobson, Bulmer 6
Hogan, Patrick 122–3
Hogan, Mr (fellow lodger) 119
Holland 295
Horgan, Jer (forest.) 200, 204, 209, 220, 223–5, 237, 291–4, 300,302
Hunters (seed merchants) 10–11, 131
Hussey, Mr (Albert) 199, 209

I
Inny, River 5
Irish Sea 244, 284, 310
Italy 142

K
Kane family (Mullahoran) 38
Kehoe, Mrs (landlady) 316
Kelleher, RIC Dist. Inspector 64
Kelly children (neighbours) 56
Kelly, Patrick (forest.) 217–8, 240–1
Keohane, Donal (forest.) 217

Kerry, County 78–9, 134, 145–7, 171, 184, 196, 200, 234, 291, 293–4
Kiernan, Kitty 45, 68
Kiernan, Larry 45, 47
Kilcash 314, 321–2
Kilcogy 34, 45, 51, 87, 113, 143
Kildare, County 145
Killinkere 10
Killurney 314–5
Killydoon 13, 25, 45, 132
Killydream 44
Killykeen 44, 51
Kilnaleck 65, 101
Kilsheelan 246, 249–61 passim, 292, 302, 305–16, 318, 320–1
Kinnity 265–74, 280, 291, 312
Kinnity (Castle) Forestry School 267, 274, 280
Knight family 51

L
Laois, County 3, 213, 218
Laragh 234, 237, 243
Legwee River 33
Leitrim, County 3–4, 78, 147, 192, 229, 276
Lemass, Seán 120–1
Lenihan, Brian 21
Leonard, Alfie (forest.) 256, 259, 261, 264–6
Leonard Mr (senior) 266
Leonard Mrs 266
Liffey, River 114
Limekiln Field 41–2, 100, 102
Lisnatinny 87
London 67, 203, 244–5, 248, 271
Lonergan, Mr (forest.) 320
Long Ashton Research Station 173
Longford, County 4, 10, 14, 18, 63, 70, 105, 147, 164, 168, 172, 191, 196, 229, 253, 276, 293
Longford Town 36, 44, 48, 93, 253
Loughduff 33
Loughrea 273, 279, 281
Lough Sheelin 2–5, 51, 100, 128, 149, 239
Lovers' Leap 209, 300
Low Garden 26

Lynam, John (botanist) 276
Lynch, Mr (Aughrim) 262
Lynch, Mrs (Aughrim) 258, 262–3
Lynch, Mrs (Clonoose) 166–7
Lynch, Mrs (Grousehall) 73, 74–5
Lynch, Paddy 31–2, 72–4, 85, 89, 93, 99, 109, 122, 132, 178
Lynch, Tommy 99

M
MacEoin, Seán 6, 63, 68, 70
Macneill, Eoin 73
Macroom 200
McCann, Ellie 46, 72–4, 95, 102
McCarthy, Cal (forest.) 224–5, 291–4, 300–1
McCarthy, Jack (forest.) 305–6
McCarthy, Mick (forest.) 217, 264
McCarthy, Seoirse 217
McCarthy, Tim (forest.) 217
McCool, Mr (forest.) 249–53, 259
McDermott, Tom 6, 32–4, 37, 58, 62, 71, 95, 102, 107, 136, 139
McEntee, Seán 120
McGee, Matt 32
McGee Mrs 32
McGerty, Eugene/Owney (fellow lodger) 114–23 passim, 200–2, 205
McGowan, John 194
McGuire, Dan (forest.) 164, 168, 170–4, 177, 179–80, 207–28, 237, 244–5, 255–6, 265, 291, 293–4, 296–7, 300–2
McGuire family (neighbours) 61
McGuire, Sean 218
McNamara, Mick (forest.) 217
Maginot Line 295
Mahon, Joe (forest.) 273–4, 278–81, 284
Mahon family 278–9
Mahony, Tom (forest.) 293
Maloney, Mr (Ballyhaise) 175
Maxwell, Mr 9
Mayo, County 161, 167, 172, 183–4, 186, 196, 217, 240, 293
Meath, County 4, 9, 196
Mission Cross 309

Monaghan, County 62, 74, 147, 172, 183, 293, 306, 313
Mooney family (Slieve Blooms) 267, 273
Mooney, John 267
Moore, Thomas 300
Mount Bellow 266, 280, 303
Mount Bellow Agricultural College 161, 180, 182
Mount Congrave Estate 194, 204
Mountnugent 149
Mount Street Bridge 201
Moydristan 51
Mullahoran 1, 4, 11, 16, 27, 32, 44–5, 48–9, 51, 82–3, 86–8, 90, 93, 99, 101–2, 108–9, 114–5, 125, 127, 143, 147–8, 153, 155, 159, 163, 178, 196, 246, 249, 313
Mulligan, John 172, 183
Mullingar 10, 93, 113, 247
Munnelly, Joe (forest.) 172, 180, 183–4
Mussolini, Benito 184

N
New Inn 4–5
New York 80, 90, 109, 248
Ninemilehouse 322
Northern Ireland 21, 62, 73–4, 110, 149
Nyhan, Dan (forest.) 224, 238, 293, 296–8

O
O'Brien, J. 10
O'Connell Bridge 116, 125
O'Connell, Daniel 108, 197
O'Connell, John (forest.) 323
O'Connell, Master (schoolteacher) 78–9
O'Connell Street 266
Ó Dálaigh, Cearbhall 134
O'Donovan Rossa 197
O'Duffy, Eoin 142–3
O'Ferrel family 15
O'Grady, Peadar (forest.) 224, 242–5, 268, 291–5, 300–1
O'Hanlon, J. F. 13, 69
O'Hickey, Fr Michael 49
O'Hickey, Nora (wife) 51, 80, 125, 324–7

O'Kelly, Seán T. 143
O'Neill, Owen Rua 5, 102, 184
O'Reillys, Cairn (neighbours) 44, 46, 61, 82, 278
O'Reilly Clan/Ó Raghallaigh 102
O'Reilly, Eddie (uncle) 55
O'Reilly, Edward (grandfather) 4
O'Reilly, Eliza (grandmother) 4
O'Reilly family (Creevy, relatives) 10, 14, 16, 21, 112
O'Reilly, Hugh (uncle) 8
O'Reilly, 'Hughie the County' 137
O'Reilly, James (uncle) 55
O'Reilly, John (uncle) 55
O'Reilly, Lizzy (aunt) 72, 101
O'Reilly, Miss (schoolteacher) 54–5, 78–9, 133
O'Reilly, Mr (landlord) 114
O'Reilly, Mr (Drumhawnagh) 29–30
O'Reilly, Mrs (landlady)114, 117
O'Reilly, Myles the Slasher 5
O'Reilly, Rose (aunt) 72
O'Reilly, Rose (paternal grandmother) 15
O'Reilly, Fr Thomas 11
O'Reilly, T. P. (second cousin) 15, 112
O'Reilly, Mrs (Creevy) 15–6
O'Shea, Patrick (schoolteacher) 78–9, 152
Ó Súilleabháin, Dónal (see Sullivan, Dan)
O'Sullivan, Dan (see Sullivan, Dan)
O'Sullivan Beare 78
O'Sullivan, Denis/Dinny (forest.) 314, 316, 323
O'Sullivan family (Kilsheelan) 255
O'Sullivan, Tom (Ballyhaise, House Master) 160–1, 170, 179, 183, 194
Offaly, County 3, 150, 218, 265, 293
Ormond family (Kilsheelan) 255

P
Pakenhams 4
Parkgate Station 12
Parnell, Charles Stewart 11, 157, 180, 197, 214, 219
Patagonia 49
Pearse, Patrick 16, 199–201, 272, 288

Petrie, Mr (forest.) 313, 323
Phoenix Park 12, 119, 124–5
Plunkett, Dr (mother's cousin) 64
Plunkett, Harry (mother's cousin) 128
Poolbeg 26
Portlaw 80, 125–6, 217, 246, 263, 324
Power, Pat (forest.) 276
Powerscourt Estate 204
Prendergast, Kathleen 254
Prendergast, May 254
Prior, Tom (forest.) 264, 312, 314, 318

R
Rathdrum 209–11, 222, 235, 237, 240–2, 288–9
Rathnew 234, 239–41
Reilly, Mattie 92
Reynolds, Bernard 8
Reynolds family (first cousins) 8
Reynolds, Maria (aunt) 8
Rigney, Mick (forest.) 223, 240, 293
Rock Field 29, 40–2, 100, 102
Roscommon 293
Ruskin, John 199
Russellstown 309–10
Ryan, John (forest.) 225, 293

S
Scotland 222, 235, 274, 287
Shane Leslie Estate 217
Shannon, River 5, 251, 276–7, 279
Shanvalla 29, 35, 59, 95–8, 109, 116, 132, 155, 197, 248, 286, 302
Sheep Field 3–4, 64–5, 100, 229
Shelton Forestry School 274, 280
Sheugh Field 26
Siegfried Line 295
Sion Hill Secondary School 125
Skerry's College 114–5
Silken Thomas (see Tomás an tSíoda)
Slieve Aughty Mountains 3, 218, 274–7, 281
Slieve Bloom Mountains 3, 125, 218, 231, 267, 325, 327
Slievenamon 3, 218, 280, 305–6, 313–27 passim
Sligo, County 69, 194, 196, 302
Smallhorns, Jack 85
Smith, Brian 'a Park 17–8, 29

Smith, ('a Park) family 17–8, 23, 25, 43, 45, 285–6
Smith, Kate 'a Park 18
Smith, Mrs 'a Park 17, 70, 285, 295
Smith, Pat 'a Park 102, 105, 146, 197, 203, 238, 244–5, 253, 271, 285, 295
Smith, Tommy/Tom 'a Park 1, 11, 17–8, 48, 71, 196, 285
Smith, Brian (schoolboy) 81–2
Smith, James (neighbour) 44
Smith, Miss (schoolteacher) 55, 77–9, 91–2, 133
Smiths Solicitors 132, 152
Somerset 173
Sonnagh 10
St. John, Mr 319
St Mels College 93
St Stephen's Green 115–6
Suir, River 250, 255, 327
Sullivan, Dan (forest.) 200, 204, 209, 220, 223, 234, 237, 238, 289–98 passim

T
Thornhill, J.J. (forest.) 290–1, 293
Tierney children (neighbours) 56
Tierney, Luke (neighbour) 30
Tierney, Mary Jane (neighbour) 30
Tierney, Philip (neighbour) 30
Tipperary, County 3, 161, 194, 218, 255, 327
Tobercurry 69
Tomás an tSíoda 152
Toor 311
Tracey Park 307
Trinity College 121–2, 202
Tullow 225
Tully, Jimmy 174
Turbotstown 4
Tyrone, County 74
Two-Mile Bridge 250

U
Ulster 62, 67, 145, 173, 178, 234, 275

V
Vale of Avoca 237, 261, 300

Verling, Paddy (Avondale/forest.) 212–
6, 219, 223, 226–47 passim
Viceregal Lodge 12

W
Wade, Mr (forest.) 251–4
Wall Street 105, 109, 130, 279
Warrenstown Agricultural College 196–
7, 278, 302
Waterford City 194
Waterford, County 3, 80, 125, 150, 204,
218, 246, 255, 263, 282, 327
Well Field (see Black Meadow)
Westmeath, County 4–5, 10, 105, 143,
147, 169, 195
Westmoreland Street 116
Whelan, Larry (forest.) 251, 305, 309
White, Dr 254
Wicklow, County 11, 124, 205,
209–48 passim, 254–266, 286–302
Wicklow Mountains 3, 261–2
Wicklow Town 238–9
Wilson family (neighbours) 20–1
Wilson, Fr Des 21
Wilson, John (neighbour) 21
Woodford 273–5, 278–84